Ordering Information:
Quantity sales. Special discounts are available on quantity purchases by corporations, associations, and others. For details, contact ascentile@hotmail.com

Printed in the United States of America
Publishing, Design, Photo Editing: Release Publishing, Elisabeth Ann Designs, Debra Werdell

A Rational Path to Christ / Donald J. Jacques

ISBN 978-0692799055

First Edition

A RATIONAL PATH
— TO —
CHRIST

DONALD J. JACQUES

Vivencio Franada
23509 Lakeview Dr # A105
Mountlake Ter, WA 98043

FOREWORD

Few things in life are accomplished without motivation, effort, perseverance, and creativity. *A Rational Path to Christ* is no exception. However, in this case, this work was accomplished and inspired by my Lord and my God. The effort, motivation, perseverance, and creativity for *A Rational Path to Christ* derive from Him. It is my longing that this book delivers fully His inspiration.

This effort began as a lesson taught in a classroom. After several reformations, it expanded to the form contained in this book. The entire undertaking required considerable energy and focus. The sacrifice was borne directly by Diane, my wonderful and supportive wife, and Jolie and Jaime, my two daughters, created in the image of God and their stunning mother. This work is the direct result of attention diverted from them. As God knows, I love dearly my three ladies. I wish to thank them for their strong and eternal support. I praise God for guiding me to Diane, such a wonderful woman. I see glimpses of God's agape love for us His children when I see her encouraging my daughters and the youth of this age.

My Rational Path to Christ began at the home of my youth. Both a strong provider and relentless nurturer raised me in a Christian home. I witnessed every day I spent in that home Edmond, my father working to provide and protect me, my mother, my sister Donna, and brother Eddie. In the actions of my dad I learned much about how my beloved Father in Heaven desires strongly that my needs be satisfied. I learned about love, from a woman who would give her life for me like Jesus; because, in a way, she has. Shirley, my mother, is the kindest, gentlest and most devoted spirit I have encountered. Although no one has walked flawlessly in the steps of Christ, I am certain my mother's footsteps have overlapped many of His.

My Rational Path to Christ accelerated at Colorado State University and in my local church. My life changed quite unexpectedly while attending graduate school in Fort Collins, Colorado. There, I accepted Jesus Christ as my Savior. I became a spirit being with the love, persistence and guidance of many fellow students and church leaders. However, I praise God for the obedience and maturity of Andy and Marcie Stewart, Cheryl Henderson and Cheri Mummert. They were instrumental in guiding me to foundational understanding. My relationship with Christ blossomed because they loved me when I was lost.

As I was not born a writer, compiling this wealth of information and rendering it understandable was not a simple task. I extend significant gratitude to Leesa Link. Early in the process, she edited my teaching drafts and guided me closer to the expectations of publication.

On behalf of my cherished above, I dedicate this writing to those who:

- seek truth and do not have a personal relationship with Jesus,

- attend church regularly only to fulfill a perceived obligation, or

- seek to gain greater knowledge to better share their faith in Jesus Christ and the Bible.

Father, I receive your calling upon my life. Endow me with the wisdom and power to fulfill your best plans for and expectations of me to the furtherance of your Kingdom here on Earth and within me.

I praise the God and Father of my Lord Jesus Christ for His flawless plan and perfect love of humankind.

Donald J Jacques

CONTENTS

A RATIONAL PATH TO CHRIST

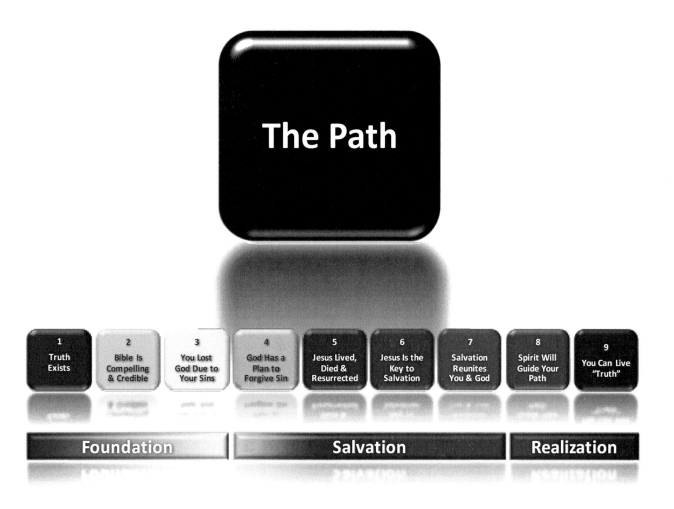

CONTENTS

ONE STEP AT A TIME

They say you need to be in great physical condition to climb a tall mountain.

While in my undergraduate engineering program at the University of Rhode Island, Mr. Russell Morgan, a classmate and friend, spoke a great deal about climbing Mt. Rainier. Almost weekly, he would entertain us with tales of this mystical earthen giant on the opposite side of the country. He would share all of the research he had done on what he would need and details about the climb. Russ would ask a group of us while studying together if we would join him on the trip. "It would be so cool," he would share to entice us into making plans and joining him.

Little did Russ know; he was prophesying over my life. He was spot-on, it was "so cool!" I climbed Mt. Rainer in 1996, but without my inspirational Mr. Morgan. I wasn't in the most amazing shape, or even the best shape of my life. At the time in 1996, exercise for me was largely running and picking up a dumbbell or two on occasion. Nevertheless, as defined by the results, I was in good enough shape to summit and feel good enough to enjoy the view from the top.

Please don't misunderstand me. Unlike Russ, it was not my goal to summit Mt. Rainier. In 1986, I moved to Seattle from Washington, DC. On my commute to and from work in the southern Seattle region, I would get glimpses of Rainier and think of it as Russ' mountain. Over time, I amassed a cadre of friends and acquaintances. One of these friends, Mr. Greg Osterloh described his goal of summiting Mt. Rainier. Like Russ, he asked if I was interested. To which, my repeated noncommittal reply was, "Let me know when you are planning the trip." I counted on Greg's idealism not requiring a decision from me. I'd climb, but it wasn't driving me…

…That was until Greg scheduled our climb, investing a deposit to secure the date with a Mt. Rainier mountaineering school and guide. I put up an argument with Greg for about fifteen minutes and quickly succumbed to my new reality of becoming a mountaineer. So, several months later, with crampons, moleskin, and ice axe in hand, we left the lowlands for the base of Rainier to receive several hours training for our climb early the next morning.

As odd as some of this sounds, during the training we were taught how to breathe, to perform a self-arrest (in case those on our rope team fell into a crevasse), and to climb "step-by-step." At the time, I had no idea of the significance the "step-by-step" training would have on the balance of my life. The teaching was simple but profound. To the best of my recollection, the procedure for each step is as follows:

1. Take a step forward solidly placing your force and weight into the center of your foot, to ensure that your crampons seat securely in the snow.

2. Take a deep breath, compressing it in your lungs.

3. Next, lock backward the knee of the same foot.

4. Pause shortly to establish a solid foundation and force the air out through your teeth, causing back pressure in your lungs. This action forced additional oxygen into your system…receive the refreshing resource.

5. Repeat each of the actions above with the opposite leg.

As simple as this technique appears, it was the key to my summiting and successfully maintaining my thoughts and clarity at over 14,411 feet in altitude.

I followed my trainer's and guide's directives listed above the entire journey. I was successful; more successful than I knew. As we ascended, we took a break every half hour or so to recover. We were nearing the top of our climb. I knew we were within several hundred feet in elevation of the summit. Our guide stopped and told us to remove our backpacks, as was customary at each previous rest break. As the second on our rope behind our guide, I quickly complained. "We are so close! Let's continue and finish!" Our guide laughed at me and said loudly, "We made it! We're there! You did it!" As you might imagine, I was excited, fulfilled, relieved and exhausted, all at the same time.

Why tell this story in a book about discovering Jesus Christ? Simply, the reason is the path and the process. I learned a great deal about life in the method used to cover tremendous ground and achieve. The path and process I followed up this magnificent mountain changed my views on improvements and achieving goals. That same path and process underlie the contents of this book.

As described above, I made it to the summit, I achieved the goal, I arrived, and did not even know it. I made it to a place I had never been before. I arrived at a location I was uncertain I could visit. Many people, some in better shape than me, fall prey to altitude sickness, among other ailments, that prevent them from summiting Rainier. Many on our trip did not summit. In fact, another in our rope team was in better shape than I. But, when we arrived at the top, he had such a bout with altitude sickness, all he could do was lie down and wait for the order to pack up for our descent. He made the journey. He took many of the same steps as me. But he did not take them as distinctly, deliberately or as focused as me. The result; he was unable to embrace the destination.

So, what did I learn? What was the valuable lesson that would help shape my philosophy going forward? I took one step at a time. I made certain that the foundation of each step was solid and secure. Next, I paused and took in a much needed breath. Then I propelled myself to the next step with great momentum. Finally, I compressed the air into my body for maximum gain. I repeated the process many times with each individual step until I reached the goal. While I understood the final destination, my focus was on each step, its foundation and the revitalization therein.

I completed a journey to an amazing place, with spectacular views, largely because my focus was on the necessary steps to achieve rather than the end destination. By following the direction of my guide, and focusing on each step individually, I was able to transport a great distance and climb to amazing heights. The next step was not important to me until I completed the current step. Only with a solid foundation and a lung full of resource was I able to continue taking additional steps. And, with each step I made progress, considerable progress. I was so focused on the steps that I failed to realize how far I had journeyed. A true lesson for life.

By following this "one step at a time" process I entered a new world and realized new things I had not seen before. It changed my life forever! My journey was a rational path to the top of Mt. Rainier. I discovered a new elevation.

Then, with a new process and point of view, what about truth?

WOULD YOUR LIFE CHANGE IF_____?

Change is complex. At times, we avoid it at all costs. Other times, we try to embrace and run with it. Accepting change in our lives can be sometimes difficult. It can initiate good or bad, based on our perspective and life's demands. At first, change may appear as a bad fit. However, when moving forward, we may gain a better understanding and realize that the change was a necessity, a crucial part of our growth.

- Is it possible that an event could change your life? What if you received something, or lost someone you highly valued? Would it change your life? Most likely, it would.

- If you learned something new and were open to it, would it change your life? Perhaps, but it may depend on the nature of that acquired knowledge.

- If faced with change, is it valuable to you or insignificant?

- If the foundation for the object of your faith becomes stronger, or becomes weakened, would it change your life? Would it be a course correction several degrees off center, or would it be a 180-degree turnaround?

Has your life ever changed? It is hard to imagine a life that has not. Merely, growing older causes change to our bodies, brains, and the way we think. These changes occur in all of us. Perhaps our greatest change stems not from within, but how we respond to experiences and situations. We use our views and ideas to react and they influence us significantly and result in change. Regardless of what motivates our reaction, change is inevitable.

Our lives change every day. We face opinions and responses from family, friends, co-workers, neighbors, society, etc. These views affect us dramatically or minimally, and persistently. Day-to-day, we do not sense our lives changing much. We are unaware of the permanent changes that emerged from one day to the next. A simple exercise will illustrate this point.

Ask yourself, "Is your life different from 10 years ago?" Where did you live? How tall were you and how much did you weigh. How much hair did you have, what color was it, and how did you style it? Who were your friends? If you had a job, where did you work? How much did you earn? What was your most important goal? What was your highest priority?

Now, take those answers and compare them to your life today. For most, a 10-year period produces many changes with family, friends, living environment, work and school, our physical being, activities, and our priorities and goals.

Your family may have expanded or withered. You may have lost touch with friends, yet acquired new ones. You may not live at the same residence or geography. Your body may have gotten bigger, smaller, stronger, or weaker. You look 10 years older, and now you do not do the same things. Some of those closest to you may no longer live, yet new influential individuals are in your life. Your job has changed as well as your living arrangements; thus, your surroundings respond to you differently. This change did not occur in one day. The change involves a host of small alterations over a period of time. This also includes those larger "shock to the system" changes.

When I was 16 years old, I set my goals. I wanted to earn a degree, get married, have children, and live in a beautiful home. I yearned to run my own company, travel, give time and money to help others, to retire at a certain age, etc. Although such goals work for a selected few, many do not realize their visions or dreams, or have it manifested to the same degree as was conceived.

Visions are not immune to change. Time delivers incentives and pressures, and we adjust. Life deals you a card from the deck that you did not anticipate in your plan. What do you do next? We play our hands differently and change our visions, as well as our dreams and expectations. Before we know it, our life has changed, and sometimes dramatically.

Our lives change continually. However, most of this change is gradual. Over time, these accumulated adjustments become a radical change in our outlook and life's path. With a longer time-frame, the change is easier to recognize.

Now, think back. Can you remember a time or event that changed your life significantly? How did the event change your life? Was the change your choice or was it unavoidable? Why did you experience it?

Although everyday occurrences change our lives, how often do we evaluate those problems, issues, and opportunities? A good exercise is identifying what can change our lives. If we recognize those influences that could have a profound effect, we can prepare ourselves for the change, or avoid it entirely. Ask, what could change your life? Many have not considered this question.

Gain and loss are what we experience in life. These may include friendships, jobs, health, finances, success, marriage, divorce, or loss of a loved one. These are examples of influences that effect what we do and the way we feel. Many of us think that life could be better, if only we had made different choices - perhaps, finding a good friend or a new job, acquiring a large sum of money, or having better health, etc. Most change is from the result of a loss or gain, such as with a relationship, trust, reward, understanding, truth, forgiveness, or sorrow. Life is a combination of anticipating and reacting to these changes.

Gaining or losing a relationship can change the way we think. It can motivate, set our priorities, and instill an attitude. This can have a dramatic effect on us. Think back at the last 10 years of your life and list all that you have gained and lost. You will have a list explaining your life's position, place, and transformed attitudes. These relationships, rewards, opportunities, information, and influences are sources that can radically change our lives.

YOU AND CHANGE

What will happen to you on your life's path? How will your life end? What legacy will you leave behind? Will you have an effect on eternity? If not, perhaps a radical change may alter your answer.

Radical change results from a shift in thinking or knowledge. We may realize at some point that we did not base our path upon Truth or authenticity. Later, with a revelation of a Truth we may discover a sweeping change. The new information alters our outlook that changes our thinking and decisions. This is when we experience a paradigm shift in our life's path.

Some dictionaries define wisdom as, "knowledge of what is true or right coupled with just judgment as to action; sagacity, discernment, or insight." Knowledge and judgment are the core of wisdom. Have you ever heard the phrase, "The older we get, the wiser we become." This is because time and experience have allowed us to grasp Truths in our lives.

If you learned a Truth that was unfamiliar, would that change your life? Would you be any wiser? Could a new understanding influence how you respond to the cards that life has dealt you? Could a Truth change your life's path, goals, or priorities? Would Your Life Change IF…?

GOD, SIN, AND ETERNITY

A Rational Path to Christ focuses on seeking inspiring information and Truth that may transform your life. Take a moment to consider the Truths that have had an influence on your thoughts and actions. Ask yourself, "Which type of information could change the way I view my life from this point on?"

Many recognize God and believe that a higher entity exists. We say, "It's in God's hands now." "God help me!" "God help you." And, "In God's time." We sign contracts that exclude "acts of God." We have heard the statement, "there are no atheists in foxholes."

Do you believe in God? Is God Truth? What if God is real and eternal life is possible? If God exists, how does He view you? What would happen to you if you died right now? Where would you go? Based upon what you know and understand, what would happen next?

If you are not certain about God and you receive information that reveals Him to you, would you change? If you recognize you do not measure up to His expectations, would you change? If God established a plan for humanity that requires you to recognize, acknowledge, and follow Him, would you change? If you recognize the sinful nature of this world that separates us from a merciful God, would you change your outlook, behavior, and priorities?

If you acknowledge that God exists and wants a meaningful relationship with you, "personally" and He is calling "you" into an eternal relationship with Him, would your life change?

QUESTIONS AND STATEMENTS

Ask someone what he or she thinks about God. Either you will get an earful or the conversation will turn silent. Society's rules dictate that we should not discuss sex, politics, or, most objectionable, spirituality so that we do not offend. Many do not wish to discuss such matters because they are uninformed while others know that their beliefs will cause controversy.

Beliefs differ for many who seek God. They embrace different levels and doctrines of faith. Christianity is a clear example. The majority of people who believe in God, believe there are many paths that lead to Him. Most Bible-based Christians believe that there is only one way to God, and the way is through Jesus Christ. Some believe in Jesus as a great man and prophet. Some believe He lived and died on a cross, but never resurrected. Others think that Jesus is the heart of a mythical story.

Opinions are rampant regarding God, Jesus Christ, and religion. Listed below are typical quotations and questions you might hear, both inside and outside a church community.

- There is no factual basis for the Bible.
- An atheist I know argues against Christianity, and I do not know what to say.
- If there is a God, why does he let us suffer?
- Sure, my life has purpose; everyone says I am beautiful, wealthy and famous.
- The Bible has lost its meaning having been translated many times.
- I do not believe in God.
- I go to church, so I am a Christian.
- I do not get it. Why is Jesus the Savior and why did He have to die?
- Why do I need a savior?
- I do not witness my faith to others because I do not know enough.
- I am a good person; therefore, I do not need forgiveness.
- I do not believe Jesus ever lived.
- I have lived a good life, so I am going to Heaven.
- If I do not have it, how do I gain salvation?
- What is the Holy Spirit and how is He empowering?
- There is no "one" Truth, we all define our own.
- How can I live a life based on Truth?
- Is there a rational path to Christ, or is it faith-based?

Who are the people asking these questions and making these statements? We might not relate to all of them, but many of us can identify with several. Whom do you know that would make these statements or ask these questions?

- Agnostics
- Atheists
- Those claiming to be Christian, but not understanding Jesus' role for salvation or the Holy Spirit's role in power

- Christian critics

- New Christians

- Christians who don't confront skeptics because they lack the tools and understanding

- Any Christian seeking to enhance witnessing

- Anyone seeking God

Can you identify with any of the groups listed above? It is likely you fit into more than one category. Which categories are you?

WHERE ARE THE ANSWERS?

This book is "A Rational Path to Christ." The core of its nine segments ("The Path") provides answers to these and other questions. We will confront numerous topics to explore Truths. When we have fully explored the evidence and arguments building each individual Path Step, we move to the next Path Step, and so on. Much like the climb to the summit of Mt. Rainier, this book is a string of defined steps. You should take each Path Step deliberately and separately. Unlike my friend who made it to the top of Rainier, but never fully realized where he was and was unable to enjoy the destination, take each step deliberately. Understand the step, ensure you have a strong foundation on each, then propel yourself to the next level.

By moving from each Path Step to the next, we will build a rational path that leads to Jesus Christ. The Path concludes with explanations of who Jesus is and His purpose, what He did and why He is the true foundation for each of us. **A Rational Path to Christ** is an enlightening experience for new, mature, and non-Christians alike. Take each step, linger for a moment, and let it refresh you as you consider its truth. Then, only after you have established a strong foundation, launch to the next step. Taken one step at a time, you will be amazed at the distance you can cover and at the view from the summit.

We begin this journey by evaluating Truth and life's purpose. We will consider historical, archaeological, and scriptural evidence of the bible, and its certainties and accuracy. While seeking Biblical credibility, we explore God's purpose for man, and find out how sin appeared in God's plan.

With this credible foundation, continuing on The Path, we learn of God's desire for reconciliation with humanity and sin. We will establish an explanation of Christ's fulfillment of God's plan with man and explore God's grace, fulfillment, and purpose for humanity.

Toward the end, you should have a clear understanding of where you are on A Rational Path, and what to research in your next path step. In the end, you will have gained the necessary elements of a life based on Truth.

THE PATH

The Path is a collection of three Phases:

- **FOUNDATION** (Phase 1): We begin by exploring the purpose of humankind and the evidence for a solid foundation.

- **SALVATION** (Phase 2): Building on the foundation, we discover in God's word, His plan for us, and the salvation He offers through grace.

- **REALIZATION** (Phase 3): The Path concludes with studying the walk of the Spirit-filled Christian and living a Truth based life, and life's purpose.

Three Phases make up A Rational Path to Christ. There are several Path Steps within each Phase. "Would Your Life Change IF…? This is a question asked in every Phase. For example, "Would Your Life Change IF you knew Jesus was the key to salvation?" This is Path Step 6.

PHASE 1 - FOUNDATION

We will ask, "Would Your Life Change IF…?"

- Truth exists, and life can be fulfilling when it is truth-based.

- The Bible is compelling and credible; evidence exists that validates the Biblical record and teachings.

- You lost God due to your sin. Humankind disobeyed God, and the result has left us withdrawn from Him and His expectations.

PHASE 2 - SALVATION

We ask the following four questions. "Would Your Life Change IF…?"

- God has a plan to forgive sin, and his definitive plan provides redemption.

- Jesus Christ actually lived, died, and resurrected.

- God defines that Jesus Christ is the key to forgiveness of our sins and our salvation.

- Salvation through Jesus Christ connects you with God.

PHASE 3 - REALIZATION

The final Phase asks, "Would your life change IF…?"

- The Holy Spirit can guide your path and provide tangible evidence of God.

- A life based on Truth can be fulfilling and meaningful.

TYING IT ALL TOGETHER

By exploring these nine Path Steps, we connect and form a Rational Path to Christ. Each of these Path Steps establishes a foundation for understanding. Then, based upon this understanding, you have a solid foundation upon which to move on to the next Path Step, and so on. Certain Path Steps along The Path are factual and historical, requiring logical thinking while others offer Biblical Scripture and insight. The journey on a Rational Path to Christ is invigorating and challenging. Embrace an open mind and heart, and let your journey begin.

Will you take hold of the information, or gain a critical viewpoint that disrupts the foundations of your understanding and existence? As we discussed previously, will you gain or lose something? Will it be significant? Will this information change your life?

LIFE PATH CHANGES

The first Phase to A Rational Path to Christ asks, **"Would your life change IF...Truth exists?"**

In this chapter, we will try to answer some questions. What could change your life? What is the purpose of life? What is your life's purpose? In the search for Truth, we will discuss: rejecting, thinking, believing, and knowing, and use them as a Truth Scale to evaluate Truth as we proceed down A Rational Path to Christ.

A RATIONAL PATH TO CHRIST

PHASE 1

1	2	3
Truth Exists	**Bible Is Compelling & Credible**	**You Lost God Due to Your Sins**

Foundation

Path Step 1

Would Your Life Change IF…?

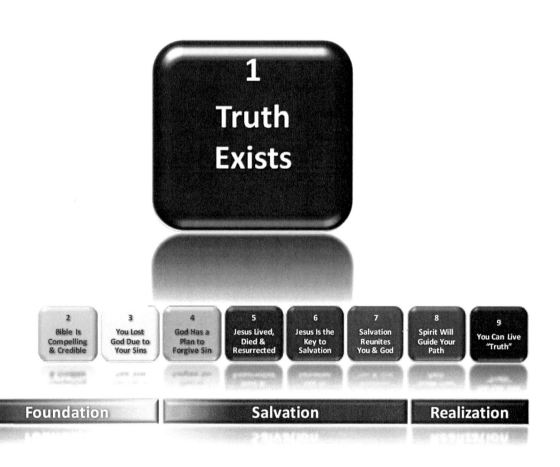

CONTENTS

THE BRIDGE TO PURPOSE

In my youth, I saw a movie that intrigued me. "The Bridge Over the River Kwai." The movie was made in 1957. Set in World War II, it starred William Holden, Jack Hawkins, Alec Guinness and Sessue Hayakawa. It won best picture at the Academy Awards. The movie is fictional but borrows from the construction of the Burma Railway in 1942–43 for its historical setting. Sessue Hayakawa plays a Japanese prisoner of war camp commander, named Saito. Saito has a bout of wills with and settles his differences with a Japanese Prisoner of War, Nicholson, a British colonel. Nicholson cooperates to oversee his regiment's construction of a railway bridge for Saito - while oblivious to a plan by the Allies to destroy it.

I was inspired by the theme of purpose, with and without foundation. Saito had a defined charge. He was commissioned to build a railroad bridge over the River Kwai so that Japanese troops and supplies could be transported by rail in the battle against an allied coalition, including the British. Saito had a well-defined and truthful foundation — strengthening of his team with a railroad bridge (for brevity, we will avoid debating the legitimacy of the opponents in this war). But, he had no sense of purpose and was unable to inspire his or the British troops. He was unable to lead and inspire his own men to build an effective bridge to cross the river, and he could not successfully force Nicholson and his men to do the same. Saito would not have been successful in his purpose had not the British Commander failed at his foundation.

On the other hand, enter British commander Colonel Nicholson. He watched as the Japanese failed in design and construction attempts. He enjoyed seeing the Japanese fail, as he was tortured for refusing to work. The Geneva Convention prevented Nicholson and his officers from manual labor, although Saito was unsympathetic. Winning the battle of wills against Saito, pride arose in Nicholson for his country and his countrymen. In a roundabout way, Colonel Nicholson led the British to design and construct a magnificent bridge that would endure long beyond the war. Despite the displeasure and disagreement of his subordinates, he led a team to quite effectively aid his enemy and hurt his country's cause. Colonel Nicholson had amazingly defined purpose, but he lacked a foundation. He was intent on building a bridge worthy of the British Empire, although it would be used as a tool to defeat the empire.

While an impressive bridge did get built, and then later was destroyed by British commandos, neither of these leaders was successful in and of themselves. In Saito's case, he had the proper foundation, but was unable to communicate and execute on his purpose. With the enemy's assistance, he was successful. More instructional for me is Colonel Nicholson. He had amazing purpose. He built a formidable bridge, despite the disagreement of his team. He gathered and organized an amazing effort, and was successful in his purpose, despite a foundation that is a polar opposite to that declared by his allies and motherland.

A great foundation provides the basis for success. But if a suitable purpose cannot be defined from its foundation, or if a solid purpose cannot be achieved, the objective is not achieved either. On the other hand, a successful purpose lacking foundation usually gets you nowhere, because work without a greater theme that does not get us to a true objective is likely meaningless. By chance, a foundationless purpose may be successful. But, the odds weigh heavy against this.

Are you Saito or Nicholson? Or, do you have a truthful foundation and a purpose consistent with your foundation that you are able to achieve?

PATH STEP 1: TRUTH EXISTS

The FOUNDATION Phase begins with Path Step 1: Truth Exists. We begin by asking the question, **"Would Your Life Change IF...Truth Exists?"**

Give this question some thought. What is Truth? If you learned of a Truth, how would you use or apply it? How do you define what Truth is? Are you confident that you know the Truth regarding important matters? Should Truth be your guideline in life? Does Truth matter to you? Does Truth define your life's purpose?

We will follow this outline:

- Your life's purpose

- Define: Rejecting, Thinking, Believing, and Knowing

- The existence of Truth

- Living Truth

- Truth and life's purpose

We will conclude this Path Step with the question asked at the beginning. Would Your Life Change IF...Truth Exists? Can you shape your life based on Truth?

Author's note: Complete the first half of the Assessment Questionnaire on Page 11. This questionnaire will help identify your beliefs prior to reading The Path. Upon completion, you will reexamine these questions to find what areas of your belief system have changed. This is a learning tool. Unless you choose to share, others will not observe your assessment.

LIFE'S PURPOSE

Does my life have a purpose? Whether or not you realize it, our life has a purpose, and you can discover what motivates it. In the previous section, change and motivation were introduced. We recognized that purpose and motivation are connected. Our purpose feeds the drive to accomplish.

Can your purpose change? Can it change by a new influence? Yes! Can change influence your life's purpose? Will Truth influence you to change? New information can change your life purpose.

What is your life's purpose? Are you satisfied with your purpose? Fears can stem from not knowing, or even considering it. Therefore, purpose can be difficult to grasp and answer.

Let us read what historical figures view as their "purpose for life":

- **Aristotle**
  "Happiness is the meaning and purpose of life, the whole aim and end of human existence."[1]

- **Maharishi Mahesh Yogi**
  "Life finds its purpose and fulfillment in the expansion of happiness."[2]

- **Dalai Lama**
  "I believe that the very purpose of life is to seek happiness."[3]

- **William James**
  "How to gain, how to keep, how to recover happiness, is in fact for most men at all times the secret motive of all they do."[4]

- **Voltaire**
  "Pleasure is the object, duty and the goal all rational creatures."[5]

- **Allen Coren**
  "To have a grievance is to have a purpose in life."[6]

- **Buddha**
  "Let us rise up and be thankful, for if we didn't learn a lot today, at least we learned a little, and if we didn't learn a little, at least we didn't get sick, and if we got sick, at least we didn't die; so, let us all be thankful."[7]

- **Ralph Waldo Emerson**
  "The purpose of life is not to be happy. It is to be useful, to be honorable, to be compassionate, TO HAVE IT MAKE SOME DIFFERENCE THAT YOU HAVE LIVED and lived well."[8]

These ideas infer that the purpose of life is some combination of being happy, useful, honorable, compassionate, and thankful. Their philosophies stem from personal interests. Although their perceptions are commendable, many of these beliefs do not provide instruction on "what" or "how." They specify an end but do not offer tools to obtain a result. Although you may gain wisdom from some or all of these statements, it is unlikely you will have derived a life purpose solely with these statements.

Christians who were God-fearing men formulated the United States of America. They signed and delivered to Great Britain a treatise for their separation from British leadership and law. This Declaration of Independence depicts why the United States severed their relationship. An excerpt from the Declaration reads, "We hold these truths to be self-evident that all men are created equal, that they are endowed by their Creator with certain unalienable Rights, that among these are Life, Liberty and the pursuit of Happiness."

In their writing, their "Creator" bestowed upon them "life" with the "right" to pursue happiness. Did these men believe that their purpose was "the pursuit of happiness?" Although they considered it humankind's right, their individual purposes differed significantly after considering the personal journeys described in the many texts and journals penned by authors of the Declaration of Indepedence.

Purpose dictates our focus and actions; therefore, a solid foundation is necessary. Emerson believed our purpose was, **"TO HAVE IT MAKE A DIFFERENCE THAT YOU HAVE LIVED."** Does it make sense to live and not make a difference? Do our actions have no purpose? Is our purpose the differences we make and leave in our wake? If so, purpose is about making a difference. A difference demands change; moving from one point to another.

How do we know our life's purpose? Situational analysis teaches that you cannot get from Point A to Point B without the following:

- An awareness of where you are right now (Point A)

- An understanding of where you want to go (Point B)

So, what compels you to act? Point B determines your motivation. We act in accordance with our motivations. Our motivations drive change. When we envision our dreams, it motivates us to act, so we may attain success. Acknowledging Point B and your process will identify your purpose.

So, what is your life's purpose? Is it happiness, money, spirituality, career, relationship, family, health, power, fame, belonging, or something else?

The answer is determined from your motivation. Motivation reveals a great deal about who you are and what you have chosen as your life's purpose. Direction will help you identify and develop it.

Let us read what historical figures have thought about life's purpose "personally:"

- **Henry David Thoreau**
  "Happiness is like a butterfly; the more you chase it, the more it will dilute you, but if you turn your attention to other things, it will come and sit softly on your shoulder."[9]

  (Focusing on purpose changes our true purpose. If you do not focus on your purpose, it will find you eventually.)

- **Dr. James Watson** (co-discoverer of the structure of DNA)
  "I don't think we're here for anything. We are just products of evolution. You can say, 'Gee, your life must be pretty bleak if you don't think there's a purpose.' But I'm anticipating a good lunch."[10]
  (Dr. Watson believes life occurs by chance. We are a random natural phenomenon, and lunch is something to be prized!!)

- **Eleanor Roosevelt**
  "The purpose of life is to live it, to taste experience to the utmost, to reach out eagerly and without fear for newer and richer experience."[11]
  (Eleanor Roosevelt started with the promise of a definition but ended with platitude.)

- **Unknown**
  "It may be that your sole purpose in life is to serve as a warning to others."[12]
  (If so, what is the purpose of life for "others?")

- **Unknown**
  "Never allow yourself to get discouraged and think that your life is insignificant and you cannot make a change. You will not have a sense of accomplishment unless you have defined the purpose of your life. Do not forget that you are a very special person and only you can fill the purpose to which you were born to accomplish."[13]
  (This is a practical thought lacking in definition.)

- **Richard Bach**
  "Here is the test to find whether your mission on earth is finished. If you're alive, it isn't."[14]
  (Started or finished, what is my purpose? Is death my sole purpose?)

- **W. Somerset Maugham**
  "Life is so largely controlled by chance that its conduct can be but a perpetual improvisation."[15]
  (Is life random? Is there a greater purpose?)

- **Moroccan Proverb**
  "He who has nothing to die for has nothing to live for."[16]
  (This is a practical guide when defining a purpose.)

- **Leonard Jacobson**
  "Everything that occurs in your life is part of God's plan to wake you up."[17]
  (What are you awakening to, and will you know when it happens?)

- **Unknown**
  "It's not enough to have lived. Be determined to live for something. It should be creating joy for others, working for the betterment of society, sharing what we have, bringing hope to the lost, and giving love to the lonely."[18]
  (Is this humankind's purpose? Is it your purpose?)

- **Robert Byrne**
  "The purpose of life is a life of purpose."[19]
  (How do we define purpose so that we can understand the purpose of life? Will any purpose do?)

- **Stacy**
  "We should give meaning to life, not wait for life to give us meaning."[20]
  (Are we to seek life's purpose and long for its meaning?)

- **Unknown**
  "God's purpose for your life does not end here on Earth; it will endure for all eternity."[21]
  (Is this Truth? How can we know? If our purpose endures for eternity, what is our purpose? How do we continue to have a purpose after we die?)

While these notions can assist us to shape our purpose, by their very nature they do not define it.

What is your life's purpose? Given some thought, here are some possibilities:

- Raise a family and prepare them for life
- Love and support your spouse
- Attain a vast amount of wealth
- Influence and shape the lives of others
- Serve others
- Leave a legacy of invention or knowledge
- Attain a vast amount of knowledge
- Attain recognition for your creativity
- Get even with others

Your purpose in life determines what you expect to be different when compared to you having not existed.

Imagine if you were never born. Now, imagine your life fully lived realizing all of your expectations. What is different? Character George Bailey played by Jimmy Stewart in "It's a Wonderful Life" received that opportunity. When George wishes he had never been born, his guardian angel shows him how his town, family, friends, and workplace would be without him. At the end, George understands his life's purpose. He realized his life touched other lives, which made a "difference." Knowing the "difference" is essential to understanding how you view your life's purpose.

PURPOSE AND TRUTH

Now, ask, why is "it" your life's purpose? More importantly, upon what is your purpose based. Why do you do what you do? Why do you want to make a difference? Are you indecisive of your purpose and motivation? Is your underlying motivation or foundation of your life's purpose based on a Truth?

A life's purpose not based on Truth can be meaningless. If your purpose has no Truth, then it is. If you do not define your purpose with Truth, it is probable your legacy will fade. Ask; will my purpose have a consequence in one year? …10 years? …100 years? …1,000 years? Into eternity? With honest consideration you might be surprised at your answers. Would it be exciting to define your purpose in life that is Truth-based and provides meaning to us and others well beyond this life and into eternity? In order to accomplish this, it is essential that you understand Truth.

SO, WHAT IS TRUTH?

Defining Truth is complex and has been a topic of discussion since before the great philosophers. They devoted considerable energy to the question, "Does Truth exist?" Some who have studied Truth journey down a path questioning whether humanity actually exists. If we do not exist, the notions quantified herein are completely irrelevant. We will not address these debates within the context of A Rational Path to Christ. With this context, let us now confront Truth and its existence.

Truth Defined

The dictionary and Internet both provide a great deal of information regarding its definition. Listed below are some of its meanings:

- An ideal or fundamental reality apart from and transcending perceived experience[22]
- An obvious or accepted fact[23]

- Conformity with fact or reality[24]

- A verified or indisputable fact, proposition, principle, or the like[25]

- Actuality or actual existence[26]

These definitions provide a sense of what Truth is, or what it is not. Although informative, these definitions do not provide a simple and practical method to evaluate evidence and Truth. As we study A Rational Path to Christ, we will evaluate issues, notions, beliefs, and their meanings. Before moving on to a subsequent Path Step, we need to evaluate the information presented and assess its Truth. We need to define a simple Truth Scale to measure Truth.

First, let us discuss Truth. In elementary school, we learn that 1 + 1 = 2. There are those that argue that one added to one equals something other than two. However, let us use the dictionary definition of Truth, "An obvious or accepted fact, a verified or indisputable fact, proposition, principle, or the like." The statement is Truth; 1 + 1 does equal 2. It is Truth.

The earth revolves around the sun. Truth! Kepler's Laws defined motion of astronomical bodies. Super-computers, star charts, and space travel have provided proof to define that the Sun is the center of the solar system. The planets follow an elliptical rotation around the Sun. This statement is Truth.

We humans were born, and we will die. Excluding any acts of God and the second coming of Jesus Christ in the Bible, is this statement true? Is there anyone alive today who was born more than 150 years ago? We sometimes live as if we are immortal, especially at a young age, but it takes an "Act of God" to change the reality that we will die. Therefore, this confirms that after we are born, we will surely die. This statement is Truth.

From a lack of knowledge and understanding, we have accepted Truths that were not. Do you know a "Truth" that was proven wrong? "The world is flat, and the sun, stars, moon and planets revolve around the Earth." In the past, it was unorthodox to believe otherwise. Because of space travel, telescopes, and astrophysics, we now "recognize" that the earth is round, revolves around the sun, and is the center of our solar system. That the world is round is a Truth.

It is likely that our descendants will observe our present 21st century philosophies and criticize our lack of understanding. Each generation benefits from the next because new data and insights are always developing. Can these benefits change Truth? No! However, they help reveal the Truth. We process information with skepticism and deliberation. Providing further evidence leads to an accurate definition of Truth. The evidence leads to an accurate assessment of Truth.

What Truths are hypotheses? One answer is evolution. Can one show evidence of Natural Selection? Yes. Is there proof that man evolved from a primate? Can we state truthfully that all species evolve from a more prominent "natural selection?" No. In fact, much evidence indicates the opposite, but many embrace it as fact. Schools worldwide teach evolution as the genesis of humankind. Does this topic require additional research? Do other hypotheses hold promise? Should we pursue these without studying the evidence and research? The answer is clear. Should we utilize logical analysis and a deliberate approach? Yes, we should.

"If all the ice melted in the Arctic Ocean, sea levels would rise." Many consider this a Truth. However, floating blocks of ice are displacing the volume of water equal to their weight. If these blocks melt, the remaining water will be equal to the blocks' displacement (ignoring the difference in density of fresh water and seawater). It is not a Truth. However, if the ice cap on Antarctica melted, sea levels would rise. The majority of the Antarctic ice blocks are supported by land and are not displacing any of its weight in water. Despite these facts, we have translated ice cap level fluctuation into sea level variations based on the "added" volume of melted ice. This is false or inaccurate, at best.

Some argue that Truth is relative. "I determine the Truth!" "What I believe is my Truth!" "I don't care about your Truth!" However, one person's belief does not define the Truth for creation. We are free to believe in whatever we choose. Some people defend a Truth that has no evidence, yet they believe it to be True. We cannot establish any notion as True unless there is evidence to support it. Regardless of your beliefs on this topic, let us pursue understanding based on evidence, on a path to truth.

OUR TRUTH SCALE

As we journey on A Rational Path to Christ, we must create descriptions of understanding and evidence in order to categorize the level and completeness of our topics. This we call a Truth Scale. We will not define Truth by the dictionary to measure our understanding, as they are too complicated. For example, is the existence of God Truth? Many say, "I don't know." If we apply a simple, but rational scale upon which to measure our level of understanding, it gives us a way to assess what we believe based on available knowledge. This simple Truth Scale enables us to progress on our journey seeking Truth.

Let us define four terms used in the Truth Scale. When examining a topic or theory on The Path, you will rate it with this scale.

- REJECT it—Does not stand up to basic scrutiny.

- THINK it—Considered a possibility, evidence exists.

- BELIEVE it—Substantial confidence due to significant available evidence.

- KNOW it—Rendered as fact based on irrefutable evidence.

REJECT, THINK, BELIEVE, OR KNOW

The Truth Scale assists with the truthfulness of a topic. For example, "the earth is round" do you:

- REJECT it

- THINK it

- BELIEVE it

- KNOW it

Your answer depends on the quantity or quality of evidence. For instance, gather the evidence that "the earth is round." Review also the information and arguments that the earth is flat. There are studies that have proven that the earth is round, so we can say that it is. For the statement "the earth is flat," is it confirmed as a proven fact? Based on the definitions above, where do you fall on your understanding of Truth? Many of us state the earth is round as a position that they Know. It is possible that someone could lack in data or understanding. Consequently, they only Think or Believe it is Truth.

As we conclude each Step on A Rational Path to Christ, we will ask, "Would Your Life Change IF...?" If your answer is "Yes," the topic is deemed important to us and possibly our life purpose. You will know that the topic requires consideration. You will then proceed to answer an additional question. Your answer is determined from the Truth Scale. Since your life would change if the topic were Truth, based on the evidence and available knowledge, will you Reject it, Think it, Believe it, or Know it.

If the topic is life changing, your answer to the question explains your understanding of the data available to you. Depending on your answer, you may want to explore the Path Step topic deeper, or proceed to the next Path Step. If proceeding, you need to be sure that the basis of your Truth is strong enough to hold up and provide a strong foundation to journey to the next course of study. As you answer these questions for all nine Path Steps, you will know where you are on A Rational Path to Christ.

A RATIONAL PATH TO CHRIST

Would Your Life Change IF...?

If you answered yes with the nine Steps, "Yes, your life would change," then identify what Truth Scale definition is accurate for each Path Step. With a Reject, you are at Point A, and that topic needs further exploration. With a Think, Believe, or Know, now you can move forward to your next, Point B.

DOES TRUTH EXIST?

We will explore whether your life's purpose is Truth-based, so we need to understand Truth. Answer the question, "Does Truth exist?" The following is an exercise regarding Truth that uses a paradox and illustrates a simple point.

Can one prove that Truth exists? Truth is a notion rendered as fact, based on evidence. This is our definition of "know." A fact is not a possibility; it is a known. Therefore, we must answer the question, "Does Truth exist?" by a yes or no.

The challenge is to prove that Truth exists. Answer this question, "Is it True there is no Truth?" Answer the question with either a yes or no. There are only two possible answers to the question; there is no maybe.

Let us presume your answer is "YES, it is true there is no Truth." If you answer yes, the question becomes the following statement, "It is True there is no Truth." The statement is "True," there is no Truth. Therefore, at least one Truth exists. "YES" proves that Truth exists, but that is only half the argument.

If the answer is "NO, it is not True, there is no Truth." It is a double negative. In the English language, when the use of two negatives are present in a single clause a double negative exists. A double negative is equivalent to the opposing answer, but without negatives; "It is True there is Truth." Therefore, "NO" proves Truth exists.

In both cases, it was necessary to presume the answer either a yes or no. Nevertheless, if only two possible answers exist to a question and both answers reveal the same outcome, by inference the outcome is sound! If we choose "Yes, Truth exists," or "No, Truth exists," then Truth exists!

Some dispute that a paradox proves nothing. Do you think it is fitting to exclude paradoxes from the evaluation of Truth? It proves the existence of "a" Truth. It does not prove any Truth besides the fact that at least this one Truth exists. Our paradox did not disclose the meaning of life or reveal humanity, origin, or destiny. It did not provide a solid foundation for your life's purpose based on Truth. It is the foundation of the first Step on a Path to discerning Truths that transform our thinking, viewpoints, and priorities.

With this understanding, seek Truth and apply it to your life. Truth is the basis of a lasting purpose. When you seek and explore Truth, you will discover more about your purpose.

DOES GOD EXIST?

In conclusion to Path Step 1, consider that many wander through life without considering, establishing, or planning for a life purpose.

- Life without purpose may be meaningless.

- Truth exists! You can prove it.

- A life's purpose not based on Truth may be meaningless.

- Most people do not invest time in seeking Truth.

The underlying question of A Rational Path to Christ asks, "What is God's purpose for my life?" If it is True that a God exists and He created you and the Universe, we can infer God created both with a purpose. Seeking God can expose or define your purpose. However, this analysis predicates on the existence of a god. So, do you believe in God? Are you an atheist? Are you an agnostic? Does your god meet your expectations of what a god should be? Does your god have the character you expect from a god? Is your god a creation of your own making? If you define "your god" with no supporting evidence, are you creating your own god? If you create a god, would that make you a god?

Either there is a God or there is not. Those that create their own god believe that Truth is relative. So, is Truth relative? No, absolute Truth exists. Does significant and compelling evidence exist substantiating your god, besides your own belief or imagination? If not, is your god truth?

The journey, A Rational Path to Christ will employ Truth to answer these questions.

1. What is the purpose of life?

2. Is there a God?

3. If there is a God, what is His purpose for us, for you?

SUMMARY

Our goal is to assist you with answering these three life-changing questions. When we get to Path Step 9, we will reexamine them. Until then, consider the following questions: What fundamentals of Truth drive your life? Can investigating Truth strengthen your life's purpose? Is your life worth investigating Truth and purpose?

In the spirit of Nicholson and Saito, is your purpose meaningful? Is your purpose effective, but lacking a truthful foundation, like Nicholson? Do you have truth as your stronghold, but cannot seem to achieve purpose that matters for your foundation, like Saito?

Realize the foundation of Saito and the purpose of Nicholson. Your purpose will have meaning that lasts.

As with each Path Step on a Rational Path to Christ, the Path Step concludes by asking the original question. Would your life change IF…Truth Exists? Yes or no? If yes:

- Do you REJECT that Truth exists?

- Do you THINK that Truth exists?

- Do you BELIEVE that Truth exists?

- Do you KNOW that Truth exists?

ASSESSMENT QUESTIONNAIRE

Name: _____ Date: _____

1.   My objectives for this study series are:

2.   Do I believe in God? YES or NO?

3.   Do I consider myself a Christian? YES or NO? *If YES to #2 & #3, go to Question #8. If NO to either, Continue.*

4.   Why do I not believe in God?

        _____

        _____

        _____

5.   Why do I not believe I am a Christian?

        _____

        _____

        _____

6.   What information, if I know were true, would convince me to be Christian?

        _____

        _____

        _____

7.   What is my life purpose? On what do I base my purpose and my decisions?

        _____

        _____

        _____

8.   Am I confident that I am "Saved"? YES or NO? *If NO, explain…if yes Go to Series Conclusion.*

        _____

        _____

9.   Even though I am saved, I have questions about Christianity? They are:

_____

_____

_____

10.   Am I able to witness to friends, family & others I know"? *YES or NO If No, why not?*

_____

_____

_____

Series Conclusion (Answer as directed in Path Step 9.)

11.   Do I believe in God? YES or NO

12.   Do I consider myself a Christian? YES or NO

13.   I can make the following three statements about Christianity that I could not make before?

_____

_____

_____

14.   I achieved some and/or all of my objectives for this series because?

_____

_____

_____

15.   I did not achieve all of my objectives for this series because?

_____

_____

_____

16.   Which (if any) is the earliest Path Step on which I do not either Believe or Know?

_____

_____

_____

17.   Since investigating deeper, I have made the following decisions/commitments for my life?

_____

_____

_____

18.   My Life Purpose is _____

_____

_____

_____

NOTES

1. "Life Quotes, Quotes about Life." Life Quotes, Quotes about Life. N.p., n.d. Web. 05 May 2012.

2. http://www.allgreatquotes.com/purpose_of_life_quotes.shtml.

3. http://www.allgreatquotes.com/purpose_of_life_quotes.shtml.

4. http://www.allgreatquotes.com/purpose_of_life_quotes.shtml.

5. http://www.allgreatquotes.com/purpose_of_life_quotes.shtml.

6. http://www.allgreatquotes.com/purpose_of_life_quotes.shtml.

7. "Let us rise up and be thankful." Think Exist. N.p., n.d. Web. 05 May 2012.

8. "The Purpose of Life Is Not to Be Happy." Think Exist. N.p., n.d. Web. 05 May 2012.

9. "Happiness Quotes." Wisdom Quotes. N.p., n.d. Web. 05 May 2012.

10. "I Don't Think We Are Here for Anything Were Just." N.p., n.d. Web. 05 May 2012.

11. "Quoteopia!" Famous Quotes & Quotations About Life -. N.p., n.d. Web. 05 May 2012.

12. FearGod.net, http://www.feargod.net/trivia.php.05 May 2012.

13. Praves World Accomplish Your Purpose." N.p., n.d. Web. 05 May 2012.14. "Here Is the Test to Fine Whether Your Mission On." Thinkexist.com. N.p., n.d. Web. 05 May 2012.

15. "Life Is so Largely Controlled by Chance That Its Conduct Can Be but a Perpetual Improvisation." Search Quotes. N.p., n.d. Web. 05 May 2012.

16. "He Who Has Nothing to Die for Has Nothing to Live for." Search Quotes. N.p., n.d. Web. 05 May 2012.

17. "Leonard Jacobson Question 5." Leonard Jacobson. N.p., n.d. Web. 05 May 2012.

18. "Purpose of Life." Http://pravstalk.com/purpose-of-life/. N.p., n.d. Web. 05 May 2012.

19. Find the Famous Quotes You Need, ThinkExist.com Quotations." Thinkexist.com. ThinkExist, n.d. Web. 05 May 2012.

20. The Quote Garden - Quotes, Sayings, Quotations, Verses." The Quote Garden - Quotes, Sayings, Quotations, Verses. N.p., n.d. Web. 05 May 2012

21. Antioch:God Purpose for Your Life." Antioch.blogspot.com. N.p., n.d. Web. 05 May 2012.

22. Dictionary.com - The World's Favorite Online Dictionary!" Dictionary.com. N.p., n.d. Web. 05 May 2012

23. Http://dictionary.reference.com/browse/truth. N.p., n.d. Web.

24. Http://dictionary.reference.com/browse/truth. N.p., n.d. Web.

25. Http://dictionary.reference.com/browse/truth. N.p., n.d. Web.

26. Http://dictionary.reference.com/browse/truth. N.p., n.d. Web.

Path Step 2

Would Your Life Change IF…?

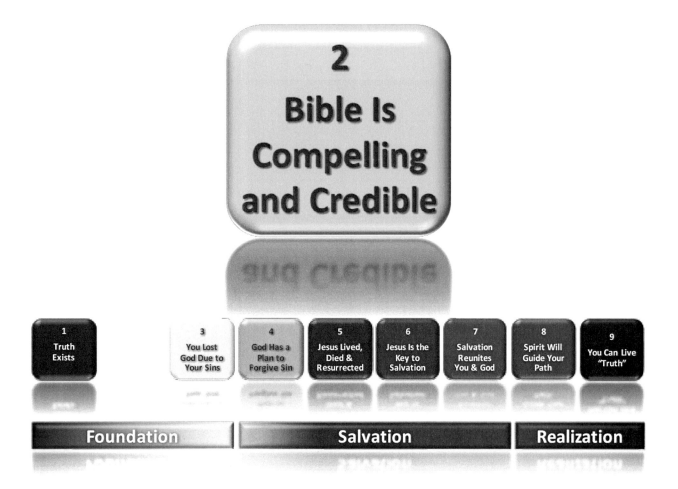

CONTENTS

Special Acknowledgement

The following pages contain photos from several sites. These photos find themselves cross-referenced and posted all over the web. Special permission has been given from these sites for use in this publication. These photos were originally accessed from a number of sites, at the end of this chapter you will see a list in the notes of the originally accessed location of the photos. Each of the photos will not be cited individually throughout this path step as many of the original cites did not obtain proper permission to use the photos within their sites and those sites have subsequently been removed from the Internet. Out of respect for the owners of these photos we spent a great deal of time finding and tracing as many of the orginal owners of the photographs and obtaining their permission to use them in this publication. Rather than cite each individual photo it was requested that this publication give a special recognition here at the opening of the chapter containing images that will take us along this Path Step in A Rational Path to Christ.

It is with great thanks that you are directed to visit the following sites for more inquiry regarding photos contained in this publication:

- wyattmusuem.com

- arkdiscovery.com

- Bible.ca

- cps.org

- ebibleteacher.com

RELIGION

I used to think of myself as religious. I recall hearing people admire others because they were "religious." "She's religious, what a good person she is!" I wanted to be religious, but I always thought that the religious among us seemed a bit stiff and rigid. Is that really what God wanted for us? I delved into the religious.

Later in life, I came to a point when religion no longer mattered as much as the basis or foundation of the religion. My God was not about religion. Rather, He just wanted me.

"Religion has done so much harm," many atheists say. "How can God be true?"

This presumes that the true God, if one exists, intended with omnipotence to establish a religion. Many of the gods that humanity has worshiped from the beginning of recorded time establish rules, guidelines and principles required to enjoy the god's professed blessings and truths. Taken to their ends, these rules and their basis are the establishment of religion. But, what if the true God, of all of the gods, did not come to establish rules and a religion? Is there evidence of such a God?

The following is a list of religions based on distinct gods:

- Muslim
- Hindu
- Buddhist
- New Age
- Sikh
- Judaism
- Baha'i

Each of these is based on a separate and distinct god (or believe in a collection of distinct and similar gods to the others in the list above), and each embraces their rules, guidelines and principles. While those human caretakers of each might not agree with my claim that each above is an established religion, the construction of its function and their followers' behavior within these groups are directed by those who maintain the idealism and foundation of their sect. Do their gods play any ongoing role, steering the sect along its progressive path?

You may be wondering about Judaism. Isn't the God of the Jews the same as the God of the Christians? Yes, that is true. However, the Jews believe only the Old Testament. The Old Testament Scriptures report a chronicle of God, but it is incomplete. The New Testament believed by the Christians completes the picture of God and defines a distinctly different nature for God than that subscribed by the Jews. With the Old Testament, humankind (the Jews) found it simple to create religion, and its respective rules. The New Testament believes in the God of Abraham, Isaac and Jacob, just as Orthodox Jews do.

Nonetheless, by strict scriptural reading, the God defined by the New Testament is quite different.

What if the evidence shows that this "fully revealed" God of the New Testament is truth, and it has not been, and is not this God's intent to establish any religion? Rather, what if God's purpose is to create an overwhelming relationship between Himself and individuals, conceived before the creation of the worlds; to have a one-on-one intimate relationship with His created? What if this relationship is predicated on humankind's God-given free will to mature and choose their own destiny? This is the God defined by the Old and New Testaments alike. The Bible defines such a god, my God. With greater understanding, this God became attractive to me.

As appealing as that may be, does the God of the Bible have foundation, a truthful foundation? Is the God of the Bible truth? It occurred to me that this God is true if the Bible is true. The Bible defines the existence and character of the one true God. But, are the claims of the Bible true? It doesn't matter what you think.

What does the evidence indicate?

Would Your Life Change IF...the Bible is Compelling and Credible?

As we move forward in the search for Truth, let us ask, "What does the Bible offer?"

Is the Bible True or is it a collection of fictional stories passed down by the Israelites and, later, the Gentile nations after 30 AD?

Does God exist?

Do Adam and Eve, Satan, the virgin conception of Mary, and Jesus rising from the dead seem far-fetched?

Surprisingly, there is more evidence verifying the Bible than any other published major writings of ancient history.

We started A Rational Path to Christ with discussions of Truth and purpose. As we progress, we will continue to identify a true and credible foundation. In Path Step 2, we will examine the fundamentals of the Bible. It is a study and review of only a sampling of available evidence that validates and verifies Scripture. Archaeologists have discovered that many of the people, locations, and findings written in the Bible are accurate.

There is an abundance of information available that allows us to see for ourselves. In fact, advances in technology continue to accelerate the rate of new discoveries. The goal of this Path Step is to explore various topics, evaluate the Bible's credibility, and seek a credible foundation from which to explore the next Path Step.

The Bible addresses a great deal about the purpose of life, humanity, and us as individuals. We will learn more about "purpose" as we continue our journey down The Path.

PATH STEP 2: THE BIBLE IS COMPELLING AND CREDIBLE

Is the Bible true? Is the Bible the word of God? Should we believe the Bible on faith alone? Does evidence exist to verify the Bible? Does the Bible prove the existence of God? Is the Bible compelling and credible?

Many have not read the Bible in its entirety. Some have read only a portion. The Bible provides an abundance of benefits if we seek its contents. Lessons and devotionals help us learn the meaning and purpose of Scriptures. With this understanding of the various parts of the Bible, you can gain a clear perspective of its larger purpose. Then, a complete read-through of the Bible will begin to make greater sense.

"Should we read the Bible?"

With which of the following statements do you identify?

- Biblical writings cannot be verified as authentic.

- When a new translation is written, the Bible loses its original meaning.

- The Bible is a collection of fictional stories with a moral agenda.

- There is little or no archaeological proof of biblical history.

- There is no proof that the Bible is the inspired word of God.

- Only parts of the Bible are true.

In Path Step 2, we will reflect on a fraction of information and evidence available, and then return to review these statements before proceeding to the next Path Step.

WHAT IS THE BIBLE?

The Bible conveys that it is the inspired word of God. The Protestant collection consists of the Old and New Testament. The duration of evidence obtained from the most dated Old Testament to the last surviving New Testament manuscripts is over 1,600 years.

Scholars believe that approximatly 40 authors wrote both Testaments. The authors wrote in Hebrew, Aramaic, and Greek while residing in the Middle East, Asia, Africa, and Europe. Since these writings, the Bible has been translated in over 2,200 languages. Billions of Bibles have been printed and distributed. No other book known to humankind has had such a profound influence in the world we live. It provides each of us a life-changing message. Is the Bibles foundation Truth?

Despite this diversity, the consistency, theme, and purpose from the beginning of the Old Testament to the ending in the New Testament are remarkable. These authors of ancient times wrote in their native language. When collated together, the Bible is a compelling narrative focused on God's reconciliation of humankind.

In Genesis, we learn of humankind's fall from grace, as well as God's plan for humankind to redeem fellowship with Him. First, we will examine the Old Testament. We will find out its value and why it was written.

THE OLD TESTAMENT

If the Bible's focus is the reconciliation of humankind, then the Old Testament supports the same idea, but with preliminary implications. The Old Testament is the first section of the Christian Bible, written prior to the birth of Jesus of Nazareth, the Son of God. It defines our world and the Universe, and the creation of Humankind—God's children.

In Path Step 3, we will discuss humanity's short-lived perfection and fall, and learn of God's expectations on how we can make amends. We will study the writings of various prophets who predicted Old Testament and New Testament events. The Old Testament is God's foundation and preparation for His son, Jesus Christ, who is the focal point of most of the prophecies.

The Bible is a progression of sequential information. It consists of prophecy and historical record written by God-inspired authors. The result is continuous, not linear. The Protestant Old Testament contains 39 books. In order: Genesis, Exodus, Leviticus, Numbers, Deuteronomy, Joshua, Judges, Ruth, 1 Samuel, 2 Samuel, 1 Kings, 2 Kings, 1 Chronicles, 2 Chronicles, Ezra, Nehemiah, Esther, Job, Psalms, Proverbs, Ecclesiastes, Song of Songs, Isaiah, Jeremiah, Lamentations, Ezekiel, Daniel, Hosea, Joel, Amos, Obadiah, Jonah, Micah, Nahum, Habakkuk, Zephaniah, Haggai, Zechariah, and Malachi.

The Pentateuch is the first five books of the Old Testament: Genesis, Exodus, Leviticus, Numbers, and Deuteronomy. It is also called the Torah which means instruction. Orthodox Rabbis believe Moses, a prominent leader of the Hebrew nation, wrote these five books with revelation from God. This occurred between 1312-1280 BC, when the Hebrew nation was located at or near Mount Sinai.

RECORDING THE OLD TESTAMENT

It was a priority to those in Old Testament times to record and teach biblical narratives, to pass information to later generations. The authors did not have use of modern day technology. Yet, they preserved the Old Testament records exactly how God commanded it.

(Psalms 12:6-7 NKJV) "The words of the LORD are pure words, Like silver tried in a furnace of earth, Purified seven times. You shall keep them, O LORD; you shall preserve them from this generation forever."

Biblical records were verbally passed down from one generation to the next and then by written media. Could this media be adequate to "preserve" the word of God? Let us review some of the materials used to record the messages from biblical writers. Papyrus, parchment, vellum, wax tablets, stone and clay tablets were the most popular means of recording a message for Old Testament writers.

Papyrus is the earliest paper used and a product of the papyrus plant. It dates back to 2400 BC. Parchment is animal skin; shaved, scraped, and then treated. Parchment became popular when papyrus and vellum were in use. It provides a smooth light colored material that absorbs ink.

Vellum is similar to parchment, but the animal skin is from a calf. It was lighter, more pliable and had fewer surface defects. Vellum dates back to 1500 BC. Animal skins were desirable as clothing and accommodated many other uses. With increasing demands for these writing materials, wax tablets were invented that could be easily erased and reused. Simply put, a wax tablet was a flat piece of wood overlaid with a thin film of wax. With a sharp pointed instrument, a writer would carve writings into the wax film. To correct a mistake, one needed only to reheat the wax and reset the film. However, as you can imagine, a disadvantage was that the tablets had to be stored in a cool environment.

Stone and clay tablets came about in the 6th century BC. The materials required to produce the tablets were plentiful. Stone and clay provided a permanent record that other methods could not. However, engravings required great work and effort and were prone to mistakes. Unlike their predecessors, if dropped they could shatter. Further, they were heavy to transport and cumbersome.

Media of different forms were available to record history from the earliest times. However, such techniques suffered due to the environment, aging, and disintegration. Although records were duplicated then passed on, the earliest copies had deteriorated, but eventually reproduced by another method. Nonetheless, various media were available and conveyed the Word and Spirit of God in the Bible for generations to present day.

TRANSCRIPTION

In earliest times, the Hebrews transmitted biblical records through verbal repetition from one generation to the next. To record and preserve these records, guarded copies were available for reproduction. This was a benefit since Hebrew records became widespread. To ensure accuracy and consistency, the Hebrews assigned specialists to produce Old Testament manuscripts. These trained specialists had a detailed set of rules. Over time, three groups of Hebrew transcribers existed.

The oldest of these transcribers were the Sopherim, who produced manuscripts from 400 BC-200 AD. To guarantee precision, a scribe would give their work to another Sopherim for validation. The scribe would count the number of verses, words, and letters of each book. The Hebrews destroyed all manuscripts that had a discrepancy.

Sopherim translation was from the Old Hebrew language that consisted of consonants and no vowels. Starting in 100 AD, the Talmudists succeeded the Sopherim. Talmudists implemented transcription services until 500 AD. Their work was similar to the Sopherim; however, they established an additional 17 rules for replicating that provided far greater accuracy. From 500-950 AD, the Masoretes who were scholars gave the final form to the Old Testament. They took the translations from the Sopherim that contained only consonants, and added vowel features.

Each of these groups duplicated manuscripts with the overriding goal of ensuring precision. After a copy was complete, another scribe would count the number of words in the Old Testament book. They would also count the number of times a specific letter appeared in a book, and then they would calculate the specific letter in the middle of a manuscript. These groups began this process at about 400 BC. Although, completed in an informal manner and format, records indicate Hebrew manuscript replication began well before 400 BC. From this point in history forward, the Sopherim, Talmudists, and Masoretes added the sanctioned, formal, and methodical process.

SCHOLARLY BOOK DATING

Scholars believe Moses wrote the Pentateuch (Genesis, Exodus, Leviticus, Numbers, and Deuteronomy) during the revelation of Torah at Mount Sinai between 1312-1280 BC. Hebrews refer to the Pentateuch as Torah or "the law" (instruction). The Nevi'im and Ketuvim are two remaining book collections of the Old Testament.

The Nevi'im, which is the second division of the Hebrew Bible, is a collection of prophetic writings. In the Hebrew canon, the prophets divide into two groups. The former prophets are Joshua, Judges, Samuel, and Kings. The latter prophets are Isaiah, Jeremiah, Ezekiel, and the Twelve (or minor prophets): Hosea, Joel, Amos, Obadiah, Jonah, Micah, Nahum, Habakkuk, Zephaniah, Haggai, Zechariah, and Malachi.

Table 1 │ Books of Nevi'im	Scholarly Dating
Book of Joshua	ca. 625 BC
Book of Judges	ca. 625 BC
Book of Samuel	ca. 625 BC
Book of Kings	ca. 625 BC
Book of Isaiah	Three main authors and an extensive editing process: 8th Century BC Isaiah 1-39 6th Century BC Isaiah 40-55 6th Century BC Isaiah 56-66
Book of Jeremiah	Late 6th Century BC or later
Book of Ezekiel	6th Century BC or later
Book of Hosea	8th Century BC or later
Book of Joel	Unknown
Book of Amos	8th Century BC or later
Book of Obadiah	6th Century BC or later
Book of Jonah	6th Century BC or later
Book of Micah	Mid-6th Century BC or later
Book of Nahum	8th Century BC or later
Book of Habakkuk	6th Century BC or later
Book of Zephaniah	7th Century BC or later
Book of Haggai	5th Century BC or later
Book of Zechariah	5th Century BC or later
Book of Malachi	Early 5th Century BC or later

The "Ketuvim" is the third division and is a collection of eschatological writings (prophetic writings of the end of the age or end times), literary wisdom and history, short stories, and worship and love poetry. Shown in Table 2 are writings from nearly 1000 BC to the middle of the 2nd century BC. Based on this information, these Old Testament books were written just after 1400 BC until the 1st century AD.

Table 2	Books of Ketuvim	Scholarly Dating
Psalms	The bulk of Psalms appears to have been written for use in the Temple, which existed from around 950-586 BC and, after rebuilding, from the 5th century BC until AD 70.
Book of Proverbs	Old material from ancient sages, some later material from 6th century BC or later, some material borrowed from the ancient Egyptian text called the Instructions of Amenemopet
Book of Job	5th century BC
Song of Songs or Song of Solomon	Scholarly estimates vary between 950 BC to 200 BC
Book of Ruth	6th century BC or later
Lamentations	6th century BC or later
Ecclesiastes	4th century BC or later
Book of Esther	4th century BC or later
Book of Daniel	Mid-2nd century BC
Book of Ezra-Book of Nehemiah	4th century BC or slightly later
Chronicles	4th century BC or slightly later

DEAD SEA SCROLLS

An archaeological find in 1947 provided evidence that the earliest version of the Old Testament translates with remarkable accuracy and precision to the version read today. The discovery of the Dead Sea Scrolls was located in caves along the northwest shore of the Dead Sea between 1947-1956, which is 13 miles east of Jerusalem and 1300 feet below sea level.

These religious scrolls represent the oldest known surviving copies of biblical, extra-biblical, and related documents. The scrolls were written in Hebrew, Aramaic, and Greek. Most of them are on parchment and others on papyrus. It is estimated that the scrolls were produced between 150 BC-70 AD.

The creators of these Old Testament scrolls identify with the ancient Jewish sect called the Essenes, a Jewish religious group from 2nd century BC to 1st century AD. The Essenes were fewer in number than the Pharisees and Sadducees, the two main Jewish religious sects in the Bible around the beginning of the AD dating system. The Essenes joined communally to a voluntary life of poverty, daily baptisms, and abstinence of worldly pleasures, which also included marriage.

Prior to this discovery, the oldest copy of the Hebrew text dated back to 1000 AD. Found in the Dead Sea caves inside clay pots were 15,000 fragments of 500 manuscripts. These scrolls dated back to 1st century BC, which was 1,100 years earlier. Remains of every book of the Hebrew canon are found (the Old Testament as the Hebrews maintained them). Of great significance were two nearly complete copies of the book of Isaiah from the Old Testament, word for word identical with the standard Hebrew Bible in more than 95 percent of the text. The five percent of variations attributes to slips of a pen and deviations in spelling.

Amongst the other findings were 19 copies of the book of Isaiah, 25 of Deuteronomy, and 30 of Psalms. These discoveries from the caves provided solid evidence that the text of the Old Testament has not changed in more than 2,000 years.

PROPHECY FULFILLED IN THE NEW TESTAMENT

The New Testament writings came after the birth, life, death, and resurrection of Jesus Christ. It is a collection of eyewitness accounts of Jesus and His ministry on Earth, as well as letters written by Jesus' disciples and apostles to Christian churches following Jesus' resurrection and ascension. The New Testament conveys the overall biblical theme of the redemption of humankind continued from the Old Testament.

The New Testament:

- Fulfills Old Testament prophecy
- Recounts the life and teachings of Jesus Christ
- Defines the forgiveness of sin through Jesus Christ
- Provides for salvation of all humankind
- Articulates prophecies fulfilled before present times, and the future.

While the Old Testament is a record of the Hebrew relationship with God, the New Testament fulfills prophecy of God's reconciliation of all humankind that includes Hebrew and Gentiles (all non-Hebrew societies) alike. The New Testament combined with the Old Testament forms the modern day Bible. All records, prophecies, commands, and values contained therein sustain a global outreach. The redemptive journey and promises in the Bible are for all humankind.

The New Testament contains 27 books: Matthew, Mark, Luke, John, Acts, Romans, 1 Corinthians, 2 Corinthians, Galatians, Ephesians, Philippians, Colossians, 1 Thessalonians, 2 Thessalonians, 1 Timothy, 2 Timothy, Titus, Philemon, Hebrews, James, 1 Peter, 2 Peter, 1 John, 2 John, 3 John, Jude, and Revelation.

The Gospels are the first four books of the New Testament: Matthew, Mark, Luke, and John. These writings recorded the life, death and resurrection of Jesus Christ. The Gospels are the proclamation of the good news. The writings were penned by specific followers of Jesus Christ, called the Apostles, most of whom walked with Jesus, witnessed, and recorded history, and were given directives to take the Gospel message to the nations.

Scholars believe that the writings of the New Testament occurred between 45 and 100 AD. However, the earliest fragments of these texts range from 100-300+ AD. Today, 24,000 manuscript copies of the New Testament exist. The writings are in Greek, Latin, and other languages and derive from apostolic writers over a few decades.

Providing a comparative reference, 643 copies of Homer's Iliad (written in the 8th Century BC) exist today, and come 400-500 years after the original. Although duplicated 1,000 years after the original, only 10-20 copies of Julius Caesar's writings (circa 50 BC) are in existence today. In comparison, the New Testament is corroborated by a great deal more manuscript copies that were written within a millennium (1/10th the time) of the original writings.

Regarding the content, the New Testament does not replace the Old Testament. The New Testament is much like a sequel to the Old Testament. The New Testament fulfills the sanctioned plan of God begun in the Old Testament and is a separation point between the first stages of God's plan (the Old Covenant) and its culmination (the New Covenant).

TRANSLATION: WORD-FOR-WORD + THOUGHT-FOR-THOUGHT

Old Testament writings are in Hebrew. However, the Hebrew alphabet and its language evolved over time. The Hebrews passed the Torah on without the burden of translating their language. The Hebrews took great care to ensure the accuracy of biblical stories from one generation to the next. Although the Hebrews received the Old Testament from God, since the days of Christ, biblical narrative is for all races, cultures, and languages of humankind. As recorded in the New Testament, the disciples of Jesus Christ received the gift of speaking in foreign tongues to deliver the message of the Gospel (Acts 2:1-6), the "Good News," to many cultures in New Testament times.

Originally, New Testament writers created manuscripts in Greek and Aramaic. Those who could not read these writings required the translation into their own language. However, words and ideas differ between languages. Greek, for instance, may not translate as a single word to the French language. Therefore, a translation could be several words replacing one, or one replacing several. Through time, biblical and language scholars gathered to develop these translations. In all cases, before translating texts they would need to establish rules. They were required to answer the question, "Do we translate the manuscripts 'word-for-word' or 'thought-for-thought?'"

Today, 25 translations exist from ancient manuscripts that convert to the English language. These vary in philosophy of word-for-word or thought-for-thought. The Interlinear and the New American Standard Bible (NASB) translations are closest to the word-for-word standard. The Living Bible and New International reader's Version (NIrV) are closer to the thought-for-thought. The popular King James Version (KJV) is closer to the word-for-word, and the New International Version (NIV) is, possibly, the most balanced.

In most cases, translators began their translation with the oldest manuscripts available. Many reject the Bible because they believe each translation builds upon a prior translation, rather than original or oldest manuscripts.

A common comparison made about the Bible is to the game "Telephone", where a message will be whispered to one person, then whispered to the next, and then so on. The resulting message is typically quite different from the original. These people believe that the Bible has lost its original meaning for a similar reason. However, this did not transpire in most biblical translations; each origin is the oldest manuscript texts and/or scholarly reproductions of the oldest texts. In a later chapter, we will review facts pertaining to New Testament manuscripts.

PROPHECIES FULFILLED

A biblical concern to Bible antagonists is that man wrote the "Word of God", so it is without divine inspiration. They struggle with its authenticity and believe the Bible is merely a moral narrative handed down from one generation to the next. An important facet of the Bible that separates it from other religious texts is the fulfillment of prophecies. While other religious texts may include prophetic prediction, very few, if any, have come true. Some biblical scholars state, "Even a blind squirrel finds a nut every now and then!" The Bible is full of prophecies in the Old and New Testaments that already have occurred and are occurring.

More than 1,500 prophecies in the Old Testament have predicted in detail future cities, and kings and kingdoms. More than 360 times in the Old Testament prophecies of the birth, life, death, and resurrection of Jesus Christ are mentioned (this is reviewed later in this text). Many have written books on fulfilled biblical prophecy.

If a prophecy occurs, many are interested, but believe that predictions eventually come true by coincidence. On the other hand, how does one explain the creation of a book that contains a vast amount of prophecy? The Bible contains over 1,500 prophecies most of which are fulfilled. Is this coincidental or written with ambiguity so that we could presume its fulfillment? Or, is this the work of visionaries? Yes, likely it is, and if so, where did they receive their visions and dreams? One plausible answer is from the Divine.

A historical overview of prophecy fulfilled in the Old Testament.

1. The prophecy of four great and powerful nations: Babylonian, Medo-Persian, Greek, and Roman (Daniel 2 and 7)

2. The prophecy specifying the date of Jesus' ministry (Daniel 9:20-26), we will review this in Path Step 8.

3. The fall of Tyre (Ezekiel 26)

4. The fall of Sidon (Ezekiel 28:22-23)

5.   The fall of Samaria (2 Kings 17):
  - City will fall violently (Hosea 13:16)
  - Will become "as a heap in the field" (Micah 1:6)
  - Vineyards will be planted there (Micah 6:15)
  - Samaria's stones will be poured down into the valley (Micah 1:6)
  - Foundations shall be "discovered" (Micah 1:6)

6.   The fall of Edom:
  - Edom will become desolation (Isaiah 34:13)
  - Will never be populated again (Jeremiah 49:18)
  - Will be conquered by heathen (Ezekiel 25:14)
  - Will be conquered by Israel (Ezekiel 25:14)
  - Shall have a bloody history (Ezekiel 35:5-6, Isaiah 34:6-7)
  - Will be made desolate as far as the city of Teman (Ezekiel 25:13)
  - Wild animals will inhabit the area (Isaiah 34:13-15)
  - Trade will cease (Isaiah 34:10; Ezekiel 35:7)
  - Spectators will be astonished (Jeremiah 49:17)

7.   The fall of Gaza-Ashkelon (Amos 1:8; Jeremiah 47:5; Zephaniah 2:4)

8.   The fall of Moab-Ammon (Ezekiel 25:3-4; Jeremiah 48:47 & 49:6)

9.   The fall of Thebes-Memphis (Ezekiel 30:13-15)

10. The fall of Nineveh (Nahum 1:8-10; 2:6; 3:10; 3:13; 3:19)

11. The prediction of Cyrus to rebuild Jerusalem (Isaiah 44:28). A heathen ruler named by the prophet Isaiah before the monarch was born.

12. Isaiah prophesied Uzziah, Jotham, Ahaz, and Hezekiah in his reign (Isaiah 1:1). His ministry occurred in the latter of the eighth century B.C. (ca. 740-701 B.C.). This was 150 years before Cyrus took his throne.

13. In 41:26, Isaiah states that the work of Cyrus was of prophecy, and not by speculation.It is a compromised faith to assume a late date for these prophecies.

14. One astounding prophecy of the Bible is in the last verse of Isaiah 44 and 45:1, where it refers to Cyrus, the King of Persia. According to the historian Herodotus (The Histories i.46), Cyrus was the son of Cambyses I. He took the Persian throne in 559 BC. Nine years later, he conquered the Medes, thus unifying the kingdoms of the Medes and the Persians as prophesied in Daniel.

It was 4,000 years ago when God called Abram out of the country to give him His promises.

"I will make you a great nation, and I will bless you and make your name great; so you shall be a blessing: And I will bless those that bless you and the one who curses you I will curse: and in you all the families of the earth shall be blessed." (Genesis 12:2, 3) "And the LORD said to Abram...'Now lift up your eyes, and look from the place where you are, northward and southward and eastward and westward; for all the land which you see, I will give it to you and to your descendants forever'" (Genesis 13-15).

God promises Abram a great nation, a great name, a blessing to all nations, and a land that shall forever belong to his descendants.

Several hundred years after God made His promises to Abram, the great nation emerged, numbering in the millions. The Israelites were about to enter the land as promised when God gave Moses His warnings. We see this in Deuteronomy, chapters 28 through 33. God warns them of disobedience and promises that He would use other nations to remove them from that land if they were unfaithful to Him. He predicted the Israelites would eventually be scattered across the earth as strangers of unfamiliar lands, and would find no rest from their wanderings. However, God in His faithfulness did promise to bring them back into their land.

What is the verdict of history? The children of Israel, even though warned, fell into idolatry, thus removed from their promised land. In 606 B.C., King Nebuchadnezzar took the Israelites captive to Babylon and returned in 588-586 B.C. After a long siege, he burned the city of Jerusalem and the Hebrew Temple.

However, as God promised, He allowed the Israelites to return to their land in 537-536 B.C., which was 70 years after (Ezra 1). Another removal from their homeland occurred in 70 A.D., when a Roman named Titus destroyed the city of Jerusalem and scattered the people.

For 1,900 years, the Jews wandered the earth as strangers, and they suffered persecution. This climaxed in the Holocaust of World War II, where the execution of six million Jews in concentration camps took place.

Nonetheless, the state of Israel was reborn on May 14, 1948, and the Jews returned to their homeland. This was the second time since becoming a nation that they have come back to their land. Since 1948, Israelites have survived several terrible conflicts; the 1967 6-Day War, and the 1973 Holy Day War. At the time of this writing, militant factions continue to surround Israel with the intent to obliterate them. This 1948 date for the creation of the Israeli nation was a prediction from the prophet Ezekiel (Chapter 4:1-6). We will review this in Path Step 8.

Through all this, the Israelite nation did not perish or lose its national identity. History proves that people who leave their homeland will eventually lose it. This happens four or five generations down the road. Their national identity then conforms into the resident country's culture. The Israelites survived, many of the nations that persecuted them perished. Ancient civilizations such as Moab, Ammon, Edom, Philistia and others had completely lost their identity or suffered defeat.

Have you ever heard of a Swedish Moabite, a Russian Philistine, a German Edomite, and an American Ammonite? Your answer is likely, "No!" The decedents of these people have been absorbed into other cultures and races. However, have you ever heard of a Swedish Jew, a Russian Jew, a German Jew, an American Jew, and an Israeli Jew? "Yes!" The Israelites have remained a distinct people since ancient times.

As prophesied in the Old Testament, Israel has not lost its identity.

- Israel will prevail over its enemies (Isaiah 41:12-14), Fulfilled—late 1900s.
- Ezekiel prophesied prosperity for modern-day Israel (Ezekiel 4:1-6, 36:11, 37:21), Fulfilled-late 1900s.
- Jerusalem would become the world's most important religious site (Micah 4:1), Fulfilled—Today.
- Zechariah prophesied the Jews return to Jerusalem (Zechariah 8:7-8), Fulfilled—1967.
- Isaiah foretold of the worldwide return of Jews to Israel (Isaiah 43:5-6), Fulfilled—late 1900s.

BIBLICAL ARCHEOLOGY

New technologies, global travel, the Internet, etc. have made research easier to confirm discoveries as factual evidence. We are able to explore, coordinate, collaborate, debate, and consolidate to prove that described Biblical events have actually occurred.

Advances in industrial and digital society are accelerating continually with information development. From the abundance of historical and archaeological evidence, biblical records indicate verification. However, can we prove beyond a reasonable doubt that any of this evidence is relevant or true? For most sources you find that relay substantial documentation supporting a biblical record, you will find others attempting to discount it. Nevertheless, overall Biblical evidence and credibility are increasing.

This review will provide evidence of several important topics in the biblical record. Is the evidence compelling? Yes! Do alternative opinions exist? Yes! Review the information with an open and critical mind. Reviewed objectively, the information can be overwhelmingly persuasive. We will consider evidence of the Exodus from Egypt, the Red Sea crossing, and the Mount Sinai encampment. If this evidence is authentic and compelling, it lays a solid foundation for the next two Path Steps. Consider the evidence and enjoy the journey!

EGYPT EXODUS AND RED SEA CROSSING

"So God led the people around by the desert road toward the Red Sea." (Exodus 13:18)

"When the king of Egypt was told that the people had fled, Pharaoh and his officials changed their minds about them and said, 'What have we done? We have let the Israelites go and have lost their services!' So he had his chariot made ready and took his army with him. He took six hundred of the best chariots, along with all the other chariots of Egypt, with officers over all of them. The LORD hardened the heart of Pharaoh, King of Egypt so that he pursued the Israelites, who were marching out boldly.

The Egyptians—all Pharaoh's horses and chariots, horsemen and troops—pursued the Israelites and overtook them as they camped by the sea near Pi Hahiroth, opposite Baal Zephon. As Pharaoh approached, the Israelites looked up, and there were the Egyptians, marching after them. They were terrified and cried out to the LORD. They said to Moses, 'Was it because there were no graves in Egypt that you brought us to the desert to die? What have you done to us by bringing us out of Egypt? Didn't we say to you in Egypt, 'Leave us alone; let us serve the Egyptians'? It would have been better for us to serve the Egyptians than to die in the desert!' Moses answered the people, 'Do not be afraid. Stand firm and you will see the deliverance the LORD will bring you today. The Egyptians you see today you will never see again. The LORD will fight for you; you need only to be still.' Then the LORD said to Moses, 'Why are you crying out to me? Tell the Israelites to move on. Raise your staff and stretch out your hand over the sea to divide the water so that the Israelites can go through the sea on dry ground. I will harden the hearts of the Egyptians so that they will go in after them. I will gain glory through Pharaoh and all his army, through his chariots and his horsemen.

The Egyptians will know that I am the LORD when I gain glory through Pharaoh, his chariots and his horsemen.' Then the angel of God, who had been traveling in front of Israel's army, withdrew and went behind them. The pillar of cloud also moved from in front and stood behind them, coming between the armies of Egypt and Israel. Throughout the night, the cloud brought darkness to the one side and light to the other side, so neither went near the other all night long. Then Moses stretched out his hand over the sea, and all that night the LORD drove the sea back with a strong east wind and turned it into dry land. The waters divided, and the Israelites went through the sea on dry ground, with a wall of water on their right and on their left. The Egyptians pursued them, and all Pharaoh's horses and chariots and horsemen followed them into the sea.

"During the last watch of the night the LORD looked down from the pillar of fire and cloud at the Egyptian army and threw it into confusion. He made the wheels of their chariots come off so that they had difficulty driving. The Egyptians said, 'Let's get away from the Israelites! The LORD is fighting for them against Egypt.' Then the LORD said to Moses, 'Stretch out your hand over the sea so that the waters may flow back over the Egyptians and their chariots and horsemen.' Moses stretched out

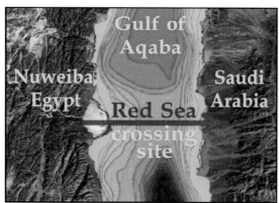

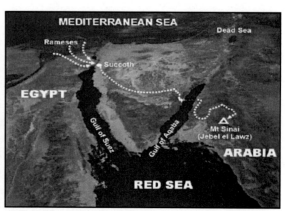

FIG 1A - PATH SUPPORTS ISRAELITE TRAVEL TO MT. SINAI

FIG 1B - HIGHLIGHTED RED SEA CROSSING OF ISRAELITE EXODUS FROM EGYPT his hand over the sea, and at daybreak, the sea went back to its place. The Egyptians were fleeing toward it, and the LORD swept them into the sea. The water flowed back and covered the chariots and horsemen—the entire army of Pharaoh that had followed the Israelites into the sea. Not one of them survived. The Israelites went through the sea on dry ground, with a wall of water on their right and on their left. That day the LORD saved Israel from the hands of the Egyptians, and Israel saw the Egyptians lying dead on the shore. When the Israelites saw the great power the LORD displayed against the Egyptians, the people feared the LORD and put their trust in him and in Moses his servant." (Exodus 14:5-31)

Evidence not shown here indicates the existence of Moses as an Egyptian prince, as well as numerous plagues, and the enslavement and release of the Israelites. As described in Exodus of the Old Testament, after Pharaoh freed the Israelites, they journeyed to Pi Hahiroth, on the Red Sea. Referenced to in figures 1A and 1B we see the evidence supporting the Israelite path to and location of Pi Hahiroth at Nuweiba, on the way to Mount Sinai.

FIG 2A - NUWEIBA PILLAR

To commemorate the Red Sea crossing of his ancestors, King Solomon placed a pair of pillars, one in Nuweiba on the Egyptian side (Fig 2A), and the other (Fig. 2B) on the Saudi side of the Gulf of Aqaba, of the Red Sea.

When first found by biblical archaeologist Ron Wyatt, (Fig. 3) the Egyptian pillar below had fallen over, was in the sea, and its inscriptions had worn off. The pillar on the Saudi side inscribed the words: Yahweh, Pharaoh, Mizraim, Moses, Death, Water, Solomon, and Edom. The Saudis have removed the pillar on the Saudi Arabian side of the Red Sea. However, the Nuweiba pillar still stands. Since this discovery, many investigators have researched the site and explored the sea floor near these pillars to confirm these findings.

FIG 2B - SAUDI SIDE PILLAR

FIG 3 - RON WYATT AT THE CROSSING

Fig 4A indicates the distance across the Red Sea at the suspected crossing location. It is about 13 kilometers across, with a maximum depth of 765 meters. The cross-section of the sea bottom is smooth and gradual. It could have been a crossing by the Israelites.

The chart (Fig 4B) shows depths of the surrounding area. It is evident that the slopes of both shores drop off very quickly

FIG 4A - RED SEA CROSSING DEPTH CHART - GULF OF AQABA

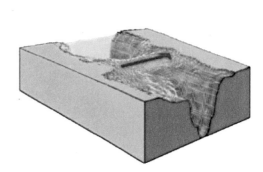

FIG 4B - UNDERSEA LAND BRIDGE | ISRAELITE PATH

to both the north and south. The slopes and terrain are so sharp, the only ocean floor path sufficient for the Israelites to cross on foot is the land unusually positioned, the submerged bridge at Nuweiba.

The ocean floor at this location is sandy sediment. Coral does not flourish in locations such as this because it needs an immovable solid object upon which to fasten and grow. To the north and south of the land bridge almost no coral exists. However, the site at the land bridge has many coral formations scattered in a line, stretching across the land bridge. Moreover, these formations have adopted non-natural shapes with right angles and other fabricated geometries. If the Red Sea parted and closed upon the Egyptian army, the land bridge should have evidence of chariots, horses, and human beings. These items would be present and make a solid formation, upon which coral could fasten and grow.

FIG 5A - SIX SPOKE EGYPTIAN CHARIOT | TIME OF EXODUS

FIG 5B - FOUR SPOKE EGYPTIAN CHARIOT HIEROGLYPHICS

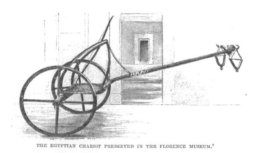

THE EGYPTIAN CHARIOT PRESERVED IN THE FLORENCE MUSEUM.'

FIG 5C - FOUR SPOKE ANCIENT EGYPTIAN CHARIOT SKETCH

Figs. 5A & B as well as 5C are actual hieroglyphics and an artist rendered depiction of chariots used by Egyptians around the time of the exodus from Egypt. There was an eight-spoke wheel used, as well. Many expeditions have investigated the sea floor and the land bridge at Nuweiba. shows coral encrusted chariot wheels, axles, and hubs. Figure 6A shows a symmetrical round object with another protruding from its center. The photo in Figure 6B shows an artist's overlay, portraying wheels and an axle beneath the coral growth. In figures 7A-7C we see coral encrusted wheels and Figure 7D an axle with an artist's illustration of a wheel embedded in coral. Coral does not form and grow as a circle with symmetrically spaced spokes originating from the center. This is evidence of Pharaoh's army destroyed by the collapsing of the parted Red Sea.

Perhaps, the most striking find is the gold overlaid, four-spoke chariot wheel shown in Figures 8A&B. The Egyptians constructed this chariot wheel of wood with thin gold plating overlaid on its surface. The wheel could not be removed after discovery, for it was too fragile because the wood disintegrated, leaving only a thin gold outer shell. The gold wheel is identifiable because coral is not able to attach to a smooth metallic plate surface. The four-spoke gold wheel and four-spoke Egyptian chariots validate to the time of Exodus. Finally, the remains of horses (Fig 9A) and humans (Figs 9B-D) are among the broken chariot fragments existing with a hard surface layer of coral. By themselves, these remains do not constitute proof that the land bridge at Nuweiba is the site of the Red Sea Crossing of Exodus. However, evidence of the Israelite journey from Egypt to the Red Sea and the land bridge shown in depth charts show the only place for crossing the Gulf of Aqaba by foot. The pillar markers on both sides of the crossing site, the existence of coral on only the suspected land bridge area, unnatural coral formations showing symmetrical and right-angled wheels, spokes, axles and hubs, and the journey to Mount Sinai shows the existence and credibility of a Red Sea crossing led by Moses.

FIG 6A - VERTICAL CHARIOT AXEL & SIX SPOKE WHEELS

FIG 6B - VERTICAL CHARIOT AXEL (OVERLAY)

FIG 7A - RED SEA CORAL ENCRUSTED WHEELS

FIG 7B - RED SEA CORAL ENCRUSTED WHEELS

FIG 7C - RED SEA CORAL ENCRUSTED WHEELS

FIG 7D - ENCRUSTED WHEELS WITH ARTIST OVERLAY

FIG 8A - RED SEA GOLD PLATED CHARIOT WHEEL

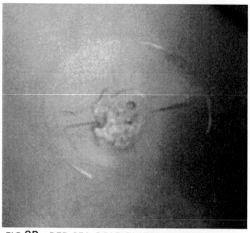

FIG 8B - RED SEA GOLD PLATED CHARIOT WHEEL

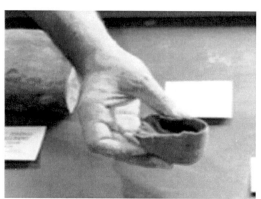

FIG 9A - RED SEA HORSE HOOF

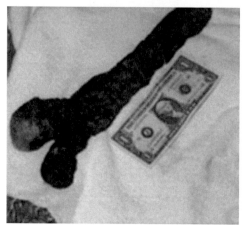

FIG 9B - RED SEA CORAL ENCRUSTED HUMAN FEMUR

FIG 9C - RED SEA CORAL HUMAN BONES

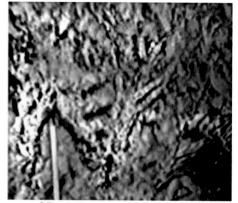

FIG 9D - RED SEA HUMAN RIB CAGE

INVESTIGATE FOR YOURSELF!

Investigate for yourself and assess your measure on the Truth Scale. Do you reject, think, believe, or know the Red Sea Crossing written in Exodus is Truth.

MOUNT SINAI

Is this Mount Sinai?

Roman Emperor Constantine appointed his mother, Helena, as "Augusta Imperatrix" and gave her unlimited access to the imperial treasury in order to locate relics of Judeo-Christian tradition. In 326-328 AD, Helena took a trip to the Holy Places in Palestine. Helena gave orders for the construction of a church in Egypt to pinpoint where she **thought** was the location of the burning bush of Sinai. The chapel at Saint Catherine's Monastery often referred to as the Chapel of Saint Helen, dates to 330 AD, and built at the base she believed to be Mount Sinai. However, this location shows little resemblance to the biblical record of the Exodus and encampment written in Leviticus. Figure 10 indicates the location of the path from the Red Sea crossing to the real Mount Sinai based on compelling evidence. The chart in Figure 11 depicts location evidence of the real Mount Sinai with respect to Jerusalem, to be explained later in Characteristic No. 3. In order to assess and identify the location of Mount Sinai, we consider biblical text as the key evidence.

FIG 10 - ROUTE TO MT. SINAI

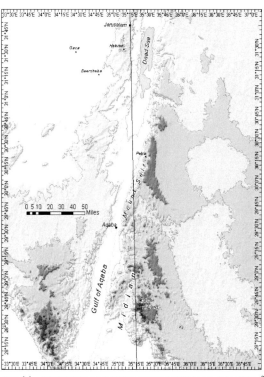

FIG 11 - MERIDIAN LOCATION OF JERUSALEM & MT. SINAI[3]

Next, examination of Scriptures will provide guidance to the location or path to Mount Sinai. The true Mount Sinai site and the path leading from Egypt would resemble and personify the characteristics in these Scriptures. Although incomplete, this text deliberates upon 21 characteristics of Mount Sinai as written in the Old and New Testament.

22 Biblical Characteristics of Mount Sinai:

Not in sequential order, the following 22 characteristics of Mount Sinai are for your deliberation. The characteristics apply to the location of the mountains, Jabal al Lawz and Jabal Maqla, in Saudi Arabia.

1. **Mount Sinai is located in Saudi Arabia, not the Sinai Peninsula as tradition states.**

"When Pharaoh heard of this, he tried to kill Moses, but Moses fled from Pharaoh and went to live in Midian, where he sat down by a well." (Exodus 2:15) Is Midian in Arabia?

"They answered, 'An Egyptian rescued us from the shepherds. He even drew water for us and watered the flock.'" (Exodus 2:19) If Moses rescued the women from shepherds, why would they clarify that he was Egyptian if he was from their land?

"So I have come down to rescue them from the hand of the Egyptians and to bring them up out of that land into a good and spacious land, a land flowing with milk and honey—the home of the Canaanites, Hittites, Amorites, Perizzites, Hivites and Jebusites. (Exodus 3:8)

"And now the cry of the Israelites has reached me, and I have seen the way the Egyptians are oppressing them. So now, go. I am sending you to Pharaoh to bring my people the Israelites out of Egypt." (Exodus 3:9-10)

"Moses said to God, 'Who am I that I should go to Pharaoh and bring the Israelites out of Egypt?'" (Exodus 3:11)

"God said, 'I will be with you. And this will be the sign to you that it is I who have sent you: When you have brought the people out of Egypt, you will worship God on this mountain.'" (Exodus 3:12) You will worship God on Mount Sinai only after the people have been "removed" from Egypt. The traditional site in Egypt does not fit.

After crossing the Gulf of Aqaba, the Israelites were out of Egypt and wandered in Arabia.

2. Some say that Mount Sinai is located in the farthest northwest corner of Arabia called, Midian.

"Now the LORD had said to Moses in Midian, 'Go back to Egypt, for all the men who wanted to kill you are dead.'" (Exodus 4:19) Midian is not in Egypt.

"Now Moses said to Hobab son of Reuel the Midianite, Moses' father-in-law, 'We are setting out for the place about which the LORD said I will give it to you. Come with us and we will treat you well, for the LORD has promised good things to Israel.' He answered, 'No, I will not go; I am going back to my own land and my own people.' Moses said, 'Please do not leave us. You know where we should camp in the desert, and you can be our eyes. If you come with us, we will share with you whatever good things the LORD gives us.' So they set out from the mountain of the LORD and traveled for three days. The ark of the covenant of the LORD went before them during those three days to find them a place to rest." (Numbers 10:29-33)

The Midianite wished to go back to his own land and people rather than to go ahead. Later, we learn that they set out from the mountain. The implication is that Midian is near Mount Sinai.

"Now Moses was tending the flock of Jethro, his father-in-law, the priest of Midian, and he led the flock to the far side of the desert and came to Horeb, the mountain of God." (Exodus 3:1) Mount Sinai is in the land of Midian.

3. Galatians placed Mount Sinai relative to Jerusalem.

"For this Hagar is Mount Sinai in Arabia, and answereth to Jerusalem which now is and is in bondage with her children. Jerusalem which is above is free, which is the mother of us all." (Galatians 4:25-26, KJV) Now Hagar stands for Mount Sinai in Arabia and corresponds to the present city of Jerusalem because she is in slavery with her children.

The geographical reinforcements of these two verses need identification. A composite of the geographical phrases yields this statement, "…Mount Sinai in Arabia…answereth to Jerusalem…which is above…" (Galatians 4:25-26, KJV).

Mount Sinai is in Arabia. Paul said this to introduce the general position of Mount Sinai relative to Jerusalem. The practice of the Hebrews was to view the world from the point of reference of Jerusalem. However, Paul specified the location of the mountain with two Greek words.

"Answereth," the first key word in the KJV, translates from the Greek word sustoicheo. It occurs only once in the New Testament, in Galatians 4:25. The meaning of sustoicheo carries the sense of corresponding, as in soldiers filing together in ranks (Strong's 1990, #4960). Aristotle used sustoichos, another form of the word, in the geographical sense of "standing on the same row or coordinate" (Liddell and Scott, 2000).

Also, used by Aristotle was *sustoichia,* which means, coordinate series. Hence, this word was useful for describing linear spatial relationships in geographical or military applications. Paul's use of *sustoicheo* seems to refer to the position of Mount Sinai relative to Jerusalem. In modern idioms, instead of *sustoicheo*, we might say that Jerusalem and Mount Sinai were on the same parallel of latitude, or on the same meridian of longitude.

Since *sustoicheo* suggests a physical geographical definition, Paul's use of it relating to Mount Sinai and Jerusalem suggest that his words imply a physical reality regarding Mount Sinai. If his idea is metaphorical, it would be structured using common Greek words for comparison, such as *homoioo*, (Strong's 1990, #3666)[2] or *parab*, but these terms do not carry the geographical meaning.

The second phrase, "Jerusalem, which is above [Mount Sinai]," clarified that Jerusalem and Mount Sinai corresponded to the same line of longitude. "Above" translates from the Greek *ano*, a word that can also mean "upward" or "on the top" (ibid. #507). It appears in the New Testament nine times. Its geographical meaning is "on the north" or "northward." The Greek historian Herodotus used this word (Liddell and Scott 1889, 83-84). Paul's inclusion of ano defined Jerusalem as being north of Mount Sinai on his line of *sustoicheo*.

With these observations, the geographical concepts in Galatians 4:25-26, summarize as follows:

- Mount Sinai was in the Arabia of Paul's day.

- *Sustoicheo*, Jerusalem and Mount Sinai are on the same line of latitude or longitude.

- Ano, Jerusalem was north of Mount Sinai.

- The north-south correlation puts Jerusalem and Mount Sinai on a similar meridian of longitude.

Galatians 4:25-26 implies that Mount Sinai and Jerusalem were located on or near the same meridian. Eastern Jerusalem is around 35-15'E in longitude. The peak of Jabal al Lawz is 215 miles south at 35-18.25'E, about 3.5 miles (5.7 km) east of that meridian. Jabal al Lawz, the tallest mountain in N.W. Saudi Arabia, is associated with the classical domain of ancient Midian. The meridian passes through the region, splitting Jabal al Lawz and Jabal Maqla. Hence, Paul placed Mount Sinai at the location of these two Arabian mountains (See Figure 11).

FIG 12 - JETHRO'S CAVES LABELED ON 1794 MAP OF ARABIA

4. Jethro, father-in-law of Moses, lived in Midian near Mount Sinai.

"Now Moses was tending the flock of Jethro his father-in-law, the priest of Midian, and he led the flock to the far side of the desert and came to Horeb, the mountain of God." (Exodus 3:1) "Now Jethro, the priest of Midian and father-in-law of Moses, heard of everything God had done for Moses and for his people Israel, and how the LORD had brought Israel out of Egypt." (Exodus 18:1) "After Moses had sent away his wife Zipporah, his father-in-law Jethro received her. (Exodus 18:2) When expelled from Egypt, Moses journeyed to Midian, where he met Jethro and his daughter Zipporah. Later, Moses returned to Jethro and Midian with the people of Israel." Figure 12 labels the Caves of Jethro in Saudi Arabia. Figure 13 is a picture of those caves.

FIG 13 - CAVES OF JETHRO[4]

5. The location of Elim, the 70 palm trees, and the 12 wells.

"Then they came to Elim, where there were twelve springs and seventy palm trees, and they camped there near the water" (Exodus 15:27)

In the Figure 15C, you can see many palm trees on Google earth, latitude/longitude (28°34'12.00"N-34°50'8.10"E). The Figures 15A and C are photographs (Figs 15 B-C) of the actual wells at this location. Although 70 palm trees no longer exist and the 12 wells are not operational, this represents another in a string of sequential and dramatic parallels to the biblical record of Exodus and the journey to Mount Sinai.(See Figure 14 for Elim location.)

FIG 14 - LOCATION OF ELIM ON PATH O MT. SINAI[5]

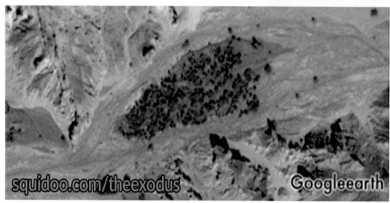

FIG 15A - 70 PALMS AND 12 WELLS AT ELIM

FIG 15 B -TWELVE WELLS

FIG 15C - SEVENTY PALMS

6. The Wilderness of Sin.

"And they took their journey from Elim, and all the congregation of the children of Israel came unto the wilderness of Sin, which is between Elim and Sinai, on the fifteenth day of the second month after their departing out of the land of Egypt." (Exodus 16:1)

Biblical narrative states, when reaching the "wilderness of sin," the Israelites began to raise objections over the lack of food as they already consumed all the corn they had brought with them from Egypt. According to Scripture, God heard their murmurings, so He provided them with an abundance of manna and quail for food. Manna described in the Bible is a fine flake-like substance, and in the book of Numbers, as arriving with the dew during the night. In Exodus, manna compares to hoarfrost in size. The Hebrews gathered it before it dissolved by the heat of the sun, and its color was white like coriander seed (See Figure 16).

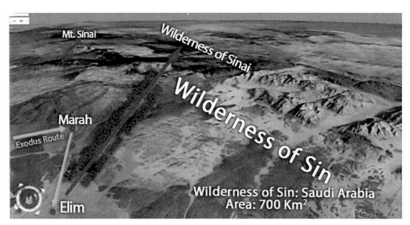

FIG 16 - WILDERNESS OF SIN LOCATION EXODUS 16:1

"I have heard the murmurings of the children of Israel: speak unto them, saying, at even ye shall eat flesh, and in the morning ye shall be filled with bread; and ye shall know that I am the LORD your God. And it came to pass, that at even the quails came up, and covered the camp: and in the morning the dew lay round about the host." (Exodus 16:12-13)

Quail are seen by two screen-captured pictures from a low-resolution YouTube video titled, "God of the Mountain" (2009), by Jim and Penny Caldwell (see Figure 17 A&B). While these photographs do show unmistakable quail, the video is far more instructive.

Figures 18A & B depict a section of a grinding mill or stone. It is likely the Israelites used this tool to grind manna in preparation for meals.

FIG 17A - QUAIL IN THE SINAI AREA

FIG 17B - QUAIL IN THE SINAI AREA

FIG 18A - EGYPTIAN-STYLE GRINDING STONES | MT. SINAI ENCAMPMENT

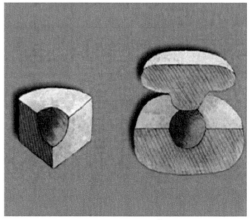

FIG 18B - EGYPTIAN-STYLE GRINDING STONES | MT. SINAI ENCAMPMENT

7. **The burning bush and, later, the camp of Israel were located on the backside of the mountain, away from the homeland of Moses and Jethro.**

"Now Moses was tending the flock of Jethro his father-in-law, the priest of Midian, and he led the flock to the far side of the desert and came to Horeb, the mountain of God. There the angel of the LORD appeared to him in flames of fire from within a bush. Moses saw that though the bush was on fire it did not burn up." (Exodus 3:1-2) (Fig 19A&B)

With no other bushes in this area and no cedar trees in this Arabian region, in the upper plateau, we see the cedar bush in figures 19 C & D, an eight-foot wide trunk (extracted from YouTube video titled, "God of the Mountain," 2009), by Jim and Penny Caldwell.

FIG 19A- ANCIENT CEDAR BUSH ON SINAI UPPER PLATEAU

FIG 19B- ANCIENT CEDAR BUSH ON SINAI UPPER PLATEAU

FIG 19C- ANCIENT CEDAR BUSH ON SINAI UPPER PLATEAU

FIG 19D- ANCIENT CEDAR BUSH ON SINAI UPPER PLATEAU

Olive trees, smaller in size in Israel, are known to be more than 2,000 years old. This ancient bush could be the 'burning bush of Moses' time.

The upper plateau is past the first ridge of mountains on Jebel Maqla and Jebel Al Lawz. In this area of Sinai, no other large bushes exist. Cedar trees do not grow in the mountains of this region of Arabia.

8. **There was an altar built of unhewn stones and pens for animals and chutes.**

"Make an altar of earth for me and sacrifice on it your burnt offerings and fellowship offerings, your sheep and goats and your cattle. Wherever I cause my name to be honored, I will come to you and bless you. If you make an altar of stones for me, do not build it with dressed stones, for you will defile it if you use a tool on it. And do not go up to my altar on steps, lest your nakedness be exposed on it." (Exodus 20:24-26) An altar structure is located at the base of Mount Sinai (see Fig 20 & 21)

As shown in Figure 22 leading up to the altar are animal pens (corrals) and chutes for holding and moving the animals staged for sacrifice. In Figure 23 men with prods walk behind the cattle toward the altar. The illustration shows the flow from right to left. It makes a corner, and then proceeds left to right and the definition of the pen area with the altar at the picture's base.

FIG 20 - LOCATION OF THE ALTAR AT THE BASE OF SINAI

FIG 21 - MOSES' ALTAR STRUCTURE

FIG 22 - OVERHEAD VIEW OF ALTAR AND LIVESTOCK CORRAL

FIG 23 - PENS, CORRAL AND CHITES AT MOSES' ALTAR

Figure 24 shows a large flat rock located in the vicinity of the altar area that has multiple petroglyphs showing men behind cattle in the chutes.

Figure 25 shows a close-up of the chute and ash receptacle at the base of Moses' Altar. As directed in Exodus chapter 20, God defined that no tools were be used to shape the stones in construction of the altar. We see flat-shaped rocks of various sizes that were gathered and laid to form a stone table with unhewn stones, believed to be Moses' altar.

FIG 24 - PETROGLYPH SHOWING MEN BEHIND CATTLE IN CHUTES

FIG 25 - PEN AREA AND ASH RECEPTACLE

9.   Moses strikes large rock at Horeb from which water flows.

"But the people were thirsty for water there, and they grumbled against Moses. They said, 'Why did you bring us up out of Egypt to make us and our children and livestock die of thirst?' Then Moses cried out to the LORD, 'What am I to do with these people? They are almost ready to stone me.'

FIG 26- COLLAGE OF CLEFT ROCK AT HOREB PHOTOS (CIRCLE IS GROUPED)

The LORD answered Moses, 'Walk on ahead of the people. Take with you some of the elders of Israel and take in your hand the staff with which you struck the Nile, and go. I will stand there before you by the rock at Horeb. Strike the rock, and water will come out of it for the people to drink.' So Moses did this in the sight of the elders of Israel." (Exodus 17:3-6)

Moses struck the rock with his staff and the rock split in two. From it flowed, perhaps, millions of gallons of water to quench the thirst of the Israel nation.

Of the evidence at the real Sinai, the split rock at Horeb may be the most prominent and convincing. Figure 26 displays a collage of six photos. The upper left photo shows the Rock of Horeb as viewed from Mount Horeb. The rock is extremely large and seen from a great distance in all directions.

The upper right photo shows the smooth erosive effects of the water flowing from the rock. Erosion is apparent where water would flow naturally. Rocks nearby and outside the path of flow are rough and jagged. However, beginning at the center of the split rock, the surfaces are smooth. As water flowed down from the rock, it carved several small riverbeds. Where the water flowed, it shows exposed rock and soft soils transported by river flow.

10. Mount Sinai had a stream.

"Also I took that sinful thing of yours, the calf you had made, and burned it in the fire. Then I crushed it and ground it to powder as fine as dust and threw the dust into a stream that flowed down the mountain." (Deuteronomy 9:21) The stream (brook) outlined by the markers, flows down from Sinai (see Figure 27).

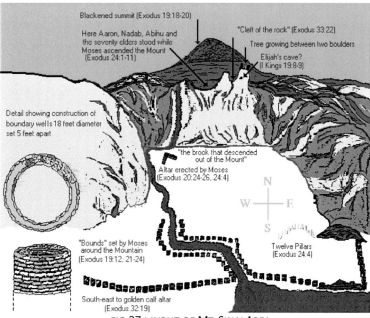

FIG 27 LAYOUT OF MT. SINAI AREA

11. An altar of the Golden Calf made within sight of the Mount Sinai.

"When Joshua heard the noise of the people shouting, he said to Moses, 'There is the sound of war in the camp.' Moses replied. 'It is not the sound of victory, it is not the sound of defeat; it is the sound of singing that I hear.' When Moses approached the camp and saw the calf and the dancing, his anger burned and he threw the tablets out of his hands, breaking them to pieces at the foot of the mountain." (Exodus 32:17-19)

Figure 28 many believe to be the golden calf altar at Mount Sinai. Figure 27 depicts an artist's rendering of the characteristics of the Mount Sinai site in Arabia. The lower left corner defines a golden calf altar to the southeast of the mountain.

FIG 28 - GOLDEN CALF ALTAR SITE

FIG 29 - ARABIAN GOVERNMENT FENCE

Shown to the left is a picture of a fence with a guard shack placed by the Saudi Arabian government. It surrounds the stone altar. (Fig 29)

(Fig 30) Peering through the fence one can see many petroglyphs on the large boulders forming the altar. This artwork is similar to the symbols for Egyptian gods.

Further, this area of Saudi Arabia has never been known to support cattle ranching or herding. However, the Israelites, after generations in Egyptian captivity, would be quite familiar with symbols and artwork for Egyptian gods and would have left Egypt with their cattle. Moses was on Mount Sinai for a considerable period talking with God. During this time, several Israelite tribes chose to rebel and worship the gods of Egypt. They recreated the Egyptian art on the altar of the golden calf.

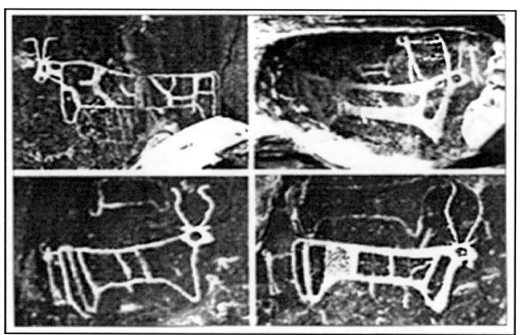

FIG 30 - EQYPTIAN CALF PETROGLYPHS ON ALTAR

12. Moses built a boundary to restrict access to the upper mountain and maintain its holiness.

"Moses said to the LORD, 'The people cannot come up Mount Sinai because you yourself warned us, 'Put limits around the mountain and set it apart as holy.'" (Exodus 19:23)

"Put limits for the people around the mountain and tell them, 'Be careful that you do not go up the mountain or touch the foot of it. Whoever touches the mountain shall surely be put to death." (Exodus 19:12)

(Fig. 31) The Mt. Sinai site overview shows two light blue colored lines that mark a stone fence. This fence may be the boundary markers built by Moses in accordance with God's boundary directive in Exodus 19.

FIG 31 - MT. SINAI SITE OVERVIEW

13. Twelve pillars were set up for each tribe.

"Moses then wrote down everything the LORD had said. He got up early the next morning and built an altar at the foot of the mountain and set up twelve stone pillars representing the twelve tribes of Israel." (Exodus 24:4)

Figures 32A & B show the remaining pillars at the Sinai encampment. There is a marble quarry on Jabal Maqla.

"Listen to me, you who pursue righteousness and who seek the LORD: Look to the rock (Fig 33) from which you were cut and to the quarry from which you were hewn." (Isaiah 51:1) The quarry holds remnants of unused pillars (Fig 34). They are rejections because they did not meet the specifications, and were broken in the cutting process.

FIG 32A - PILLARS REMAINING AT MT. SINAI

FIG 32B - PILLARS REMAINING AT MT. SINAI

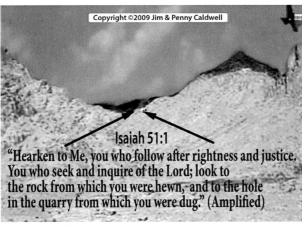

Copyright ©2009 Jim & Penny Caldwell

Isaiah 51:1
"Hearken to Me, you who follow after rightness and justice. You who seek and inquire of the Lord; look to the rock from which you were hewn, and to the hole in the quarry from which you were dug." (Amplified)

FIG 33 - LOCATION OF MARBLE QUARRY AT MT. SINAI

Copyright ©2009 Jim & Penny Caldwell

FIG 34 - MISSHAPEN PILLAR | MT. SINAI QUARRY SITE

14. Sinai had a habitable cave used by Elijah.

"So he got up and ate and drank. Strengthened by that food, he traveled forty days and forty nights until he reached Horeb, the mountain of God. There he went into a cave and spent the night. And the word of the LORD came to him 'What are you doing here, Elijah?'" (1 Kings 19:8-9)

Many believe Mount Horeb to be Jebel al Lawz, which is a smaller peak in the shadow of Jabal Maqla, the blackened top Mount Sinai. Figure 35 shows the possible location and (Fig 36 collage) view from Elijah's cave.

FIG 35 - ELIJAH CAVE AT MT. HOREB

FIG 36 - VIEW FROM ELIJAH CAVE AT MT. HOREB

15. The mountain was "exceedingly high."

Jewish historian, Josephus (ca. 37-100 A.D.) said that Mount Sinai was "the highest of all mountains that are in that country" (Josephus 1960, 70). If Josephus' information about Mount Sinai is accurate, his description agrees with the Jabal al Lawz range. In recent decades, Jabal al Maqla, a mountain within the Lawz range, gained considerable support as the precinct of the biblical Mount Sinai. Its peak is about 4.25 miles S SE of the main Lawz peak (Horeb). Between the Jabal al Lawz range and the Red Sea coast, there are no other candidates for a Mount Sinai. Jabal Maqla is the highest peak in the region.

16. The presence of God on Mount Sinai was a burning fire.

"To the Israelites the glory of the LORD looked like a consuming fire on top of the mountain." (Exodus 24:17) Unlike any other peak in the region, Jabal Maqla has a blackened top (Fig 37&38). Many speculate the blackened material is the result of a period of high heat to the upper mountain, or rock derived from a basaltic material. Although samples went to laboratory research, results have not yet been published.

FIG 37 - JABAL MAQLA, WITH HOREB TO THE LEFT

17. The Mount Sinai area had ample room for approximately 3,000,000 Israelites to camp next to the mountain.

"The Israelites journeyed from Rameses to Succoth. There were about six hundred thousand men on foot, besides women and children." (Exodus 12:37) A vast plain lies at the base of Jabal Lawz and Jabal Maqla. It would have been sufficient to accommodate three million people (Fig 39), tents and their livestock.

FIG 38 - BLACKENED PEAK OF MT. SINAI (JABAL MAQLA)

Moses' altar at base of mountain

Golden Calf Altar

Google

FIG 39 - LARGE ENCAMPMENT AREA AT BASE OF MT. SINAI

18. **From the campsite at the foot of the mountain, the children of Israel could see the presence of God.**

"Then Moses led the people out of the camp to meet with God, and they stood at the foot of the mountain. Mount Sinai was covered with smoke because the LORD descended on it in fire. The smoke billowed up from it like smoke from a furnace, the whole mountain trembled violently." (Exodus 19:17-18)

The picture to the right (Fig 40) shows the mountain base with direct and clear visibility to view (Jabal Maqla) as described in Exodus chapter 19 of Mount Sinai.

Thousands of flat land acres are near Mount Sinai, and ancient tent circles (Figs 41 A & B) formed by large rocks are evident in the areas of the split rock at Horeb, and near the base of Jabal Maqla.

FIG 40 - JABAL MAQLA PEAK FROM ENCAMPMENT

FIG 41A - A TENT CIRCLE FOUND NEAR HOREB ROCK AND MT. SINAI

FIG 41B - TENT CIRCLES FOUND NEAR HOREB ROCK AND MT. SINAI

19. **A plateau for Aaron, Nadab and Abihu, and seventy elders of Israel from which to view Jabal Maqla peak.**

"Then he said to Moses, 'Come up to the LORD, you and Aaron, Nadab and Abihu, and seventy of the elders of Israel. You are to worship at a distance, but Moses alone is to approach the LORD; the others must not come near. And the people may not come up with him.'" (Exodus 24:1-2)

A large secluded plateau exists on the eastern side of Mount Sinai, approximately half way up the mountain as shown in Figure 42. The elders were to worship at a distance. Figure 43 shows the view the elders had from the secluded plateau.

FIG 42 - MT. SINAI EAST FACING PLATEAU

FIG 43 - VIEW OF MT. SINAI FROM PLATEAU

20. A graveyard large enough to bury 3,000 Israelites, after the golden calf incident.

"When Moses approached the camp and saw the calf and the dancing, his anger burned and he threw the tablets out of his hands, breaking them to pieces at the foot of the mountain." (Exodus 32:19)

"So he stood at the entrance to the camp and said, 'Whoever is for the LORD, come to me.' And all the Levites rallied to him. Then he said to them, 'This is what the LORD, the God of Israel, says: Each man strap a sword to his side. Go back and forth through the camp from one end to the other, each killing his brother and friend and neighbor.' The Levites did as Moses commanded, and that day about three thousand of the people died." (Exodus 32:26-28)

North and east of Mount Sinai and Mount Horeb pinpoints a graveyard (see Figure 44). The graveyard is large enough to bury 3,000 people, with many grave markers (Figs 45-47) still upright (Fig 48).

FIG 44 - DEPICTS GRAVE AREA AT JEBEL EL LAWZ (SINAI)

FIG 45 - PRE-ISLAMIC ANCIENT GRAVEYARD

FIG 46 - OVERVIEW OF JEBEL EL LAWZ GRAVESITE

FIG 47 - GRAVEYARD AT JEBEL EL LAWZ

FIG 48 - UPRIGHT GRAVESTONE AT ARABIAN SINAI SITE

21.   A rectangular location is where the tabernacle and Tent of Meeting resided.

"Then have them make a sanctuary for me, and I will dwell among them. Make this tabernacle and all its furnishings exactly like the pattern I will show you." (Exodus 25:8-9)

Exodus describes at Mount Sinai, Moses' instructions for a tent-like sanctuary that was the center of Israel's worship. The sanctuary was referred to as the tabernacle (dwelling) and the Tent of Meeting.

The courtyard of the tabernacle was 150 feet long and 75 feet wide, had a washbasin for the priests, and an altar for burnt offerings. The tabernacle itself was 45 feet long and 15 feet wide. The inner court housed the Ark of the Covenant, which contained the tablets on which the Ten Commandments were written.

Moses moved the tabernacle to the outskirts of the Mount Sinai area. Outside the encampment is a rectangular foundation (Fig 49) the approximate size of the tabernacle. The Israelites took the tabernacle and Tent of Meeting with them as they traveled through the wilderness from Mount Sinai to Canaan.

FIG 49 -TABERNACLE LOCATION OUTSIDE ENCAMPMENT AFTER GOLDEN CALF INCIDENT

22.   Hebrew Petroglyphs

Perhaps, one of the most striking discoveries in Arabia is located near the Mount Sinai site at Jabal Maqla. In 2006, South Korean doctor, Sung Hak Kim found a large rock with petroglyphs. The petroglyphs are Hismaic graffito, with artwork that looks like a menorah. The menorah was designed by God and delivered to the Israelites for use in the Holy Place of the tabernacle. It is highly unlikely any other culture in the Sinai area would have the design or conceive of something similar in the same historical period. (Fig 50)

FIG 50 - MENORAH FOUND NEAR JEBEL MAQLA BY S. KOREAN DR. SUNG HAK KIM IN 2006

If this discovery and petroglyph can date to the time of The Exodus, it demonstrates that the Israelites journeyed to Arabia. This and the evidence surrounding Jabal al Lawz and Jabal Maqla would prove that the Israelite nation encampment was in Arabia, and Mount Sinai is not in Egypt, in favor of Saudi Arabia. However, based on all evidence thus far, the probability that Mount Sinai is not located in Saudi Arabia is minimal and grows weaker as time progresses.

SUMMARY

Much of this evidence coordinates closely with the biblical record. It is more difficult to argue against its credibility than it is to maintain its truth. The evidence for the Egypt Exodus, Red Sea crossing, and Mount Sinai (and the Hebrew encampment established there) are impressive and significant. This information serves to provide a foundation for Path Step 3 and Path Step 4 of A Rational Path to Christ.

A Rational Path: Path Step 3

Moses receives two tablets containing the Ten Commandments. He received them on Mount Sinai.

A Rational Path: Path Step 4

- Moses receives additional laws defining sin, forgiveness and sacrifice.

- Moses receives Instructions for building a Holy Place for God, the construction of a tabernacle, and directions for the sin offering. He received them at Mount Sinai.

In Path Step 5, we will review New Testament evidence in detail. This evidence includes, the Gospels, the Pauline epistles (written by the Apostle Paul), other written accounts, early Christian sources outside the New Testament, archeology, and prophecy leading to Jesus Christ's second coming corroborated by Old Testament prophets. The Old Testament accurately prophesied Jesus over 360 times. Prophecies of Jesus' Second Coming in the Old Testament, corroborates with New Testament prophecy, including the book of Revelation.

If one undertakes an objective study of the biblical record and historical evidence, the observations of the Bible presented earlier in this Path Step, we come to some interesting conclusions.

"Original writings cannot be verified as authentic."

The Bible provides more proof than any prominent manuscripts of the same period, and the process used to propagate its writings is precise and more detailed than any other record in history.

"Each time a new translation is written the Bible loses its original meaning."

Regarding the premise for authenticity, most modern-day translations derive from oldest existing manuscripts rather than translating a previous translation.

"It is a collection of fables, stories with a moral agenda."

Moral agenda…Yes. A short study of the Bible reveals a clear moral tone and design. The characters, places, and occurrences are historically based on authenticity and translation, as well as other historical records.

"No archaeological proof of biblical history."

Historical evidence/archeology is abundant at the very least, with greater evidence as time passes.

"There is no way to prove the Bible is the inspired word of God."

Unlike any other religion, Christianity (and Judaism) as defined in the biblical record employs prophecy extensively. In addition, much of these prophecies have transpired as recorded. The Bible proves an all-powerful God, with the power to create, inspire and influence!

"Only parts are true."

The Bible contains a historical record, descriptions, prophecy and lectures/letters to various groups and factions. It is difficult to prove the entire Bible. As many have realized, it is far more difficult to disprove it.

In the past 100 years, biblical proof through archeology has been plentiful. More factual, historical, archaeological, and fulfilled prophecy evidence supports the Bible than any other document in antiquity. An abundance of information exists in periodicals, non-fiction and on the Internet. One needs only to initiate an investigation to learn that the evidence is remarkable and significant.

As with each Path Step on A Rational Path to Christ, the Path Step ends with the same question from its beginning. Would your life change IF…the Bible is compelling and credible? Yes or no? If yes:

- Do you REJECT the Bible is compelling and credible?
- Do you THINK the Bible is compelling and credible?
- Do you BELIEVE the Bible is compelling and credible?
- Do you KNOW the Bible is compelling and credible?

Notes

1. "Mount Sinai and the Apostle Paul." Ancient Exodus. N.p., 08 Apr. 2016. Web. 05 June 2012.

2. "Mount Sinai and the Apostle Paul." Ancient Exodus. N.p., 08 Apr. 2016. Web. 05 June 2012.

3. "Mount Sinai and the Apostle Paul." Ancient Exodus. N.p., 08 Apr. 2016. Web. 05 June 2012.

4. "Bible Ca." Bible.ca. N.p., 05 June 2012. Web. 05 June 2012.

5. "Mt Sinai." Ark Discovery. N.p., 05 June 2012. Web. 05 June 2012.

6. "The Exodus Discovered! Egypt to Arabia." HubPages. HubPages, 05 June 2012. Web. 05 June 2012.

7. "The Exodus Route: Wilderness of Sin: Manna, Quails, Sabbath." The Exodus Route: Wilderness of Sin: Manna, Quails, Sabbath. N.p., 05 June 2012. Web. 05 June 2012.

8. "Flood." Flood. Cps.org, 30 May 2012. Web. 23 July 2016.

9. AllOtherNamesUsed. "Jim and Penny Caldwell - God of the Mountain [2009] SUBTITULOS EN ESPAÑOL." YouTube. YouTube, 23 Dec. 2011. Web. 05 June 2012.

10. AllOtherNamesUsed. "Jim and Penny Caldwell - God of the Mountain [2009] SUBTITULOS EN ESPAÑOL." YouTube. YouTube, 23 Dec. 2011. Web. 05 June 2012.

11. "Evidence at Jebel El Laws." Wyatt.redrokk.com. Wyatt.redrokk.com, 05 June 2012. Web. 05 June 2012.

12. AllOtherNamesUsed. "Jim and Penny Caldwell - God of the Mountain [2009] SUBTITULOS EN ESPAÑOL." YouTube. YouTube, 23 Dec. 2011. Web. 05 June 2012.

13. "Mount Sinai Featured on PAX Television." Mount Sinai Featured on PAX Television. N.p., 05 June 2012. Web. 05 June 2012.

14. "Discovery News." : The REAL Mount Sinai Is in Saudi Arabia. Discoverynews1.blogspot.com, 05 June 2012. Web. 02 June 2012.

15. "Mount Sinai." Wyatt Archaeological Research. Wyatt Museum, 08 Sept. 2011. Web. 05 June 2012.

16. "Mt. Sinai Found." Mt. Sinai Found. Ark Discovery, 05 June 2012. Web. 05 June 2012.

17. "Flood." Flood. N.p., Web. 02 June 2012.

18. AllOtherNamesUsed. "Jim and Penny Caldwell - God of the Mountain [2009] SUBTITULOS EN ESPAÑOL." YouTube. YouTube, 23 Dec. 2011. Web. 05 June 2012.

19. "Mount Sinai." Wyatt Archaeological Research. Wyatt Museum, 08 Sept. 2011. Web. 05 June 2012.

20. "The True Location of the Red Sea Crossing." Biblebelievers.org. Bible Believers, 05 June 2012. Web. 05 June 2012.

21. "Mt Sinai 10 Commandments Stone Tablets." Possibleimpossible.com. Possibleimpossible.com,, 02 June 2012. Web. 02 June 2012.

22. "Mount Sinai Found: Discovery in Saudi Arabia." HubPages. HubPages, 02 June 2012. Web. 02 June 2012.

23. "Mount Sinai." Wyatt Archaeological Research. Wyatt Museum, 08 Sept. 2011. Web. 05 June 2012.

24. "Mount Sinai." Wyatt Archaeological Research. Wyatt Museum, 08 Sept. 2011. Web. 05 June 2012.

25. AllOtherNamesUsed. "Jim and Penny Caldwell - God of the Mountain [2009] SUBTITULOS EN ESPAÑOL." YouTube. YouTube, 23 Dec. 2011. Web. 05 June 2012.

26. "Mount Sinai Found: Discovery in Saudi Arabia." HubPages. HubPages, 05 June 2012. Web. 05 June 2012.

27. "Mount Sinai and the Apostle Paul." Ancient Exodus. Ancient Exodus, 05 June 2012. Web. 05 June 2012.

28. "Newprovidencebc.com." Newprovidencebc.com. N.p., 05 June 2012. Web. 05 June 2012.

29. "Mt. Sinai Found." Mt. Sinai Found. Ark Discovery, 05 June 2012. Web. 05 June 2012.

30. AllOtherNamesUsed. "Jim and Penny Caldwell - God of the Mountain [2009] SUBTITULOS EN ESPAÑOL." YouTube. YouTube, 23 Dec. 2011. Web. 05 June 2012.

31. AllOtherNamesUsed. "Jim and Penny Caldwell - God of the Mountain [2009] SUBTITULOS EN ESPAÑOL." YouTube. YouTube, 23 Dec. 2011. Web. 05 June 2012.

33. AllOtherNamesUsed. "Jim and Penny Caldwell - God of the Mountain [2009] SUBTITULOS EN ESPAÑOL." YouTube. YouTube, 23 Dec. 2011. Web. 05 June 2012.

34. AllOtherNamesUsed. "Jim and Penny Caldwell - God of the Mountain [2009] SUBTITULOS EN ESPAÑOL." YouTube. YouTube, 23 Dec. 2011. Web. 05 June 2012.

Path Step 3

Would Your Life Change IF…?

HAVE YOU EVER TALKED WITH SOMEONE ABOUT GOING TO HEAVEN?

I have, many times.

It's curious that a majority of the people I have encountered believe they are clearly destined for Heaven. Isn't Heaven based on the Bible? It sure is. But doesn't the Bible tell us that, in the end, not everyone will go to Heaven. "The Bad" people are destined for Hell. But, that's not me!"

The Bible teaches that sin is unacceptable to God and that "sinners" will go to Hell, while the rest enjoy Heaven. So then, what is a sinner? Am I a sinner? Are you a sinner? The answer to both is likely, "Yes!"

Some think a more important question is, "Who is the biggest sinner?" Or, maybe, "I believe I'm a better person than he or she is. I'm going to Heaven, but she won't!" Another important question for them is, "Have I done more good things than bad?"

Would you believe that even Mother Theresa had so great a sin nature that by her own doing she would not be permitted into Heaven without assistance from God? Are you a better person than she? I know I am not!

Sin nature - what does it mean to be a sinner?

I know that I have sinned-many times, and I know that I have done considerable good in my lifetime. We will deal with the good works that we all accomplish later in this teaching. Let's start with a simple question.

Are you acceptable to God?

Would Your Life Change IF...You Lost God Due to Your Sins?

"According to the Ten Commandments, everyone has sinned, so what!"

"The Ten Commandments are not relevant today."

PATH STEP 3: YOU LOST GOD DUE TO YOUR SINS

In our search for Truth, we explored the Red Sea Crossing, and the "real" Mount Sinai site.

Let us consider the evidence of Mount Sinai.

Do you REJECT, THINK, BELIEVE, or KNOW it is Truth? If so, what implications does this have on the authenticity of Moses receiving two stone tablets on Mount Sinai, which are God's Ten Commandments?

THE FOUNDATIONS OF HUMANKIND

What is Sin? Sin is defined by the Bible as a violation of the Law of God:

- "Everyone who sins breaks the law; for sin is the transgression of the law." (1 John 3:4) Therefore, based on the laws, sin is any action, word, thought, or failure to act or go against the character of God, or against faith and confidence in Him.

- "All unrighteousness is sin." (1 John 5:17)

Based on Biblical text, God views sin as self-destructive and defiling:

- "Let not an evil speaker be established in the earth: evil shall hunt the violent man to overthrow him." (Psalm 140:11) Sin is more destructive to the sinner than to the person wronged by him.

- "Sin hunts the sinner down and overthrows him. Solomon said, but he that sinneth against me wrongeth his own soul: all they that hate me love death." (Proverbs 8:36)

- "Surely the arm of the LORD is not too short to save, nor his ear too dull to hear. But your iniquities have separated you from your God; your sins have hidden his face from you so that he will not hear." (Isaiah 59:1-2)

From the Old Testament, we draw the conclusion that sin separates man from God's purpose. If humankind had no sin, we would exist within God's purpose for us. So, does humankind have a purpose? We will discuss this topic soon, so let us continue.

The New Testament does not waiver on sin. "For the wages of sin is death." (Romans 6:23) Later, we will discuss this in the 6th and 8th Path Steps on A Rational Path; "a gift of God is eternal life." God wants us to share eternal life with Him. However, if we are sinners and we have not received forgiveness, death is our promise. This may appear to be a disparity, but God wants us to share His blessings and life with Him forever.

Nevertheless, we are sinners, all of us, and He will not accept sin. It would seem irrational that humankind's purpose on earth would involve overcoming sin to find favor with God. Should God choose to forgive all humankind and give us favor? The missing piece of this puzzle is understanding God's original and continuing purpose for man. Let us explore what the Bible says about humankind's purpose.

We will explore the book of Genesis, which relates to the creation of the Universe, and the first man and woman. For many, Jews, Christians, and agnostics alike, believing in Biblical creation and Adam and Eve is problematic. They do not accept that God created the Universe as recorded in the Bible, nor do they believe that humankind is rooted from a man and woman over 6,000 years ago. As one begins a study of biblical records, these precepts may be obstacles. For many who understand and believe, creation according to the book of Genesis is logical and substantiated. However, without proof, and clenching to theories as the universal big bang and evolution, many think that creation, and Adam and Eve, are only stories to justify humankind.

If you identify with these thoughts as you continue on this journey, do not let them become a roadblock. If you have a difficult time understanding biblical facts and fitting them into your way of thinking, study the text and understand its meaning. Familiarize yourself with the Bible and later return to the book of Genesis. Also, consider the biblical record of Adam and Eve in light of the archaeological evidence that validates a notable portion of the Old Testament following the first few chapters of Genesis. By doing so, you may have a different point of view. Perhaps, studying archeology of the Bible or a tangible experience with God may change your perspective. In any case, keep an open mind and seek to understand the biblical record.

IS THERE A GOD?

"In the beginning, God created the heavens and the earth." (Genesis 1:1) These questions confuse man:

- What is the beginning?
- When was the beginning?
- What was before the beginning?
- Did time exist before the beginning?
- Why did God create us?
- Am I a product of universal forces, or did a being of higher measure create humankind and me?

Because you have no definitive answer to all these questions, you leave it up to your imagination.

So, do these questions prove there is a god or a higher-level of being? Well, they do not disapprove it. When considering them without evidence, it is easier to accept there is a god than to believe that nothing ever existed. Some believe the creation of the Universe resulted from natural forces. However, there was no substance or energy in existence prior to universal creation with which to create it!

Can we be an atheist and say with certainty that there is no God? You either believe there is a God or not. If we are agnostic, we believe God may or may not exist. Because of our lack of understanding, we may not believe there is a higher being or a God. However, we cannot with certainty (Truth), know for sure, there is no God. If you believe in the big bang theory of universal creation, then who or what caused it to occur. Who created all things before the "bang" and when did it all begin? What is beyond the boundaries of our Universe? By not having answers to these questions, how can anyone claiming to be an atheist know for sure that there is not a God, and be fully Truthful?

MAN'S PURPOSE

"In the beginning, God created the heavens and the earth. Now the earth was formless and empty, darkness was over the surface of the deep, and the Spirit of God was hovering over the waters. And God said, 'Let there be light,' and there was light. God saw that the light was good, and he separated the light from the darkness. God called the light 'day,' and the darkness he called 'night.' And there was evening, and there was morning—the first day.

And God said, 'Let there be a vault between the waters to separate water from water. So God made the vault and separated the water under the vault from the water above it. And it was so. God called the vault 'sky.' And there was evening, and there was morning—the second day.

And God said, 'Let the water under the sky be gathered to one place, and let dry ground appear. And it was so. God called the dry ground 'land,' and the gathered waters he called 'seas.' And God saw that it was good.

Then God said, 'Let the land produce vegetation: seed-bearing plants and trees on the land that bear fruit with seed in it, according to their various kinds. And it was so. The land produced vegetation: plants bearing seed according to their kinds and trees bearing fruit with seed in it according to their kinds. And God saw that it was good. And there was evening, and there was morning—the third day.

And God said, 'Let there be lights in the vault of the sky to separate the day from the night, and let them serve as signs to mark seasons and days and years, and let them be lights in the vault of the sky to give light on the earth.' And it was so. God made two great lights—the greater light to govern the day and the lesser light to govern the night. He also made the stars. God set them in the vault of the sky to give light on the earth, to govern the day and the night, and to separate light from darkness. And God saw that it was good. And there was evening, and there was morning—the fourth day.

And God said, 'Let the water teem with living creatures, and let birds fly above the earth across the vault of the sky. So God created the great creatures of the sea and every living and moving thing with which the water teems, according to their kinds, and every winged bird according to its kind. And God saw that it was good. God blessed them and said, 'Be fruitful and increase in number and fill the water in the seas, and let the birds increase on the earth.' And there was evening, and there was morning—the fifth day.

And God said, 'Let the land produce living creatures according to their kinds: livestock, creatures that move along the ground, and wild animals, each according to its kind. And it was so. God made the wild animals according to their kinds, the livestock according to their kinds, and all the creatures that move along the ground according to their kinds. And God saw that it was good.

Then God said, 'Let Us make man in Our image, according to Our likeness; let them have dominion over the fish of the sea, over the birds of the air, and over the cattle, over all the earth and over every creeping thing that creeps on the earth. So God created human beings in His own image, in the image of God He created them; male and female he created them. God blessed them and said to them, 'Be fruitful and increase in number; fill the earth and subdue it. Rule over the fish in the sea and the birds in the sky and over every living creature that moves on the ground.'

Then God said, 'I give you every seed-bearing plant on the face of the whole earth and every tree that has fruit with seed in it. They will be yours for food. And to all the beasts of the earth and all the birds in the sky and all the creatures that move on the ground—everything that has the breath of life in it—I give every green plant for food. And it was so. God saw all that he had made, and it was very good. And there was evening, and there was morning—the sixth day." (Genesis Chapter 1)

God spoke the Universe into existence. He did not form it in His hands. He did not throw the stars into the vastness. He spoke all things into existence. As we further our studies, it is beneficial to understand the power of words, or the Word (Bible). Words have power. Many have not valued the power they possess in speech, to create and destroy. The power of life and death is in the tongue. Many have been either built up or torn down by the words of others.

In Genesis, we read several times that man is to rule. God gave humankind dominion over the earth. So, is man's purpose to rule the earth and all the creatures on it? Since God gave humankind dominion over the planet, does God rule over the earth? Let us continue.

HUMANKIND'S RESPONSIBILITY

"Thus the heavens and the earth were completed in all their vast array. By the seventh day, God had finished the work he had been doing so on the seventh day he rested from all his work. Then God blessed the seventh day and made it holy because on it he rested from all the work of creating that he had done. This is the account of the heavens and the earth when they were created, when the LORD God made the earth and the heavens.

Now no shrub had yet appeared on the earth and no plant had yet sprung up, for the LORD God had not sent rain on the earth and there was no one to work the ground, but streams came up from the earth and watered the whole surface of the ground. Then the LORD God formed a man from the dust of the ground and breathed into his nostrils the breath of life, and the man became a living being. Now the LORD God had planted a garden in the east, in Eden; and there he put the man he had formed. The LORD God made all kinds of trees grow out of the ground—trees that were pleasing to the eye and good for food.

In the middle of the garden were the Tree of Life and the Tree of the Knowledge of Good and Evil. A river watering the garden flowed from Eden; from there it was separated into four headwaters. The name of the first is the Pishon; it winds through the entire land of Havilah, where there is gold. (The gold of that land is good; aromatic resin and onyx are also there.) The name of the second river is the Gihon; it winds through the entire land of Cush. The name of the third river is the Tigris; it runs along the east side of Ashur. And the fourth river is the Euphrates.

The LORD God took the man and put him in the Garden of Eden to work it and take care of it. And the LORD God commanded the man, 'You are free to eat from any tree in the garden; but you must not eat from the Tree of the Knowledge of Good and Evil, for when you eat of it you will certainly die.' The LORD God said, 'It is not good for the man to be alone. I will make a helper suitable for him. Now the LORD God had formed out of the ground all the wild animals and all the birds in the sky. He brought them to the man to see what he would name them, and whatever the man called each living creature, that was its name.

So the man gave names to all the livestock, the birds in the sky and all the wild animals. But for Adam no suitable helper was found. So the LORD God caused the man to fall into a deep sleep, and while he was sleeping, he took one of the man's ribs and then closed up the place with flesh. Then the LORD God made a woman from the rib he had taken out of the man, and he brought her to the man. The man said, 'This is now bone of my bones and flesh of my flesh; she shall be called woman, for she was taken out of man.' For this reason a man will leave his father and mother and be united to his wife, and they will become one flesh. The man and his wife were both naked, and they felt no shame." (Genesis, Chapter 2)

In Genesis 2:7-9, God created humankind. In Genesis, chapters 1-2, we learn that God's intent was for humankind to rule the Garden of Eden and the earth. "The LORD God took the man and put him in the Garden of Eden to work it and take care of it." (Genesis 2:15) Here, the Old Testament reminds us that God gave man the earthly creation to work it and take care of it. The Scriptures do not state that God gave man the Garden of Eden and that He would show up once a week to mow and edge, or gather food for humankind's stores!

We learned that God began the creation of the physical world, and the place to create man and establish His kingdom. Humankind would be God's representative on earth. God began a family of offspring like Him, created by His own Spirit, in His image.

"Then God said, 'Let us make man in Our image, in Our likeness, and let them rule over the fish of the sea and the birds of the air, over the livestock, over all the earth, and over all the creatures that move along the ground. So God created man in His own image, in the image of God He created him; male and female He created them.' God blessed them and said to them, 'Be fruitful and increase in number; fill the earth and subdue it. Rule over the fish of the sea and the birds of the air and over every living creature that moves on the ground.'" (Genesis 1:26-28) God gave humankind dominion and authority (rule) over the entire earth and everything that lives upon it. From the beginning, God's plan for humankind was to have a personal relationship with Him and vice versa.

"For God so loved the world…" (John 3:16) It was love that motivated the God of the Universe to create children (called humankind) to share ruling of His kingdom. God created humankind for ruling and relationship. He wanted to extend his heavenly kingdom on earth, have a family of sons and daughters, not assistants; a kingdom of sons and daughters; a commonwealth of citizens, not Jews or Christians. Genesis makes it clear that God created humankind for a relationship, not religion.

Reading the biblical text, we learn that man's purpose is to rule the earth and love and honor God in fellowship. Therefore, what does God expect from us? Why did He create us? Genesis explains, "To rule the earth and exalt and love God in fellowship." God wanted us to glorify and love Him. He did not want us to be worship slaves, ones to love Him by force. Rather, He wanted a relationship with us based on love. He wanted us to appreciate His creation of humankind. It is His desire that we yearn to be with Him and worship Him, above all else.

"Know that the LORD is God. It is He, who made us, and we are His; we are His people, the sheep of His pasture." (Psalms 100:3) Genesis and Psalms advise us that God is the creator. He created us.

Still, what is God's purpose for Humankind? In Genesis 1 we understand that "In the beginning God created the heavens and the earth." Then, sometime thereafter, God created humankind and gave them dominion over all the earth. God gave humankind authority to rule over the entire planet. Psalms confirms this.

 "The highest heavens belong to the LORD, but the earth he has given to man." (Psalm 115:16)

Does this mean that God created humankind with the sole purpose of assuming dominion over the planet earth? While the assignment is a true and correct statement, it does not define the purpose for humankind.

Prior to Chapter 1, verse 1 in Genesis, wouldn't it be instructive to know what God was thinking before He created the universe and planet earth? If we could learn what He was thinking, could that illustrate His purpose for humankind? The answer is, "Quite possibly!" So, is there any way to learn what God was thinking before the foundation of our world? Yes, there is!

Read the three verse selections following. When taken together, they form a picture of God's thoughts, expectations, and plan, remarkably before the foundations of the world were in place. At this time, there was no physical world; only the spirit world and spirt beings. These scriptures give meaning to the entire text of the Bible from Genesis through Revelation, and reveal Humankind's purpose from God.

"In him we were also chosen, having been predestined according to the plan of him who works out everything in conformity with the purpose of his will, in order that we, who were the first to hope in Christ, might be for the praise of his glory. (Ephesians 1:11-12)

"For those God foreknew he also predestined to be conformed to the likeness of his Son, that he might be the firstborn among many brothers." (Romans 8:29)

"For he chose us in him before the creation of the world to be holy and blameless in his sight. In love he predestined us to be adopted as his sons through Jesus Christ, in accordance with his pleasure and will. (Ephesians 1:4-5)

Notice Ephesians 1:4-5 refers to the time "before the creation of the world." Therefore, we can get a glimpse into what God was doing prior to Genesis 1:1. It says that a selection of Humankind was to be with God ("in His sight") and that they are to be "holy and blameless," meaning without sin. The attribute of humankind becoming holy and blameless defines humankind's journey through almost the entire Bible. Next, the same verses define that God predestined those same people to be adopted as God's children through Jesus Christ. The word 'predestined' has caused disagreement amongst theologians. However, simply, it means 'to predetermine.' So, we can conclude that God predetermined before the creation of the worlds that God wanted to create a people who were holy and blameless in His presence, and He predetermined that in order to make them holy and blameless that they be adopted as children through Jesus Christ. How is that accomplished?

Review Romans 8:29. Here we have another similar verse using predestination. It says that God predetermined that this population, His children be conformed to the image of Christ. As we will learn later, being conformed to Christ's image would make one holy and blameless in God's sight. Another predestination scripture is Ephesians 1:11-12. There, we learn that God predetermined according to His plan that this same population has their hope in Christ. All three verse selections agree that God predetermined that He would create a race of humans that would be conformed to the image of Jesus Christ, and are, therefore, before God holy and blameless.

Further, in Ephesians 1:11-12 and 1:4-5, we learn that these people conformed to Christ's image would be His 'chosen' people, whom He could love and bless. Romans 8:29 indicates further that God foreknew all that would be conformed to Christ's image. Simply, this means that God, in his omnipotence and omniscience, was able to see all of humanity who by their free will would accept and be born again (conformed the image of Jesus Christ). He saw the completed collection of Humankind with whom He would spend an eternity in a loving, blessed relationship.

To summarize these verses, we learn the following regarding purpose:

- Before creation, God foresaw those who would accept His Son, Jesus Christ

- God predetermined that those He foresaw accept and be conformed to the image of Jesus

- A foundational element of Humankind's purpose is to accept the image of Jesus Christ to become "holy and blameless" in the presence of God.

- Humankind must exercise their free will to accept this purpose

- God would bless and love these conformed people, and they would become His Chosen.

- These, His Chosen, will freely worship and love God, satisfying God's desire in this relationship.

Part of humankind's purpose is to be conformed to the image of Jesus Christ. We will reveal more about this in Path Step 8.

"The highest heavens belong to the LORD, but the earth he has given to man." (Psalm 115:16)

No matter what we do, we are to glorify God. God established conditions of His relationship to earth through humankind. He did not say, "Let us…" rather, "Let them rule…over all the earth." Humankind has authority over the earth, we have power of attorney to act on God's behalf. What humankind chooses to do with it is humankind's decision, as it was in the time of Adam and Eve. Humankind has control over the earth. If God wants to make a change or influence it, He does it through humankind as He did by taking human form as Jesus Christ.

God made a covenant with a chosen people, the Israelites. Because the Israelites showed irresponsibility, God offered a perfect covenant to overcome humankind's failings. When initiating this new covenant, God did not threaten man's authority or his freedom to choose. God came to Earth to assist man in his weakness. Since it was humankind's planet, God took on the form of man to retrieve the authority humankind had yielded to evil. He became flesh and came to provide a covenant that would overcome humankind's failings (see Path Step 6). To change a matter concerning man, God became a man, but He never withdrew man's freedom to choose and free will.

Humankind's Purpose is to rule the earth, and glorify and love God in fellowship holy and blameless … conformed to the image of His Son, Jesus Christ. With this theme understood, as you read any section, you can begin to sense how God's greater purpose underlies all that is in Biblical writings, connecting both Old and New Testaments, as well as Old and New Covenants, alike.

FREE WILL

Some Christians believe that God exercises His sovereignty by manipulation; therefore, we do not have free will. They believe that God plans and controls all actions or activities on earth. Does God implement this level of control over humankind? No! Biblical text says that man has free will to exercise authority. (Proverbs 16:9, John 7:17, Revelation 3:20, John 1:12-13, 2 Timothy 2:26, Genesis 2:16-17, Galatians 5:16-17, Deuteronomy 30:19-20, Romans 10:9-10, Mark 8:34, 1 Timothy 2:4, Ezekiel 18:30-32, Romans 13:2, Deuteronomy 11:26-28, Genesis 4:6-7, 2 Corinthians 9:7, James 4:7, Isaiah 55:6-7, Ephesians 2:8-9, John 8:24, John 6:44, Jeremiah 13:23, Romans 9:16, Proverbs 21:1-31, Proverbs 1:29, Romans 6:23, Revelation 22:19, 1 John 2:2, 2 Timothy 2:25-26, Galatians 5:1, Romans 10:13, Romans 6:16, 2 Peter 3:9, John 3:16-17) God gave humankind the earth to manage and rule. More importantly, God desires our love and worship. To satisfy this desire, He could have created humankind that had no alternative but to love and worship Him. He could have instilled this in each of us, as an element of our nature. He could have controlled everything we say or do, to ensure that He received the glory and worship He desired.

However, if God operated in this manner, He would not receive that for which He created us. For love and worship to have true meaning, it is essential for God to supply free will. He wants us to worship Him because of His nature, because of His love for us, and not because we do not have a choice. Free will is the basis of true love, not just for God, but also for us. We get fulfillment when we are loved for who we are and what we do. We do not get fulfillment when told they love us, when we know they do not. When someone exercises love by free will, we experience validation. In life, nobody has to love us, but one may choose to love us by employing his or her free will.

"This day I call Heaven and earth as witnesses against you that I have set before you, life and death, blessings and curses. Now choose life, so that you and your children may live." (Deuteronomy 30:19) God gives each of us a choice, life or death, blessings or curses. Not only did God give us free will, He provided the correct answer…choose life. (See Path Steps 6, 8 and 9).

When we accept Jesus, we choose life, and fulfill God's purpose and destiny. God wanted us to choose Him and His righteousness, from a position of knowing that His way is the only way. Knowing that we could go awry with free choice, He wanted us to select righteousness of our free will and choose to love Him. God gave us free will to choose from good and evil. If by our free will we understood the condemnation of sin, we would know the goodness and joy of choosing His righteousness. Nevertheless, in the end, if we understand the love of God for humankind and each of us individually through Jesus Christ, and we choose Jesus Christ as our path, we receive the blessings of being predestined to be conformed to the likeness of His Son.

Humankind's purpose is in a loving, worship relationship with God, being conformed to God's image in Jesus Christ.

A perfect plan indeed. The cornerstone of this plan is free will. With something so precious and integral, what did humankind do with its free will?

THE FALL

We see that God gave humankind authority to rule the earth and have free will. What have we learned?

"The LORD God formed the man from the dust of the ground and breathed into his nostrils the breath of life, and the man became a living being." (Genesis 2:7) God created man.

"The LORD God took the man and put him in the Garden of Eden to work it and take care of it. And the LORD God commanded the man, 'You are free to eat from any tree in the garden, but you must not eat from the Tree of the Knowledge of Good and Evil, for when you eat of it you will surely die.' The LORD God said, 'It is not good for the man to be alone. I will make a helper suitable for him.'

Now the LORD God had formed out of the ground all the beasts of the field and all the birds of the air. He brought them to the man to see what he would name them, and whatever the man called each living creature, that was its name. So the man gave names to all the livestock, the birds of the air and all the beasts of the field. But for Adam no suitable helper was found. So the LORD God caused the man to fall into a deep sleep, and while he was sleeping, he took one of the man's ribs and closed up the place with flesh. Then the LORD God made a woman from the rib he had taken out of the man, and he brought her to the man. The man said, 'This is now bone of my bones and flesh of my flesh; she shall be called woman, for she was taken out of man.' For this reason, a man will leave his father and mother and be united to his wife, and they will become one flesh. The man and his wife were both naked, and they felt no shame." (Genesis 2:15-25) God created woman.

"The Serpent said, for God knows that when you eat of it your eyes will be opened, and you will be like God, knowing good and evil.' When the woman saw that the fruit of the tree was good for food and pleasing to the eye, and also desirable for gaining wisdom, she took some and ate it. She also gave some to her husband, who was with her, and he ate it. Then the eyes of both of them were opened, and they realized they were naked, so they sewed fig leaves together and made coverings for themselves.

Then the man and his wife heard the sound of the LORD God as he was walking in the garden in the cool of the day, and they hid from the LORD God among the trees of the garden. But the LORD

God called to the man, 'Where are you?' He answered, 'I heard you in the garden, and I was afraid because I was naked; so I hid.' And he said, 'Who told you that you were naked? Have you eaten from the tree that I commanded you not to eat from?' The man said, 'The woman you put here with me—she gave me some fruit from the tree, and I ate it.' Then the LORD God said to the woman, 'What is this you have done?' The woman said, 'The serpent deceived me, and I ate.'" (Genesis 3:5-13) Woman sins. Man sins.

"So the LORD God said to the serpent, 'Because you have done this, cursed are you above all the livestock and all the wild animals! You will crawl on your belly, and you will eat dust all the days of your life. And I will put enmity between you and the woman, and between your offspring and hers; he will crush your head, and you will strike his heel.'

To the woman he said, 'I will greatly increase your pains in childbearing; with pain you will give birth to children. Your desire will be for your husband, and he will rule over you.' To Adam he said, 'Because you listened to your wife and ate from the tree about which I commanded you, you must not eat of it, cursed is the ground because of you; through painful toil you will eat of it all the days of your life. It will produce thorns and thistles for you and you will eat the plants of the field. By the sweat of your brow, you will eat your food until you return to the ground since from it you were taken; for dust you are and to dust you will return.' Adam named his wife Eve because she would become the mother of all the living. The LORD God made garments of skin for Adam and his wife and clothed them. And the LORD God said, 'The man has now become like one of us, knowing good and evil. He must not be allowed to reach out his hand and take also from the Tree of Life and eat, and live forever.'

So the LORD God banished him from the Garden of Eden to work the ground from which he had been taken. After he drove the man out, he placed on the east side of the Garden of Eden cherubim and a flaming sword flashing back and forth to guard the way to the Tree of Life." (Genesis 3:14-24) Humankind fell.

God created His angels with free will, just as He did for humankind. The angels witnessed God's power and glory, and they worshiped Him in obedience. When studying the fallen angel, Satan, you will learn that he rejected God's authority and believed he could be God's equal. Satan, also known as the Devil, exercised his free will, and sought to reject God, and take over His kingdom and authority. God sent Satan to the Garden of Eden in Satan's pre-fallen state to support all creation. Motivated by pride, Satan desired worship. He implemented his free will and desired to be greater than God.

Satan used tactics such as subtlety, craftiness, and charm in the Garden of Eden. Employing deceit, he instilled in Adam and Eve that they could be as great as or greater than God.

"How you have fallen from Heaven, morning star, son of the dawn! You have been cast down to the earth, you who once laid low the nations! You said in your heart, 'I will ascend to Heaven; I will raise my throne above the stars of God; I will sit enthroned on the mount of assembly, on the utmost heights of Mount Zaphon. I will ascend above the tops of the clouds; I will make myself like the Most High.'" (Isaiah 14:12-14)

"The word of the LORD came to me: Son of man, take up a lament concerning the king of Tyre and say to him: This is what the Sovereign LORD says: You were the seal of perfection, full of wisdom and perfect in beauty. You were in Eden, the garden of God; every precious stone adorned you: carnelian, chrysolite and emerald, topaz, onyx and jasper, lapis lazuli, turquoise and beryl. Your settings and mountings were made of gold; on the day you were created they were prepared. You were anointed as a guardian cherub, for so I ordained you. You were on the holy mount of God; you walked among the fiery stones. You were blameless in your ways from the day you were created till wickedness was found in you. Through your widespread trade you were filled with violence, and you sinned.

So I drove you in disgrace from the mount of God, and I expelled you, guardian cherub, from among the fiery stones. Your heart became proud on account of your beauty, and you corrupted your wisdom because of your splendor. So I threw you to the earth; I made a spectacle of you before kings. By your many sins and dishonest trade you have desecrated your sanctuaries. So I made a fire come out from you, and it consumed you, and I reduced you to ashes on the ground in the sight of all who were watching. All the nations who knew you are appalled at you; you have come to a horrible end and will be no more." (Ezekiel 28:11-19)

"And there was war in Heaven. Michael and his angels fought against the dragon (Satan), and the dragon and his angels fought back. But he was not strong enough, and they lost their place in Heaven. The great dragon was hurled down—that ancient serpent called the devil, or Satan, who leads the whole world astray. He was hurled to the earth, and his angels with him." (Revelation 12:7-9) As a result, Satan's dominion became the earth.

Satan appropriated humankind's authority when humankind yielded to him. He was cast out of the heavenly realms. Now, he seeks to contain man's power of authority over the earth, destroy man, and distract man from worshiping God. This distraction began in the Garden of Eden.

Temptation comes from Satan, whose desire is to be as God. It is not by coincidence that Satan's first attempt at coercing humankind was to offer humans what he desired. Most of humankind's sin is the result of pride. Yielding authority to evil, man selects a god of his own choosing or elevates himself to a godly stature. Pride was the undoing of Adam and Eve, and it represents humankind's greatest downfall, even today.

With free will, humankind chose to disobey God. Sin entered the physical world. At that moment, humankind became unworthy of eternal fellowship with God.

What does Genesis teach us about God and man?

- God created humankind in His image.

- God gave humankind free will and authority to rule over the earth.

- God gave humankind one rule to follow. He may eat from any tree except the Tree of the Knowledge of Good and Evil, "For when you eat of it you will surely die!"

"And the LORD God said, 'The man has now become like one of us, knowing good and evil. He must not be allowed to reach out his hand and take also from the Tree of Life and eat, and live forever.'" (Genesis 3:22)

Adam and Eve disobeyed God's rule. From temptation, they ate fruit from the Tree of the Knowledge of Good and Evil. They broke the rule, disobeyed, and did not glorify God. Man "surely did die" when banished from the Garden, because God did not desire for humankind to live forever in a fallen state. At that moment, humankind was not allowed to live forever. Sin entered the world. The fall of man was complete. Not by God's choosing, but the free will of Satan seeking his glory and tempting man, and man, exercising his free will.

God banished Humankind from the Garden, not because man sinned, but rather that he and she became corrupted. Remember, it is God's plan to fellowship with a people that are holy and blameless in His sight. After the fall and the corruption of humankind, humankind is not holy and blameless in God's sight, not without divine assistance. God ejected humankind from the Garden so they could not eat from the Tree of Life and live forever in a state not fulfilling His purpose for humankind to be holy and blameless. This realization depicts a picture of God's nature and character generally not portrayed by a good deal of the Christian church at large.

Man and woman disobeyed. As Scripture states, toil and pain entered man's existence. The earth is no longer the Garden of Eden. Eternal fellowship with God was lost, but God understood humankind and resumed with His plan.

The biblical record describes how God desires for humankind to regain stature, to overcome sin, and again become worthy of God's fellowship eternally. God has not rescinded humankind's free will, and His power of attorney to rule the earth was restored with the embodiment of Jesus Christ. Earth is man's to rule. Jesus is referred to as the Son of God and the Son of Man. **He has the sovereignty of God and the authority of humankind.** However, God gave humankind free will. We will soon learn about an opportunity for humankind's free will that can save us from an otherwise certainty of death.

SIDE NOTE—THE GARDEN OF EDEN

Is it possible to find the Garden of Eden? If the Garden is on earth as described in Genesis, a remnant or fossil should be discoverable. Currently, there is no archaeological proof of the Garden of Eden, or Adam and Eve. However, theories flourish. Genesis states that God sealed the way into the Garden.

"After he drove them out, he placed on the east side of the Garden of Eden cherubim and a flaming sword flashing back and forth to guard the way to the Tree of Life." (Genesis 3:24)

A conclusion is that since God sealed Eden, man will not discover it or find any evidence of its existence. Considering Genesis 3:24, is it possible that the Tree of Life exists only in the spiritual and not our physical realm.

Based on biblical indications, some believe that the location of the Garden of Eden is somewhere in the Mediterranean, east of Israel, or in Saudi Arabia as shown in Figures 51, 52, and 53.

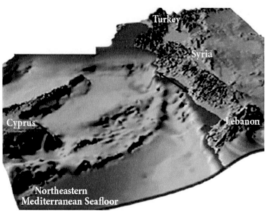

FIG 51 - EDEN SITE CONJECTURE[1]

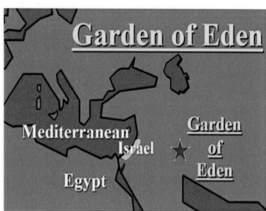

FIG 52 - EDEN SITE CONJECTURE[2]

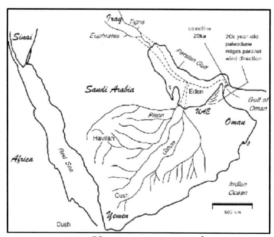

FIG 53 - EDEN SITE CONJECTURE[3]

Genesis, the first book of the Bible, records all creation. However, many believe that man evolved from a lower form of creature. Over time, through periodic changes, or evolution, emerged the human being of today, known as Homo Sapiens.

After studying Genesis and regarding the theory of evolution, it is most probable that creationism and the theory of evolution cannot coexist. Creationism states that God created man and woman, in the image of God. When created, man had language and free will. It does not state that man evolved from a primordial soup, to an ape, and then to Homo Sapien. Government funded and many privately funded schools in the United States teach the theory of evolution as scientific fact without regard to biblical creationism. Evolution is a theory, speculation without validity or proof.

As in Path Step 2, evidence exists confirming biblical accuracy. Many believe that Moses wrote Genesis, which is included in the Pentateuch.

The creation of man was to glorify and love God in fellowship. With free will, humankind was tempted, and sin entered the world. Humankind lost paradise and favor with God. Can humankind regain fellowship with God? Will God reclaim fellowship with humankind? The Bible describes our journey after man's expulsion from the Garden of Eden. Shortly after the exodus from Eden, God issues a covenant to man.

TEN COMMANDMENTS

What do we know about the Ten Commandments? For many of us, we relate to a bearded Charlton Heston in the Cecil B. Demille movie, "The Ten Commandments." Moses has long white hair and is barefooted, and he wore a Hebrew robe, and descends from Mount Sinai. When he arrives at the bottom of the mountain, Moses witnesses the Israelites dancing and worshiping a golden calf. Although the movie does not represent the biblical record perfectly, it provides an eloquent image of the Exodus from Egypt, the Red Sea Crossing, and the Ten Commandments.

Biblical records state that Moses received the Ten Commandments from God on behalf of the Israelites while he was on the top of Mount Sinai. Refer back to the evidence regarding the Red Sea Crossing and the Mount Sinai encampment in Path Step 2.

The evidence includes:

- The blackened mountaintop, the twelve pillars, the altar for the golden calf, and hieroglyphics of the Egyptian calf god displayed on the altar.

- The graveyard of the 3,000, the rock at Horeb that God split in the middle, and the water erosion from the millions of gallons of water on the rock at Horeb.

- Elijah's cave, Moses' altar to God, the boundary markers set by Moses, the 12 palms and the wells, and the caves of Moses' father-in-law, Jethro.

- Mount Sinai's geographical position, which is in accordance with the biblical text, has a foundation stone outline of the tabernacle that housed the Ark of the Covenant, and tablets of the Ten Commandments.

This evidence is so compelling that the Saudi government has fenced the area and has it guarded against all unauthorized entries.

If there is ample evidence of the Egypt Exodus, the Mount Sinai encampment and its location, and Gods' deliverance of the Ten Commandments, is it likely that Moses on Mount Sinai received the Ten Commandments, and then stored them in the tabernacle? The tablets of the Ten Commandments written by God were stored in the Ark of the Covenant (Path Step 4). The Israelites placed the Ark of the Covenant in the tabernacle. As shown in Path Step 2, evidence exists showing the rectangular stone outline of the tabernacle. This wealth of archaeological evidence, when compared to the biblical record, gives much credibility to the location and existence of Mount Sinai, and the journey of the nation of Israel. Then, is it not highly likely that the Ten Commandments are authentic?

"Moses was there with the LORD forty days and forty nights without eating bread or drinking water. And he wrote on the tablets the words of the covenant—the Ten Commandments. When Moses came down from Mount Sinai with the two tablets of the Testimony in his hands, he was not aware that his face was radiant because he had spoken with the LORD." (Exodus 34:28-29)

Moses received two stone tablets of the Ten Commandments that God inscribed with his own finger. Why did God give us His Ten Commandments?

PURPOSE OF THE COMMANDMENTS

"Then Moses went up to God, and the LORD called to him from the mountain and said, 'This is what you are to say to the house of Jacob and what you are to tell the people of Israel: You yourselves have seen what I did to Egypt, and how I carried you on eagles wings and brought you to myself. Now if you obey me fully and keep my covenant, then out of all nations you will be my treasured possession.'" (Exodus 19:3-5)

The Ten Commandments are a list of God's laws and the foundation of the covenant between God and His people. God specifies that if the Israelites obey His commandments, they will be his treasured possession, His chosen people.

"These are the commandments the LORD proclaimed in a loud voice to your whole assembly there on the mountain from out of the fire, the cloud and the deep darkness; and he added nothing more. Then he wrote them on two stone tablets and gave them to me. When you heard the voice out of the darkness, while the mountain was ablaze with fire, all the leaders of your tribes and your elders came to me.

And you said, 'The LORD our God has shown us his glory and his majesty, and we have heard his voice from the fire. Today we have seen that people can live even if God speaks with them. But now, why should we die? This great fire will consume us, and we will die if we hear the voice of the LORD our God any longer. For what mortal has ever heard the voice of the living God speaking out of fire as we have, and survived? Go near and listen to all that the LORD our God says. Then tell us whatever the LORD our God tells you. We will listen and obey.'

The LORD heard you when you spoke to me, and the LORD said to me, 'I have heard what this people said to you. Everything they said was good. Oh, that their hearts would be inclined to fear me and keep all my commands always so that it might go well with them and their children forever! Go; tell them to return to their tents. But you stay here with me so that I may give you all the commands, decrees, and laws you are to teach them to follow in the land I am giving them to possess. So be careful to do what the LORD your God has commanded you; do not turn aside to the right or to the left. Walk in obedience to all that the LORD your God has commanded you so that you may live, prosper, and prolong your days in the land that you will possess.'" (Deuteronomy 5:22-33)

God Himself provided the Ten Commandments to the Hebrews that lead to a full and victorious life. They reveal the majestic glory and holiness of God, showing that a barrier exists between Him and "fallen" humankind. Deuteronomy says that God required a mediator to represent humankind. Here, we see that God exposed His heart to humankind. These elements go beyond the Ten Commandments and the Old Covenant and lead to the revelation of Jesus Christ, the mediator, and the New Covenant.

STRUCTURE

The first four commandments given by God sum up to love God above all else, and the remaining six to love your neighbor as yourself.

Later, we will study the life, death, and resurrection of Jesus Christ. Although we have not yet supported an argument that the evidence for Christ is plentiful and compelling, for brevity as we review these commandments from God, amplification of each commandment is in accordance with the teachings of Jesus Christ in the New Testament.

Exodus, Chapter 20, lists the Ten Commandments and describes the circumstances of their delivery to the people of Israel.

"And God spoke all these words:" (Exodus 20:1)

COMMANDMENT #1
SHALL HAVE NO OTHER GODS

"I am the LORD your God, who brought you out of Egypt, out of the land of slavery. You shall have no other gods before me." (Exodus 20:1-3)

In the New Testament, Jesus said, "You shall worship the LORD your God, and Him only you shall serve" (Matthew 4:10), and "No one can serve two masters. Either he will hate the one and love the other, or he will be devoted to the one and despise the other. You cannot serve both God and Money" (Matthew 6:24).

"You shall have no other gods before me." God is a jealous god. He desires our undivided love and worship. The first commandment states that we are solely to worship God and put nothing above Him.

In your life, what you serve IS your god. Where do you spend your time? On what do you focus? What do you worship? What IS your god?

COMMANDMENT #2 - SHALL NOT WORSHIP IDOLS

"You shall not make for yourself an idol in the form of anything in Heaven above or on the earth beneath or in the waters below. You shall not bow down to them or worship them; for I, the LORD your God, am a jealous God, punishing the children for the sin of the fathers to the third and fourth generation of those who hate me, but showing love to a thousand {generations} of those who love me and keep my commandments."
(Exodus 20:4-6)

In the New Testament, Jesus said, "You shall worship the LORD your God and Him only you shall serve" (Matthew 4:10). "God is spirit, and those who worship Him must worship in spirit and truth" (John 4:24). "But I have a few things against you because you have there those who hold the doctrine of Balaam...To eat things sacrificed to idols" (Revelation 2:14).

You shall not make for yourself an idol in the form of anything in Heaven or on the earth, or from the waters below. Do we put others or things above God?

- Money
- Celebrity
- Power
- Family
- Appearance
- Belonging

How do you spend your time and energy, and what do you focus upon every day? The answer to that question defines your idol. Is it the God of Abraham and Moses?

This commandment is a promise of reward for compliance. "I, the LORD your God, am a jealous God, punishing the children for the sin of the fathers to the third and fourth generation of those who hate me, but showing love to a thousand {generations} of those who love me and keep my commandments."

God says that He is jealous. Is God jealous of your idol?

COMMANDMENT #3
SHALL NOT MISUSE THE LORD'S NAME

"You shall not misuse the name of the LORD your God, for the LORD will not hold anyone guiltless who misuses his name."(Exodus 20:7)

In the New Testament, Jesus said, "Therefore I say to you, every sin and blasphemy will be forgiven men, but the blasphemy against the Spirit will not be forgiven men" (Matthew 12:31), and "For ut of the heart proceed evil thoughts...Blasphemies. These are the things which defile a man" (Matthew 15:19-20).

Have you misused the name of God? Have you used the name of Jesus Christ, God, or the Holy Spirit in vain? This commandment follows #1 and #2. Worship God; do not mock Him.

COMMANDMENT #4 - KEEP SABBATH HOLY

"Remember the Sabbath day by keeping it holy. Six days you shall labor and do all your work, but the seventh day is a Sabbath to the LORD your God. On it you shall not do any work, neither you, nor your son or daughter, nor your manservant or maidservant, nor your animals, nor the alien within your gates. or in six days the LORD made the heavens and the earth, the sea, and all that is in them, but he rested on the seventh day. Therefore, the LORD blessed the Sabbath day and made it holy."(Exodus 20:8-11)

The first day of the biblical week is Sunday. The seventh day is Saturday. According to the Old Testament the Sabbath is Saturday, beginning at 6 p.m. on Friday. Jews have observed the seventh day from the time of Abraham, and they still keep it today. Nations around the world continue to observe a Sabbath they have known for more than 4,000 years. The Sabbath Day is for man to worship, study, reflect, and pray, as a reminder of our relationship with God. In Hebrew, Sabbath, or Shabbat means to cease, or rest.

In the New Testament, Jesus said, "Then he said to them, 'The Sabbath was made for man, not man for the Sabbath. So the Son of Man is Lord even of the Sabbath.'" (Mark 2:27-28) "Come to me, all who labor and are heavy laden, and I will give you rest. Take my yoke upon you, and learn from me, for I am gentle and lowly in heart, and you will find rest for your souls. For my yoke is easy and my burden is light." (Matthew 11:28-30)

In these Scriptures, Jesus states that He is our Sabbath, our rest. The New Testament says, "That is why I was angry with that generation, and I said, 'Their hearts are always going astray, and they have not known my ways.' So I declared on oath in my anger, 'They shall never enter my rest.'" (Hebrew 3:10-11) Here, the Holy Spirit declares that some will not enter His Sabbath rest, which means that those within whom the Holy Spirit rests will enjoy a Sabbath rest.

"There remains, then, a Sabbath-rest for the people of God; for anyone who enters God's rest also rests from his own work, just as God did from his. Let us, therefore, make every effort to enter that rest, so that no one will fall by following their example of disobedience." (Hebrew 4:9-11)

The Apostle Paul provides guidance in the following verses. "One man considers one day more sacred than another; another man considers every day alike. Each one should be fully convinced in his own mind. He, who regards one day as special, does so to the Lord." (Romans 14:5–6) If you accept Jesus Christ and do not consider one day more sacred from another, then every day is available to you as a Sabbath rest.

"Therefore do not let anyone judge you by what you eat or drink, or with regard to a religious festival, a New Moon celebration, or a Sabbath day. These are a shadow of the things that were to come; the reality, however, is found in Christ." (Colossians 2:16–17) Find your rest in Jesus Christ. Do not judge anyone by his or her Sabbath day.

After the resurrection of Jesus Christ, He became our Sabbath rest. We are encouraged to take our Sabbath rest continually, not just on one day per week. However, if you believe that Sabbath occurs on a given date or schedule, celebrate it and, as you do so, honor God.

Do you honor the Sabbath by taking your rest in Jesus Christ, the Son of God?

COMMANDMENT #5
HONOR FATHER AND MOTHER

"Honor your father and your mother, so that you may live long in the land the LORD your God is giving you." (Exodus 20:12) In the New Testament, Jesus said, "For God commanded saying, 'Honor your father and your mother' and 'He who curses father or mother, let him be put to death'" (Matthew 15:4), and "You know the commandments…Honor your father and your mother" (Luke 18:20).

Family is at the core of Godly relationships and is the basis of decent society. Just as God is our Father and desires us to honor Him, He desires us to honor our parents. Honor provides a solid foundation for society. God promises a blessing for obedience, "To live long in the land the Lord God is giving you."

Do you honor God? Do you honor your parents?

COMMANDMENT #6 - SHALL NOT MURDER

"You shall not murder." (Exodus 20:13) In the New Testament, Jesus said, "You have heard that it was said to those of old, 'You shall not murder', and whoever murders will be in danger of the judgment. But I say to you that whoever is angry with his brother without a cause shall be in danger of the judgment" (Matthew 5:21-22), "For out of the heart proceed evil thoughts, murders…These are the things which defile a man" (Matthew 15:19-20). "You shall not murder" (Matthew 19:18).

In Hebrew, the word "rasah" means to kill a human being, to murder, or the criminal act of killing. In Hebrew, the word "harag" means to kill, the taking of life in all forms. The original text of this commandment is in Hebrew, rasah. Here, we learn that it is possible to kill, but not murder. Christ says one is guilty of breaking this commandment if they practice hate or anger toward someone without justification. Hate in your heart is murder, rasah.

Do you murder? Did you murder today?

COMMANDMENT #7 - SHALL NOT COMMIT ADULTERY

"You shall not commit adultery." (Exodus 20:14) In the New Testament, Jesus said, "You have heard that it was said to those of old, 'You shall not commit adultery'. But I say to you that whoever looks at a woman to lust for her has already committed adultery with her in his heart" (Matthew 5:27-28). "But I say to you that whoever divorces his wife for any reason except sexual immorality causes her to commit adultery; and whoever marries a woman who is divorced commits adultery" (Matthew 5:32). "For out of the heart proceed evil thoughts… adulteries, fornications…These are the things which defile a man" (Matthew 15:19-20).

God forbids adultery. Jesus says that if we lust in our hearts, we are guilty of breaking this commandment. All sex or lust outside a marriage is adultery. Have you committed adultery? Have you lusted for another in your heart?

COMMANDMENT #8 - SHALL NOT STEAL

"You shall not steal." (Exodus 20:15) In the New Testament, Jesus said, "It is written, 'My house shall be called a house of prayer,' but you have made it a den of thieves" (Matthew 21:13). "For out of the heart proceed evil thoughts…thefts…These are the things which defile a man" (Mat 15:19-20).

Do not take what does not belong to you. Have you stolen? Throughout the Old and New Testaments, God tells us to be generous with what He has provided to us. Are you generous? Do you steal?

COMMANDMENT #9
SHALL NOT LIE

"You shall not give false testimony against your neighbor." (Exodus 20:16)
In the New Testament, Jesus said, "Again you have heard that it was said to those of old, 'You shall not swear falsely, but shall perform your oaths to the Lord. But I say to you, do not swear at all" (Matthew 5:33-34). "For out of the heart proceed evil thoughts... false witness...These are the things which defile a man" (Matthew 15:19-20). "And you have tested those who say they are apostles and are not, and have found them liars" (Revelation 2:2).

The commandment is do not lie. It does not justify the lie by excusing lies that are a means to an end.

Do you ALWAYS tell the truth?

COMMANDMENT #10 - SHALL NOT COVET

"You shall not covet your neighbor's house. You shall not covet your neighbor's wife, or his manservant or maidservant, his ox or donkey, or anything that belongs to your neighbor." (Exodus 20:17) In the New Testament, Jesus said, "Do not worry about your life, what you will eat or what you will drink, nor about your body, what you will put on" (Matthew 6:25). "For out of the heart proceed thefts...These are the things which defile a man" (Matthew 15:19-20), and "covetousness...All these evil things come from within and defile a man" (Mark 7:22-23)

Do you envy or lust for what your neighbor has? Must you earn more to keep up with society? With all that you have, is it not enough? Coveting distracts your focus from God. Do you covet God? Have you coveted? Have you coveted today?

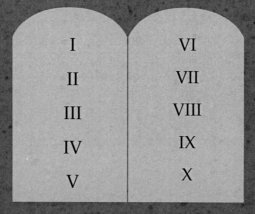

THE NEED FOR LAWS

A Covenant Guarantee

God created human beings with the need to be in relationship with Him. When Adam and Eve sinned, they damaged their perfect relationship with God. However, later God fulfilled His plan of salvation that would fully restore His children to Him. To understand the depth of His love and commitment, God chose to seal the relationship with a cultural form for the Israelites, THE COVENANT.

A covenant is an agreement between two or more. It is a commitment to do or not do something specific. The participants in the covenant make the promises. When each party adheres to the agreement, it becomes a binding contract. The covenant is a foundational element in the Bible. In fact, the Bible is a historical record, and a narrative on God's covenants with humankind.

The Pentateuch (first five books of the Bible referred to as the books of the law, or Torah) is the instruction for Israel relating to the covenant made with God. The Old Testament pertains to the historical accounts of Israel, as well as other writings and prophecies. The Pentateuch recounts Israel's accomplishment with respect to the covenant made with God.

Jesus and the Covenant

The Ten Commandments (and other laws) were God's covenant with Israel, and they are a foundation for His covenant with all of humanity. The commandments are God's will for society. It is to hear God say, "I am God, and I love you enough to make a covenant (be in relationship) with you." When we explore Jesus Christ in Path Steps 5 and 6, we will learn how God fulfilled the promise to the Hebrews of giving His own life to fulfill and seal the covenant.

APPLY THE COMMANDMENTS

The Sin Checklist

Try this exercise. Make a copy of The Sin Checklist on the next page. It is a list of the Ten Commandments from Exodus, Chapter 20. Review the Ten Commandments as we discussed. Remember the supplementary details Jesus added to the commandments. Carefully and thoughtfully, make an evaluation.

Did you write "Yes" to any of your answers? Did you check all ten? Do we all have sin? Do you know anyone who can make a claim that they have no checks? Probably not. We all fall short of God's glory. "For all have sinned and fall short of the glory of God" (Romans 3:23).

Many will argue, "I have done more good things than bad, and therefore I am acceptable to God." It may be that you have been virtuous, but you have violated the Ten Commandments and you are a SINNER. Later, we will discuss "good works." Any sin is unacceptable to God. Can we ask God to forgive our sin? Yes! So, what do we do AND how do we do it?

"Behold, the LORD'S hand is not shortened that it cannot save; neither his ear heavy that it cannot hear: But your iniquities have separated between you and your God, and your sins have hid his face from you that He will not hear." (Isaiah 59:1-2)

We need forgiveness from our sinful nature… we need to be saved! The next Path Step asks, Would Your Life Change IF…God Had a Plan to Forgive Your Sin?

The Sin Checklist

Command	Have you violated these laws?	Yes, or No
1	You shall have no other gods before me	
2	You shall not make for yourself an idol in the form of anything in Heaven or earth or in the waters below.	
3	You Shall not misuse the name ov the LORD your God, for the Lord will not hold anyone guiltless who misuses His Name.	
4	Rember the Sabbath day by keeping it holy. Six days you shall labor and do all your work, but the seventh day is a Sabbath to the LORD your God. On it, you shall not do any work	
5	Honor your father and your mother, so that you may live long in the land the LORD your God is giving you	
6	You shall not murder	
7	You shall not commit adultery	
8	You shall not steal	
9	You shall not give false testimony against your neighbor	
10	You shall not covet your neighbor's house. You shall not covet your neighbor's wife, or his manservant or maidservant, his ox or donkey, or anything that belongs to your neighbor	

SUMMARY

- God created humankind for the purpose of fellowship and worship.

- Sin is a violation of the character of God and His laws as revealed on the pages of Scripture.

- Sin may be acceptable and respectable to the world, but it is destructive to the sinner.

- Humankind has sinned and fallen short of the glory of God.

- God defined a code of conduct—the Ten Commandments.

- All are sinners and need forgiveness.

- God offers a plan of salvation (next Path Step), so that you may fulfill the Law.

We have concluded the first three Path Steps on A Rational Path to Christ, which completes the FOUNDATION Phase of our journey. What is your life purpose? On which Truth do you base your life purpose? Is the Bible Truth? Substantial evidence exists making the Bible compelling and credible. We are sinners, every one of us.

In man's current form, we all sin. However, God will not accept sin. Without help, humankind's relationship with God is tainted and we have no promise of reuniting with Him for all eternity. The FOUNDATION of our Journey on A Rational Path to Christ is in place. With this understanding, we study the next Phase, SALVATION. What help do we need, and how will we get it?

As with each Path Step on A Rational Path to Christ, the Path Step ends with the same question from its beginning. Would your life change IF…You lost God due to your sins? Yes or no? If yes:

- Do you REJECT you lost God due to your sins?

- Do you THINK you lost God due to your sins?

- Do you BELIEVE you lost God due to your sins?

- Do you KNOW you lost God due to your sins?

Notes

1. "Lost States: Garden of Eden - Located!" Lost States: Garden of Eden - Located! N.p., n.d.
    Web. 04 June 2012.

2. "Old Testament Maps." EBibleTeacher. N.p., n.d. Web. 04 June 2012.

3. "Eden Map." Crystal Links. N.p., n.d. Web. 04 June 2012.

A RATIONAL PATH TO CHRIST

PHASE 2

4	5	6	7
God Has a Plan to Forgive Sin	Jesus Lived, Died & Resurrected	Jesus Is the Key to Salvation	Salvation Reunites You & God

Salvation

Path Step 4

Would Your Life Change IF…?

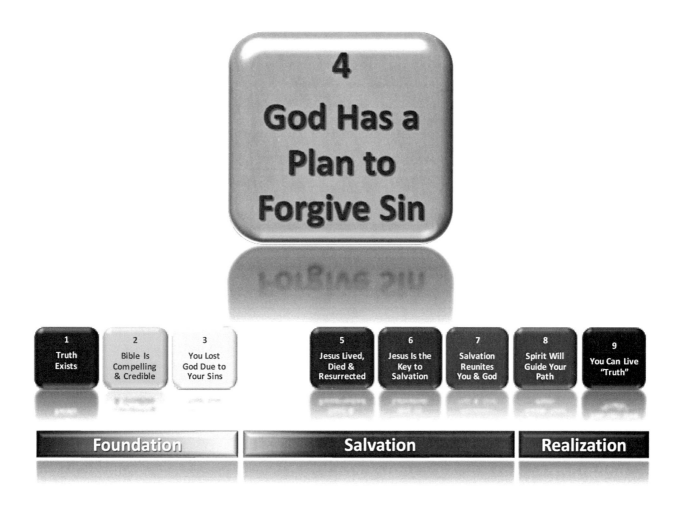

CONTENTS

> ## ENLIGHTENMENT
>
> I was raised attending a Catholic Church. In fact, I served as an altar boy for many years. I did not understand a good deal about Christianity and the foundations of the Bible. I did understand that I could earn some money providing services at both weddings and funerals.
>
> Through many years of listening to readings from the New Testament and the Gospels, and singing hymns on Sunday mornings, I became familiar with the following notions:
>
> - Jesus Christ died and was resurrected
>
> - For some good reason, Jesus is referred to as the Lamb of God
>
> - There is something very special about the blood of Jesus
>
> However, through these teachings I did not understand the basis for any of these claims. Nor did I understand the deeper meaning creating their prominence and the nature of the relationship between them. The Catholic parish that I attended did little to encourage me to read, study, and analyze the Bible independent of Sunday service readings.
>
> A neighborhood friend and classmate at the University of Rhode Island, Mr. Andy Stewart, graduated a semester before I did. He moved to Fort Collins, Colorado to attend graduate engineering school at Colorado State University. Skipping many details, Andy was instrumental in my acceptance into the same program. With many questions about life and Christianity unanswered for many years, I moved to Fort Collins and benefited from having Andy as my housemate.
>
> Andy is one of the most intelligent and genuine people I have ever known. On multiple occasions, we discussed our beliefs. I continued to attend Catholic church, while Andy enjoyed his fellowship at Immanuel, at the time, a local Southern Baptist church. Tagging along with Andy to fellowship at fun events with the Baptist Student Union of CSU, I was introduced to the freedom and ability to open the Bible, read it, and study it on my own. I befriended many of the delightful souls I met there and began to attend regularly Immanuel Baptist Church. Within 6 months, I accepted Jesus Christ as my Savior and was baptized by immersion.
>
> Discussions with Andy and many of my fellow students and teachers at Immanuel laid a foundation for me to understand better the basis of the bullets listed above. The information contained in this Path Step has been augmented through the years. However, years back in Fort Collins, the main thrust of its content satisfied my analytical need to understand and provide meaning and purpose to Jesus Christ. It made real to me a relationship with my creator, something I had not known previously. Wow, did my life change! These core foundational elements I learned at this church provided a basis for many deeper revelations to follow.
>
> This information transformed my life. While in our present form, we cannot fully comprehend Jesus Christ. In light of the previous Path Steps, the information contained herein provided for me the necessary connection and purpose to Jesus Christ, my Lord and Savior.
>
> Understanding the need for a lamb to be unblemished and learning about the "secret ingredient" turned on the light for me.
>
> **Now, I can see clearly. The darkness will never return.**

Would Your Life Change IF...God Has a Plan to Forgive Sins?

"I'm a good person; I have no need for forgiveness."

"I've lived a good life, I'm going to Heaven."

"Ok, I have sinned and fall short of God… now what?"

Under the first covenant in the Old Testament, God offers a plan of redemption for His chosen people, the Israelites. Although there is a fault in the first covenant between God and humankind, in that all humanity has sinned (we will explore this topic in this Path Step), God chose a second "perfect" covenant that is different, but has the same foundation as the first.

Path Step 4 explains how God forgives sin.

SALVATION

In the Foundation Phase, we read of Truth and studied life's purpose based on Truth. We reviewed evidence that supports the accuracy and credibility of the Bible.

From the evidence found on Mount Sinai and the Israelite encampment, the Foundation Phase identifies God's purpose for humankind. It also verifies the Ten Commandments delivered to Moses, which Jesus Christ illuminates and fulfills in the New Testament.

Due to sin, there is a separation between humankind and God, our creator. The next section defines God's plan to remove sin, then conveys how we can receive forgiveness and salvation as described in the New Testament. It concludes with a description of salvation and God's promise, and the outcome for those who reject it.

Path STEP 4: GOD HAS A PLAN TO FORGIVE SINS

The Necessary Ingredient

The central theme of the Bible is the redemption of humankind from its sin, that when achieved leads to eternal fellowship with God. God explains His process for forgiveness of sins in the Old Testament, under the Old Covenant. God perfects this process in the New Testament, under the New Covenant. Path Step 4 explores God's process for atonement (to make amends or reparation) of sin. To obtain forgiveness, God requires a "secret" ingredient. Without this ingredient, there is no forgiveness. This necessary component provides eternal salvation. Do you know what the necessary ingredient is for forgiveness?

PASSOVER—BEGINNINGS OF REDEMPTION

The original Passover originated when God delivered His chosen, the Hebrew people, from their suffering in Egypt. Thereafter, He confirmed that relationship with a covenant. The original Passover is God's display of redemption. While slaves in Egypt, the Israelites were delivered from God's plagues. He redeemed them from death by the blood of a lamb without defect, painted over and around their doors.

"The LORD said to Moses and Aaron in Egypt, 'This month is to be for you the first month, the first month of your year. Tell the whole community of Israel that on the tenth day of this month each man is to take a lamb for his family, one for each household. If any household is too small for a whole lamb, they must share one with their nearest neighbor, having taken into account the number of people there are. You are to determine the amount of lamb needed in accordance with what each person will eat.

The animals you choose must be year-old males without defect, and you may take them from the sheep or the goats. Take care of them until the fourteenth day of the month, when all the people of the community of Israel must slaughter them at twilight. Then they are to take some of the blood and put it on the sides and tops of the door frames of the houses where they eat the lambs. That same night they are to eat the meat roasted over the fire, along with bitter herbs, and bread made without yeast.

Do not eat the meat raw or cooked in water, but roast it over the fire—head, legs and inner parts. Do not leave any of it till morning; if some is left till morning, you must burn it. This is how you are to eat it: with your cloak tucked into your belt, your sandals on your feet and your staff in your hand. Eat it in haste; it is the LORD's Passover. On that same night, I will pass through Egypt and strike down every firstborn—both men and animals—and I will bring judgment on all the gods of Egypt. I am the LORD.

The blood will be a sign for you on the houses where you are, and when I see the blood, I will pass over you. No destructive plague will touch you when I strike Egypt. This is a day you are to commemorate; for generations to come you shall celebrate it as a festival to the LORD—a lasting ordinance." (Exodus 12:1-14)

God gives a vast amount of instruction in Scripture. The Passover is a day we are to commemorate; for generations to come. God's command to observe Passover is of great importance. As a tradition, He insisted the original Passover celebration would continue into future generations, so they too would understand and benefit from its meaning. Soon, we learn that Passover is a festival and is to be celebrated.

Summarizing the original Passover:

- A one-year old lamb without blemishes is to be sacrificed

- Any first-born animal or man is stricken by God

- Lamb's blood is painted over a door that saves (redeems) the Israelites from God's wrath

- Offenses of the Egyptians are punished

- At the celebration, they ate lamb, bitter herbs, unleavened bread, salt, etc.

Afterwards, a Passover feast consisting of four cups of wine is to celebrate the four expressions of forgiveness and redemption—deliverance that God had promised. In Exodus, God proclaimed the first covenant to the Hebrews, "I will bring out," "I will deliver," "I will redeem," and "I will take you as my people."[1,2,3]

"Therefore, say to the Israelites: 'I am the LORD, and I will bring you out from under the yoke of the Egyptians. I will free you from being slaves to them, and I will redeem you with an outstretched arm and with mighty acts of judgment. I will take you as my own people, and I will be your God. Then you will know that I am the LORD your God, who brought you out from under the yoke of the Egyptians." (Exodus 6:6)

In this Exodus Scripture, we see God's impending covenant deliver and redeem His chosen people, the Israelites. We will discuss this and the four cups of the Passover feast in Path Step 6.

THE OLD (FIRST) COVENANT

In the spirit of the first Passover, God has a plan for forgiveness. This plan is the primary focus of the Bible. God establishes His plan in the Old Testament and expands it in the New Testament. We will cover these in the next two Path Steps.

"When Moses had proclaimed every commandment of the law to all the people, he took the blood of calves, together with water, scarlet wool and branches of hyssop, and sprinkled the scroll and all the people. He said, 'This is the blood of the covenant, which God has commanded you to keep.'" (Hebrews 9:19-20)

To perfect the covenant, Moses mixed water and blood, and sprinkled it on the scrolls and the Ark of the Covenant. The covenant included the Ten Commandments, a tabernacle, a sin offering, and a Day of Atonement sacrifice, along with other elements. There are many books, commentaries, and studies written on the Old Covenant. Forgiveness is the main topic we will examine in A Rational Path to Christ. Our focus will begin with the Ten Commandments, the tabernacle, and the process for cleansing sin.

THE SIN OFFERING

God defines the sin offering as the means to cleanse man's sin. What is a sin offering? How does it work?

God's plan to forgive sin required the Israelites to construct a holy place. God gave these requirements to Moses at Mount Sinai. If the data supporting Mount Sinai is accurate, that same evidence justifies that Moses wrote about the first covenant between God and the Israelites, which is in Exodus, Leviticus, and Deuteronomy. The Pentateuch, which is the first five books of the Bible, contains the specific knowledge and commands God gave to Moses on Mount Sinai.

THE TABERNACLE

The first task of the Old Covenant was to build a tabernacle with precise detail from God. It included the Ark of the Covenant, the Most Holy Place, a veil, a holy place, the priestly garments, a lampstand (menorah), a brazen altar and an altar of incense, a table of showbread, a courtyard, a washbasin, anointing oil, and other essentials. Archaeological evidence studied in Path Step 2 shows rectangular outlines of the tabernacle containing these items left behind by the Israelites as described by God and Moses in the Scriptures (see Figures 68 in Path Step 2 and Figure 55 on page 6).

"The LORD said to Moses, 'Tell the Israelites to bring me an offering. You are to receive the offering for me from each man whose heart prompts him to give. These are the offerings you are to receive from them: gold, silver and bronze; blue, purple and scarlet yarn and fine linen; goat hair; ram skins dyed red and hides of sea cows; acacia wood; olive oil for the light; spices for the anointing oil and for the fragrant incense; and onyx stones and other gems to be mounted on the ephod and breastpiece.

Then have them make a sanctuary for me, and I will dwell among them. Make this tabernacle and all its furnishings exactly like the pattern I will show you. Have them make a chest of acacia wood—two and a half cubits long, a cubit and a half wide, and a cubit and a half high. Overlay it with pure gold, both inside and out, and make a gold molding around it. Cast four gold rings for it and fasten them to its four feet, with two rings on one side and two rings on the other.

Then make poles of acacia wood and overlay them with gold. Insert the poles into the rings on the sides of the chest to carry it. The poles are to remain in the rings of this ark; they are not to be removed. Then put in the ark the Testimony, which I will give you. Make an atonement cover of pure gold—two and a half cubits long and a cubit and a half wide. And make two cherubim out of hammered gold at the ends of the cover. Make one cherub on one end and the second cherub on the other; make the cherubim of one piece with the cover, at the two ends. The cherubim are to have their wings spread upward, overshadowing the cover with them. The cherubim are to face each other, looking toward the cover.

Place the cover on top of the ark and put in the ark the Testimony, which I will give you. There, above the cover between the two cherubim that are over the ark of the Testimony, I will meet with you and give you all my commands for the Israelites. Make a table of acacia wood—two cubits long, a cubit wide and a cubit and a half high. Overlay it with pure gold and make a gold molding around it. Also, make around it a rim a handbreadth wide and put a gold molding on the rim. Make four gold rings for the table and fasten them to the four corners, where the four legs are. The rings are to be close to the rim to hold the poles used in carrying the table. Make the poles of acacia wood, overlay them with gold and carry the table with them. And make its plates and dishes of pure gold, as well as its pitchers and bowls for the pouring out of offerings. Put the bread of the Presence on this table to be before me at all times.

Make a lampstand of pure gold and hammer it out, base and shaft; its flower like cups, buds and blossoms shall be of one piece with it. Six branches are to extend from the sides of the lampstand—three on one side and three on the other. Three cups shaped like almond flowers with buds and blossoms are to be on one branch, three on the next branch, and the same for all six branches extending from the lampstand.

And on the lampstand there are to be four cups shaped like almond flowers with buds and blossoms. One bud shall be under the first pair of branches extending from the lampstand, a second bud under the second pair, and a third bud under the third pair—six branches in all. The buds and branches shall all be of one piece with the lampstand, hammered out of pure gold. Then make its seven lamps and set them up on it so that they light the space in front of it. Its wick trimmers and trays are to be of pure gold. A talent of pure gold is to be used for the lampstand and all these accessories. See that you make them according to the pattern shown to you on the mountain.'" (Exodus 25:1-40)

God's command from Mount Sinai is to build the holy place. God's details on the construction of the sacred articles are in Exodus, Chapters 26 and 27. A segment of the Pentateuch explains how the Israelites were to use the facility and articles. Each of the items described by God in Exodus 25 through 27 had great symbolic meaning to the Israelites of Moses' time. Moreover, the significance of their meaning persists today. Some biblical scholars believe that the Ark of the Covenant has not yet served its complete intended purpose.

We will not explore the meanings of each symbol; however, if you continue studying the tabernacle and its contents, you will discover that their design communicates the nature of God. The book of Hebrews in the New Testament describes that the tabernacle is a model of the tabernacle in Heaven.

"The point of what we are saying is this: We do have such a high priest, who sat down at the right hand of the throne of the majesty in Heaven, and who serves in the sanctuary, the true tabernacle set up by the Lord, not by man. Every high priest is appointed to offer both gifts and sacrifices, and so it was necessary for this one also to have something to offer. If he were on earth, he would not be a priest, for there are already men who offer the gifts prescribed by the law. They serve at a sanctuary that is a copy and shadow of what is in Heaven. This is why Moses was warned when he was about to build the tabernacle: 'See to it that you make everything according to the pattern shown you on the mountain." (Hebrews 8:1-5)

From God's instruction, the Israelites constructed the tabernacle and the items He commanded with precision. The tabernacle contained a secluded area called the Most Holy Place. This area was set apart for the presence of God (also known as the Shekinah glory) and separated from the tabernacle by columns and a thick veil. The Most Holy Place contained the Ark of the Covenant, and the tablets of stone, upon which were written by the finger of God the Ten Commandments. They were stored in the ark for safekeeping.

Figure 54 is an illustration of the tabernacle. Clockwise, starting in the upper left corner is the menorah lampstand, table of showbread, brazen altar, incense altar, and the Ark of the Covenant. Figure 55 is a rectangular stone foundation believed to be the location of the tabernacle at Mount Sinai (see Path Step 2). Figure 56 is a scale model of the original tabernacle in the mountainous desert of Mount Sinai. Figure 57 and Figure 58 are the location of the tabernacle and articles with dimension, map, and compass orientation as described by God to Moses.

FIG 54 - TABERNACLE ITEMS[4]

FIG 55 - TABERNACLE LOCATION[6]

FIG 56 - REPLICA OF MOUNT SINAI TABERNACLE[5]

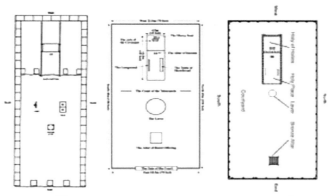

FIG 57 - TABERNACLE LAYOUT AND COMPAS ORIENTATION [7]

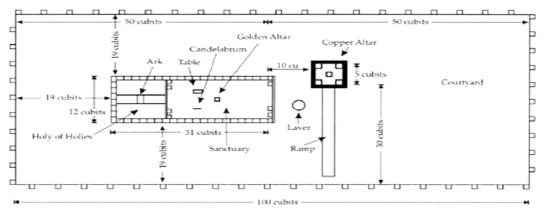

FIG 58 - ARTICLE PLACEMENT IN THE TABERNACLE[8]

On top of the Ark of the Covenant was the mercy seat used in special ceremonies. On the Day of Atonement, the high priest would perform a blood sacrifice from a specific offering, wash with water in the laver, anoint himself with oil, fill the holiest place with the mist of incense to obscure, and then spill blood of the sacrifice upon the mercy seat. The mercy seat was the resting place for God on Earth. Above the ark was the Shekinah glory, the glowing presence of God. At night, His glowing presence stretched to the sky so that the Israelite encampment was aware that He dwelled among them (Figure 59).

FIG 59 - NIGHT VIEW OF SHEKINAH GLORY[9]

Figure 60 is an illustration of how the Shekinah glory might have appeared above the Ark of the Covenant. Figure 61 shows a view of how the most holy may have looked with the curtains drawn from the holy place. Those that looked directly at the Shekinah glory died instantly. The only one allowed to enter the Most Holy Place was the chief priest but at certain times and under specific conditions. In order to enter, the chief priest burned incense to create a smoke fog to obscure God and prevent death of the priest.

FIG 60 - ARK OF THE COVENANT[10]

As shown in Figure 61 and Figure 62, the Most Holy Place (or the holy of holies) was the most controlled and constrained area of the tabernacle. A thick curtain separated it from the holy place, the next room to the right in Figure 62. Only priests spent time there attending to daily worship and tasks. Beyond the entrance to the holy place was the

FIG 61 - HOLY OF HOLIES W/ CURTIANS DRAWN[11]

FIG 62 - HOLY OF HOLIES[12]

open-air courtyard. This is where the sacrifices took place, and only members of an Israelite family possessing the family's blessing could enter. Shown in Figure 63 the brazen (or bronze) altar sits in the courtyard. It plays a key role with sin and burnt offerings. The Tent of Meeting surrounded the perimeter of the tabernacle.

THE PROCESS

As written, the tabernacle is a holy place for God and is the designated place for the Israelite nation to atone for their sins. What does the Old Testament require for sin atonement? How do we accomplish atonement? What are we to sacrifice, and what is a sin offering?

FIG 63 - BRAZEN ALTER[13]

"The LORD called to Moses and spoke to him from the Tent of Meeting. He said, 'Speak to the Israelites and say to them: When you bring an offering to the LORD, bring as your offering an animal from either the herd or the flock. If the offering is a burnt offering from the herd, you are to offer a male without defect. You must present it at the entrance to the Tent of Meeting so that you may be acceptable to the LORD. You are to lay your hand on the head of the burnt offering, and it will be accepted on your behalf to make atonement for you.'" (Leviticus 1:1-5)

"You are to slaughter it before the LORD, and then Aaron's sons the priests shall bring the blood and splash it against the sides of the altar at the entrance to the Tent of Meeting. If the offering is a burnt offering from the flock, from either the sheep or the goats, you are to offer a male without defect. You are to slaughter it at the north side of the altar before the LORD, and Aaron's sons the priests shall splash its blood against the sides of the altar." (Leviticus 1:11-12)

A sin offering is the process God describes with detail that when followed would forgive all sins confessed by a family. Forgiveness of sin occurs through the family's representative who then enters the Tent of Meeting with the appropriate living sacrifice.

In summary, the process has several steps. A requirement is to slaughter a young lamb, bull, or bird, depending on the nature of sin or family standing in the Israelite community. The sacrifice must be male, under one year old, and without blemish or weakness. They must bring the appropriate sacrifice to the priest for inspection at the Tent of Meeting. After the animal passes inspection, the family representative lays their hand on the animal's head. He then confesses (transfers) the family's sin into the animal. Next, the family representative slaughters (sacrifices) the animal in the courtyard, in front of the Tent of Meeting. The priest sprinkles the blood on the altar and all sides of the entrance to the Tent of Meeting, suggestive of the door and lintel on the original Passover.

God forgives sin only with a sacrifice. With this process, the family made atonement for their known sins, or their sins of commission. The transfer of sins then dies with the young, unblemished sacrifice. The particular sacrifice must be male, under one year old, and without blemish or weakness. Why?

"The soul who sins is the one who will die…" (Ezekiel 18:20)

"For the wages of sin is death." (Romans 6:23)

Sin requires sacrifice and death. The sin transferred in a sacrifice must die with bloodshed. If someone has an imperfection, (symbolic of sin) his or her sacrifice removes only its sin, and not the sin transferred to it. Only an unblemished (sin free) sacrifice can be a substitute for another's sin. A sin free (unblemished) sacrifice can accept the sin of another and the sin can be removed completely by the being's sacrifice, bloodshed, and death.

"For the life of a creature is in the blood, and I have given it to you to make atonement for yourselves on the altar; it is the blood that makes atonement for one's life." (Leviticus 17:11)

Blood absorbs your sin. Blood carries your sin. The shedding of your blood pays the penalty for sin when you die. However, what if a person has no sin? Their blood is sin free. Query: Can it absorb the sin of others?

Why does an unblemished lamb work for God's purpose? How is an unblemished (sin free) lamb able to absorb sins? A simple analogy is instructive. The lamb is analogous to a sponge and water is the sin, as depicted in Figures 64 through 68.

FIG 64   FIG 65   FIG 66   FIG 67   FIG 68

As shown in Figure 64, if you sin once, you are a sinner. Either you are a sinner or you are not. Every man and woman is an imperfect sinner. Because you are a sinner, consider yourself a sopping wet sponge. This is the same as for a blemished lamb. The blemished lamb, with its imperfections, cannot take on the blemishes (sin) of another. The sponge in Figure 65, is you as a sinner and a blemished lamb. You have sin, so cannot assume another's sin.

As shown in Figure 65, a blemished lamb is a sponge fully soaked in water. It cannot soak up fluid (or sin). Therefore, it cannot assume (receive) the sins of another. Because the lamb has blemish (water), it cannot soak up additional sin (water) from others.

However, note the dry sponge in Figure 66. It has no water (sin). Therefore, it can soak up fluid (or sin). This sponge is the unblemished lamb with no sin.

An unblemished lamb is a dry sponge. It can soak up much. A dry, perfect sponge has no water, and is able to absorb water, as depicted in Figure 67. The water represents the sin of all humankind. The blood of an unblemished lamb is able to absorb and erase a multitude of sins.

The sponge above was dry and was able to soak up all of the water, as shown in Figure 68. As we all have sin, we need an unblemished lamb who can assume our sin. With our analogy, the unblemished lamb has no sin and can soak up all the sin of humankind.

This procedure is a foreshadowing of the New Covenant (see Path Step 6).

AN OFFERING WALK-THROUGH

Let us do a walk-through of the process with you as the family representative.

1. First, select a lamb from your herd.

    - Male

    - Under one year old

    - Unblemished, without defect

2. Bring the lamb into your home to clean and feed in preparation, before taking it into the tent. If the family had children, they were the likely candidates to prepare and wash it, much like a pet for the time, the lamb was taken into the tent. It represents your heart and the heart of your family. It is your family's personal lamb. It serves its purpose only if accepted by the priests. If rejected, the family would be overcome with shame. The lamb must be the most valued you have and without flaws so that it will be approved for sacrifice. Likely, the family named the lamb as they became close to it. Let us give your lamb a Hebrew name called, Yehoshua.

3. Bring Yehoshua to the priests at the Tent of Meeting.

4. Tell the priest the family name you represent.[16]

5. Respond to the question, "Is this your personal lamb?" (To take a lamb from another family in substitution was unacceptable.)[17]

6. The priest inspects Yehoshua for any defects (broken bones, disease, mange, scars, etc.).

7. After approval, lay your hands on Yehoshua's head.

8. Confess (transfer) into Yehoshua yours and your family's sins.

9. Sacrifice Yehoshua in front of the Tent of Meeting.

10. The priest collects and sprinkles Yehoshua's blood on the brazen altar and the entrance to the Tent of Meeting.

God forgives sin only with a sacrifice. The sins transferred into the lamb die with the sacrifice. With this process, God has shown the family how to make atonement for their known sins. The sin offering was unable to make atonement for unknown sins or sins of omission, as the sins needed confession. To remedy, God provided the Day of Atonement.

HEBREW DAY OF ATONEMENT

Yearly, at 3:00 p.m., on the Day of Atonement, the chief priest sacrifices a lamb for the nation of Israel. For this event, God permitted the chief priest to enter the Most Holy Place of the Tent of Meeting to sprinkle the blood on the Mercy Seat of the Ark of the Covenant. Be reminded, the mercy seat on top of the Ark of the Covenant in the Most Holy Place is where the essence of God resided.

Originally, the Israelites called the Ark of the Covenant the Ark of the Testimony. Several important Items are stored in the Ark as a testimony to later generations. The Ark contains:

- Aaron, Moses' brother's staff from an almond tree (that later budded showing God's favor) to remind the Israelites of their rebellion against God's majesty.

- A container of manna to remind Israel of God's provision and of their ungratefulness in the desert.

- The stone tablets to remind the Israelites of their failure to keep the Ten Commandments and the laws.

In the Most Holy Place, the blood of a sacrifice covered the transgressions (sins) of Israel. However, a sacrifice on the Day of Atonement was for sins of omission. These are sins the Israelites did not realize they had committed or for actions they failed to take.

God established a process for forgiveness of sins. An Israelite family could receive forgiveness of their sins through an atonement process. The sin offering is for individuals (and their families), and their known sins. A sacrifice on the Day of Atonement is for forgiveness of sins of omission for the Hebrew nation. The sin offering and the Day of Atonement sacrifice together remove and atone for the transgressions of the Mosaic Laws.

BEYOND MOUNT SINAI

The Temple

Long after God handed plans for the Tent of Meeting and tabernacle to Moses at Mount Sinai, King Solomon built a temple in Jerusalem, in 960 BC. It was much like the original, but larger and more ornate. In this new tabernacle, offerings specified in Levitical Law (explained in Exodus, Leviticus, and Deuteronomy) are identical to what God instructed, and its implementation. As the original tabernacle, the temple housed the Ark of the Covenant, which was central for Judaism and worshiping God. In 587 BC, the Babylonians destroyed the temple built by Solomon.

In 538 BC, Cyrus the Great, of Persia, authorized the Israelites return to Jerusalem, permitting that a second temple is built by 516 BC. Later, in 70 AD, the Romans destroyed that temple. Then, as prophesied in the Bible, there will be a third temple (which form is at issue among Bible scholars) at the time of the second coming of Jesus Christ.

Do Jews Still Sacrifice for Forgiveness?

Sacrificial practice stopped in 70 AD, when a Roman army destroyed the temple in Jerusalem. The Torah instructs not to offer sacrifices unless it is where God has chosen.

"Be careful not to sacrifice your burnt offerings anywhere you please. Offer them only at the place, the Lord will choose in one of your tribes, and there observe everything I command you." (Deuteronomy 12:13-14)

It is a sin to offer sacrifices in a place not chosen by God, for it would be similar to stealing bread and wine to observe the Sabbath or Passover. Sacrificial practices resumed during the Bar Kokhba revolt (Jewish War) of 132-136 AD.[18] The revolt established an independent state of Israel over parts of Judea for over two years. However, a Roman army of over six legions escalating with another six legions finally crushed it. Sacrificial practices ended permanently after the war was lost.

Orthodox Jews do not believe that Jesus Christ is the Messiah as prophesied in the Old Testament (see Path Step 6). They are waiting for His "first" arrival so He may reign as king. Christians believe Jesus Christ is the Messiah and He has already appropriated His seat over His kingdom. Unlike Jews, Christians await Jesus' second coming as prophesied in the Old and New Testaments.

If the Jews do not have a location that God specifies for sacrificial purposes, and they do not believe that Jesus Christ is the path to God through forgiveness, how do Orthodox Jews gain forgiveness? Many Jews put emphasis on two Scriptures from the Old Testament for resolution: 1 Kings 8:46-50 and Hosea 14:2.

"When they sin against you—for there is no one who does not sin—and you become angry with them and give them over to the enemy, who takes them captive to his own land, far away or near; and if they have a change of heart in the land where they are held captive, and repent and plead with you in the land of their conquerors and say, 'We have sinned, we have done wrong, we have acted wickedly'; and if they turn back to you with all their heart and soul in the land of their enemies who took them captive, and pray to you toward the land you gave their fathers, toward the city you have chosen and the temple I have built for your Name; then from Heaven, your dwelling place, hear their prayer and their plea, and uphold their cause. And forgive your people, who have sinned against you; forgive all the offenses they have committed against you, and cause their conquerors to show them mercy." (1 Kings 8:46-50)

This reference describes a situation in which the Israelites turn away from God to worship idols and sin against God. To be captive to their enemies is the result of their sin. Solomon asks God to forgive them based on their repentance. However, as a penalty for their transgressions, he asks that they not be freed. He asks only that their captors show them mercy. It is not clear in 1 Kings that this Scripture permits Orthodox Jews to gain forgiveness from repentance.

"'Take words with you and return to the LORD. Say to him: 'Forgive all our sins and receive us graciously, that we may offer the fruit of our lips or offer our lips as sacrifices of bulls.'" (Hosea 14:2)

Hosea was a prophet. He encourages Israel to consider their words they bring to God and repent of their sins. This appeal would be offered to God as the "fruit of our lips" or "offer our lips as sacrifices of bulls" depending on the translation. The Orthodox Jewish interpretation of this Scripture permits Jews to obtain forgiveness from repentance, rather than animal sacrifices. More likely, this short and simple verse is one of many prophecies of the coming new covenant from God for reconciliation of humankind.

Orthodox Jews do not believe Jesus Christ is the Messiah. They believe a new covenant is yet to come (see Path Step 6). They believe that when the Messiah comes, God will provide them a place for sacrificial purposes.

Until then, they believe forgiveness comes through repentance, prayer, and good deeds, in accordance with these two Scriptures.

There is a sect of modern day Jews that DO believe that Jesus Christ was the Messiah. They are known as messianic Jews. This is an ever-growing group in the Hebrew community.

God told Abraham in Genesis 12:2-3 that we are to bless Israel, and God will bless those that do.

WHY WAS THE OLD COVENANT FAULTY?

OFFER

"Then Moses went up to God, and the Lord called to him from the mountain and said, 'This is what you are to say to the house of Jacob and what you are to tell the people of Israel: You yourselves have seen what I did to Egypt, and how I carried you on eagles' wings and brought you to myself. Now if you obey me fully and keep my covenant, then out of all nations you will be my treasured possession. Although the whole earth is mine, you will be for me a kingdom of priests and a holy nation.'" (Exodus 19:3-6) God asks Moses to present His offer to the people.

These are the elements of a true covenant:

- Conditions and promises are set for both sides
- If the children of Israel accept God's proposal, then a covenant is established

So, how did they respond to the offer?

ACCEPTANCE

"And Moses came and called for the elders of the people, and laid before their faces all these words which the Lord commanded him. And all the people answered together, and said, All that the Lord hath spoken we will do. And Moses returned the words of the people unto the Lord." (Exodus 19:7-8)

In this verse, all answered that they would abide by the laws. When God heard their answer, the basis for the Old Covenant was accepted and established. However, before it was established, the Israelites needed to confirm the covenant.

This covenant was not the law, but made regarding "all these words." The Ten Commandments are the foundation for the agreement, as well as the 613 laws given to the Israelites in the Torah. The people promised to keep that law, and in return, God promised to bless them.

A weakness to the promise came from Israel. Nothing suggests that they could not conform to God's requirements. Neither was there any request for God's assistance. "We can do it," they insisted. This is an example of a man leaning on his own flawed abilities (flesh) and trusting human strength. Self-confidence filled their hearts and minds. "All that the Lord hath said will we do…" and be obedient.

FAILURE

Were the Israelites able to keep their promise? Because of their human weaknesses, they broke their promise to God before Moses returned from the mountain with the stone tablets. From their weak promises, the Old Covenant was established. Did God maintain his commitment to the covenant?

The books of Jeremiah and Hebrews give insight to the broken promises. God states "finding fault with them."

"But God found fault with the people and said: 'The time is coming, declares the Lord, when I will make a new covenant with the house of Israel and with the house of Judah. It will not be like the covenant I made with their forefathers when I took them by the hand to lead them out of Egypt because they did not remain faithful to my covenant, and I turned away from them, declares the Lord.'" (Jeremiah 31:31-32, Hebrews 8:8-9)

God places blame on the human side of the mutual agreement. The writer of Hebrews addresses the Old Covenant in Hebrews. He points out judgment and self-criticism and directs them to the prophecy in Jeremiah 31 of the New Covenant.

The Old Covenant proved faulty and the Jews broke their promise to God. The Jews did not have or request God's assistance, "Yes we can do it!" The Israelites did not seal the Old Covenant with their hearts, so a New Covenant was necessary, one with better promises and divine intervention. The New Covenant would need to come from the heart.

"The days are coming, declares the LORD, when I will make a new covenant with the house of Israel and with the house of Judah. It will not be like the covenant I made with their ancestors when I took them by the hand to lead them out of Egypt because they broke my covenant, though I was a husband to them, declares the LORD. This is the covenant I will make with the house of Israel after that time, declares the LORD. I will put my law in their minds and write it on their hearts. I will be their God, and they will be my people. I will put my law in their minds and write it on their hearts." (Jeremiah 31:31-33)

God shows the need for divine assistance. Later, we will review being "born again" through the resurrection of Jesus Christ, and the coming of the Holy Spirit. The New Covenant fulfillment is with divine intervention through Jesus Christ. We will study Jesus Christ and the New Covenant in the next two Path Steps.

THE SECRET INGREDIENT

The Israelites received the Ten Commandments and agreed to the Old Covenant. God describes the building of a tabernacle that contains a dwelling place for Him among men. He provided other laws to the Jewish nation, including sacrificial offerings, and particularly the sin offering. The sin offering is for a family and establishes a penalty for their sinful nature.

How is sin forgiven? What is God's underlying requirement? Is it possible to receive forgiveness by sacrificing food, jewels, etc.? What is the "ingredient" God requires for forgiveness of sins? The answer is in the Old and New Testaments.

"For the life of a creature is in the blood, and I have given it to you to make atonement for yourselves on the altar; it is the blood that makes atonement for one's life." (Leviticus 17:11)

"When Moses had proclaimed every commandment of the law to all the people, he took the blood of calves, together with water, scarlet wool and branches of hyssop, and sprinkled the scroll and all the people. He said, 'This is the blood of the covenant, which God has commanded you to keep.' In the same way, he sprinkled with the blood both the tabernacle and everything used in its ceremonies. In fact, the law requires that nearly everything be cleansed with blood and without the shedding of blood there is no forgiveness." (Hebrews 9:19-22)

THE 11TH COMMANDMENT (UNOFFICIALLY)

Do you know the key to forgiveness, to the Old Covenant and New Covenant? A single element perfects God's plan in the forgiveness of sins. **The "secret" ingredient is blood.**

"… it is the blood that makes atonement for one's life …" (Leviticus 17:11)

"… without the shedding of blood there is no forgiveness (of Sin)" (Hebrews 9:22)

Sin results in sacrificial death. "For the wages of sin is death." (Romans 6:23) In death, there is bloodshed. With the appropriate sacrifice and shedding of blood, the sin borne dies forever. Sin perishes with the bearer. Ultimately, all sin will perish. A death will occur for every sinner that committed or will commit sin; the only variables are the timing of death and who will realize the death penalty (see Path Step 7).

"But only the high priest entered the inner room (the Most Holy Place of the tabernacle), and that only once a year, and never without blood, which he offered for himself and for the sins the people had committed in ignorance." (Hebrews 9:7)

As fallen beings with sin, not one of us, not even the high priest, can be in the presence of God without the blood of a perfect sacrifice to make us righteous and holy before Him. The blood of a perfect sacrifice, shed on behalf of our sins, cleanses us and allows us to regain fellowship with God. Where is the perfect blood that will permit you to be reconciled with your God, the Creator?

"PURE" AND SIMPLE

There is only one man who walked this earth without sin. He was Jesus Christ, the Son of God. His blood was perfect and pure. He became a vessel for sin. Yet, He never committed a sin.

How did you rate on the sin checklist? Whether it is a sin of commission or omission, we all fail the sin checklist (see Path Step 3). It is irrelevant how many sins you have committed or how many times you have sinned in comparison to others. You might sin less frequent than your neighbor may. You might have only committed "small" sins. Your sins might be secretive. You might have performed an abundance of good deeds that you believed would overcome your sin. They did not. You are a sinner in God's view. As such, without assistance to remove your sin, you are unworthy of God and you will suffer death.

SUMMARY

God provided the first Passover and the sin offering to redeem His people. Without sacrifice and the shedding of blood, there is no redemption or forgiveness of sin. However, the sacrifice and blood must meet God's criteria. It cannot come from an ordinary or random source. The blood is yours or it MUST be from a young unblemished sacrifice, approved by a priest and chosen by God.

The Jews were unfaithful to the Old Covenant. God promised a New Covenant that would place the law in our minds and in our hearts. How do YOU find forgiveness of your sins given God's process to forgive sins? Where is the blood that will forgive YOUR sins? Remember, the blood of a creature that has sinned sheds its own blood when it dies to pay for its sin. However, a creature that has not sinned, and is unblemished can accept the sin of another. The death of this unblemished creature can forgive the sins of others.

When the God who created and who loves YOU pronounces judgment, which blood will pay for YOUR sins?

Do YOU know a sinless substitute, with perfect unblemished blood, who can assume your sin and die with it so that you are forgiven completely? If YOU do not, the atoning blood is flowing through YOUR arteries and veins, and YOU will pay the price.

Is there a substitution for YOUR sacrifice that is without sin, which can pay the penalty for YOUR ungodliness and grant YOU relationship with God?

There is no more important a question you will answer in your life!

As with each Path Step on A Rational Path to Christ, the Path Step ends with the same question from when it began. Would your life change IF…God has a plan to forgive sins. Yes or no? If yes:

- Do you REJECT God has a plan to forgive sins?

- Do you THINK God has a plan to forgive sins?

- Do you BELIEVE God has a plan to forgive sins?

- Do you KNOW God has a plan to forgive sins?

Notes

1. "A Mishnaic Commentary on Matthew 26.29 and 39." Bible.org. Bible.org, 05 June 2012. Web. 05 June 2012.

2. "The Passover Seder." The Passover Seder. Teachinghearts.com, 02 June 2012. Web. 02 June 2012.

3. "Passover Seder." Wikipedia. Wikimedia Foundation, 02 June 2012. Web. 02 June 2012.

4. "Parashat Terumah - The Eight Aliyot of Moses." Parashat Terumah - The Eight Aliyot of Moses. John J. Parsons, 02 June 2012. Web. 02 June 2012.

5. AllOtherNamesUsed. "Jim and Penny Caldwell - God of the Mountain [2009] SUBTITULOS EN ESPAÑOL." YouTube. YouTube, 23 Dec. 2011. Web. 02 June 2012.

6. "Koti.phnet.fi." Koti.phnet.fi. Koti.phnet.fi, 02 June 2012. Web. 02 June 2012.

7. "The Desert Tabernacle." : Tabernacle Layout: The Key Questions Checklist. The Dessert Tabernacle, 05 June 2012. Web. 05 June 2012.

8. "Examples of 3-fold Truths in the Tabernacle of Moses." Temple Builders Ministry. N.p., 05 June 2012. Web. 05 June 2012.

9. "413.) 1 Kings 8:1 – 21." DWELLING in the Word. N.p., 01 Dec. 2010. Web. 05 June 2012.

10. "Protected Blog." Rising River Youth. Rising River Youth, 30 Sept. 2009. Web. 05 June 2012.

11. Talbot, Louiss T. "Christ in the Tabernacle." Biblebaptistbelievers.com. Bible Baptist Believers, 05 June 2012. Web. 05 June 2012.

12. "Biblical Adventist Truths." Biblical Adventist Truths. N.p., 05 June 2012. Web. 05 June 2012.

13. "The Bronze Altar in the Outer Court of the Tabernacle of Moses (Bible History Online)." The Bronze Altar in the Outer Court of the Tabernacle of Moses (Bible History Online). N.p., 05 June 2012. Web. 05 June 2012.

14. "Shofar - The Shofar Man Is Your Israel Shofars Connection." Shofar - The Shofar Man Is Your Israel Shofars Connection. Dr. Terry Harman, 05 June 2006. Web. 05 June 2012.

15. "Shofar - The Shofar Man Is Your Israel Shofars Connection." Shofar - The Shofar Man Is Your Israel Shofars Connection. Dr. Terry Harman, 05 June 2006. Web. 05 June 2012.

16. "Shofar - The Shofar Man Is Your Israel Shofars Connection." Shofar - The Shofar Man Is Your Israel Shofars Connection. Dr. Terry Harman, 05 June 2006. Web. 05 June 2012.

17. "Shofar - The Shofar Man Is Your Israel Shofars Connection." Shofar - The Shofar Man Is Your Israel Shofars Connection. Dr. Terry Harman, 05 June 2006. Web. 05 June 2012.

18. "Judaism 101: Qorbanot: Sacrifices and Offerings." Judaism 101: Qorbanot: Sacrifices and Offerings. N.p., 05 June 2012. Web. 05 June 2012.

Path Step 5

Would Your Life Change IF…?

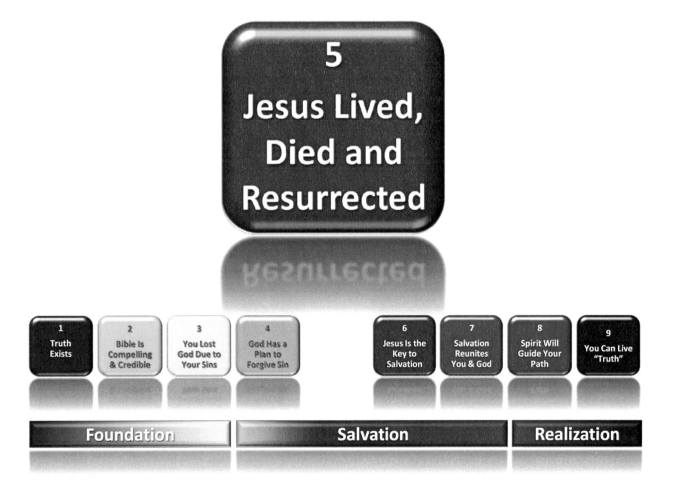

CONTENTS

THE SON OF MAN

I imagine I always considered Jesus to be real; to be truth. Mainly by association, I was raised to believe He was the truth. For many years, I had not considered the claims of the Bible defining Jesus' life and reality. With considerable study, the Bible exposed me to a compelling report of God's purpose, which is fulfilled completely by the Son of God and the Son of Man. Without revelation and enlightenment, the Bible might appear to be a collection of loosely connected fables. But for me, the reality of Jesus is so perfect. I grow more and more amazed as I am exposed to His purpose.

God gave humankind authority and dominion over the planet. Humankind surrenders authority to a fallen angel. God takes on human form to regain and operate in human authority. Jesus is born both as the Son of God and the Son of Man. God gave authority on earth only to humankind. Through Jesus, humankind can overcome the evil and fallen nature of this world with the shared authority of Jesus. Through Jesus, man can be made righteous and acceptable in the view of their creator. With greater study, the perfection of God's plan and His purpose for Jesus Christ is astonishing.

In my opinion, a more pure narrative has not been testified in recorded history. Who is this Son of God and Son of Man. Are His deeds recorded in the Bible factual? As recorded, Jesus performed amazing feats and astonishing tasks.

Regardless of the faith you may or may not possess, you need to answer a definite and simple question. The response changes everything.

Query: Did Jesus live, die and resurrect?

Would Your Life Change IF...Jesus Lived, Died, AND Resurrected?

"I don't believe Jesus ever lived."

"There is no factual basis for the Bible."

"The Apostles stole Jesus' body from the tomb."

In order to receive forgiveness of our sins, there needs to be sacrifice and blood. The blood must be from a qualified source. In the Old Testament, God specifies His commandments and covenant for forgiveness. However, there is a new covenant.

Biblical prophets predicted a new covenant between God and humankind. It was a new foundation for a relationship. The prediction suggests two characteristics of the first covenant made on Mount Sinai. The Sinai covenant was temporary, serving a short-term purpose, and it was not God's ultimate plan in reconciling with humankind. The new covenant would last forever and provide eternal life.

"If there had been nothing wrong with that first covenant, no place would have been sought for another." (Hebrews 8:7)

What was wrong with the Old Covenant?

The writer of Hebrews tells us "God found fault with the people." (Hebrews 8:8) God told Moses that the Old Covenant was temporary.

"God foretold this to Moses: 'These people will soon prostitute themselves to the foreign gods of the land they are entering. They will forsake me and break the covenant I made with them. On that day, I will become angry with them and forsake them.'" (Deuteronomy 31:16-18)

The Israelites did not obey the laws. Since God's blessings depended on the Israelites' obedience, the covenant was limited. The Israelites promised to comply, but the covenant and commandments were not in their hearts! When making the covenant with God, they did not ask God for His divine help to maintain their obligations.

Isaiah used symbolism to describe a special servant of God.

"Here is my servant, whom I uphold, my chosen one in whom I delight; I will put my Spirit on him, and he will bring justice to the nations. He will not shout or cry out, or raise his voice in the streets. A bruised reed he will not break, and a smoldering wick he will not snuff out. In faithfulness, he will bring forth justice; he will not falter or be discouraged till he establishes justice on earth. In his teaching, the islands will put their hope.

"This is what God the LORD says—he who created the heavens and stretched them out, who spread out the earth with all that springs from it, who gives breath to its people and life to those who walk on it: 'I, the LORD, have called you in righteousness; I will take hold of your hand. I will keep you and will make you to be a covenant for the people and a light for the Gentiles, to open eyes that are blind, to free captives from prison and to release from the dungeon those who sit in darkness.'" (Isaiah 42:1-7)

A servant of God will establish justice on earth, and a covenant for the non-Jews. Could Isaiah have been referring to Jesus Christ?

Who and what is Jesus Christ?

REALIZATION

The SALVATION Phase explains the principles and process defined by God for removing sin. In the Old Testament, it states that sacrifice and bloodshed are necessary practices to remove a sin. In a prophecy in Jeremiah that is disclosed by the author in his letter to the Hebrews, we learn that the plan for forgiveness was faulty under the Old Covenant. Because the Mosaic Law was not in the minds and hearts of the Israelites, they continued to sin. The Old Testament, it predicts a new and better covenant that addresses the failed nature of the first covenant and still meets the original criteria by God for the atonement of sin.

Jesus Christ is the center of the New Covenant. A prominent purpose of the New Testament is to teach the foundations of the New Covenant and of Jesus Christ. How do we know that the New Testament is legitimate, and Jesus Christ lived, and was crucified? Did He rise from the dead? Path Step 5 provides evidence supporting the life, death, and resurrection of Jesus Christ.

PATH STEP 5: JESUS LIVED, DIED AND RESURRECTED

In the New Testament, Jesus Christ fulfilled the prophecy in Isaiah 42. Jesus is the New Covenant. He is the new foundation that allows a relationship between God and His people. As you read in Isaiah, "He will bring justice to the nations." God does not wish for anyone to perish. He intended for all humankind to learn from His relationship with His chosen people, the Israelites. God's people expanded from the Israelites to the Gentiles (non-Jewish people). Under the New Covenant, it is only through Jesus Christ that we can have an eternal relationship with God.

"The Redeemer will come to Zion, to those in Jacob who repent of their sins." (Isaiah 59:20) The redeemer is Jesus Christ, and He would come through the Israelites (Zion), "to those in Jacob." In the Gospel of John 14:6, Jesus answered, "I am the way and the truth and the life. No one comes to the Father except through me."

"As for me, this is my covenant with them," says the LORD. "My Spirit, who is on you, and my words that I have put in your mouth will not depart from your mouth or from the mouths of your children, or from the mouths of their descendants from this time on and forever," says the LORD. (Isaiah 59:21)

This is the New Covenant. God places His Spirit and words on and in us. The New Covenant perfects what the Old Covenant lacked.

Question: How would God place His Spirit and words on and in us? See Path Step 8 - The Spirit Will Guide Your Path.

WHAT IS CHRISTIANITY?

The definition of Christianity is as follows: the study and belief in Jesus Christ, the Son of God, who lived as a man and who was sacrificially crucified as an offering to forgive the sins of humankind. He rose from the dead to provide a new beginning to those who call Him Savior. This is a short synopsis of Christianity. It is faith and belief in Jesus Christ, as a means to regain fellowship with God. This is consistent with John 14:6 above.

If Christ existed, does that signify Christianity is Truth? Not necessarily. However, if Jesus Christ lived, died, and resurrected, then Christianity is Truth. All three are essential in order for Christianity to be true. In that case, who is Jesus Christ and what claims does the Bible make of Him? The following are eleven claims of Jesus Christ from the Bible:

- Son of God
- Born of a virgin
- Hebrew descendant of Abraham
- Born in approximately 4 to 1 BC, in the town of Bethlehem
- Was a carpenter most of His life
- Ministered during His last 3½ years of life
- Preached love and forgiveness
- Performed miracles
- Crucified by Romans

- Resurrected from the dead
- Will return at the end of the age

What evidence supports these claims?

EVIDENCE TYPES

Let us evaluate Jesus Christ's existence and crucifixion, and if He rose from the dead. We will examine a small portion of the available evidence and data from the following categories:

- Eyewitness testimony - the Bible is evidence
- Archeology - does physical evidence exist?
- Non-biblical writings - do you believe that non-Christian and other biblical writers recorded the life and influences of Jesus Christ?
- Pontius Pilate - He was a prominent figure in Jesus Christ's trial and death; did he exist?
- Conspiracy theories - if the death or resurrection of Jesus was a hoax, why or how could they have carried out their plot?
- Effect on culture - after His resurrection, did Christ have an enduring influence on culture?
- Prophecy - the Old Testament has over 360 prophecies of Christ, so how many did He fulfill?
- Astronomy recorded in the Bible - what do the stars tell us?
- Logic - How does the evidence come together?

EYEWITNESS TESTIMONY

In the Gospels and New Testament, there is documentation, written evidence of Jesus Christ. The Gospels, the writings of Matthew, Mark, Luke, and John come from namesakes, eyewitnesses of Jesus Christ. They documented His life, teachings, death, and resurrection. Their testimonies of the life of Jesus are from their own perspective. Though the writings are similar about the Son of God, these four books do not replicate the other. They do recount many of the same occurrences, but each writer documented from a different vantage point.

"Many have undertaken to draw up an account of the things that have been fulfilled among us, just as they were handed down to us by those who from the first were eyewitnesses and servants of the word. Therefore, since I myself have carefully investigated everything from the beginning, it seemed good also to me to write an orderly account for you, most excellent Theophilus, so that you may know the certainty of the things you have been taught." (Luke 1:1-4)

Luke's writings explain the certainty of the accounts he is about to deliver. He writes his Gospel so others will know the truth.

The New Testament contains letters by the eyewitnesses and other apostolic writers to the new Christian churches throughout the Mediterranean region. The Apostle Paul, formerly Saul of Tarsus, writes much of the New Testament.[1] Before his conversion to Christianity, Paul studied in the Pharisee Academy of Gamaliel (Acts 22:3).

A Pharisee is a member of a Jewish sect that was in existence prior to the resurrection of Christ. They studied the strict observance of the rites and ceremonies of the Jewish (Old Testament) law and made their own traditions concerning the law. Prior to his conversion to Christianity, the Apostle Paul previously believed that the early Christians were blasphemous. Paul was involved in the death of Stephen, a disciple of Jesus Christ (Acts 8:1). He felt they were preaching against God. He believed in the imprisonment of Christians and their extradition. He conspired with Roman authorities seeking and persecuting new Christian "renegades." In the many letters he wrote to the early churches, Paul recounts his conversion to Christianity and interaction with Jesus Christ, who appeared to him.

The apostles wrote many letters to the early churches. They did not publish the collected works defined as the Bible we find in bookstores today. The original manuscripts were hand copied (as described in Path Step 2) and dispersed by and to the early Christian churches found throughout Asia and the Middle East (see Figure 69). There are over 24,000 manuscript copies of the New Testament identified by clergy, researchers, and historians. These manuscripts are written within a few decades of the apostolic writers (as described in Path Step 2). These manuscripts were assembled by the Council of Nicaea in 325 A.D. and comprise what is known now as the Bible.

The 24,000 is significant when compared to other popular writings. To date, there are only 643 copies of Homer's Iliad written in the 8th Century BC. Scholars date the earliest copy at 400 BC. That is 500 years after the original. Further, 10-20 copies of the writings of Julius Caesar exist. Copies of the oldest are approximately 1,000 years after the original.

FIG 69 - EARLIEST MANUSCRIPT COPY OF LUKE[2]

Ancient books and writings are evidence of people and civilizations. As with all records in history, the New Testament provides evidence of Jesus Christ. However, the mere existence of these manuscripts does not prove His existence. The number of early manuscripts written after Christ's resurrection, and the widespread distribution of these texts throughout the region after Christ's death confirms that the New Testament Gospels and Epistles are remarkable and relevant.

Have you considered and evaluated the assertions of Jesus Christ written in the New Testament? Let's continue.

ARCHEOLOGY

The New Testament states that Jesus Christ resurrected from the dead. Evidence shows that no remains of Him have been located or identified. However, the New Testament reports Jesus traveling throughout Jerusalem and the surrounding area and interacting with prominent figures in the establishment at the time just following his death and reported resurrection.

These are a sampling of sites and archaeological data that report sites and circumstances surrounding Jesus' activity, as reported in the New Testament:

- (Mark 1:21-28) Figure 70 the synagogues foundation in Capernaum where Jesus cured a man with an unclean spirit and delivered the sermon on the bread of life (John 6:25-59).[3]

FIG 70 -CAPERNAUM SYNAGOGUE FOUNDATION[3]

- (John 4) Figure 71, Jacob's well where Jesus spoke to the Samaritan woman.[4]

- (Matthew 26:57) Figure 72, Caiaphas, the Jewish high priest's Sarcophagus. Caiaphas protected the ways of Jewish tradition and the Mosaic Law. His leadership led Jesus to His death. (Matthew 8:14-16)

FIG 71 - JACOB'S WELL[4]

FIG 72 - SARCOPHAGUS OF CAIAPHAS THE JEWISH HIGH PRIEST[5]

- Figure 73, the house of Peter in Capernaum, where Jesus healed Peter's mother-in-law and others.

- (Acts 23:33-35) Figure 74, Herod's palace at Caesarea, where Paul is guarded.[9]

FIG 73 - PETER'S HOUSE AT CAPERNAUM

FIG 74 - HEROD'S PALACE AT CAESAREA

- (Acts 19:29) Figure 75, the theater at Ephesus, Turkey, where the riot of silversmiths occurred.[8]

- (Acts 18:12-17) Figure 76, the tribunal at Corinth, where Paul was tried.[7]

FIG 75 - THEATER AT EPHESUS

FIG 76 - TRIBUNAL AT CORINTH

- (John 5:1-14) Figure 77, the Pool of Bethesda in Jerusalem, where Jesus healed a crippled man.[5]

- (John 9:1-4) Figure 78, the Pool of Siloam in Jerusalem, where Jesus healed a blind man.[6]

FIG 77 - JERUSALEM POOL OF BETHESDA   FIG 78 - POOL OF SILOAM

- Figure 79, bones of Apostle Peter in Saint Peter's Basilica, Rome.[10]

- Figure 80, remains of Apostle Andrew stored at the Cathedral of Saint Andrews Scotland for many years. The majority of the remains are now in the town of Amali, Italy.[11]

- Fig 81 shows the iron spike location which sealed the rolling stone over the entrance of the tomb and Fig 82 shows the garden tomb believed to be the burial site of Jesus Christ.[12]

- Figs 83 and 84 depict Golgotha, the "Place of the Skull," believed to be the location of the crucifixion of Jesus Christ (Matthew 27:33). You can see the expanded view of a human skull likeness showing eye sockets and a nose bridge.[13]

FIG 79 - PETER'S TOMB UNDER STANT PETER'S BASILICA

FIG 80 - CATHEDRAL ST. ANDREWS SITE OF ANDREW REMAINS

FIG 81 - SPIKE TO RESTRAIN LARGE STONE

FIG 82 - GARDEN TOMB

FIG 83 - EXPANDED VIEW OF SKULL

FIG 84 - ROCK FAE OF GOLGOTHA ESCARPMENT

Do any of these sites prove that Jesus Christ lived and resurrected? No, but the data supports the New Testament and provokes more in-depth exploration and scrutiny.

NON-BIBLICAL HISTORICAL EVIDENCE

Beyond a Reasonable Doubt

Simon Greenleaf was born in 1783 in Suffolk, England. He is a famed attorney known for his teachings on legal evidence. His understandings shaped European and United States law, and doctrines on evidence and its permissibility in courtroom activities. Many legal institutions require the study of his teachings and works.[14]

Greenleaf applied the standards of proof to defend Christian belief. In his book, *The Testimony of the Evangelists*, he examines evidence of the resurrection of Jesus Christ, and talks of becoming a Christian. This book has become a model for many legal apologists and their works.[15] Greenleaf applied the standards of the Ancient Document Rule to establish the authenticity of the gospels. He cross-examined principles of those who witnessed the crucifixion and resurrection of Christ. Originally, he set out to prove that there was not sufficient evidence to establish Jesus Christ as Truth. After applying the legal evidence to the data, he concluded that the life, death, and resurrection of Jesus Christ to be valid "beyond a reasonable doubt."

His reasoning is reflected in the apologetic (a branch of theology which defends or proves the truth of Christian doctrines) works by John Warwick Montgomery, Josh McDowell, and Ross Clifford.[16]

NON-CHRISTIAN WRITERS ON CHRISTIANITY

Many non-Christian writers reported and commented on Jesus Christ, the early Christian movement, and the early church. Below is a list of these writers, along with their writings that are without commentary. Library and Internet searches are useful for gaining additional background on bibliographies and work collections.

Cornelius Tacitus (55-120 AD), the greatest historian of ancient Rome, annals 15.44

"Such indeed were the precautions of human wisdom. The next thing was to seek means of propitiating the gods, and recourse was had to the Sibylline books, by the direction of which prayers were offered to Vulcanus, Ceres, and Proserpina.

Juno, too, was entreated by the matrons. First in the capitol, then on the nearest part of the coast, whence water was procured to sprinkle the fane and image of the goddess. And there were sacred banquets and nightly vigils celebrated by married women. But all human efforts, all the lavish gifts of the emperor, and the propitiations of the gods, did not banish the sinister belief that the conflagration was the result of an order.

Consequently, to get rid of the report, Nero fastened the guilt and inflicted the most exquisite tortures on a class hated for their abominations, called Christians by the populace. Christus, from whom the name had its origin, suffered the extreme penalty during the reign of Tiberius at the hands of one of our procurators, Pontius Pilate, and a most mischievous superstition, thus checked for the moment, again broke out not only in Judea, the first source of the evil, but even in Rome, where all things hideous and shameful from every part of the world find their centre and become popular.

Accordingly, an arrest was first made of all who pleaded guilty; then, upon their information, an immense multitude was convicted, not so much of the crime of firing the city, as of hatred against mankind. Mockery of every sort was added to their deaths. Covered with the skins of beasts, they were torn by dogs and perished, or were nailed to crosses, or were doomed to the flames and burnt, to serve as a nightly illumination, when daylight had expired.

Nero offered his gardens for the spectacle, and was exhibiting a show in the circus while he mingled with the people in the dress of a charioteer or stood aloft on a car. Hence, even for criminals who deserved extreme and exemplary punishment, there arose a feeling of compassion; for it was not, as it seemed, for the public good, but to glut one man's cruelty, that they were being destroyed."

Gaius Suetonius Tranquillas, chief secretary of Emperor Hadrian (117-138 AD)

"First mention from *The Life of Claudius*: 'Because the Jews at Rome caused continuous disturbances at the instigation of Chrestus, he expelled them from the city.' The word *Chrestus* is a variant spelling of Christ. This event is referred to in Acts 18:2. Second mention from *The Lives of the Caesars*: "After the great fire at Rome… punishments were also inflicted on the Christians, a sect professing a new and mischievous religious belief."

Flavius Josephus (37-97 AD), court historian for Emperor Vespasian. Major work, *The Antiquities* (90 AD)

"At this time there was a wise man who was called Jesus. His conduct was good and (he) was known to be virtuous. And many people from among the Jews and other nations became his disciples. Pilate condemned him to be crucified and to die. But those who had become his disciples did not abandon his discipleship. They reported that he had appeared to them three days after his crucifixion, and that he was alive; accordingly he was perhaps the Messiah, concerning whom the prophets have recounted wonders."

Julius Africanus (160-240 AD) Chronography, XVIII refers to writings by Thallus and Phlegon concerning the darkness during the Crucifixion

"On the whole world, there pressed a most fearful darkness, and the rocks were rent by an earthquake, and many places in Judea and other districts were thrown down. This darkness Thallus, in the third book of his History, calls, as appears to me without reason, an eclipse of the sun…Phlegon records that, in the time of Tiberius Caesar, at full moon, there was a full eclipse of the sun from the sixth hour to the ninth - manifestly that one of which we speak."

Thallus, who wrote a history of the Eastern Mediterranean around 52 AD

"In a lost work referred to by Julius Africanus in the third century, the pagan writer Thallus reportedly claimed that Jesus' death was accompanied by an earthquake and darkness. However, the original text is in fact lost, and we can confirm neither the contents of the text or its date. It is possible that Thallus was merely repeating what was told to him by Christians, or that the passage, which Africanus cites, is a later interpolation. Outside of the New Testament, no other references to earthquakes or unusual darkness occur in the contemporary literature. This is very surprising; given the effect these sorts of events would presumably have had on the populace."

Pliny the Younger, Roman governor of Bithynia in Asia Minor around 112 AD. Pliny the Younger, Letters 10.96-97—to the Emperor Trajan

"'[The Christians] were in the habit of meeting on a certain fixed day before it was light, when they sang in alternate verses a hymn to Christ, as to a god, and bound themselves by a solemn oath, not to any wicked deeds, but never to commit any fraud, theft or adultery, never to falsify their word, nor deny a trust when they should be called upon to deliver it up; after which it was their custom to separate, and then reassemble to partake of food—but food of an ordinary and innocent kind.' Pliny added that Christianity attracted persons of all societal ranks, all ages, both sexes, and from both the city and the country. Late in his letter to Emperor Trajan, Pliny refers to the teachings of Jesus and his followers as excessive and contagious superstition."

Emperor Trajan, in reply to Pliny, Ep. 10.97

"The method you have pursued, my dear Pliny, in sifting the cases of those denounced to you as Christians is extremely proper. It is not possible to lay down any general rule, which can be applied as the fixed standard in all cases of this nature. No search should be made for these people; when they are denounced and found guilty they must be punished; with the restriction, however, that when the party denies himself to be a Christian, and shall give proof that he is not (that is, by adoring our gods) he shall be pardoned on the ground of repentance, even though he may have formerly incurred suspicion. Information's without the accuser's name subscribed must not be admitted in evidence against anyone as it is introducing a very dangerous precedent, and by no means agreeable to the spirit of the age."

Emperor Hadrian (117-138 AD), in a letter to Minucius Fundanus, the Asian proconsul

"'I do not wish, therefore that the matter should be passed by without examination so that these men may neither be harassed, nor opportunity of malicious proceedings be offered to informers. If, therefore, the provincials can clearly evince their charges against the Christians, so as to answer before the tribunal, let them pursue this course only, but not by mere petitions, and mere outcries against the Christians. For it is far more proper if anyone would bring an accusation that you should examine it.' Hadrian further explained that if Christians were found guilty they should be judged 'according to the heinousness of the crime.' If the accusers were only slandering the believers, then those who inaccurately made the charges were to be punished."

The Jewish Talmud, compiled between 70 and 200 AD

"On the eve of the Passover Yeshu was hanged. For forty days before the execution took place, a herald went forth and cried, 'He is going forth to be stoned because he has practiced sorcery and enticed Israel to apostasy. Anyone who can say anything in his favour, let him come forward and plead on his behalf.' But since nothing was brought forward in his favour he was hanged on the eve of the Passover." [Further, another early reference in the Talmud speaks of five of Jesus' disciples and recounts their standing before judges who make individual decisions about each one, deciding that they should be executed. However, no actual deaths are recorded.]

Lucian, a second century Greek satirist

"'The Christians, you know, worship a man to this day—the distinguished personage who introduced their novel rites, and was crucified on that account. You see, these misguided creatures start with the general conviction that they are immortal for all time, which explains the contempt of death and voluntary self-devotion which are so common among them; and then it was impressed on them by their original lawgiver that they are all brothers, from the moment that they are converted, and deny the gods of Greece, and worship the crucified sage, and live after his laws. All this they take quite on faith, with the result that they despise all worldly goods alike, regarding them merely as common property.' Lucian also reported that the Christians had 'sacred writings' which were frequently read. When something affected them, 'they spare no trouble, no expense.'"

Mara Bar-Serapion, of Syria, writing between 70 and 200 AD from prison to motivate his son to emulate wise teachers of the past

"What advantage did the Athenians gain from putting Socrates to death? Famine and plague came upon them as a judgment for their crime. What advantage did the men of Samos gain from burying Pythagoras? In a moment, their land was covered with sand. What advantage did the Jews gain from executing their wise king? It was just after that their kingdom was abolished. God justly avenged these three wise men: the Athenians died of hunger; the Samians were overwhelmed by the sea; the Jews, ruined and driven from their land, live in complete dispersion. But Socrates did not die for good; he lived on in the teaching of Plato. Pythagoras did not die for good; he lived on in the statue of Hera. Nor did the wise king die for good; he lived on in the teaching which he had given."

GNOSTIC-BASED HISTORICAL EVIDENCE

The Gospel of Truth, assumed by Valentinus, around 135-160 AD

"'For when they had seen him and had heard him, he granted them to taste him and to smell him and to touch the beloved Son. When he had appeared instructing them about the Father. For he came by means of fleshly appearance.' Other passages affirm that the Son of God came in the flesh and 'the Word came into the midst, it became a body.'

'Jesus was patient in accepting sufferings…since he knows that his death is life for many…he was nailed to a tree; he published the edict of the Father on the cross. …He draws himself down to death through life…eternal clothes him. Having stripped himself of the perishable rags, he put on imperishability, which no one can possibly take away from him.'"

The Treatise on Resurrection, by uncertain author of the late second century, to Rheginos

"The Lord…existed in flesh and…revealed himself as Son of God…Now the Son of God, Rheginos, was Son of Man. He embraced them both, possessing the humanity and the divinity, so that on the one hand he might vanquish death through his being Son of God, and that on the other through the Son of Man the restoration to the Pleroma might occur; because he was originally from above, a seed of the Truth, before this structure of the cosmos had come into being.

For we have known the Son of Man, and we have believed that he rose from among the dead. This is he of whom we say, 'He became the destruction of death as he is a great one in whom they believe.' Great are those who believe.

The Savior swallowed up death…He transformed himself into an imperishable Aeon and raised himself up, having swallowed the visible by the invisible, and he gave us the way of our immortality.

Do not think the resurrection is an illusion. It is no illusion, but it is Truth. Indeed, it is more fitting to say that the world is an illusion, rather than the resurrection which has come into being through our Lord the Savior, Jesus Christ.

…already you have the resurrection…why not consider yourself as risen and already brought to this? Rheginos was thus encouraged not to 'continue as if you are to die.'"

The Gospel of Thomas, **probably from 140-200 AD, contains many references to and alleged quotations of Jesus.**

The Aprocryphon of John, probably by Saturninus, around 120-130 AD

"It happened one day when John, the brother of James,—who are the sons of Zebedee—went up and came to the temple that a Pharisee named Arimanius approached him and said to him, 'Where is your master whom you followed?' And he said to him, 'He has gone to the place from which he came.' The Pharisee said to him, 'This Nazarene deceived you with deception and filled your ears with lies and closed your hearts and turned you from the traditions of your fathers.'"

Phlegon, born about 80 AD, as reported by Origen (185-254 AD), mentioned that Jesus made certain predictions, which met fulfillment.

CHRISTIAN WRITINGS OUTSIDE THE BIBLE

Clement, elder of Rome, letter to the Corinthian church (95 AD)

"The apostles received the Gospel for us from the Lord Jesus Christ; Jesus Christ was sent forth from God. So then, Christ is from God, and the apostles are from Christ. Both therefore came of the will of God in the appointed order. Having therefore received a charge, and having been fully assured through the resurrection of our Lord Jesus Christ and confirmed in the Word of God with full assurance of the Holy Ghost, they went forth with the glad tidings that the kingdom of God should come. So preaching everywhere in the country and town, they appointed their first fruits, when they had proved them by the Spirit, to be bishops and deacons unto them that should believe."

Ignatius, bishop of Antioch, letter to the Trallians (110-115 AD)

"Jesus Christ who was of the race of David, who was the son of Mary, who was truly born and ate and drank, was truly persecuted under Pontius Pilate, was truly crucified and died in the sight of those in Heaven and on earth and those under the earth; who moreover was truly raised from the dead, His Father having raised Him, who in the like fashion will so raise us also who believe on Him."

Ignatius, letter to the Smyrneans (110-115 AD)

"He is truly of the race of David according to the flesh, but Son of God by the Divine will and power, truly born of a virgin and baptized by John that all righteousness might be fulfilled by Him, truly nailed up in the flesh for our sakes under Pontius Pilate and Herod the tetrarch (of which fruit are we—that is, of his most blessed passion); that He might set up an ensign unto all ages through His resurrection.

For I know and believe that, He was in the flesh even after the resurrection; and when He came to Peter and his company, He said to them, 'Lay hold and handle me, and see that I am not a demon without body.' And straightway they touched him, and they believed, being joined unto His flesh and His blood. Wherefore also they despised death, nay they were found superior to death. And after His resurrection He ate with them and drank with them."

Ignatius, letter to the Magnesians (110-115 AD)

"Be ye fully persuaded concerning the birth and the passion and the resurrection, which took place in the time of the governorship of Pontius Pilate; for these things were truly and certainly done by Jesus Christ our hope."

Quadratus, to Emperor Hadrian about 125 AD

"The deeds of our Saviour were always before you, for they were true miracles; those that were healed those that were raised from the dead, who were seen, not only when healed and when raised, but were always present. They remained living a long time, not only whilst our Lord was on earth, but likewise when He had left the earth. So that some of them have also lived to our own times."

(Pseudo) Barnabas, written 130-138 AD

"He must need be manifested in the flesh. He preached teaching Israel and performing so many wonders and miracles, and He loved them exceedingly. He chose His own apostles who were to proclaim His Gospel. But He Himself desired so to suffer; for it was necessary for Him to suffer on a tree."

Justin Martyr, to Emperor Antoninus Pius about 150 AD

"After referring to Jesus' birth of a virgin in the town of Bethlehem, and that His physical line of descent came through the tribe of Judah and the family of Jesse, Justin wrote, 'Now there is a village in the land of the Jews, thirty-five stadia from Jerusalem, in which Jesus Christ was born as you can ascertain also from the registers of the taxing made under Cyrenius, your first procurator in Judea.

Accordingly, after He was crucified, even all His acquaintances forsook Him, having denied Him and afterwards, when He had risen from the dead and appeared to them, and had taught them to read the prophecies in which all these things were foretold as coming to pass, and when they had seen Him ascending into Heaven, and had believed, and had received power sent thence by Him upon them, and went to every race of men, they taught these things, and were called apostles.'"

Justin Martyr to Emperor Antoninus Pius about 150 AD, in Dialogue with Trypho, around 150 AD

"For at the time of His birth, Magi who came from Arabia worshiped Him, coming first to Herod, who then was sovereign in your land.

For when they crucified Him, driving in the nails, they pierced His hands and feet; and those who crucified Him parted His garments among themselves, each casting lots for what he chose to have, and receiving according to the decision of the lot.

Christ said amongst you that He would give the sign of Jonah, exhorting you to repent of your wicked deeds at least after He rose again from the dead…yet you not only have not repented after you learned that He rose from the dead, but as I said before, you have sent chosen and ordained men throughout all the world to proclaim that a godless and lawless heresy had sprung from one Jesus, a Galilean deceiver, whom we crucified, but His disciples stole Him by night from the tomb, where He was laid when unfastened from the cross, and now deceive men by asserting that He has risen from the dead and ascended to Heaven.

For indeed the Lord remained upon the tree almost until evening, and they buried Him at eventide; then on the third day He rose again."

If the apostles and early disciples fabricated the existence and mission of Jesus Christ, why did non-Christians, Gnostics and Christian writers outside the Bible record His accounts and the effects He had on culture from His life, death, and resurrection?

PONTIUS PILATE

Pontius Pilate is known as the fifth Roman procurator of Judea, under whose administration Jesus was executed. [17] The New Testament records the dealings of Pontius Pilate and Jesus Christ in various verses in the Gospels of Matthew, Mark, Luke, John, the book of Acts, and in 1 Timothy.

In addition to the writings listed above by Justin Martyr concerning Jesus Christ, reports from Justin Martyr sent from Pilate to Tiberius refer to the Acts of Pontius Pilate.[18]

Therein he states, "And the expression, 'They pierced my hands and my feet,' was used in reference to the nails of the cross which were fixed in His hands and feet. And after he was crucified, they cast lots upon His vesture, and they that crucified Him parted it among them. And that these things did happen you can ascertain from the 'Acts of Pontius Pilate.'"

Later Justin Martyr lists several healing miracles and asserts, "And that He did those things, you can learn from the Acts of Pontius Pilate."

Did Pontius Pilate exist? The Acts of Pontius Pilate does not say Pilate wrote it, but does claim to have derived from Acts at the praetorium in Jerusalem. Beyond the Acts of Pontius Pilate, evidence does exist of the Roman authority who presided over the death of Jesus Christ.

Fig 85 and 86 are bronze coins engraved by Pontius Pilate and made at the Jerusalem mint between 26 and 36 AD, including the year of Jesus Christ's crucifixion.[19]

FIG 85 - COIN HONORING PILATE

FIG 86 - BRPMZE PRUTAH MINTED BY PILATE

Discovered in 1961 is compelling evidence relating to Pilate. In the ruins of a theater in ancient Rome, an Italian archaeological expedition uncovered a block of limestone, known as The Pilate Stone (Figs 87 & 88). [20] This block of limestone was discovered in Caesarea Maritima (Fig 89), the capital of the province of Judea (Iudaea). A worker overturned a stone that was used for one of the stairways. On the other side was a partially obscured inscription in Latin, "Caesariensibus Tiberium Pontius Pilate Praefectus Iudaeae." (To the people of Caesarea Tiberium Pontius Pilate Prefect of Judea)

FIG 87 - FLAT STONE FOUND IN THEATER

FIG 88 - INSCRIPTION ON PILATE STONE

FIG 89 - THEATER RUINS AT CAESAREA

The dedication states that Pilate of Tiberieum was ECTVS IUDA, read as praefectus Iudaeae, prefect of Judea. The governors of Judea were of prefect rank. A group led by Antonio Frova and dated to AD 26-37 discovered the inscription. The inscription is now in the Israel Museum, Jerusalem, and a replica stands at Caesarea.

CONSPIRACY THEORIES

Is the Bible a conspiracy or stories fabricated from writings over a multitude of generations?

As disclosed in Path Step 2, the Bible is written over a 1,600-year period, by more than 40 authors, in Hebrew, Aramaic, and Greek languages, and written in the Middle East, Asia, Africa, and Europe. If the Old and New Testament were a conspiracy against Jesus, it is likely that a conspirator would have come forward to expose it. Many apostles and disciples of Jesus who wrote about Him were tortured and martyred for their unwavering belief. How could such a conspiracy be achieved, coordinated, and spread with such diversity over time, geography, perspective, and language? The earliest assumption of a conspiracy was that the disciples stole the body of Jesus.

In Matthew 28:11-15, we have a record of the reaction of the chief priests and the elders when the guards gave them the news that the body of Jesus was gone. They gave the soldiers money and told them to say that the disciples came in the night and stole Jesus' body while they slept. That account was so absurd that Matthew devoted no effort to disprove it.

Furthermore, a psychological and ethical impossibility arises. If the disciples stole the Body of Christ, it would contradict the character of the disciples as recorded in the Bible.[21] It would mean that they were perpetrators of a deliberate lie that was responsible for the deception and death of thousands of people. It is inconceivable that if even a few disciples conspired and pulled off this theft, they would have never told the others, who later were tortured and killed for their beliefs. It is highly out of character that they could overpower Roman soldiers to execute their devious plot. Traditionally, if a Roman guard failed his task, it would cost him his life.

Each of the disciples faced the test of torture and martyrdom for his statements and beliefs. Men and women will die for what they believe is to be true, though it may actually be false. They do not die for what they know is false. If ever a man tells the truth, it is on his deathbed. No records exist of any disciple giving a dying testimony against Jesus Christ, but rather for Him. Moreover, if the disciples had taken the body, and Christ had not arisen, an issue explaining His post-resurrection appearances remains.

A second hypothesis is that the authorities, Jewish and/or Roman, moved the body.

Why? Roman authorities, in alliance with Jewish leadership were in control of the gravesite of Jesus. With guards at the tomb, what would be their reason for moving the body? In addition, what about the silence of the authorities toward the apostles that preached about the resurrection in Jerusalem? The Jewish religious leaders were angry and tried to prevent the spread of the message that Jesus raised from the dead. They arrested Peter and John. They beat and threatened them in an attempt to keep them silent (see Acts 4:1-31).[22]

However, there was a simple solution to their problem. If they had Christ's body, they could have marched it through the streets of Jerusalem. They would have successfully extinguished Christianity in its infancy. That the authorities did not do this is compelling evidence they did not possess Jesus' body.

In 70 AD, the Romans invaded and destroyed Jerusalem and most of Israel, slaughtering its inhabitants. At the hand of the Romans, entire cities were burned to the ground. Many of Jesus' eyewitnesses would have been killed. This limits the number of survivors, and testimonies of Jesus. Arguably, substantial evidence of Jesus' existence was destroyed, which could have disproved many of the conspiracy theories. Despite this mockery, manuscript copies of the Gospels and New Testament letters flourished to motivate billions today through biblical translations.

CULTURE EFFECT

No other religion in history has influenced more people than the God of Abraham and Jesus Christ. A comprehensive demographic study of more than 200 countries finds that there are 2.2 billion people who claim to be Christians of all ages around the world. They represent a third of the 2010 global population of 7.2 billion.[23] Christians are also geographically widespread. No single continent or region can indisputably claim to be the center of global Christianity.

A century ago, this was not the case. In 1910, about two-thirds of the world's Christians lived in Europe, where the bulk of Christians had been for a millennium, according to the Center for the Study of Global Christianity. Today, only about a quarter of all Christians live in Europe (26%). More than a third now live in the Americas (37%). One in every four Christians lives in sub-Saharan Africa (24%) and about one in eight are found in Asia and the Pacific (13%). The number of Christians around the world has quadrupled in the last 100 years, from about 600 million in 1910 to more than 2 billion in 2010. However, the world's population increased rapidly, from an estimated 1.8 billion in 1910 to 6.9 billion in 2010. As a result, Christians make up about the same portion of the world's population today (32%) as they did a century ago (35%).

PROPHECY

No other religion establishes and embraces prophecy like Judaism and Christianity. Unlike other religious texts, the Bible has over 1,500 prophecies, most of which have already been realized. Over 360 of these prophecies found in the Old Testament predict the details of the Messiah (prophecies of the Christ that died and rose again in 33 AD). Listed are some Old Testament prophecies concerning Jesus Christ that correspond to New Testament fulfillment.

- "He would be a descendant of Abraham." (Genesis 12:1-3; 18:18; 22:18; Matthew 1:1-2,17; Galatians 3:8,16)

- "His name would be Immanuel." (Isaiah 7:14; Matthew 1:21-23) Immanuel in Hebrew means "God with us."

- "He would be a descendant of David." (2 Samuel 7:4-5, 12-13; 1 Chronicles 17:11-14; Psalm 132:11; Luke 1:32-33, 67-69; Acts 2:29-30; Matthew 1:17; Romans 1:3)

- "He would be from the tribe of Judah." (Genesis 49:8-10; Hebrews 7:14; Revelation 5:5)

- "He would be born in Bethlehem." (Micah 5:2; Matthew 2:4-6; John 7:42)

- "He would be from Nazareth and be called a Nazarene." (Matthew 2:23; Luke 1:26-27; John 1:45; Judges 13:5-7, 4)

- "He would be born of a virgin." (Isaiah 7:14; Matthew 1:20-23; Galatians 4:4; Genesis 3:15)

- "He would be a prophet like Moses." (Deuteronomy 18:15; John 1:45; Acts 3:20-23)

- "His name would be the Messiah." (Daniel 9:25-26; John 1:41) The word Christ in English comes from the Greek word Christos, which means "The Anointed One." Christos in Greek is the word Mashiah in Hebrew, which also means "The Anointed One." The word Mashiah means "Messiah" who is Jesus.

- "He would be the Son of God and God would be His Father." (Psalm 89:26-27; 2 Samuel 7:8,12-14; 1 Chronicles 22:7-10; Hebrews 1:1-2,5; Mark 14:36; John 20:30-31)

- "He would be circumcised the eighth day according to the law of purification." (Luke 2:21-24; Leviticus 12:1-6)

- "Young babies would die in an attempt to kill Jesus at His birth." (Jeremiah 31:15; Matthew 2:16-18)

- "He would be the only begotten Son of God." (Psalm 2:2, 6-7; John 1:14; Acts 13:33; Hebrews 1:1-2,5)

- "He would go to Egypt and return to the land of Israel." (Hosea 11:1; Matthew 2:13-15)

- "He would be preceded by a messenger who would prepare the way of the Lord" (Malachi 3:1; Luke 1:13,76; Matthew 11:7,10) A type of Elijah (Eliyahu) known as John (Yochanan) the Immerser (Baptist).

- "Jesus would be rejected by His own people Israel" (Psalm 69:8; 31:11; 88:8,18; Job 19:13; John 1:11; 7:3,5) Corporately. Note that many Jews were believers in the Messiah during the first century. Study Matthew, Mark, Luke, John, and the book of Acts.

- "The messenger, John (Yochanan) the Immerser (Baptist), would be preaching in the wilderness." (Isaiah 40:3-5; Luke 1:13, 80, 3:2-6)

- "He would be anointed of the Holy Spirit" (Isaiah 11:1-2; 42:1; Matthew 3:16) Ruach HaKodesh.

- "He would preach and teach in the temple" (Malachi 3:1; Luke 4:16; Matthew 26:55; John 7:28; 8:1-2) Beit HaMikdash.

- "His ministry would be to heal the sick, set the captives free, and preach deliverance." (Isaiah 61:1-2; Luke 4:16-21; Matthew 4:23; 9:34-35; Acts 2:22; 10:38) This is known as the basar (gospel) in Hebrew.

- "Jesus was to be the shepherd of Israel because Israel had no shepherd." (Ezekiel 34:5-10; 1 Kings 22:17; Zechariah 10:2; Genesis 49:22,24; Psalm 23:1; 80:1; Isaiah 40:10-11; Ezekiel 34:23-24; 37:24; John 10:11,14-15)

- "Jesus would be received by the Gentiles" (Isaiah 11:10; 42:6; 49:6,22; 54:3; 60:3,5,11,16; 61:6,9; 62:2; 66:12,19; Malachi 1:11; Luke 2:30-32; Acts 28:28) Corporately. Note that many Gentiles do not believe in Jesus, and others are believers in name only and not true followers with their hearts. "The believers in the Messiah are commanded to follow God with all of their heart" (Deuteronomy 6:4-9).

- "Jesus is the stone that the builders rejected." (Psalm 118:22; Isaiah 3:10-12; Romans 9:11)

- "He would speak in parables." (Psalm 78:2-4; Matthew 13:34-35)

- "The ministry of Jesus would be in Galilee." (Isaiah 9:1-2; Matthew 4:12-16, 23)

- "His message would not be believed." (Isaiah 53:1; John 12:37-38)

- "The meek would praise Him." (Psalm 8:1-2; Matthew 21:15-16)

- "Illegal merchandise trading would be done in the temple." (Psalm 69:9; John 2:13-17; Isaiah 56:7; Matthew 21:12-13)

- "He would be hated." (Psalm 69:4; 35:19; 109:2-3; 119:161; John 15:24-25)

- "He would be a reproach to the people." (Psalm 69:9; 89:50-51; Romans 15:3)

- "He would not seek publicity." (Isaiah 42:1-2; Matthew 12:15-19; 9:30; 8:4)

- "He can be trusted and would be compassionate." (Isaiah 42:3; Matthew 12:15, 20-21)

- "No evil words would proceed from His mouth." (Isaiah 53:9; Luke 23:41; 1 Peter 2:21-22; 2 Corinthians 5:21)

- "His disciples would forsake Him." (Zechariah 13:7; Matthew 26:31-35, 56)

- "He was not physically attractive, in a worldly form to be desired." (Isaiah 53:2; Psalm 22:6; Mark 6:1-3; Philippians 2:7)

- "He would publicly enter Jerusalem (Yerushalayim) before the time of His crucifixion - He would ride into Jerusalem (Yerushalayim) on a donkey." (Zechariah 9:9; Matthew 21:5)

- "He would be betrayed for 30 pieces of silver." (Zechariah 11:12; Matthew 26:14-16)

- "His betrayal price would be given for a potter's field." (Zechariah 11:13; Matthew 27:3, 7-10)

- "He would be betrayed by a friend." (Psalm 41:9; John 13:18-21)

- "Both Jew and Gentile would conspire against Him." (Psalm 2:1-2; Acts 4:27-28; Matthew 26:3; 27:1-2)

- "He would be nailed to a tree." (Deuteronomy 21:22-23; Psalm 22:16; John 19:18; 20:25)

- "He would suffer for others." (Isaiah 53:6; Matthew 20:28)

- "He would die for our sins." (Isaiah 53:5; 1 Corinthians 15:3; 1 Peter 2:24)

- "He would be mocked." (Psalm 22:7-8; Matthew 27:39-43)

- "He would die with the transgressors." (Isaiah 53: 12; Mark 15:27-28)

- "He would make intercession for His murderers." (Isaiah 53:12; Luke 23:34)

- "He would be smitten." (Micah 5:1; Isaiah 50:6; Lamentations 3:30; Matthew 26:67; 27:30)

- "He would be spit upon." (Isaiah 50:6; Matthew 26:67, 27:30)

- "He would be forsaken by God." (Psalm 22:1; Matthew 27:46)

- "He would be given gall and vinegar to eat and drink." (Psalm 69:21; Matthew 27:34, 48)

- "He opened not His mouth when accused." (Isaiah 53:7; Matthew 26:63-64; 27:12-14)

- "His garments would be parted." (Psalm 22:18; Matthew 27:35)

- "Not one bone would be broken." (Psalm 34:20; John 19:33, 36)

- "He would be pierced." (Zechariah 12:10; John 19:34, 37)

- "He would be like a lamb going to the slaughter." (Isaiah 53:7; Acts 8:26-35)

- "He is King of the Jews" (and the world) (Psalm 2:6; John 18:33, 37; 19:19-22)

- "He would be buried with the rich." (Isaiah 53:9; Matthew 27:57-60)

- "He would die." (Isaiah 53:12; Matthew 27:50)

- "His soul would not be left in Hell." (Psalm 16:10; 49:15; 56:13; Acts 2:27, 31; 13:33-35)

- "He would rise from the dead." (Psalm 16:10; Luke 24:6, 31, 34; Acts 2:27-31; 13:35)

- "Others would rise from the dead with Him." (Psalm 68:18; Ephesians 4:8; Matthew 27:52-53)

- "He would rise the third day from the grave." (Jonah 1:17; 1 Corinthians 15:4; Luke 24:45-46; Matthew 12:40)

- "He would ascend into Heaven." (Psalm 68:18; Acts 1:9; Luke 24:50-51)

- "He would sit at the right hand of God." (Psalm 110:1; Hebrews 1:2-3; Ephesians 1:20-21; 1 Peter 3:22)

- "He would usher in a New Covenant" (Jeremiah 31:31; Luke 22:20) Brit Hadashah.

- "He would be a sure foundation to all who believe." (Isaiah 28: 16; Romans 10:11; 1 Peter 2:4-6)

- "The exact time of His crucifixion was known." (Daniel 9:25; Nehemiah 2:1-8; 5:14 – the Seventy Sevens Prophecy) 483 years from the decree to build the temple and was around 444 BC.

Daniel's Seventy "Sevens" Prophecy

Perhaps the most awe-inspiring prophecy of Jesus Christ is the Seventy Sevens of Daniel.

"Know and understand this: from the issuing of the decree to restore and rebuild Jerusalem until the Anointed One, the ruler, comes, there will be seven 'sevens' and sixty-two 'sevens.' It will be rebuilt with streets and a trench, but in times of trouble. After the sixty-two 'sevens,' the Anointed One will be cut off and will have nothing. The people of the ruler who will come will destroy the city and the sanctuary. The end will come like a flood: war will continue until the end, and desolations have been decreed. He will confirm a covenant with many for one 'seven.' In the middle of the 'seven', he will put an end to sacrifice and offering. And on a wing of the temple he will set up an abomination that causes desolation, until the end that is decreed is poured out on him." (Daniel 9:25-27)

It is believed that Daniel provided this prophecy around 150 BC. He prophesies that after seven sevens and 62 sevens the Anointed One comes. The Hebrew word the Anointed One means Mashiah, translating in many texts as Messiah. Jesus Christ was prophesied as the coming Messiah in the Old Testament and assumed that role and title in the New Testament. The prophecy delivered a time schedule for the coming of the Messiah, as a ruler. This is a critical clue to uncovering the meaning of the prophecy.

The trigger point of the prophecy is, "Know and understand this: from the issuing of the decree to restore and rebuild Jerusalem…It will be rebuilt with streets and a trench, but in times of trouble." This is the starting point of the time schedule.

"In the month of Nisan in the twentieth year of King Artaxerxes...the king said to me, 'What is it you want?' Then I prayed to the God of Heaven, and I answered the king, "If it pleases the king and if your servant has found favor in his sight, let him send me to the city in Judah where my fathers are buried so that I can rebuild it.'...And because the gracious hand of my God was upon me, the king granted my requests." (Nehemiah 2:1-8) King Artaxerxes gave a decree, "In the month of Nisan in the twentieth year of King Artaxerxes." According to the historical record, the first Nisan in the 20th year of King Artaxerxes is March 5, 444 BC.

The 'sevens' referred in Daniel are sevens of years. Rebuilding Jerusalem will require seven sevens, or 49 years. After that, in another 62 sevens, the Anointed One comes. In total, the Anointed One comes in 69 sevens, or 483 years from Artaxerxes decree to rebuild Jerusalem. However, when Daniel wrote this prophecy, the Hebrews used a 360-day lunar calendar, not the 365-day solar calendar of today.

- 483 lunar years x 360 days/lunar year = 173,880 days
- 173,880 days from the 1st of Nisan in 444 BC is Nisan 10, or March 30, 33 AD

By analyzing the dates of Jewish festivals and other clues in the Bible (see ASTRONOMY IN THE BIBLE later in the Path Step); we learn that the crucifixion of Jesus Christ occurred on April 3, 33 AD. The 173,880th day from the decree is March 30th or 4 days prior to the crucifixion of Jesus. On that day, what prominent event occurred? Did any activity occur that matches the prophecy, the Anointed One comes?

"As he approached Bethphage and Bethany at the hill called the Mount of Olives, he sent two of his disciples, saying to them, 'Go to the village ahead of you, and as you enter it, you will find a colt tied there, which no one has ever ridden. Untie it and bring it here. If anyone asks you, Why are you untying it? Tell him, The Lord needs it.' Those who were sent ahead went and found it just as he had told them.

As they were untying the colt, its owners asked them, 'Why are you untying the colt?' They replied, 'The Lord needs it.' They brought it to Jesus, threw their cloaks on the colt and put Jesus on it. As he went along, people spread their cloaks on the road. When he came near the place where the road goes down the Mount of Olives, the whole crowd of disciples began joyfully to praise God in loud voices for all the miracles they had seen: 'Blessed is the king who comes in the name of the Lord! Peace in Heaven and glory in the highest!' Some of the Pharisees in the crowd said to Jesus, 'Teacher, rebuke your disciples!' 'I tell you' he replied, 'if they keep quiet, the stones will cry out.'" (The Gospel of Luke 19:29-40)

By taking the calendar of Jewish festivals and applying them to the time of Jesus Christ, we learn that Jesus arrived triumphantly in the city of Jerusalem on March 30, 33 AD, and was crucified four days later by the Jews. Jesus Christ, the Anointed One, the Messiah (Mashiah), was presented to the Israelite people of Jerusalem as the King (ruler), who came to redeem His people. Did the Anointed One come? As history records, Jesus Christ arrived in the manner that was prophesied, precisely on schedule.

- "After the sixty-two 'sevens,' the Anointed One will be cut off and will have nothing." (Daniel 9:26) Translating from the Hebrew, cut off means to be killed.

- "He came to that which was his own, but his own did not receive him." (John 1:11) When Jesus was crucified, he was "cut off" and he had nothing because His own did not receive Him.

- In Daniel 9:26-27, a final seven remains and, generally, is believed to describe end time events. While the topic and imagery are fascinating, we will not explore it herein.

Because of historical confirmation, few historians argue that Jesus Christ did not exist. Based on evidence, they agree that Jesus was killed during the period that Pontius Pilate was prefect of Judea. Some historians dispute the claim Jesus resurrected from the dead and ascended to Heaven. Nevertheless, Jesus Christ fulfilled Daniel's prophecy of presentation to His people as a ruler after 69 sevens from the decree to rebuild Jerusalem. Daniel's same prophecy identified Jesus Christ as the Messiah (we will explore this deeper in Path Step 6). If an element of Daniel's prophecy proved so precise, it would be ignorant to dismiss the balance.

PROBABILITY OF JESUS CHRIST FULFILLING PROPHECY

What is the probability that Jesus Christ could fulfill all the Old Testament prophecies of the Messiah? Let us investigate the probability of Christ fulfilling a subset of the prophecies pertaining to Him. For additional information, see http://www.goodnewsdispatch.org/math.html.[25]

First, for perspective, let us consider probabilities of occurrences with which we can identify.

- Being struck by lightning in a year = 7×10^5 or 1 in 700,000

- Being killed by lightning in a year = 2×10^6 or 1 in 2,000,000

- Becoming president = 1×10^7 or 1 in 10,000,000

- A meteorite hitting your house = 1.8×10^{14} or 1 in 180,000,000,000,000

- You will eventually die = 1 in 1

As you can see, the probabilities of being struck or killed by lightning, becoming president, or having a meteorite hit your house, are small and diverse. However, someone, somewhere will be that one and that someone could be you.

What is the probability of a man fulfilling the prophecies of the Messiah? With over 360 prophecies to fulfill, the chance of one person accurately satisfying all of them is incalculable and small. However, a mathematician performed a probability analysis and derived an interesting conclusion.

Dr. Peter Stoner is the author of *Science Speaks*. [26] He applied the principle of probability. It states that if the chance of one thing happening is "1 in M", and the chance of another independent thing happening is "1 in N", then the chance of them both happening is "1 in M x N", pertaining to the fulfillment of biblical prophecies. He analyzed the probability that a random man in the time of Jesus Christ could have fulfilled the many prophecies of the Messiah in the Old Testament. (http://sciencespeaks.dstoner.net/Christ_of_Prophecy.html) [27]

The Bible has over 1,500 prophecies, either events that have happened already or events that will happen in the future. In *Science Speaks*, Dr. Stoner looks at the probability that one man, Jesus Christ, could have fulfilled eight of the 360 prophecies relating to the Messiah in the Bible.

Let us look at eight prophecies from the Old Testament, their fulfillment by Christ in the New Testament, the probability of one man fulfilling each prophecy, and analysis of one man fulfilling all eight prophecies (See Table 5-1). Keep in mind, the time span between the prophecies of the Old Testament and the New Testament range from hundreds to thousands of years.

To answer the question, "What is the probability of one man fulfilling all eight prophecies?" we apply the principal of probability by multiplying all eight probabilities together.

Table 5-1 - Probability of Prophecy Fulfillment

Old Testament Prophecy	New Testament Fullfilment	Probability
Christ to be born in Bethlehem (Micah 5:2)	And Herod asked where Christ had been born… they answered Bethlehem (Matt 2:4-6)	2.8×10^5 or 1 in 280,000
Forerunner of Christ (Malachi 3:1)	John the Baptist, the forerunner of Christ (Mark 1:2-8)	1×10^3 or 1 in 1,000
Christ to enter Jerusalem riding on a donkey (Zech 9:9)	Christ to enter Jerusalem riding on a donkey (Zech 9:9)	1×10^2 or 1 in 100
Christ to be betrayed by a friend (Psalm 41:9)	Judas betrayed Jesus (Luke 22:21)	1×10^3 or 1 in 1,000
Christ to be betrayed for 30 pieces of silver (Zech 11:12)	Judas sold out Jesus for 30 pieces of silver (Matt 26:15)	1×10^3 or 1 in 1,000
30 pieces of silver casted down and used to buy a potter's field (Zech 11:13)	30 pieces of silver used to buy a potter's field (Matt 27:3-10)	1×10^5 or 1 in 100,000
Although innocent, Christ kept silent when on trial (Isaiah 53:7)	Jesus kept silent when questioned (Mark 14:60-61)	1×10^3 or 1 in 1,000
Christ crucified (Psalm 22:16)	Jesus was crucified (John 19:17, 18)	1×10^4 or 1 in 10,000

(1 times $2.8 \times 10^5 \times 10^3 \times 10^2 \times 10^3 \times 10^3 \times 10^5 \times 10^3 \times 10^4$) gives us 2.8×10^{28}, or for simplicity 1×10^{28} or 1 in 10,000,000,000,000,000,000,000,000,000.

Given a probability analysis and the time span between the writings of the Old Testament and the fulfillment by Christ in the New Testament, either God revealed the prophecies to the Old Testament prophets, or the prophets wrote them as they thought fit. With Christ fulfilling all 8 prophecies (and over 352 other prophecies), what are the odds the prophets were just guessing?

ASTRONOMY IN THE BIBLE

There are signs that emerged in the heavens proclaiming the conception, birth, life, and death of Jesus Christ. Does the Bible predict these signs? What guidance does the Bible give for astronomical phenomena?

Attorney Frederick A. (Rick) Larson did a study on the star of Bethlehem described in Matthew. He made a DVD called, "The Star of Bethlehem," and has a website, bethlehemstar.com.[28] It is detailed and fascinating. Larson articulates the story of Jesus revealed in the heavens with signs during His life, in agreement with the biblical text.

He used astronomy software that predicts with great physical precision the motion of celestial bodies. If the software could predict where these bodies are destined, he used the same tool to find out where they had been, specifically in times of Jesus Christ. Matching biblical astronomical signs and the revelations shown in the DVD, it is nothing short of a dramatic and compelling proclamation of God and Jesus Christ. The following are short subjects of the DVD.

"Lift your eyes and look to the heavens: Who created all these? He who brings out the starry host one by one and calls them each by name. Because of his great power and mighty strength, not one of them is missing." (Isaiah 40:26) "He is the Maker of the Bear and Orion, the Pleiades and the constellations of the south." (Job 9:9) Isaiah and Job tell us that God is the creator of all things. Even so, in creating the Universe, He organized the stars to create His intended signs and the shapes of the constellations.

"For the director of music. A psalm of David. The heavens declare the glory of God; the skies proclaim the work of his hands. Day after day, they pour forth speech; night after night they display knowledge. There is no speech or language where their voice is not heard. Their voice goes out into all the earth, their words to the ends of the world. In the heavens, he has pitched a tent for the sun." (Psalm 19:1-4) In the Old Testament, the psalmist prophesies and instructs us to look to the heavens, for they declare knowledge. Within them is declared the glory of God.

Jesus Christ offers direct counsel on the topic of astronomy. "There will be signs in the sun, moon and stars. On the earth, nations will be in anguish and perplexity at the roaring and tossing of the sea." (Luke 21:25) In Luke, when prophesying, Jesus instructs us to look for signs in the sun, moon, and stars. These are prophetic words for His second coming as written in Revelation, and signs marking His crucifixion. We will begin with His birth.

"A great and wondrous sign appeared in Heaven: a woman clothed with the sun, with the moon under her feet and a crown of twelve stars on her head. She was pregnant and cried out in pain as she was about to give birth." (Revelation 12:1-2) As written in Revelation, the Scripture describes Jesus Christ's conception by the Virgin Mary. In September of 3 BC, the picture in Revelation was displayed in the sky. Figure 90 shows the lower portion of the constellation Virgo, which is a symbol of the virgin, with the sun at her side, and the new moon next to her left foot. Note that the new moon is to the right of her left foot. It is contained in the lens flare effect of the software. The time was Rosh Hashanah, the festival of the new moon. Rising in the sky before this is Jupiter, the "king" planet, circling Regulus, the "royal" star, three times with retrograde motion, all occurring in the constellation of Leo, the lion (see Figure 91).

FIG 90 - WOMAN CLOTHED IN THE SUN & MOON AT HER FEET

FIG 91 - JUPITER CIRLING REGULAS

Jesus was born of the Israelite tribe of Judah, whose symbol is the lion. With the new moon symbolizing Jesus Christ, this sign marks the conception in September of 3 BC. If so, what occurred in the skies approximately nine months later?

Figure 92 shows that in June of 2 BC, nine months after the conception signs, show the "king" planet, Jupiter moving toward Venus. It did not fully eclipse, but created the brightest star in the sky anyone had ever seen. It is symbolic that Jupiter, known as the "king" planet while Venus is the "mother" planet. These planets came together, and then the "king" planet departed. Larson believes this phenomenon is the star of Bethlehem, which is a symbol of the Virgin Mary and her son Jesus.

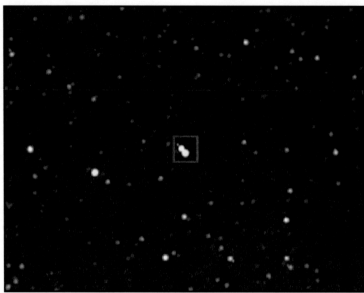

FIG 92 - COINCIDENCE OF PLANETS JUPITER AND VENUS IN JUNE 2 BC

Much is stated in the Bible about the journey of the magi as they traveled to Herod and then on to Bethlehem in search of the child king.

"After Jesus was born in Bethlehem in Judea, during the time of King Herod, Magi from the east came to Jerusalem and asked, 'Where is the one who has been born king of the Jews? We saw his star in the east and have come to worship him.' When King Herod heard this, he was disturbed, and all Jerusalem with him.

When he had called together all the people's chief priests and teachers of the law, he asked them where the Christ was to be born. 'In Bethlehem in Judea,' they replied, 'for this is what the prophet has written: 'But you, Bethlehem, in the land of Judah, are by no means least among the rulers of Judah; for out of you will come a ruler who will be the shepherd of my people Israel.' Then Herod called the Magi secretly and found out from them the exact time the star had appeared. He sent them to Bethlehem and said, 'Go and make a careful search for the child. As soon as you find him, report to me so that I too may go and worship him.'

After they had heard the king, they went on their way, and the star they had seen in the east went ahead of them until it stopped over the place where the child was. When they saw the star, they were overjoyed."

The planet Jupiter withdrew from Venus at the time of Jesus' birth and moved, confirming the biblical text surrounding the Magi from the East. Larson demonstrates how the star guided the magi and stopped over Bethlehem (result of precision astrophysics and retrograde motion). He demonstrates the star (Jupiter) stopping in the sky on December 25, in 2 BC, when Jesus would have been an infant child and the magi would have delivered their gifts, in accordance with Scripture. See the DVD, "The Star of Bethlehem" for Larson's details of this and other events.

Perhaps the most dramatic astronomical signs occurred at the time of Jesus' crucifixion. Let us review Old Testament prophecy.

"I will show wonders in the heavens and on the earth, blood and fire and billows of smoke. The sun will be turned to darkness and the moon to blood before the coming of the great and dreadful day of the LORD." (Joel 2:30-31) In the New Testament, "I will show wonders in the Heaven above and signs on the earth below, blood and fire and billows of smoke. The sun will be turned to darkness and the moon to blood before the coming of the great and glorious day of the Lord. And everyone who calls on the name of the Lord will be saved. 'Men of Israel, listen to this: Jesus of Nazareth was a man accredited by God to you by miracles, wonders and signs, which God did among you through him as you yourselves know.'" (Acts 2:19-22)

Joel projected that a totally-eclipsed "blood" moon would preside over the death of Jesus Christ. In Acts, Peter recalls his prophesy and reminds the Israelites that they have seen the signs and prophesy come true.

Using New and Old Testament Scriptures with an understanding of Jewish festivals, the date of Jesus' crucifixion can he confirmed to April 3, 33 AD. Recreating the sky on that date with astrophysics, Figure 93 and Figure 94 show the heavens at 3:00 pm Jerusalem local time, on the predicted date in 33 AD.

FIG 93 - BLOOD MOON AT VIRGO S FEET APRIL 3, 33 AD

FIG 94 - APRIL 3, 33 AD WITH VIRGO OVERLAY

As Jesus died, a lunar eclipse occurred, causing a blood moon due to the red shift of the sun's light refracting through the earth's atmosphere, much as we see with a sunset. Just as Joel predicted and as Peter proclaimed, the Jews had witnessed, the blood moon. Further, in the same position when Jesus was conceived with a new moon, the full moon was at the feet of the virgin, the constellation Virgo. A new moon for the life conceived, and a full moon for the life ended. This is an astonishing fulfillment of biblical prophecy.

Perhaps the most remarkable discovery in "The Star of Bethlehem" occurred at the time of the blood moon and Jesus' death, but from another vantage point. A lunar eclipse places the earth directly between the sun and the moon. A blood moon is seen from the earth. From this perspective, we see a breath-taking glimpse into the God of the Universe's intelligent design.

Figure 95 shows the lunar eclipse from the moon, at the exact moment of Jesus Christ's death. The sun is blotted out; it is fully obstructed from the earth. However, when constellation outlines are added, we learn the eclipsed sun and earth are located within the constellation Aries. To the Jewish people, the constellation Aries is the Paschal Lamb, or Passover Lamb.

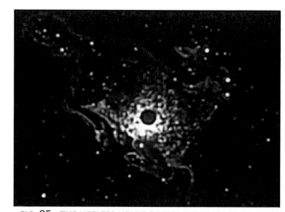

FIG 95 - THE LIFELESS HEART OF THE PASCHAL LAMB, ARIES

"Get rid of the old yeast that you may be a new batch without yeast—as you really are. For Christ, our Passover lamb has been sacrificed." (1 Corinthians 5:7)

As written in the New Testament, Jesus Christ was our Passover Lamb sacrifice (see Path Step 6). The sun is obscured, blotted out by the earth, and is over the heart of Aries. At 3:00 pm on April 3, 33 AD, the Passover Lamb died, and its heart was blotted out. The symbolism is breathtaking and testimony of a Creator who breathed wisdom and truth into biblical writings.

REALITIES OF CHRIST

Biblical Account: The New Testament is a written historical record with many of the manuscripts written within decades of Christ's crucifixion. More manuscript copies exist of the New Testament than any others of that same period.

- Archaeology—Archaeology supports a multitude of locations visited by Jesus and other New Testament characters.

- Non-biblical writing of evidence—More than 40 Non-Christian historians and authors either write about or refer to the influence of Christ in society.

- Pontius Pilate writings and archeology—manuscript, script, and archaeological proof exist of the man in authority who contributed to Jesus' crucifixion.

- Prophecy evidence—Over 360 prophecies are recorded in the Old Testament that predict many facets of Jesus and His life. Some prophecies in manuscript copies are pre-dating Jesus Christ by several hundred years; defining the date of His triumphal entry into Jerusalem and His crucifixion. Moreover, what is the probability of anyone fulfilling all these prophecies by chance? Analyses of only eight of these prophecies yield a unreasonably low probability and asserts the probability that chance defined the events in the New Testament is zero.

- Biblical circumstances—The apostles were martyred; they were not part of a hoax. If the Old and New Testaments were a deception someone would have come forward to expose it. Paul, formerly Saul of Tarsus, perhaps the greatest Christian persecutor of his time, became the greatest Christian evangelist after a vision with Christ and conversion.

- Jesus' death faked—Disciples moved the bodies and then were tortured to say they were not Christians, but not one of them succumbed. If the Romans or Pharisees had Jesus' body, would they not have paraded it through the streets to repress the growing Christian following?

- Jesus' effect on culture—Approximately 2.18 billion people today believe Jesus Christ lived, died, and resurrected. This is a cause for consideration. Christianity is the largest religious affiliation on the globe.

SUMMARY

Did Jesus Live? As portrayed in the Gospels, evidence of Jesus' life and death is convincing.

The Bible is about redemption and fulfillment of the covenant at Mount Sinai. Jesus as Messiah/Savior is prophesied over 360 times in the Old Testament. Prophecies of Jesus' life and His death written in the Old Testament are fulfilled in the New Testament.

- Eyewitness accounts (Gospels) recorded in the New Testament.

- Disciples wrote Gospels and Epistles, and died while spreading the good news of Jesus Christ.

- 19 non-biblical writers capture and record Jesus as a "real" person and comment on His death, and the turmoil it created.

- Validation of biblical events and dates are established by astronomy.

- Proven prophecy and a zero probability of any man of Jesus' time replicating His fulfillment of Scripture.

- If Jesus Christ had not resurrected, His body would have been exhumed and displayed.

With Historicity, by the standard of a court of law, convincing evidence substantiates that Jesus Christ existed, died, and resurrected.

Do you know who Jesus Christ is, really?

As with each Path Step on A Rational Path to Christ, the Path Step ends with the same question from when it began. Would your life change IF…Jesus lived, died, and resurrected. Yes or no? If yes:

- Do you REJECT Jesus lived, died, and resurrected?

- Do you THINK Jesus lived, died, and resurrected?

- Do you BELIEVE Jesus lived, died, and resurrected?

- Do you KNOW Jesus lived, died, and resurrected?

NOTES

1 "ApoLogika – Who Wrote Most of the New Testament?" www.apologika.blogspot.com, May 3, 2014.

2 "Jeremy Norman's - From Cave Paintings to the Internet." www.historyofinformation.com, June 11, 2012, www.historyofinformation.com/index.php?=3058.

3 "Associates for Biblical Research." www.biblearcheology.org, June 12, 2012, http://www.biblearchaeology.org/post/2007/08/Three-Woes!.aspx.

4 "Finding My Way." June 12, 2012, cwpilgrimage.wordpress.com.

5 "Israel Photos IV – Pilgrimage." dqhall59.com , June 12, 2012, http://dqhall59.com/israelphotosIV/hotsprings.htm.

6 "Religion & Spirituality." Christian, About.com, June 12, 2012, http://christianity.about.com/od/symbolspictures/ig/Israel-Tour-Pictures/06IsraelPoolSiloam800x600.htm.

7 "Wide Open Hearts." First Christian Church, heartofeugene.org, June 12, 2012, http://www.heartofeugene.org/Sermons/2009/WideOpenHearts.htm.

8 "About Kusadasi Guide, Ephesus Tour." Private, June 12, 2012, http://www.aboutkusadasi.com/ephesus-tours/ephesus-tour-halfday.html.

9 "Voyage to Rome." welcome to hosanna.com, June 12, 2012, http://www.welcometohosanna.com/PAULS_MISSIONARY_JOURNEYS/4voyage_2.html.

10 "The Confessio." Stpetersbasilica.org, June 12, 2012, http://saintpetersbasilica.org/Confessio/Confessio.htm.

11 "St Andrews Cathedral." https://en.wikipedia.org/wiki/St_Andrews_Cathedral, August 17, 2016.

12 "A Visit to the Garden Tomb." http://discoverynews.us, 2016, /DISCOVERIES/BibleLandsDisplay/Garden_Tomb/garden_tomb_part_2.html.

13 "A Visit to the Garden Tomb." http://discoverynews.us, 2016, /DISCOVERIES/BibleLandsDisplay/Garden_Tomb/garden_tomb_part_2.html.

14 "Simon Greenleaf." en.wikipedia.org. Wikipedia Foundation, Inc., July 21, 2016. en.wikipedia.org/wiki/Simon_Greenleaf.

15 "Simon Greenleaf." en.wikipedia.org. Wikipedia Foundation, Inc., July 21, 2016. en.wikipedia.org/wiki/Simon_Greenleaf.

16 "Simon Greenleaf." en.wikipedia.org. Wikipedia Foundation, Inc., July 21, 2016. en.wikipedia.org/wiki/Simon_Greenleaf.

17 "Pontius Pilate." en.wikipedia.org. Wikipedia Foundation, Inc., August 8, 2016. https://en.wikipedia.org/wiki/Pontius_Pilate.

18 "Pontius Pilate." en.wikipedia.org. Wikipedia Foundation, Inc., August 8, 2016. https://en.wikipedia.org/wiki/Pontius_Pilate.

19 "Pontius Pilate." en.wikipedia.org. Wikipedia Foundation, Inc., August 8, 2016. https://en.wikipedia.org/wiki/Pontius_Pilate.

20 "Pontius Pilate." www.bibleistrue.com. Lion Tracks Ministries, www.bibleistrue.com/qna/pqna29.htm

21 "Stolen Body Hypothesis." en.wikipedia.org. Wikipedia Foundation, Inc., July 19, 2016. en.wikipedia.org/wiki/Stolen_body_hypothesis.

22 "Evidence for the Resurrection." www.leaderu.com. Josh McDowell, 1992, www.leaderu.com/everystudent/easter/articles/josh2.html.

23 "List of Religious Populations." https://en.wikipedia.org, August 16, 2016, https://en.wikipedia.org/wiki/List_of_religious_populations.

24 List of Religious Populations, en.wikipedia.org. Wikipedia Foundation, Inc. August 16, 2016, en.wikipedia.org/wiki/List_of_religious_populations.

25 "Odds of Christ Fulfilling Prophecy." www.goodnewsdispatch.org. Good News Dispatch, 2008. www.goodnewsdispatch.org/math.html.

26 "Odds of Christ Fulfilling Prophecy." www.goodnewsdispatch.org. Good News Dispatch, 2008. www.goodnewsdispatch.org/math.html.

27 "Chapter 3 – The Christ of Prophecy." www.sciencespeaks.dstoner.net. November 2005. www.sciencespeaks.dstoner.net/Christ_of_Prophecy.html.

28 "The Star of Bethlehem." Frederick A. Larson. www.bethlehemstar.com.

Path Step 6

Would Your Life Change IF…?

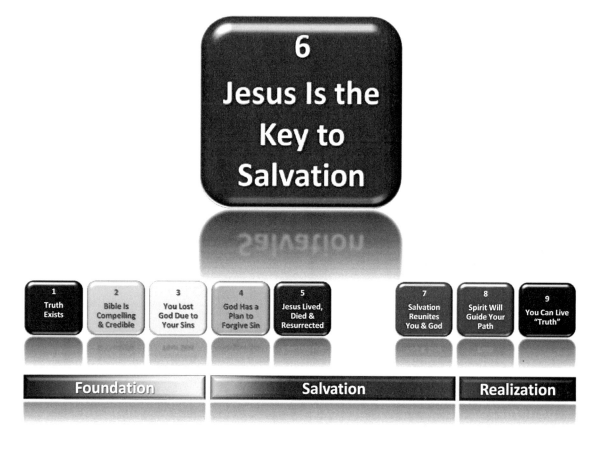

6

Jesus Is the Key to Salvation

| 1 Truth Exists | 2 Bible Is Compelling & Credible | 3 You Lost God Due to Your Sins | 4 God Has a Plan to Forgive Sin | 5 Jesus Lived, Died & Resurrected | 7 Salvation Reunites You & God | 8 Spirit Will Guide Your Path | 9 You Can Live "Truth" |

Foundation   **Salvation**   **Realization**

CONTENTS

THE VOICE

Have you ever heard a voice that changed everything?

I grew up in a medium-sized town, Pawtucket, Rhode Island, a suburb of Providence. After school and during summers, friends and I would ride our bikes all over the neighborhood. After collecting a few friends, we'd gather at someone's house to play street hockey, football, hide and seek, or the like. Even though we were hungry, nothing could take us away from game time.

That is…nothing except the "voice." Starting at about 5:30, you'd hear the first call. "David, dinner!" Next up, "Scott, time to come home!" Followed by, "Kevin!" Simple but effective. The voice would call out with a piercing shriek, beckoning my friends to their welcoming destinations, and, they'd succumb. The last few remaining would give up and leave as a quorum for the game at hand no longer existed. It was time to go home.

I remember hearing the voice call out "Donald, time to eat!" countless times. In just as many cases, I heard, "It's time to come home!" I knew when I arrived there, awaiting me was a welcome hug, warm smile and delicious home-cooked meal that would fill me to the brim. As I grew older and ceased running around the neighborhood, in favor of driving to sports practice or other "less childish" destinations, the voice stopped calling. I remember missing the voice, but being glad to move on not needing it anymore. The voice that called me to a welcome place with rest and refreshing had departed never to return. Or, so I thought.

Many who accept Jesus as their Lord and Savior and are born again, hear an inner voice. They get urges, unctions and sensations, that they say guide them through situations and inspire them. That describes me. As I grew closer to my God in my daily walk, this inner voice grew louder and more distinct.

I learned over time that the more distinct the inner voice, the more prominent and important was the message. Sometimes I'd hear no inner voice in disappointment. In those moments I'd wonder why I could not audibly hear the voice of my Lord. "Why not?" I'd ask, "My ears work?" I guessed that if I pressed in closer and it was important enough, I could and would hear the audible voice of my God. That was my prayer. My prayer was answered. Up until the time of this writing, I have heard the audible voice of God twice.

Years later, while researching Path Step 6, centered on establishing the basis for salvation through Jesus Christ, something remarkable happened. I was sitting at my computer editing a Power Point presentation for the 6th Path Step for a class I was scheduled to teach. I was reading about and researching the wine soaked sponge lifted to Jesus' lips just prior to His death upon the cross. As I was typing, I heard an audible voice. It was clear and it sounded like its origin was directly behind me. The voice was masculine, but not too deep. I turned, startled, to find no one. My pulse quickened, "What was that?"

After collecting my wits, I calmed down. I recall asking myself, "What did the voice say?" Before I could finish the thought, the voice again issued, "The 4th Cup." Startled again, but with a sliver of clarity, my fingers frantically pecked at the keyboard, typing "the 4th Cup" into the search line of Google.

After about six months of on and off research, and continued development of Path materials, 4th Cup revelations were coming fast and furious. I was amazed at the meanings and discoveries. But, a connection point was missing. The 4th Cup needed a tie between the Old and New Covenants.

Despite this, my understanding and faith in my Christ had never been stronger. That is, until I heard the voice call a second time.

There is a main street near my home in Washington State that tracks down a hill to the town center. I liked to run it to feel the burn as I ran back up the hill back toward my home. This day, and this run, was like many others. I felt the sweat pouring down my forehead as I struggled back up the hill. About half way up the hill I heard the Voice, once, clearly and distinctly. "Jeremiah, chapter 31, verses 31 through 33!"

I stopped in my tracks. "What?" That wasn't a word, it was a sentence. And, it was very specific. Though I did not time it, I am certain I have never run a faster pace in my life than that time I ran home. I ran with excitement. What could this string of verses mean? I bolted through the garage, ran to my computer, opened my digital Bible and read Jeremiah, chapter 31, verses 31 through 33.

I felt the warm hug, the warm smile, and I was filled to the brim. I wept for the next fifteen minutes and praised my God!

Would Your Life Change IF...Jesus Is the Key to Salvation?

"Why do I need a Savior?"

"Why is Jesus the Lamb of God?"

"Jesus was just a Great Prophet."

God has a plan for the forgiveness of sin. Through sacrifice, the Israelite Day of Atonement and the sin offering, God designed a way for us to overcome our sins. God's conditions and processes are specific and definitive. Archaeological evidence, prophecies, non-biblical writers, astronomical signs, cultural effects, and New Testament accounts demonstrate beyond a reasonable doubt that Jesus Christ lived, died, and resurrected.

Due to human imperfections in the Old Covenant, the Old Testament prophesies a New Covenant. There are numerous prophecies of a Messiah who would come and redeem His people from bondage. Jesus Christ is the center of this New Covenant, who would provide salvation to any who would believe in Him and follow His teachings.

Is Jesus the key to Salvation and if so, how do we gain salvation through Him?

Salvation

The SALVATION Phase explains the principles and process defined by God for removing sin from humankind. The Old Testament states that sacrifice and bloodshed are necessary practices to remove a sin. We learn that the plan for forgiveness was faulty under the Old Covenant. The writer disclosed this shortcoming in the letter to the Hebrews recalling a prophecy in Jeremiah. Because the Mosaic Law was not in the minds and hearts of the Israelites, they continued to sin. The Old Testament predicts a new and better covenant that addresses the failed nature of humanity in the first covenant and still meets the original criteria by God for the atonement of sin.

Path Step 6 is the third of four Path Steps in the SALVATION Phase. In this Path Step, the objective is to understand the purpose and role of Jesus Christ. In the final SALVATION Path Step, we will focus on the realities of salvation and what lies ahead for those who fail to meet the criteria.

PATH STEP 6: JESUS IS THE KEY TO SALVATION

The Bible verifies God's first covenant. The basis for the covenant was the Ten Commandments. These commandments defined the will of God. The covenant provided a means of forgiveness for the people when they violated His laws. God makes it clear that there is no forgiveness of sin without a sacrifice and the shedding of blood, and that sacrifice would be specific and with qualified blood.

The Old Covenant describes the forgiveness of sin, but the covenant itself proved faulty with the Israelite people. The Jews made promises that they broke; the covenant was flawed. They promised God they would keep His commandments, but did not request His assistance. They declared their acceptance and the covenant was sealed.

Did the Israelite people believe they could fully honor God's laws? The people failed to obey and fulfill the agreement because they had human frailty and the covenant was not in their hearts or minds.

God delivered the Israelites as celebrated in the original Passover. Later, He made a covenant with them at the Mount Sinai encampment. Though the covenant proved faulty, it established the basis for God's expectations of humankind and His process for forgiveness of sins. Old Testament prophets described a new and better covenant, where a Messiah would become king and offer God's redemption to the Israelites and Gentiles. The Messiah would deliver His people from bondage.

We studied the evidence that Jesus Christ lived, died, and resurrected. Is He the deliverer, the Messiah, prophesied in the Old Testament?

THERE IS A NEW COVENANT

If the Old Covenant were faulty, sealed with a broken promise by the Hebrews, the New Covenant would change everything. Paul reports that the covenant was not in the hearts of the people, and they felt there was no need for God's assistance. The New Covenant delivered greater promise and would not fail; it is a "perfect" covenant (See Path Step 8).

In Path Step 3, God gave humankind the "power of attorney" to subdue and rule the earth. God established the conditions of His relationship to earth through humankind. He did not say, "Let us…" rather, "Let them rule over all the earth." This means that humankind has authority over the earth. We have "power of attorney" on God's behalf. What humankind chooses to do with it is humankind's decision solely, as it was in the time of Adam and Eve. Man has control over the earth. If God wants to make a change or influence it, He does it through humankind.

"The highest heavens belong to the LORD, but the earth he has given to man." (Psalm 115:16)

God made the Old Covenant with His chosen people, the Israelites. When they failed to honor the covenant, God offered a better, "perfect" covenant that could not fail as the first. In order to perfect the New Covenant, God did not threaten man's authority or his freedom to choose. God came to earth to assist man. Since it was man's planet to rule, God took on the form of a man. God became flesh and came to provide a covenant that could not fail. He came to change earthly matters, but never rescinded man's free will or took back the authority given to man.

Jesus Christ is the focal point of the New Covenant. Who is Jesus Christ? Why is He the center of the covenant? How is the covenant perfect because of Jesus? The Old Testament says that God will make a covenant with people who repent. "His Spirit will be upon them, and His words will remain in them." (Isaiah 59:21) This is the foundation and improvement applied in the New Covenant.

We have a new covenant; however, as God defined at Mt. Sinai, for forgiveness we still need sacrifice and qualified blood. Where do we find the qualified blood? The Old Testament tells us that a sacrifice should be male, young, unblemished, and without defect. Did the crucifixion of Jesus Christ have anything to do with this requirement?

"When everything had been arranged like this, the priests entered regularly into the outer room to carry on their ministry. But only the high priest entered the inner room, and that only once a year, and never without blood, which he offered for himself and for the sins the people had committed in ignorance. The Holy Spirit was showing by this that the way into the Most Holy Place had not yet been disclosed as long as the first tabernacle was still standing. This is an illustration for the present time, indicating that the gifts and sacrifices being offered were not able to clear the conscience of the worshiper. They are only a matter of food and drink and various ceremonial washings—external regulations applying until the time of the new order." (Hebrews 9:6-10)

The author of Hebrews tells us that the sacrifice and offerings under the Old Covenant were ceremonial. They had little effect on the hearts and minds of the Jews. Although they continued to sin, they were still replicating ceremonial duties in an effort to cleanse their sin. The imperfection was that their offering was unable to clear their conscience. Therefore, God designed the New Covenant to overcome this flaw.

"And by that will, we have been made holy through the sacrifice of the body of Jesus Christ once for all. Day after day, every priest stands and performs his religious duties; again and again, he offers the same sacrifices, which can never take away sins. But when this priest had offered for all time one sacrifice for sins, he sat down at the right hand of God." (Hebrews 10:10-12)

Although the priests of the Old Covenant performed religious duties in accordance with the Old Testament, these duties did not remove any sin from the Israelites. Nevertheless, the sin offering and Day of Atonement pointed to the only true unblemished sacrifice to remove any sin of humankind. It would be the Messiah, Jesus Christ.

"When Christ came as high priest of the good things that are already here, he went through the greater and more perfect tabernacle that is not man-made, that is to say, not a part of this creation.

He did not enter by means of the blood of goats and calves, but he entered the Most Holy Place once for all by his own blood, having obtained eternal redemption. The blood of goats and bulls and the ashes of a heifer sprinkled on those who are ceremonially unclean sanctify them so that they are outwardly clean. How much more, then, will the blood of Christ, who through the eternal Spirit offered himself unblemished to God, cleanse our consciences from acts that lead to death, so that we may serve the living God! As chief priest, Christ went through the tabernacle in Heaven." (Hebrews 9:11-14)

The writer of Hebrews tells us that although the sin offering made the Jews outwardly clean, they remained inwardly corrupt. Jesus Christ is the offering to God that cleanses our consciences. He makes us outwardly clean and inwardly righteous. We will discuss this in detail when we review our new spirit in Christ (see Path Step 8).

"For this reason, Christ is the mediator of a new covenant, that those who are called may receive the promised eternal inheritance—now that He has died as a ransom to set them free from the sins committed under the first covenant." (Hebrews 9:15) The eternal inheritance is everlasting life in a perfected state. We will discuss this in Path Step 8.

The author of Hebrews wrote this letter to the Hebrews regarding issues of the Old Covenant and expressed how the New Covenant is flawless and complete. Jesus Christ is the New Covenant. He is the Savior.

So, what is a Savior? Christ means "Messiah". Messiah means "deliverer, anointed one." "'The Redeemer will come to Zion, to those in Jacob who repent of their sins,' declares the LORD." (Isaiah 59:20) Prophecy reveals Christ as the redeemer. A Savior is defined as "one who rescues you from harm or danger." In Path Steps 3 and 4, we discussed our sinful nature and rejection by God.

Do you need a Savior?

Do you need Jesus Christ?

THE BREAD OF LIFE

"Then the LORD said to Moses, 'I will rain down bread from Heaven for you. The people are to go out each day and gather enough for that day. In this way, I will test them and see whether they will follow my instructions.'" (Exodus 16:4)

Shortly after leaving Egypt, the Israelite community entered the Desert of Sin on the way to Mount Sinai. They were hungry and feared that they would die of starvation. To sustain His people, once a day, God rained down manna from Heaven.

"The people of Israel called the bread manna. It was white like coriander seed and tasted like wafers made with honey." (Exodus 16:31)

However, the food came with instructions that the Israelites violated. They were to take only what they needed for the day, and not gather any on the Sabbath.

God's provision was sweet and pleasing. As a sign, God provided bread from Heaven to nourish His people, and provide everything they needed. Was this a sign to the Israelites that God would provide food for them in the future?

"Jesus said to them, 'I tell you the truth, it is not Moses who has given you the bread from Heaven, but it is my Father who gives you the true bread from Heaven. For the bread of God is he who comes down from Heaven and gives life to the world.' 'Sir,' they said, 'from now on give us this bread.' Then Jesus declared, 'I am the bread of life. He who comes to me will never go hungry, and he who believes in me will never be thirsty.'" (John 6:32-35)

Jesus said He is the bread from Heaven. Without Jesus as our Savior, humankind will die as a punishment for our sins. If you accept Jesus, you will have life, you will never be hungry, and you will not thirst.

"I tell you the truth; he who believes has everlasting life. I am the bread of life. Your forefathers ate the manna in the desert, yet they died. But here is the bread that comes down from Heaven, which a man may eat and not die. I am the living bread that came down from Heaven. If anyone eats of this bread, he will live forever. This bread is my flesh, which I will give for the life of the world." (John 6:47-51)

Jesus was not referring to each of us eating His body. If you are born again in Him, he becomes a part of you. Jesus is the bread that does more than sustain—He gives everlasting life. If you "eat of this bread," you will live forever. If you are reborn in Jesus, you will not die. He is the true Passover Lamb, eaten to save and redeem. Many elements of a traditional Hebrew Passover celebration provide basis for Jesus and the New Covenant. Next, we will investigate a remarkable relationship between Jesus' Passover celebration and His purpose here on earth.

THE 4TH CUP OF THE PASSOVER FEAST

Jesus and the 4th Cup of Passover validates the nature and purpose of Jesus Christ's death and resurrection. Unfamiliar with Jewish traditions, the 4th Cup is not widely understood by Christians. Because Orthodox Jews deny the validity of the New Testament (Jesus and/or His resurrection), the Passover and Christ are not celebrated.

However, the Passover celebration illuminated prophecies of the New Covenant and Jesus' sacrifice. Great meaning and purpose are found with the fulfillment of the 4th Cup. Understanding the Jewish Passover in the time of Christ, one can see the similarity with the Last Supper of Christ and the Passover. What Jesus accomplished and why He performed it is the cornerstone and fulfillment of the New Covenant.

Reviewing the 4th Cup of Passover

To provide a rational approach for understanding, this study is divided into four definable Units:

Unit I.   Explanation—Jewish Tradition

Describes the creation of the Passover celebration and the connection to Jesus Christ.

Unit II.   Application—Relevance with Jesus

Compares the Passover celebration and the 4th Cup to Jesus Christ's last supper and crucifixion.

Unit III.   Implication—Personal meaning

Describes Jesus Christ's achievements related to the 4th Cup and their meaning to all God's people.

Unit IV.   Revelation—Jesus Revealed

Reveals Jesus Christ's character and what He did for humankind by celebrating the 4th Cup.

Path Step 6 explains Units 1, 2, and the beginning of 3. We will conclude Unit 3 in Path Step 8 and Unit 4 in Path Step 9. We will begin with the explanation of the Jewish Passover celebration and tradition.

UNIT I: EXPLANATION—JEWISH TRADITION

Exodus 12:1-13 describes the first Passover. Following verse 13 is God's directive for Passover. He issues the following command:

"This is a day you are to commemorate; for the generations to come you shall celebrate it as a festival to the LORD - a lasting ordinance." (Exodus 12:14)

God proclaimed a "day to commemorate" for generations to come. Passover would become a tradition, a lasting ordinance. God has great meaning in the Passover tradition. In Exodus 12:14 we learn that Passover is a festival, a festival to the Lord. Festival, in the (Encarta) dictionary means "a day or period of celebration, often one of religious significance." This is what God intended because he commanded, "for generations to come you shall celebrate it." Passover is a celebration. The celebration includes a feast. It is a festival to the Lord.

Why would God command the Israelites to commemorate Passover yearly? God wanted the Israelites to maintain the Passover for tradition purposes, to embrace a sensitivity or insight for a future message or event. Is Exodus 12:14 a reminder to remember and celebrate God's deliverance and His chosen people? Do the signs and clues foreshadow what is to come - a supplementary deliverance? Let us investigate.

"The LORD said to Moses and Aaron in Egypt, 'This month is to be for you the first month, the first month of your year. Tell the whole community of Israel that on the tenth day of this month each man is to take a lamb for his family, one for each household. If any household is too small for a whole lamb, they must share one with their nearest neighbor, having taken into account the number of people there are. You are to determine the amount of lamb needed in accordance with what each person will eat. The animals you choose must be year-old males without defect, and you may take them from the sheep or the goats. Take care of them until the fourteenth day of the month, when all the people of the community of Israel must slaughter them at twilight.

Then they are to take some of the blood and put it on the sides and tops of the door frames of the houses where they eat the lambs.

That same night they are to eat the meat roasted over the fire, along with bitter herbs, and bread made without yeast. Do not eat the meat raw or cooked in water, but roast it over the fire—head, legs and inner parts. Do not leave any of it till morning; if some is left till morning, you must burn it. This is how you are to eat it: with your cloak tucked into your belt, your sandals on your feet and your staff in your hand. Eat it in haste; it is the LORD's Passover. On that same night I will pass through Egypt and strike down every firstborn—both men and animals—and I will bring judgment on all the gods of Egypt. I am the LORD. The blood will be a sign for you on the houses where you are, and when I see the blood, I will pass over you. No destructive plague will touch you when I strike Egypt.'" (Exodus 12:1-13)

A family must select their lamb and prepare it before the Passover celebration in accordance with the Old Testament. In the time of Jesus, the majority of sheep that were sacrificed were owned by the Sadducees. The Sadducees were a sect of the upper echelon in the Hebrew community that fulfilled various political and religious roles, including maintaining the temple.

Jewish Historians indicate that the Sadducees brought lambs in pens to Bethlehem from the south to Jerusalem. The lambs entered the city walls through the northeast gate, called the "Sheep Gate," and were led down the main streets to the temple.[1] To comply with Exodus 12, they chose the lambs in the afternoon on the 9th day of Nisan to be with the family from the 10th day at sundown through the 14th day. Four days before Passover, high priests selected an unblemished lamb for the entire Israel nation. The selected lamb is led to Jerusalem through the Sheep Gate and then to the temple, for all to witness.

On the 14th day of Nisan (day before Passover), after the lamb was declared pure and unblemished, it was placed on the altar at 9:00 a.m. Three hours were required to prepare the slain lamb for the Passover feast. The feast began on the 15th day of Nisan. However, the Hebrew calendar indicates, a day began and ended at 6:00 p.m. The lamb was on the altar at 9:00 AM, and then sacrificed at 3:00 p.m., thus providing three hours for preparation. At 3:00 pm, the high priest would say, "I thirst" and then he would wet his lips. He then cut the lamb's throat at 3:00 pm (twilight). While performing the sacrifice, he would say in Hebrew, "Ze Nigmar!" (Meaning, "It Is Finished!").[2]

Passover Celebration

The Israelites celebrated a traditional Passover for nearly 1,350 years. The first Passover occurred prior to the time of the Exodus from Egypt. Evidence dates the Exodus from Egypt to approximately 1,270 BC but some theologians argue that it was 1,446 BC.[3] Considering the abundance of evidence, 1,270 BC is favored herein. Although the actual date is insignificant, the length and period of the Passover celebration is relevant. The Romans destroyed the temple in Jerusalem in 70 AD, the sacrificial Passover could not continue as specified in Deuteronomy, chapter 12. This calculates from 1,270 BC to 70 AD, yielding 1,339 years.

However, the Passover celebration did evolve after the destruction of the temple. It is likely that its customs transformed during the 1,350-year period. Some believe that the four cups of wine celebrating the deliverance in Egypt and God's preference came about in 63 BC. Jesus and His apostles celebrated supper with cups of wine; this confirms its practice.[4]

The Four Cups of Passover

Each of the four cups associates with a different part of the Passover celebration and represents four expressions of Gods deliverance.

"Therefore, say to the Israelites, I am the LORD. I will free you from the forced labor of the Egyptians, and I will deliver you from their slavery. I will redeem you by my outstretched arm and with mighty acts of judgment. I will take you as my people, and I will be your God." (Exodus 6:6-7)

Exodus 6 describes the basis for the four cups of wine celebrated at the Passover Feast. Below is an outline.

"Therefore say to the children of Israel 'I am the LORD;

1ST CUP: Cup of Sanctification

> I will BRING YOU OUT from under the burdens of the Egyptians,

2ND CUP: Cup of Deliverance

> I will DELIVER YOU from their bondage, and

3RD CUP: Cup of Redemption

> I will REDEEM YOU WITH AN OUTSTRETCHED ARM and with great judgments.

4TH CUP: Cup of Restoration

> I will TAKE YOU AS MY PEOPLE, and I WILL BE YOUR GOD.

Each cup has a specific meaning and ties to the Egyptian deliverance. Nevertheless, how does this fit into a Passover celebration, especially in the time of Jesus?

Summary in the time of Jesus

Today, the Passover celebration has a great deal of ceremony, which includes a specific meal. Based on the years of tradition, the Passover process has a specified order and instruction. After the destruction of the temple, the celebration changed by necessity, a lamb could no longer be sacrificed. However, the mandate to practice traditions and the ceremonial process remained. At the time of Jesus, reciting, praising God, and reclining were customary in the Passover celebration. During the Last Supper, these traditions were present as well.

The following is a summary of a Passover feast at the time of Christ. It describes only the major elements and does not account for every tradition or its details.

Passover Summary in the Time of Jesus:

1. 3:00 p.m.—Ze Nigmar!

2. 1st Cup—I Will Free You

3. 2nd Cup—I Will Deliver You

4. Breaking of the Bread

5. Passover Meal

   • Lamb

   • Unleavened Bread

   • Bitter Herbs

6. 3rd Cup—I Will Redeem You

7. Sing Hallel—Song of Praise

8. 4th Cup—I Will Take You

"Then came the day of Unleavened Bread on which the Passover lamb had to be sacrificed. Jesus sent Peter and John, saying,'Go and make preparations for us to eat the Passover. Where do you want us to prepare for it?' They asked. He replied, 'As you enter the city, a man carrying a jar of water will meet you. Follow him to the house that he enters, and say to the owner of the house, 'The Teacher asks, where is the guest room, where I may eat the Passover with my disciples?' He will show you a large upper room, all furnished. Make preparations there.' When the hour came, Jesus and his apostles reclined at the table. And he said to them, 'I have eagerly desired to eat this Passover with you before I suffer.'" (Luke 22:7-15)

Luke writes that Jesus organized the Last Supper and established it as a Passover feast. There are 14 uncanny parallels between the record of the Last Supper and a Passover celebration (see Joachim Jeremias, *The Eucharistic Words of Jesus*, 3rd ed. 1960).

We return to the question asked at the beginning of the Explanation unit. "Why would God command the Israelites to commemorate Passover yearly? Jesus Christ is the Messiah, the deliverer, and the Son of God. The New Testament describes Jesus' Last Supper, and His Passover feast in detail. Could it provide signs or clues of a supplementary deliverance?

UNIT II: APPLICATION—RELEVANCE WITH JESUS

"'What do you want me to do for you?' He asked. They replied, 'Let one of us sit at your right and the other at your left in your glory.' 'You do not know what you are asking,' Jesus said. 'Can you drink the cup I drink or be baptized with the baptism I am baptized with?'" (Mark 10:36-38)

This Scripture in Mark tells the story of James and John, the sons of Zebedee, misunderstanding the kingdom Jesus was to create. When Jesus was to assume His throne, they wished to be on His right side and left side to take up seats of power. This displayed their desire for worldly glory. Jesus would bring the Kingdom of Heaven, a spiritual kingdom.

To which cup and baptism are Jesus referring? Did Jesus receive a special cup? If so, does the cup relate to the Passover?

Exodus chapter 6 defines the purpose of each of the four cups. Beyond the drinking of wine at the Last Supper, does the Bible contain any prediction of another occasion similar to the circumstances celebrated as the 4th Cup from Exodus?

4th Cup In Prophecy

Exodus 6:6-7 is the basis for the traditional four cups consumed at a Passover feast. From those verses, this is God's blessing with the 4th Cup, "I will take you as my people, and I will be your God." (Exodus 6:6-7) It is the celebration of God's promise and preference. Where in the Bible does this notion and prophecy again occur? The Old Testament is full of prophecy of the New Covenant.

"'The days are coming,' declares the LORD, 'when I will make a new covenant with the house of Israel and with the house of Judah. It will not be like the covenant I made with their ancestors when I took them by the hand to lead them out of Egypt because they broke my covenant, though I was a husband to them,' declares the LORD. 'This is the covenant I will make with the house of Israel after that time,' declares the LORD. 'I will put my law in their minds and write it on their hearts. I will be their God, and they will be my people.'" (Jeremiah 31:31-33)

When Jeremiah declares, "I will put my law in their minds and write it on their hearts," he is referring to the New Covenant written in Jeremiah 3:31. This is God's instruction how Jesus Christ will correct the fault of the people under the Old Covenant. The Jews, under the leadership of Moses, made a covenant promising to follow God's laws. However, the covenant failed. Prophesied was Jesus Christ as the deliverer of a new and perfect covenant. With Christ, God would place His law in the minds of His people and write them on their hearts. This time, God will supply the "divine assistance" the first covenant lacked.

The New Testament validates the prophecy of the New Covenant as a testimony. In the book of Hebrews, it refers to the prophecy by Jeremiah to evangelize the Jews during His time of ministry.

"For if there had been nothing wrong with that first covenant, no place would have been sought for another. But God found fault with the people and said: 'The time is coming, declares the Lord, when I will make a new covenant with the house of Israel and with the house of Judah. It will not be like the covenant I made with their forefathers when I took them by the hand to lead them out of Egypt because they did not remain faithful to my covenant, and I turned away from them, declares the Lord. This is the covenant I will make with the house of Israel after that time, declares the Lord. I will put my laws in their minds and write them on their hearts. I will be their God, and they will be my people. No longer will a man teach his neighbor, or a man his brother, saying, 'Know the Lord,' because they will all know me, from the least of them to the greatest. For I will forgive their wickedness and will remember their sins no more.'" (Jeremiah 31:31-33) By calling this covenant new, He has made the first one obsolete; and what is obsolete and aging will soon disappear.

Jeremiah 31:33 predicts, "I will be their God, and they will be my people." The promise of the 4th Cup written in Exodus 6:7 is a declaration that ties it to the prophecy of Jesus Christ and the New Covenant.

Jesus' Passover Celebration

The objective of this text is not to describe with detail the differences and protocols of a Passover celebration. Therefore, we will use the following eight components of the Passover Feast.

1. 3:00 p.m.—Ze Nigmar! (Sacrifice of the lamb)

2. 1st Cup—I Will Free You

3. 2nd Cup—I Will Deliver You

4. Breaking of the Bread—Breaking of the Middle Matzoh

5. Passover Meal—Traditional feast with lamb as defined in Exodus 12

   - Lamb

   - Unleavened Bread

- Bitter Herbs

6. 3rd Cup - I Will Redeem You

7. Sing Hallel—Song of Praise (Singing and reciting the "Great Hallel," Psalm 113-118)

8. 4th Cup—I Will Take You

Although more traditions exist that are recorded in the Gospels, they are not essential to draw parallels to the 4th Cup and Jesus Christ.

We will apply the eight components to investigate parallels and meanings of the Last Supper. First, we must modify the Passover summary. The sacrifice of the lamb, and the declaration of "Ze Nigmar" by the chief priest occurs three hours before the Passover celebration (Passover starts on Nisan 15), in preparation of the lamb. However, the New Testament states Jesus died the day before the traditional Passover celebration (Nisan 14). Jesus intentionally celebrated the Passover feast a day early. Therefore, the sacrifice of the Passover lamb for the Israel nation did not occur before His feast, but rather, at its conclusion. Therefore, "Ze Nigmar" will be moved to the end, Item 8. As we progress, the foundation for this revision by Jesus becomes apparent.

Let us assess for parallels of Jesus' Passover feast.

1. 1st Cup—I Will Free You

2. 2nd Cup—I Will Deliver You

3. Breaking of the Bread

4. Passover Meal

- Lamb

- Unleavened Bread

- Bitter Herbs

5. 3rd Cup—I Will Redeem You

6. Sing Hallel—Song of Praise

7. 4th Cup—I Will Take You

8. 3:00 p.m.—Ze Nigmar!

The Gospels define the Last Supper as a Passover celebration. Using the Gospels, in chronological order, we will match the Passover feast with Scripture. However, the purpose of the Gospels was to describe notable events in Jesus Christ's life. They do not record every facet of the Jewish festival, nor do they record every action taken at Jesus Christ's Last Supper.

1. 1st Cup—I Will Free You

"After taking the cup, he gave thanks and said, 'Take this and divide it among you.'" (Luke 22:17) This is the first cup of wine mentioned by Luke. It is the celebration of "I will free you." Luke mentions another cup later in his Gospel.

2. 2nd Cup—I Will Deliver You

The second cup of wine celebrated at the Last Supper was for praising and worshiping God. There is no mention of the second cup in the Gospels. However, many Passover meal traditions are not mentioned, including much of the early activities of Jesus' Passover celebration. It is possible that the cup mentioned in Luke 22:17 is the second cup of the Passover feast. Later, we will learn that other Scripture anchors the third cup. We can pronounce that the cup described in Luke is either the first or second cup.

3. Breaking of the Bread

Next, the Matzo (unleavened bread) is broken. Luke records the breaking of the bread. "And he took bread, gave thanks and broke it, and gave it to them, saying, 'This is my body given for you; do this in remembrance of me.'" (Luke 22:19-20) Throughout the Old Testament, leavening represents sin. As a Passover feast is prepared, all were to avoid contact with leavening (yeast), and it could not be present during the celebration. Symbolically, the Passover experience removes sin. In the Old and New Testament, Jesus is referred to as the 'Bread of Life.' Further, Jesus was the only man without sin. The unleavened bread symbolizes Jesus' body, which was broken for us and without sin.

4. Passover Meal

Prior to destruction of the temple, a traditional Passover meal included lamb, unleavened bread, and bitter herbs. In the Gospel of Luke, Jesus sends two disciples to make preparations for the Passover.

"Jesus sent Peter and John, saying, 'Go and make preparations for us to eat the Passover.'" (Luke 22:8)

"The disciples left, went into the city and found things just as Jesus had told them. So they prepared the Passover." (Mark 14:16) Mark reports that Jesus gave instruction of what to gather for the Passover meal. What was on Jesus' grocery list—wine, a lamb, bread, bitter herbs? The Gospels provide clues, but few details.

"While they were eating, Jesus took bread, gave thanks and broke it, and gave it to his disciples, saying, 'Take and eat; this is my body.'" (Matthew 26:26) Matthew writes, "While they were eating, Jesus took bread." We can assume that they were eating food other than bread, but it is not conclusive.

"Jesus replied, 'The one who has dipped his hand into the bowl with me will betray me.'" (Matthew 26:23) Matthew refers to Judas who dipped his hand into the sop bowl with Jesus. Often, a bowl of salt water sits on the table for dipping bitter herbs during the meal.

Jesus maintained tradition, and we know that other food was there besides bread. Did the disciples sacrifice the lamb a day early in the proper method that was in accordance with Jewish tradition? We do not know enough about the meal to make it conclusive. However, Jesus "gave instructions." Would not these Jewish men, after participating in many Passover feasts, already know what to gather and how to prepare it? Did any of them violate procedure and custom for sacrificing the lamb a day early? Did the disciples take a lamb to the temple a day early to have it slain? Jesus may have had a roasted lamb at the Last Supper, but it is unlikely. In any event, Jesus makes the next statement.

"While they were eating, Jesus took bread, gave thanks and broke it, and gave it to his disciples, saying, 'Take and eat; this is my body.'" (Matthew 26:26) God redeemed His people with the first Passover lamb. Jesus was the lamb of the "New" Passover. In 1 Corinthians 5:7 it states, "Get rid of the old yeast, so that you may be a new unleavened batch—as you really are. For Christ, our Passover lamb, has been sacrificed." Jesus provided the sacrificed Passover lamb. It was His own unblemished body that would be sacrificed for humankind.

5. 3rd Cup—I Will Redeem You

"Then he took the cup, gave thanks and offered it to them, saying, 'Drink from it, all of you. This is my blood of the covenant, which is poured out for many for the forgiveness of sins.'" (Matthew 26:27-28)

"In the same way, after the supper he took the cup, saying, 'This cup is the new covenant in my blood, which is poured out for you.'" (Luke 22:20) "In the same way, after supper he took the cup, saying, 'This cup is the new covenant in my blood; do this, whenever you drink it, in remembrance of me.'" (1 Corinthians 11:25) Paul tells us that the cup Jesus shared as His blood, was shared after the meal. This necessitates it to be the third cup, based on Hebrew tradition.

From Jewish tradition, we know the cup following supper is the third cup. It is the Cup of Redemption and represents "I will redeem you" in Exodus 6. Jesus refers to this as the cup, or blood, of the New Covenant. This is the cup celebrated as the Eucharist in non-protestant churches.

Something unconventional occurs after the third cup. Jesus states, "I tell you, I will not drink of this fruit of the vine from now on until that day when I drink it anew with you in my Father's kingdom"

(Matthew 26:29).

Did Jesus not understand the Passover feast? We know that Jesus returned to Jerusalem to celebrate Passover. Luke 2:41, "Every year Jesus' parents went to Jerusalem for the Festival of the Passover." Nonetheless, Jesus states at this point in the Passover celebration that He would not drink "Fruit of the Vine." Fruit of the vine is an integral part of the Passover Feast. How could the Passover Feast end (the Last Supper) without celebrating the 4th Cup? Did Jesus not want it to end? Did He want it to end later? If so, where is the 4th Cup?

Matthew 26:29 is perhaps one of the most significant verses in the New Testament as it unites important components of the New Covenant. In Path Step 8, we delve deeper into the meaning of this verse.

6. Sing Hallel—Song of Praise

Next in the Passover celebration, participants sang the Great Hallel. This chant derives from Psalms 113 to 118.

"When they had sung a hymn, they went out to the Mount of Olives." (Matthew 26:30) After the third cup, Matthew records that Jesus and the disciples sang a hymn and then went to the Mount of Olives. Jesus and the disciples sang praise and worshiped God as specified by Passover tradition.

7. 4th Cup—I Will Take You

Next in the celebration is the drinking of the 4th Cup to conclude the celebration. Did Jesus drink the 4th cup and conclude the Passover celebration? If he did, where is the record of a 4th Cup? There is no mention of the 4th Cup at the Last Supper. We read in Mathew 26:30, "When they had sung a hymn, they went out to the Mount of Olives." It appears the Last Supper had concluded. How can this be? There is no mention of the 4th Cup. Let's continue on Jesus' perfect journey.

Garden of Gethsemane

Jesus journeys to the Garden of Gethsemane with His disciples.

"Then he said to them, 'My soul is overwhelmed with sorrow to the point of death. Stay here and keep watch with me.' Going a little farther, he fell with his face to the ground and prayed, 'My Father if it is possible, may this cup be taken away from me. Yet not as I will, but as you will.' He went away a second time and prayed, 'My Father if it is not possible for this cup to be taken away unless I drink it, may your will be done.'" (Matthew 26:38-39, 42)

To which cup is Jesus referring? Let us continue to examine Jesus' path to His crucifixion.

Jesus Arrested

Led by Judas, the betrayer of Jesus, the soldiers arrive at the garden and arrest Jesus.

"Jesus answered, 'I told you that I am he. If you are looking for me, then let these men go.' This happened so that the words he had spoken would be fulfilled: 'I have not lost one of those you gave me.' Then Simon Peter, who had a sword, drew it and struck the high priest's servant, cutting off his right ear (The servant's name was Malchus). (John 18:8-10)

"Jesus commanded Peter, 'Put your sword away! Shall I not drink the cup the Father has given me?'" (John 18:11)

Jesus refers to a cup that He must drink. However, it is not clear to which cup He refers.

Beaten and Brought to Golgotha

The Gospels record the many turns and twists that occur prior to the crucifixion. Jesus endures public disgrace, inhumane torture, and physical and mental abuse as Roman soldiers bring him to

Golgotha to be nailed to a cross.

"They brought Jesus to the place called Golgotha (which means 'The Place of the Skull'). Then they offered him wine mixed with gall, but he did not take it. And they crucified him." (Mark 15:22-24)

Some translations refer to the wine additive as myrrh, in place of gall. Historians say, sour wine and gall, or myrrh, were given to those to be crucified. This would intoxicate them, dull their senses and diminish their suffering. When combining the myrrh or gall with sour wine, it creates an anesthetic that can lessen the pain. The Roman soldiers tried to numb Jesus with this narcotic to make crucifixion easier for the Romans.

However, in accordance with Jesus' statement in Matthew 26:29, Jesus was not ready to drink wine as He promised, though it would have diminished his suffering.

Crucifixion and the 4th Cup

The culminating step of Christ's passion is the crucifixion. It is at this moment when Jesus concludes His Passover Feast and celebration by receiving the 4th Cup.

"Later, knowing that all was now completed, and so that the Scripture would be fulfilled, Jesus said, 'I thirst.'" (John 19:28)

"A jar of wine vinegar was there, so they soaked a sponge in it, put the sponge on a stalk of the hyssop plant, and lifted it to Jesus' lips. (John 19:29)

"When he had received the drink, Jesus said, 'It is finished.' With that, he bowed his head and gave up his spirit. (John 19:30)

Jesus waited before it was time to give His soul and receive the 4th and final cup of the Passover feast.

Note: The Greek word "pneuma" is translated into spirit when referring to God or the Holy Spirit. It is translated as a "living soul" for humankind. As Jesus was both the Son of God and the Son of Man, it is not clear which meaning was intended. However, as Jesus asked, "My God, my God, why have you forsaken me?" implying the divine Spirit abandoned Jesus already, it is possible that the Spirit left Him. With no Spirit remaining, only Jesus' human soul remained to be given up upon His death.

4th Cup - I Will Take You

The 4th Cup is the Cup of Restoration. In Exodus, we read, "I will take you as my people, and I will be your God." This is what the 4th Cup celebrates in the traditional Passover celebration. Later, we will study more on tradition, the fulfillment of prophecy, and the New Covenant.

8.   3:00 p.m.—Ze Nigmar!

On the 14th day of Nisan (day before Passover), after the nation's lamb was declared pure and unblemished, it was placed on the altar at 9:00 a.m. Three hours were required to prepare the slain lamb for the Passover feast. The feast began on Nisan 15. However, on the Hebrew calendar, a day began and ended at 6:00 p.m. The lamb waited on the altar at 9:00 a.m. until 3:00 p.m., thus providing the three hours for preparation. At 3:00 p.m., the high priest said, "I thirst" and then wet his lips. Then, he cut the throat of the nation's lamb at 3:00 pm (twilight). As he performed the sacrifice, he said in Hebrew, "Ze Nigmar!" In English, Ze Nigmar means, "It Is Finished."

It was the 3rd hour (9:00 AM) when they crucified him. (Mark 15:25)

From the 6th hour (noon) until the 9th hour (3:00 p.m.), darkness came over all the land. About the 9th hour, Jesus cried out in a loud voice, "My God, my God, why have you forsaken me?" (Matthew 27:45-46)

Jesus (the New Passover Lamb) is on the altar (the cross) at 9:00 a.m. and sacrificed at 3:00 p.m., just as the Nation of Israel's Passover lamb. The symbolism of the crucifixion is rich with Hebrew tradition.

Later, knowing that everything had now been finished, and so that Scripture would be fulfilled, Jesus said, "I thirst." (John 19:28)

As the Chief Priest, Jesus issues the same declaration, "I thirst!"

When he had received the drink, Jesus said, Teleo (in Greek means "It is finished"). With that, he bowed his head and gave up his spirit. (John 19:30)

As the Chief Priest, Jesus declared Ze Nigmar (in Hebrew "It is finished") at the death of the lamb.

Jesus is both chief priest and the Passover lamb of the New Covenant, the "Second" Passover. Many signs show that Jesus Christ was the chief priest presiding over His own sacrifice.

Passover—Old and New

If the New Covenant represents a "Second" Passover, how do the expressions from Exodus 6 apply under the Old and New Covenants.

"Therefore, say to the Israelites: I am the LORD. I will free you from the forced labor of the Egyptians, and I will deliver you from their slavery. I will redeem you by my outstretched arm and with mighty acts of judgment. I will take you as my people, and I will be your God." (Exodus 6:6-7) These two verses center on God's redemption and deliverance of His chosen people. It is the foundation of the Old Covenant.

These verses prophesied the first Passover.

> 1st Passover—In 1,280 BC, God redeemed and delivered His people from slavery and bondage.

Under the New Covenant, God redeemed and delivered His people.

> 2nd Passover— In 33 AD, God (Jesus) redeemed and delivered His people from slavery of sin.

Did God command the Israelites to commemorate the Passover yearly as a reminder of an impending act of redemption and deliverance? Did He command a tradition for a promise and future deliverance?

UNIT III: IMPLICATION—PERSONAL MEANING

Jesus died "as a perfect sacrifice" to save humankind from sin. Jesus' last action before He gave up His spirit was to conclude the Passover feast. This indicates His Passover ceremony to be significant.

Mark Chapter 10 was used to introduce the II—APPLICATION Unit. In verse 35, James and John, the sons of Zebedee ask Jesus if they may sit on Jesus' right and left hand side. They wished to sit in the seats of honor and authority as Jesus assumed His throne as the King of the Jews.

"'What do you want me to do for you?' He asked. They replied, 'Let one of us sit at your right and the other at your left in your glory.' 'You don't know what you are asking,' Jesus said. 'Can you drink the cup I drink or be baptized with the baptism I am baptized with?' 'We can,' they answered. Jesus said to them, 'You will drink the cup I drink and be baptized with the baptism I am baptized with, but to sit at my right or left is not for me to grant. These places belong to those for whom they have been prepared.'" (Mark 10:36-40)

Jesus replies that it is not for Him to decide who sits at His right or left, and deflects the conversation by countering that they do not understand the nature of His reign as King. In order to qualify to sit on His right or left, he specifies certain criteria saying, "drinking the cup He drinks or being baptized with the baptism he is baptized with." The brothers respond by stating, "We can." Then, Jesus declares that they WILL drink the same cup as He, and be baptized as he is baptized.

Which cup and baptism can we share with Jesus? (We will study the baptism in Path Step 8)

4th Cup and Cup of God's Wrath

Which cup can we share with Jesus?

"This is what the LORD, the God of Israel, said to me: 'Take from my hand this cup filled with the wine of my wrath and make all the nations to whom I send you drink it.'" (Jeremiah 25:15) The Old Testament defines a "cup filled with the wine of God's wrath." God is issuing a judgment against nations by commanding they "take from His hand" that cup. Can we share this cup with Jesus?

"God remembered Babylon the Great and gave her the cup filled with the wine of the fury of his wrath." (Revelation 16:19) Revelation contains elements of history from the beginning through the time of Jesus Christ and thereafter. However, considerable portions of prophecies in Revelation are fulfilled before modern time. God handed the cup of His wrath to a nation as punishment, and it perishes. Can we share this cup with Jesus?

"A third angel followed them and said in a loud voice: 'If anyone worships the beast and his image and receives his mark on the forehead or on the hand, he, too, will drink of the wine of God's fury, which has been poured full strength into the cup of his wrath. He will be tormented with burning sulfur in the presence of the holy angels and of the Lamb.'" (Revelation 14:9-10)

With great symbolism, this passage refers to Hell and the fiery pit, "In the presence of the holy angels and of the Lamb." Those experiencing this fate "drink of the wine of God's fury, which has been poured full strength into the cup of his wrath." Drinking the Cup of God's Wrath is death, the punishment for sin as noted in Romans 6:23.

Nevertheless, Jesus drank the 4th Cup on the cross. The 4th Cup is the Cup of Restoration, the cup Jesus referred to in the Garden of Gethsemane and received on the cross. However, the Cup of Restoration is bound to the Cup of God's Wrath, God's punishment, and death.

"For the wages of sin is death, but the gift of God is eternal life in Christ Jesus our Lord." (Romans 6:23) When someone sins, a penalty is paid. The penalty (wage) of sin is death. Under the Old Covenant, the sacrifice of an unblemished animal paid the penalty for a man's sin. We will all die at some point, whether we have forgiveness or not. The death that results from sin is the loss of eternal life with God (see Path Step 7).

Jesus restores us as in the Cup of Restoration, when He takes the Cup of God's Wrath from our hands. He takes our penalty, our death, and makes us righteous in God's eyes. As we become righteous in God's eyes, we are restored (reconciled) to His favor.

The Cup of Restoration celebrates God's deliverance as written in Exodus. "I will be your God, and I will take you as my people." How does the 4th Cup and the crucifixion of Jesus fulfill this statement of restoration? With a Savior!

Savior Defined

What is the definition of "savior?" One that saves from danger or destruction. Jesus is the Savior because He takes the penalty of death for His people. He pays the price for sin. With Jesus' sacrifice, His followers are reconciled in God's eyes.

"If you declare with your mouth, 'Jesus is Lord,' and believe in your heart that God raised him from the dead, you will be saved." (Romans 10:9) We must accept Jesus as Lord in order to receive salvation.

"This is good and pleases God our Savior." (1Timothy 2:3) God is our Savior. We call on the name of Jesus to be made whole and righteous (holy and acceptable) in the eyes of God. God saves us.

"Jesus answered, 'I am the way and the truth and the life. No one comes to the Father except through me.'" (John 14:6) We are not worthy of God unless Jesus makes atonement for our sinful fallen state. Jesus is the only unblemished sacrifice acceptable to God to atone for our sins. Without Him, we have no access to God's grace and redemption.

We need a savior. We become God's people when we accept Jesus as Savior. "I will be your God, and I will take you as my people." As a savior, Jesus accepts all of our sins, sheds His blood and dies with our sin to remove it forever. This is how Jesus fulfills the final statement in Jeremiah's prophecy of the 4th Cup.

4th Cup: Cup of Restoration—I will be your God and I will take you as my people

When we ask Jesus to be our Savior, He becomes our Lord, King, and Messiah. He celebrates the Cup of Restoration. To fulfill His role and discharge His duty as our Savior, Jesus takes from us and drinks for us the Cup of God's Wrath.

Let us rephrase and "personalize" this transaction to learn about His covenant.

- I accepted Jesus as my Savior and took Him as my God. He celebrated and received the Cup of Restoration to restore me to my Creator.

- To be my Savior, Jesus accepted from my hand the Cup of Wrath that God placed in my hands as a sinner. Jesus took it from me and drank it as my substitute. He drank the Cup of Wrath for me! By paying the penalty for my sin, Jesus justified me, paid my penalty and made me acceptable to God. He made me righteous in the eyes of God.

- On the cross, Jesus Christ received the 4th Cup for me. They gave Jesus a sponge soaked in sour wine on the stalk of a hyssop plant, which signifies the Cup of Restoration and the Cup of God's Wrath!

- He received the 4th Cup for me and ANYONE who will call Him SAVIOR!

Never to Drink Again

"This is what your Sovereign LORD says, your God, who defends his people: 'See, I have taken out of your hand the cup that made you stagger; from that cup, the goblet of my wrath, you will never drink again.'" (Isaiah 51:22-23) At that moment, for all time! Isaiah describes a profound promise from God. Once you have accepted Christ from your heart, the Cup of God's wrath is taken from your hands. You are made righteous in the sight of God. With your new spirit in Christ, (see Path Step 8) God accepts you. You will not worry about having to drink of God's wrath ever again because you are righteous forever!

"He went away a second time and prayed, 'My Father, if it is not possible for this cup to be taken away unless I drink it, may your will be done.'" (Matthew 26:42) Jesus acknowledged in the Garden of Gethsemane that the cup would not be taken away (as defined above in the prophecy of Isaiah) unless He drank it. This is a remarkable acknowledgment that Jesus took the Cup of God's Wrath for anyone who would call on Him to be their Savior.

We will continue with the 4th Cup study in Path Step 8.

SIN OFFERING

On Mount Sinai, Moses received specific instruction of the behavior God would accept from His chosen people. In the covenant, ratified by the Israelites, God designed a process so that each Israelite family could atone for their sins. The purpose of the Day of Atonement sacrifice was to make restitution for those sins committed by omission for the entire nation of Israel. In addition, we discovered God's process for making restitution for sins of commission. The name of this process is the sin offering.

Sin Offering Review

The necessary steps for the sin offering

1. Select a lamb from the herd.

   - Male

   - Under 1 year old

   - Unblemished and without defect

2.   Take the lamb into the home to clean and feed it in preparation. It represents your heart and the heart of your family. It is your family's personal lamb. The lamb represents the family's heart. Likely, the family prepared and washed it much like a pet before taking it to the tent. They took special care of it because it was the best of the herd. It is likely that they also gave it a name. For this review, we will give the lamb a Hebrew name, Yehoshua.

3.   Bring Yehoshua to the priests at the Tent of Meeting.

4.   Tell the priest the family name you represent.

5.   Answer the question, "Is this your personal lamb?" (To take a lamb from another family in substitution was forbidden).

6.   The priest inspects Yehoshua for defects (e.g. broken bones, disease, mange, scars, etc.).

7.   After the priest approves the lamb, lay your hands on Yehoshua's head.

8.   Confess (transfer) onto him your family's sin.

9.   Sacrifice Yehoshua by slitting its throat in front of the Tent of Meeting.

10. Priest collects blood in a bowl and sprinkles Yehoshua's blood on the brazen altar and entrance to the Tent of Meeting.

Is Jesus a Savior?

The definition of a savior is one that saves you from danger or destruction. Do you need a savior?

God intended to have a relationship with humankind. Through His New Covenant, He provided a means to forgive sin and allow humankind to be reconciled with Him.

Jesus is the key to the New Covenant, through the Passover. Does this make Jesus Christ your savior? To redeem us from sin, there must be a sacrifice and blood. Our substitution must be unblemished, without sin, and must die with our sins. This sin offering is our Savior; it saves us from danger and destruction.

Was Jesus a sin offering?

- "For what the law was powerless to do because it was weakened by the sinful nature, God did by sending his own Son in the likeness of sinful humanity to be a sin offering. And so he condemned sin in human flesh." (Romans 8:3)

- "Yet it was the LORD's will to crush him and cause him to suffer, and though the LORD makes his life a guilt offering, he will see his offspring and prolong his days, and the will of the LORD will prosper in his hand." (Isaiah 53:10)

- "And live a life of love, just as Christ loved us and gave himself up for us as a fragrant offering and sacrifice to God." (Ephesians 5:2)

- "But with the precious blood of Christ, a lamb without blemish or defect." (1 Peter 1:19)

The Scripture states that Jesus was a sin (guilt) offering. He gave himself as an offering, a sacrifice. He was a lamb without blemish or defect.

"Now it was the day of Preparation, and the next day was to be a special Sabbath. Because the Jews did not want the bodies left on the crosses during the Sabbath, they asked Pilate to have the legs broken and the bodies taken down. The soldiers therefore came and broke the legs of the first man who had been crucified with Jesus, and then those of the other. But when they came to Jesus and found that he was already dead, they did not break his legs. Instead, one of the soldiers pierced Jesus' side with a spear, bringing a sudden flow of blood and water." (John 19:31-34) At the crucifixion, Jesus' blood spills, like a sin offering. Jesus Christ is a sin offering!

In Path Step 4, we learned the specifics of a sacrifice. It must be male, under one year old, and without blemish or weakness. Romans 6:23 states, "for the wages of sin is death." To remove sin, there must be a sacrifice and a death. Sin transfers into that sacrifice. It must die with blood shed for atonement of the sin. Because of our imperfections (sin), a sacrifice only removes its inherent sin, and not the sin transferred to it. An unblemished (sin-free) sacrifice can substitute for another's sin. A sin-free (unblemished) sacrifice can accept the sin of another; the creature's death will remove it. The unblemished lamb is the foundation of the sin offering. We used an analogy of a sponge and water to illustrate the blemished and unblemished lamb, and each's ability to soak up water (appropriate the sin of another). Jesus was born without sin. He never sinned, not on earth nor in Heaven. He is the only unblemished lamb.

Using the sponge analogy from Path Step 4, because He was a "sponge with no water," or a lamb with no sin, He was able to absorb the sin of all humankind.

Jesus Christ is the only man to walk the earth without committing a sin. He came to earth as a perfect sacrifice for the forgiveness of sin. As a new sacrificial offering, He became our Savior. He provides us an eternal spirit as promised in the New Covenant. "I will put my law in their minds and write it on their hearts. I will be their God, and they will be my people." (Jeremiah 31:33) An animal from the herd was incapable of this task, it was not suitable. Jesus Christ is and was the perfect sin offering.

Jesus Is the Lamb

If Jesus Christ is our Savior and sin offering, we must walk with Jesus through the sin offering process as written in the Old Testament. The New Testament does not define a new sin offering. Though Jesus Christ was a man and not an animal from the herd, the principles of the Old Testament still apply to the New Testament sin offering. The Old Testament sin offering was a "type" to the New Testament sin offering "anti-type." We will now walk through the sin offering process with our Savior as our lamb.

1. Select a lamb from the herd.

   - Male

   - Young

   - Unblemished, and without defect or sin

   We must select an unblemished savior, who is without sin, and perfect in every way.

2. Take the lamb into the home to clean and feed it in preparation. It represents your heart and the heart of your family. It is your family's personal lamb. The lamb represents the family's heart. Likely, the family prepared and washed it much like a pet before taking it to the tent. They took special care of it because it was the best of the herd. It is likely that they also gave it a name. For this review, we will give the lamb a Hebrew name, Yehoshua.

   In Hebrew, Yehoshua means Jesus. Before we become a Christian, we begin a study of Jesus Christ. Over time, we gain knowledge, understanding, and affiliation. We learn that He lived a sinless life, and that He did it because He loved us so much. Jesus wants you to ask Him to be your Savior. He viewed it as joy to be a Savior for you. Is He your personal lamb?

3. Bring Yehoshua to the priests at the Tent of Meeting.

   Jesus needs to be a lamb approved by a chief priest. He is a Chief Priest approving himself.

4. Tell the priest the family name you represent.

   Under the Old Covenant, a lamb was slain for the family's sin. Under the New Covenant, the sin offering is individual based.

5. Answer the question, "Is this your personal lamb?" (To take a lamb from another family in substitution was forbidden.)

   Is Jesus our personal Savior? Is He yours? Have you confessed Jesus to be your Savior, to forgive you of your sin?

6. The priest inspects Yehoshua for defects (e.g. broken bones, disease, mange, scars, etc.).

   Let the Priest (God) inspect the lamb for defects. "And the Holy Spirit descended on him in bodily form like a dove. And a voice came from Heaven: 'You are my Son, whom I love; with you I am well pleased.'" (Luke 3:22) Jesus never committed a sin. Though Jesus may be a chief priest, there is no question that God approved Him as such.

7. After the priest approves the lamb, lay your hands on Yehoshua's head.

   This is a personal moment where the sinner and the sacrifice connect. The moment that you realize and acknowledge that Jesus Christ is the necessary connection to your God, your fleshly heart softens and you open your heart to Him. You become bonded to Jesus.

8. Confess (transfer) onto Him your family's sin.

   Confess your sins and your sinning nature to Jesus, your Savior. Transfer to Jesus every sin you have ever committed and ever will commit while on earth.

9. Sacrifice Yehoshua by slitting its throat in front of the Tent of Meeting.

   Understanding in our request that Jesus be our Savior is our request for Him to die for our transgressions. Jesus was not killed. He gave His human life on the cross (see Path Step 9). Jesus responds to all who ask Him to be their Savior. Even if you were the only person to ask Jesus to be your Savior, He would have given His life for you.

10. Priest collects blood in a bowl and sprinkles Yehoshua's blood on the brazen altar and entrance to the Tent of Meeting, as for the Day of Atonement sacrifice. The blood of the lamb is placed on the Mercy Seat of the Ark of the Covenant.

    Jesus delivered His perfect blood shed to the true tabernacle in Heaven. His blood was placed on the mercy seat, atop the Ark in Heaven.

"Who his own self bare our sins in his own body on the tree that we, being dead to sins, should live unto righteousness: by whose stripes you were healed." (1 Peter 2:24)

"For you know that it was not with perishable things such as silver or gold that you were redeemed from the empty way of life handed down to you from your forefathers, but with the precious blood of Christ, a lamb without blemish or defect. He was chosen before the creation of the world but was revealed in these last times for your sake." (1 Peter 1:18-20)

Jesus Christ, the Lamb of God, gave his life and His blood to redeem and make righteous, those who would call Him, Savior.

We will explore the sin offering and the crucifixion in more detail in Path Step 9.

THE TEMPLE AND THE OLD COVENANT

While Jesus was giving up His spirit on the cross at 3:00 p.m. on Nisan 14 (April 3, 33 AD), at the same time the temple priests in Jerusalem were in the holy place sacrificing the young, unblemished Passover lamb, and spilling its blood in the Most Holy Place.

Jesus cries, "It is finished!" (Matthew 27:51) at that moment the curtain of the temple was torn in two from top to bottom. The earth shook, and the rocks split.

"The law is only a shadow of the good things that are coming—not the realities themselves. For this reason, it can never, by the same sacrifices repeated endlessly year after year, make perfect those who draw near to worship. If it could, would they not have stopped being offered? For the worshipers would have been cleansed once for all, and would no longer have felt guilty for their sins. But those sacrifices are an annual reminder of sins because it is impossible for the blood of bulls and goats to take away sins.

Therefore, when Christ came into the world, he said, 'Sacrifice and offering you did not desire, but a body you prepared for me; with burnt offerings and sin offerings you were not pleased.' Then I said, 'Here I am—it is written about me in the scroll— I have come to do your will, O God.' First He said, 'sacrifices and offerings, burnt offerings and sin offerings you did not desire, nor were you pleased with them' (although the law required them to be made).

Then He said, 'Here I am, I have come to do your will.' He sets aside the first to establish the second. And by that will, we have been made holy through the sacrifice of the body of Jesus Christ once for all. Day after day, every priest stands and performs his religious duties; again and again, he offers the same sacrifices, which can never take away sins. But when this priest had offered for all time one sacrifice for sins, he sat down at the right hand of God. Since that time, he waits for his enemies to be made his footstool because by one sacrifice he has made perfect forever those who are being made holy. The Holy Spirit also testifies to us about this. First, he says, 'This is the covenant I will make with them after that time, says the Lord. I will put my laws in their hearts, and I will write them on their minds.' Then he adds, 'Their sins and lawless acts I will remember no more.' And where these have been forgiven, there is no longer any sacrifice for sin." (Hebrews 10:1-18)

The Old Covenant was not bound to the people's hearts. However, after Jesus' crucifixion, God no longer resided in the Most Holy Place as the Shekinah Glory. Rather, He dwells in the hearts and minds of those who He has made perfect with the righteousness purchased by the sacrifice of Jesus Christ. From Christ's perfect and complete sacrifice, there is no longer any sacrifice for sin. The Old Covenant became obsolete, all sacrifices ended. This is fulfillment of the New Covenant. Now, God resides in the hearts of those who come to Him through Jesus Christ (see Path Step 8).

THE BIBLE AND PURPOSE

The Bible contains two main collections, the Old Testament and New Testament (See Path Step 2). The Bible has 66 separate books, and more than 40 different authors over a 1,600-year span. Original manuscripts from these authors are in Hebrew, Aramaic and Greek, in the Middle East, Asia, Africa, and Europe.

The idea that an organization of conspirators devised a narrative that was so substantial, meaningful, and perfect is a remote impossibility.

JESUS CHRIST

The Scripture has many terms to describe Jesus Christ.

- Son of God

- Son of Man

- The Bread of Life

- The Passover Lamb

- Lamb of God

- Messiah

- Redeemer

- Savior

If Jesus is the Savior, is He your Savior? What must you do to have a savior? (See Path Step 7)

SUMMARY

Jesus Christ fulfilled prophecies of Jeremiah and received the 4th Cup of the Passover feast before He died on the cross and celebrated all of those who would follow Him. For anyone who believes in Him and calls Him Savior, Jesus takes from his or her hand and drinks the Cup of God's Wrath. At the same time, He celebrated the Cup of Restoration for each of His followers and restored them to their God.

Jesus sacrificed Himself, as the Lamb of God and perfect sin offering, and then died with the sins of those who confessed Him as their Savior. His sacrifice is complete and puts an end to sacrifice forever. Through their faith in Him, followers of Jesus Christ become righteous and gain salvation.

As we revealed earlier, Scriptures tell us the purpose God has for humankind, or at minimum, the critical element of humankind's destiny.

"For those God foreknew he also predestined to be conformed to the likeness of his Son, that he might be the firstborn among many brothers." (Romans 8:29)

God predetermined that those who would spend an eternity with Him in a loving relationship be conformed to the image of Jesus. Jesus is the key to salvation. Accepting Him as a sufficient sacrifice for your sin is a foundational step for humankind.

The final Path Step in the SALVATION section explores the meaning and implications of salvation.

As with each Step on A Rational Path to Christ, this Path Step ends with the same question from when it began. Would your life change IF…Jesus is the key to salvation? Yes or no? If yes:

- Do you REJECT Jesus is the key to salvation?

- Do you THINK Jesus is the key to salvation?

- Do you BELIEVE Jesus is the key to salvation?

- Do you KNOW Jesus is the key to salvation?

NOTES

1 "Fishing the Abyss - Holy Week I: Lamb Selection Day." www.fishingtheabyss.com.
www.fishingtheabyss.com/archives/137

2 "Feasts of the Lord - Part 1:The Feast of Passover." www.bereanbiblechurch.com, David B. Curtis. April 28, 2013.
http://www.bereanbiblechurch.org/transcripts/leviticus/lev-23_04-05_feast-passover.htm.

3 "The Date of the Exodus: 1446 BC." www.bible.ca. http://www.bible.ca/archeology/
bible-archeology-exodus-date-1440bc.htm

4 Passover In the Time of Jesus, www.bible.org, May 28, 2004, https://bible.org/article/passover-time-jesus.

Path Step 7

Would Your Life Change IF…?

CONTENTS

WHERE ARE YOU GOING?

"Heaven is under our feet as well as over our heads." - Henry David Thoreau, *Walden*

"The critical question for our generation—and for every generation—is this: If you could have Heaven, with no sickness, and with all the friends you ever had on earth, and all the food you ever liked, and all the leisure activities you ever enjoyed, and all the natural beauties you ever saw, all the physical pleasures you ever tasted, and no human conflict or any natural disasters, could you be satisfied with Heaven, if Christ were not there? " - John Piper, *God Is the Gospel: Meditations on God's Love as the Gift of Himself*

"I am still in the land of the dying; I shall be in the land of the living soon." (His last words) - John Newton

"Aim at Heaven and you will get earth thrown in. Aim at earth and you get neither." - C.S. Lewis

"To enter Heaven is to become more human than you ever succeeded in being on earth; to enter Hell, is to be banished from humanity." - C.S. Lewis, *The Problem of Pain*

"If there were no Hell, the loss of Heaven would be Hell." - C.H. Spurgeon

"Go to Hell!" - Anonymous (you and me)

"Go to Hell!" "Go to Hell?" **If only you and I knew.**

Do you know what the Bible says about Heaven and Hell? You might be surprised! Including those who identify as Christians, many have never read what is written in the Bible.

Would Your Life Change IF…Salvation Reunites You and God.

"There is no such thing as Heaven or Hell."

"Those who don't believe in Christ will spend an eternity in Hell."

"I go to church, I'm a Christian!"

In the last three Path Steps, we established a path to salvation. Salvation is the objective of Christianity. However, what is salvation? What does it mean to be saved? In Path Step 7, we will study Scripture to find what the Bible says about Heaven, Hell and the path leading to each.

Salvation

In the FOUNDATION Phase, we characterized truth and life's purpose based on truth. The examination showed evidence supporting biblical accuracy and its credibility. Evidence founded at Mount Sinai and the Israelite encampment reviews God's purpose for humankind. We learned that Jesus Christ in the New Testament amplified, through His teachings, the Ten Commandments given to Moses. We also learned that because of sin, a gap exists between humankind and God the Creator. In our fallen state, we do not experience the fullness of God, God's endowment for humankind.

In Path Step 4, we learned the process God requires for the forgiveness of sin. In the 5th and 6th Path Steps, we examined evidence that verifies the life, death, and resurrection of Jesus Christ, and how He fulfills the New Covenant between God and humankind. In Path Step 7, we will examine Bible teachings defining what it means to be saved, what happens to those who are not saved, and how to obtain salvation through Jesus Christ.

PATH STEP 7: SALVATION REUNITES YOU AND GOD

EARNING SALVATION

God created man and desires his fellowship. We learned that humankind sinned and lost the fullness of God for eternity. Salvation means cleansing and removing sin so that we are acceptable to God. Those who receive salvation are reconciled with God. Sozo is the Greek word of the New Testament translated as salvation. Sozo is the same Greek word translated as saved, healed, and made whole. Its direct meaning is "to be made whole." Salvation through Jesus Christ and His sacrifice makes us worthy of God's original purpose and state for humankind.[1] Thus, we obtain acceptance into Heaven and into God's presence. Salvation is fulfilling God's plan and purpose for humankind for eternal life, love, and worship. How does this operate if we are fallen sinners?

We are justified by the sacrifice of Jesus Christ if He is our Savior.

"Yet we know that a person is justified, not by the works of the law but through faith in Jesus Christ. And we have come to believe in Christ Jesus so that we might be justified by faith in Christ, and not by doing the works of the law because no one will be justified by the works of the law." (Galatians 2:16)

We are acceptable to God if we have faith in Jesus Christ as our Savior. Then, He removes our sin, justifying us before God.

An analogy: Let us say you must go to court because of an unpaid parking ticket. The judge declares that you are guilty so you must pay the penalty. Just as you were to pay the fine, someone steps up to the judge and says, "Release the party now; I will pay the fine in full."

Each of us is a sinner. We have broken God's laws, so we are not worthy of Him. We are imperfect. When we accept Jesus Christ as our Savior, He justifies us before God by accepting punishment for our sins. Jesus paid the fine and He did so at the crucifixion!

"For the wages of sin is death, but the gift of God is eternal life in Christ Jesus our Lord." (Roman 6:23)

We gain salvation by His justification. God accepts Jesus' death as our substitute. We are still sinners, but God accepts us because Jesus paid the penalty for our sins, which is death. Jesus Christ has paid the penalty for our misdeeds. He paid it in full; therefore, our sin is no longer.

Many take comfort in the belief that they have done more good things in life than bad:

"I am a good person."

"I used to be bad, but now I am good."

"I've done more good in my life than bad, so I'm going to Heaven."

In the Old and New Testament, God declares He will not accept sin. We cannot appreciate the purity, perfection, and holiness of God. We judge our situations with only our fallen, earthly perspective. As defined in the Bible, the goodness and purity of God is beyond our comprehension. From our limited perspective, we might judge ourselves good and worthy of our God. However, we have violated God's laws. Our good intentions and morals do not erase our sins, not even one of them. God is not about karma. He is about living and being holy (pure and without sin), and righteous (free from guilt and sin). This is His expectation and it leads to happiness and joy. Evil is the absence of good. When we are not righteous, guilty of even only one sin, evil accrues to our ledger and we are sinners.

SALVATION THROUGH FAITH, NOT WORKS!

The Bible defines "works" as deeds that are acceptable to God. Many refer to this as legalism. The New Testament teaches that we gain salvation and fellowship with God, through our faith in Him and in His Son, Jesus Christ. However, many believe that if they are good, they will gain this salvation. Let us review a few verses from the New Testament.

- "For we hold that a person is justified by faith apart from works prescribed by the law." (Romans 3:28)

- "For it is by grace you have been saved, through faith—and this, not from yourselves, it is the gift of God—not by works so that no one can boast." (Ephesians 2:8-9)

- "For God so loved the world that he gave his one and only Son that whoever believes in him shall not perish but have eternal life." (John 3:16)

From Romans 3:28, when we accept Jesus as our Savior, He justifies us, assumes the penalty for our sin (death) and reconciles us to God.

It is by God's grace (unmerited divine favor) that we are saved. All of us are sinners; we are not acceptable to God. Nevertheless, He loves us so much that He displayed immense grace by providing His Son to take the death penalty for our sins. If we believe that Jesus died for our sins and we accept Him as our Savior, God saves us. Through Jesus Christ, we are saved. We cannot save ourselves. Ephesians states that salvation is a gift from God. We cannot earn salvation. Pride and boasting are major obstacles for humankind. If we cannot work our way to salvation, then we cannot boast nor lift ourselves above another.

John 3:16 states that if you believe (have faith) in Jesus Christ you will not perish but receive eternal life. It does not say because you have faith in Christ and do good works, you will be eternally saved.

On our own, we are incapable of being pure as Jesus. Good works, good deeds, and acts of kindness cannot save us. **NO ONE CAN EARN HIS OR HER SALVATION.** We cannot earn our way into God's presence.

Ask the following question to many of those who do not understand the principles of Christianity and do not know Jesus Christ. "Are you going to Heaven?" Commonly, an immediate response is, "Yes!" When asked why they were going, the typical response was, "I am generally a good person. I do more good things than I do bad things." This may be so. But, it is not acceptable to God. It does not admit them into Heaven; no amount of good works can save them. It is only the grace of God and their faith in Jesus Christ as Savior that grants salvation.

Nevertheless, good works are important. It comes from our faith in Christ and inner transformation. Jesus asked us to believe in Him and follow His teachings.

"In the same way, faith by itself, if it is not accompanied by action (works), is dead." (James 2:17)

We are saved by faith. Through faith in Christ, our good works are evident. James teaches us that faith in Jesus, without good works, is not a true faith. Good works earns us nothing. However, it is the evidence of our saving faith.

WHEN WE DIE

Before discussing our final destination, we must understand what happens when we die.

"Where do we go when we die?"

"Exactly what happens to us when we die?"

"Is there an afterlife?"

"Do we cease to exist as many atheists proclaim?"

Throughout history, the afterlife has been a mystery. Almost all religions believe in an afterlife. It is either a life in a spiritual realm, in an imprecise location, or eternal life in Heaven. The immortality of the soul is hopeful by all. This has been a subject of debate within the church for centuries. Does the Bible teach that we exist after death, or do we cease to exist?

"And the LORD God said, 'The man has now become like one of us, knowing good and evil. He must not be allowed to reach out his hand and take also from the Tree of Life and eat, and live forever.' So the LORD God banished him from the Garden of Eden to work the ground from which he had been taken." (Genesis 3:22-23)

After humankind sinned, God banished man from paradise. Genesis states that humankind was separated from the Tree of Life. In humankind's fallen state, we were NOT permitted to live forever. "He must not be allowed to live forever." God has a profound love for His created humankind. God does not wish for humankind to live forever in a corrupted state. Man was banished from the Garden so that He could not eat from the Tree of Life and live forever.

Hence, the soul is not immortal. However, a born again spirit is eternal! More to come!

While Hell is not a destination to be favored, two opposing views have their origin in biblical Scripture. One theology cites verses that contend those destined for Hell live in a far less than ideal existence for an eternity (burn in Hell forever). For the contrary theology, other verses, as well as some of the same, make a strong case that the soul of all those who go to Hell perish (cease to exist) for eternity and, hence, suffer eternal punishment.

This topic and its answers are not critical to an understanding of salvation. Again, Hell is not a destination to be desired. This writing favors that the souls destined for Hell perish, completely, in the lake of fire on earth. Investigate the theology and Scriptures supporting both cases. You will find it to be a rewarding pursuit.

Bodies After Death

"Then death and Hades were thrown into the lake of fire. The lake of fire is the second death. All whose names were not found written in the book of life were thrown into the lake of fire." (Revelation 20:14-15)

The Bible describes Hell as "fiery." This passage reinforces the destruction of the soul for eternity. The first death is the death of the body on earth. The soul rises, from the dead, to be judged. Sinners will be cast into the fiery lake and undergo the second death, which is the destruction of the soul. The body dies the first death and rests on earth until judgment.

- "Then David rested with his ancestors and was buried in the City of David." (1 Kings 2:10)

- "Now when David had served God's purpose in his own generation, he fell asleep; he was buried with his ancestors and his body decayed." (Act 13:36)

- "Brothers, I can tell you confidently that the patriarch David died and was buried, and his tomb is here to this day." (Act 2:29)

The Bible states that David, the great patriarch, died and rests in his grave.

- "When your days are over, and you rest with your ancestors, I will raise up your offspring to succeed you, who will come from your own body, and I will establish his kingdom." (2 Samuel 7:12)

- "Therefore, we are always confident and know that as long as we are at home in the body we are away from the Lord." (2 Corinthians 5:6)

We come to two assertions:

1. If we are in the body, we are away from the Lord.

2. Upon death, we are with the Lord; we no longer are in our body, but wait for a glorified body.

"Do not be amazed at this, for a time is coming when all who are in their graves will hear his voice and come out—those who have done what is good will rise to live, and those who have done what is evil will rise to be condemned." (John 5:28-29)

Upon death, the saved and unsaved both lie in their graves. Those that are living will be raised for judgment. Though their spirits and souls may be elsewhere, the dead are in the earth.

> "...and the dust returns to the ground it came from, and the spirit returns to God who gave it." (Ecclesiastes 12:7)

Our born again spirit and soul go to Heaven.

After death, our bodies "rest" in the grave.

OLD TESTAMENT SOULS

If we do not meet the criteria for salvation before we die on earth, and our body remains in the grave after we die, what becomes of our soul?

The Old Testament describes a holding place for all the dead, called Sheol. In Hebrew, Sheol means, "abode of the dead; underworld." The word Sheol is Hebrew and translates as "in the grave" or "Hell" by modern day translators.[2] Sheol is a holding place equivalent to Hades as described in the New Testament.

The following are Old Testament verses that refer to a Sheol.

- "The LORD brings death and makes alive; he brings down to Sheol (the grave) and raises up." (1 Samuel 2:6)

- "Deal with him according to your wisdom, but do not let his gray head go to Sheol (down to the grave) in peace. But show kindness to the sons of Barzillai of Gilead and let them be among those who eat at your table. They stood by me when I fled from your brother Absalom. And remember, you have with you Shimei son of Gera, the Benjamite from Bahurim, who called down bitter curses on me the day I went to Mahanaim. When he came down to meet me at the Jordan, I swore to him by the LORD: 'I will not put you to death by the sword.' But now, do not consider him innocent. You are a man of wisdom;

you will know what to do to him. Bring his gray head down to Sheol (the grave) in blood.'" (1 Kings 2:6-9)

- "They will say, 'As one plows and breaks up the earth, so our bones have been scattered at the mouth of Sheol (the grave).'" (Psalms 141:7)

- "Whatever your hand finds to do, do it with all your might, for in Sheol (the grave), where you are going, there is neither working nor planning nor knowledge nor wisdom." (Ecclesiastes 9:10)

- "I said, 'In the prime of my life must I go through the gates of Sheol (death) and be robbed of the rest of my years?'" (Isaiah 38:10)

- "I will ransom them from the power of Sheol (the grave); I will redeem them from death. Where, O death, are your plagues? Where, O grave is your destruction? I will have no compassion." (Hosea 13:14)

Sheol is the location of all the souls who died in Old Testament times, prior to Christ's resurrection.

WITHOUT SALVATION

Jesus Christ spoke a great deal about the fate of the unsaved. He used two words, which translates in the New Testament as Hell - Hades, and Gahenna.

The New Testament defines Hades as a temporary place for souls awaiting final judgment.

"The sea gave up the dead that were in it and death and Hades gave up the dead that were in them, and each person was judged according to what he had done." (Revelation 20:13)

One thousand years after the second coming of Christ, God judges the unsaved souls. Revelation 20:13 indicates that Hades will "give up" the dead to be judged. The dead are awaiting judgment, which is located in Hades prior to judgment.

Gehenna refers to the Valley of Hinnom near Jerusalem, which served as a dump where garbage was burned. Close in proximity to the first temple, this valley was the place where the people of Judah offered their children to the fire god Molech and to Baal (Jeremiah 7:31; 32:35) which, Jeremiah warned, would pay with the destruction of the temple and exile. In light of the sacrifices to the fire god, the latter name gave rise to the word Gehenna, which over time Jesus uses as a synonym for Hell.[3]

"Then death and Hades were thrown into the lake of fire. The lake of fire is the second death. If anyone's name was not found written in the book of life, he was thrown into the lake of fire." (Revelation 20:14-15)

Jesus used the term Gehenna because it had meaning to the population surrounding Jerusalem. Live sacrifices were thrown into a pit of fire and burned to death. Jesus used this imagery to describe the final fate of non-believers.[4]

"Then death and Hades were thrown into the lake of fire. The lake of fire is the second death. If anyone's name was not found written in the book of life, he was thrown into the lake of fire." (Revelation 20:14-15)

In Revelation 20, it says that Hades (in the New Testament, all of those in Hell) are thrown into the lake of fire. Here Gehenna refers to the lake of fire or Hell.

CHRIST IN HADES

"Jesus said, 'Do not hold on to me, for I have not yet ascended to the Father (after rising the 3rd day).'" (John 20:17)

If Jesus did not ascend to His Father, where did He go after the crucifixion and before the resurrection?

"For Christ died for sins once for all, the righteous for the unrighteous, to bring you to God. He was put to death in the body but made alive by the Spirit, through whom also he went and preached to the spirits in prison who disobeyed long ago when God waited patiently in the days of Noah while the ark was being built." (1 Peter 3:18-20)

Peter indicates that Jesus was dead in His body, but alive in His Spirit before the resurrection.

"I, the LORD, have called you in righteousness; I will take hold of your hand. I will keep you and will make you to be a covenant for the people and a light for the Gentiles, to open eyes that are blind, to free captives from prison and to release from the dungeon those who sit in darkness." (Isaiah 42:6-7)

The prophet Isaiah predicted that the New Covenant would be a light to the Gentiles. Jesus will open the eyes that are blind and bring out the prisoners from the dungeon who sit in darkness.

Jesus went to Sheol or Hades, to preach salvation to the Old Testament souls. He preached that He was the sacrifice, the only unblemished lamb that would save them.

"This is why it says: 'When he ascended on high, he led captives in his train and gave gifts to men.'" (Ephesians 4:8-10) What does "He ascended" mean except that He also descended to the lower, earthly regions? He who descended is the very one who ascended higher than all the heavens, in order to fill the whole Universe.

Jesus descended into the lower regions of the earth. This is the dwelling of the dead, the underworld. After preaching, He ascended on high; He led captives in His train and gave gifts to men. He preached that salvation was through Him, and He gave the gift of salvation to those who followed Him.

Although the destiny of those that did not accept Christ in Hades is not clear, it is believed by some based on Jesus' teachings that a portion of the Old Testament dead remained there. The souls of those that did not follow Him remained in Hades, awaiting the promises of the book of Revelation.

"The sea gave up the dead that were in it and death and Hades gave up the dead that were in them, and each person was judged according to what he had done." Revelation 20:13

The verse in John 20:17 above indicates that Jesus may not have been in Hades before Mary touched Him. Depending on the translation, many believe that Jesus was telling Mary "not to cling to him", as He was not leaving (nor would he for another fifty days). A few verses later in John chapter 20, Jesus encourages the disciples to touch him, especially Thomas. Therefore, we can draw the conclusion that Jesus either preached in Hades and gave gifts to men before the stone rolled away and He walked out of the tomb, or He arose to the Father before He met the apostles in the upper room, after Mary touched Him.

WITH SALVATION

Jesus preached to the souls of the Old Testament so they may have salvation. Those that responded received the gift of eternal life. When Jesus resurrected, the unsaved souls went to Hades to await their fate as written in Revelation 20. Then, where do the saved go? Three New Testament verses will help to establish a foundation.

- "No one has ever gone into Heaven except the one who came from Heaven - the Son of Man. Until His resurrection, Jesus states that no man has ever gone to Heaven." (John 3:13)

- "But Christ has indeed been raised from the dead, the first fruits of those who have fallen asleep." (1Corinthians 15:20)

- "And he is the head of the body, the church; he is the beginning and the firstborn from among the dead so that in everything he might have the supremacy." (Colossians 1:18)

Of all who have died, Jesus is the first to resurrect and rise to Heaven. As the first to be raised, He will reign supreme. With this as our foundation, where do the saved go when they die? Will their bodies rest in the grave? The Apostle Paul reveals a great deal on this topic.

- "Therefore, we are always confident and know that as long as we are at home in the body we are away from the Lord. We live by faith, not by sight. We are confident, I say, and would prefer to be away from the body and at home with the Lord." (2 Corinthians 5:6-8)

- "If I am to go on living in the body, this will mean fruitful labor for me. Yet what shall I choose? I do not know! I am torn between the two: I desire to depart and be with Christ, which is better by far; but it is more necessary for you that I remain in the body." (Philippians 1:21-24)

According to Paul, when we are away from our body, we are with Jesus Christ in Heaven. After Jesus rose from the dead and ascended to Heaven, He unlocked a path for the saved souls to enter Heaven with Him.

If the saved spirits go to Heaven, to which Heaven would they go? Is there more than one? Let us continue.

TO WHAT END?

In Genesis, God created humankind to rule the earth, and to glorify and love Him in fellowship. God created the heavens and the earth, and Adam and Eve. Adam and Eve sinned against God, and He expelled them from the Garden of Eden. Humankind yielded to sin and lost God's eternal fellowship, so we became separated and lost the connection to the fullness of God. Humankind lost paradise because we were corrupt.

Salvation allows us to fellowship and have an eternal relationship with God. It is paradise regained. However, what happens if we do not gain salvation? Where do we go? What happens to us?

The Bible defines one choice, eternal life or perishing. What does the Bible proclaim about Heaven and Hell?

Heavenly Perceptions

Most people have a fabricated illustration of Heaven and Hell. Without studying the Bible, hearsay and doctrine can shape our perception. When asked about Heaven, typical responses are: pearly gates, paradise, in the clouds, pure light, adorned in gold, jewels and pearls, and fellowship with God for eternity. Though each may represent a sampling of Scripture from the Bible, they do not define the nature and preparation of Heaven or eternity.

Hell—Common Beliefs

When asked, "What is Hell?" What is your answer? A burning pit, lake of fire, pain and suffering, exists today with a host of eternal inhabitants, or the place where the devil lives wielding his pitchfork?

Some think Hell is seeing God and being cast aside and rejected or being forsaken by God. The biblical description of Hell is confusing to most.

PUNISHMENT RECEIVED BY JESUS

If Jesus paid the price for ours sins, did He experience Hell for us, too?

- "My God, my God, why have you forsaken me? Why are you so far from saving me, so far from the words of my groaning?" (Psalm 22:1)

- "About the ninth hour, Jesus cried out in a loud voice, 'Eloi, Eloi, lama sabachthani?' —which means, "My God, my God, why have you forsaken me?" (Matthew 27:46)

The psalmist prophesies Matthew's record describing Jesus on the cross, taking the sins of all who call on Him as Savior. Therefore, with sin, God forsakes and abandons Him. So, is this what the Bible describes as perishing?

When forsaken by God, is this punishment for humankind's sin? Yes, the Bible promises it for those whose sins are not justified by Jesus. However, is this the Hell that all unsaved sinners will receive?

Let us study what the Bible says about Heaven and Hell.

HEAVEN AND HELL

When we die, our bodies are reserved in the grave until called. People who trust in Jesus go with Him to Heaven when they die. Non-believers (those without salvation) or those who trust in their own goodness, go to Hades. On the second coming, Jesus Christ returns to earth. All believers who are living and dead will reign with Him for 1,000 years (this term could mean a period or the end of an age).

After the 1,000-year period, enter "The Great White Throne of Judgment." God empties Hades and judges those on their actions. Non-believers (those without salvation), are thrown into the lake of fire. God restores the heavens and the earth, and believers spend eternity with Him in a restored earth, in the New Jerusalem.**Where?**

Without Salvation—Hell

We learned in Path Step 6 that Jesus Christ removes the Cup of God's Wrath from the hands of His followers and drinks it on their behalf. Revelation defines the meaning of drinking from the Cup of God's Wrath.

"A third angel followed them and said in a loud voice: 'If anyone worships the beast and his image and receives his mark on the forehead or on the hand, he, too, will drink of the wine of God's fury, which has been poured full strength into the cup of his wrath. He will be tormented with burning sulfur in the presence of the holy angels and of the Lamb.'" (Revelation 14:9-10)

This prophecy in Revelation describes the lake of fire or Hell. Those who have not united with God receive the beast's mark on their hand or forehead and will be tormented with burning sulfur. Jesus, the Lamb, and His host of angels will oversee this. However, as we learned in Path Step 6, Jesus prevents His believers from having to drink the Cup of God's Wrath.

- "Jesus told them another parable: 'The kingdom of Heaven is like a man who sowed good seed in his field. But while everyone was sleeping, his enemy came and sowed weeds among the wheat and went away. When the wheat sprouted and formed heads, then the weeds also appeared. The owner's servants came to him and said, 'Sir, didn't you sow good seed in your field? Where then did the weeds come from?' 'An enemy did this,' he replied. The servants asked him, 'Do you want us to go and pull them up?' 'No,' he answered, 'because while you are pulling the weeds, you may root up the wheat with them. Let both grow together until the harvest. At that time, I will tell the harvesters: First collect the weeds and tie them in bundles to be burned; then gather the wheat and bring it into my barn.'" (Matthew 13:24-30)

- "This is how it will be at the end of the age. The angels will come and separate the wicked from the righteous and throw them into the fiery furnace, where there will be weeping and gnashing of teeth." (Matthew 13:49-50)

- "I saw thrones on which were seated those who had been given authority to judge. And I saw the souls of those who had been beheaded because of their testimony about Jesus and because of the word of God. They had not worshiped the beast or his image (the enemy) and had not received his mark on their foreheads or their hands. They came to life and reigned with Christ a thousand years. (The rest of the dead did not come to life until the thousand years were ended.) This is the first resurrection." (Revelation 20:4-5)

- "Do not be afraid of those who kill the body but cannot kill the soul. Rather, be afraid of the One who can destroy both soul and body in Hell." (Matthew 10:28)

- "For God so loved the world that he gave his one and only Son that whoever believes in him shall not perish but have eternal life." (John 3:16)

The choice is clear. Choose Jesus to receive forgiveness of your sins and have eternal life in fellowship with God, or choose to perish.

When they perish, where will the unsaved be?

Where Is Hell?

"And I saw an angel coming down out of Heaven, having the key to the Abyss and holding in his hand a great chain. He seized the dragon, that ancient serpent, who is the devil, or Satan, and bound him for a thousand years." (Revelation 20:1-2)

If an angel comes down out of Heaven, is the abyss on earth?

"At that time, the sea, death, and Hades will give up the dead for judgment. Then death and Hades were thrown into the lake of fire. The lake of fire is the second death. All whose names were not found written in the book of life were thrown into the lake of fire." (Revelation 20:13-15)

The sea on earth gives up its dead. Hades gives up its dead from the underworld, and they are thrown into the lake of fire, the abyss, by angels who come down out of Heaven.

"By the same word, the present heavens and earth are reserved for fire, being kept for the day of judgment and destruction of ungodly men. ...The heavens will disappear with a roar; the elements will be destroyed by fire, and **the earth and everything in it will be laid bare.**" (2 Peter 3:7,10)

The earth is reserved for fire and kept for the Day of Judgment. This reference refers to the Day of Judgment in Revelation. This statement directly links the lake of fire to earth.

2 Peter 3:10 states that the elements will be destroyed by fire and **everything** in it will be laid bare. After the lake of fire, the earth will be destroyed and consumed by fire until it is made anew.

"Then I saw a new Heaven and a new earth, for the first Heaven and the first earth had passed away, and there was no longer any sea. I saw the Holy City, the New Jerusalem, coming down out of Heaven from God, prepared as a bride beautifully dressed for her husband." (Revelation 21:1-3)

The lake of fire, the elements, the earth as we know it today, and those cast into the fire will cease to exist. Hell will not last forever. Eternal damnation refers to the destruction of the soul, the second death. For all eternity, the soul will be destroyed. Revelation and 2 Peter state that the lake of fire is on earth. If the first Heaven and the first earth have passed away (are restored), then everyone suffering in the lake of fire (Hell) has passed away into oblivion. When a sinner accepts Jesus Christ as Savior, they die and are reborn. The same is true of the fallen earth. The earth will die, and then it will renew when sin no longer exists. Any remnant of the old existence will be gone forever. All sin will perish with all sinners (those with sin and without salvation).

How Long Does Hell Last?

The Bible is clear that all who die on earth will rise again, to live into eternity with God or to die the second death. Terms such as "eternal damnation" refer to the second death from which there is no resurrection. One such as this is eternally damned.

In the Bible, the term "forever," means a period of time, limited or unlimited, and is written 56 times in connection with all that has already ended. It is comparable to the word "tall," which means something different in describing men, trees, or mountains. In Jonah 2:6, forever means three days and nights (see Jonah 1:17).

In Deuteronomy 23:3, forever means ten generations. This means as long as he lives or until death (see 1 Samuel 1:22, 28; Exodus 21:6; Psalm 48:14). The wicked will burn in the fire as long as they live or until death. The fiery punishment for sin will vary according to the degree of sins for each individual. However, after the punishment the fire will go out.

"For every living soul belongs to me, the father as well as the son-both alike belong to me. The soul who sins is the one who will die." (Ezekiel 18:4)

The prophet Ezekiel in the Old Testament confirms Matthew's warning, where he states that souls whose sins that are not forgiven will perish.

"In a similar way, Sodom, Gomorrah, and the surrounding towns gave themselves up to sexual immorality and perversion. They serve as an example of those who suffer the punishment of eternal fire." (Jude 1:7)

Many believe that the fire in Hell is symbolic of pain and suffering, or the magnificence of God who casts out the sinners. Jude states that the burning sulfur and fire that destroyed Sodom and Gomorrah are an example of what will occur to those whose sins are not justified.

Does eternal fire mean it burns for eternity? Though stated as an eternal fire, Sodom, Gomorrah, and the cities of the plain did cease to smolder and became extinguished. As the cities of the plain, Hell does not burn forever. God is the eternal fire.

While the verses above may lead you to a robust conclusion, Bible scholars disagree on the duration of Hell.

In fact, the following is one verse regarded by many as a strong case for burning in Hell for an eternity.

"Their worm does not die, and the fire is not quenched." (Mark 9:44 NKJV)

Here, Jesus speaks and refers to Hell. He states "their worm does not die," and the "fire is not quenched." Many argue that as Jesus reports, the fire and worms continue forever. The conclusion is that the fires of Hell burn the unrighteous unsaved forever and ever, into eternity.

However, the verse does not state anything about the unsaved. We read in Revelation about the first and second death. The naysayers of the burn forever theology believe that the worm and fire continuing mean that no resurrection or additional life is permitted for eternity. A worm is attributed to eating flesh after death. They believe that the unsaved souls perish forever by worms that never cease and fire that is never quenched. This argument is similar to the eternal flame or eternal damnation discussion above.

Let us recognize that eternity in fellowship with God is desirable; however, we should avoid Hell at all costs.

With Salvation—Heaven

"For God so loved the world that he gave his one and only Son that whoever believes in him shall not perish but have eternal life." (John 3:16) John states that we can either perish (go to Hell) or have eternal life (go to Heaven and know God).

"Let not your hearts be troubled. Believe in God; believe also in me. In my Father's house are many rooms. If it were not so, would I have told you that I go to prepare a place for you? And if I go and prepare a place for you, I will come again and will take you to myself, that where I am you may be also." (John 14:1-3) John states that Jesus will prepare a place in Heaven for His followers. He promises that He will return to earth a second time to retrieve His followers.

In Isaiah 65:17, the prophet Isaiah foretells the destruction of Hell as a former thing and the old earth. He states that after this occurs the saved will not remember them or that they ever existed.

Revelation 20:4-5 states they had not worshiped the beast or his image and had not received his mark on their foreheads or their hands. They came to life and reigned with Christ a thousand years. The rest of the dead did not come to life until the thousand years were ended. This is the first resurrection. At the second coming of Jesus Christ, the saved are raised from the dead and will reign with Him for the 1,000 year period.

"Listen, I tell you a mystery: We will not all sleep, but we will all be changed - in a flash, in the twinkling of an eye, at the last trumpet. For the trumpet will sound, the dead will be raised imperishable, and we will be changed. For the perishable must clothe itself with the imperishable and the mortal with immortality." (1 Corinthians 15:51-53) Believers and their resurrected bodies will rise into the clouds to meet Jesus so they may escort Him back to earth. This is similar to a Jewish wedding, where guests would meet at the bride's house. They would greet the groom, and then they would escort him to the wedding banquet (see Matthew 25:1-13).[5]

When Jesus returns, the Bible states that He will establish His kingdom on earth for one thousand years. Believers will reign with Him and they will serve as priests to the nonbelievers who survive the tribulation (see Revelation 20:6)

- "Then I saw a new Heaven and a new earth, for the first Heaven and the first earth had passed away, and there was no longer any sea. I saw the holy city, the New Jerusalem, coming down out of Heaven from God, prepared as a bride beautifully dressed for her husband. And I heard a loud voice from the throne saying, 'Look! God's dwelling place is now among the people, and he will dwell with them. They will be his people, and God himself will be with them and be their God.'" (Revelation 21:1-3)

- "And he carried me away in the Spirit to a mountain great and high, and showed me the holy city, Jerusalem, coming down out of Heaven from God. It shone with the glory of God, and its brilliance was like that of a very precious jewel, like jasper, clear as crystal. It had a great, high wall with twelve gates and with twelve angels at the gates.

  On the gates were written the names of the twelve tribes of Israel. There were three gates on the east, three on the north, three on the south and three on the west. The wall of the city had twelve foundations, and on them were the names of the twelve apostles of the Lamb. The angel who talked with me had a measuring rod of gold to measure the city, its gates and its walls.

  The city was laid out like a square, as long as it was wide. He measured the city with the rod and found it to be 12,000 stadia in length, and as wide and high as it is long. He measured its wall, and it was 144 cubits thick, by human measurement, which the angel was using. The wall was made of jasper, and the city of pure gold, as pure as glass. The foundations of the city walls were decorated with every kind of precious stone.

  The first foundation was jasper, the second sapphire, the third agate, the fourth emerald, the fifth onyx, the sixth ruby, the seventh chrysolite, the eighth beryl, the ninth topaz, the tenth turquoise, the eleventh jacinth, and the twelfth amethyst. The twelve gates were twelve pearls, each gate made of a single pearl. The great street of the city was of gold, as pure as transparent glass." (Revelation 21:10-21)

In essence, this is a return to Eden, a restored, improved Eden. The earth is recreated, all sin and unsaved sinners are obliterated, Jesus establishes an earthly kingdom, and all of remaining humankind is conformed to the image of God's Son, Jesus Christ.

God's plan is fulfilled. From Genesis, "Let us create man in our image," He created man in the image of God, for love and worship. God gave humankind the choice between life and death. By free will, those accepting Jesus repented of evil ways and accepted the form and glory of their Savior, Jesus Christ. God's plan is fulfilled.

Heaven Or Hell?

Hell:

- After death, bodies are reserved in the grave
- Unsaved souls go to Hades
- Hell occurs 1,000 years after Christ's return
- Hades returns its dead to earth and judgment occurs
- Hell, the lake of fire, is on earth

- Earth and everything on it is consumed in fire
- Hell fire will destroy the body and soul
- Hell does not yet exist, and it does not continue forever

Heaven:

- After death, souls and spirits of the saved go to Heaven
- Bodies are reserved in the grave
- During the second coming of Christ, bodies are resurrected and will rise to Jesus
- The saved reign on earth with Christ for a 1,000 year period
- After 1,000, years and the rebirth of the heavens and earth, God and man reunite on earth (New Jerusalem)
- Heaven comes to earth
- God and humankind enjoy eternal existence

These are the two paths and destinations. God gives one choice.

"For God so loved the world that he gave his one and only Son that whoever believes in him shall not perish but have eternal life." (John 3:16)

Perish, or have eternal life?

Will Jesus justify you before God?

Is Jesus Christ your savior?

God requires sacrifice and bloodshed for the forgiveness of sin. Will your bloodshed provide forgiveness, pay for your sins, or will someone pay the penalty for your sins?

A substitute for a sacrifice must be unblemished and perfect. As outlined in Path Step 3, you are a sinner. You must die and shed your blood to pay the price (penalty) for your sins, which is Hell. However, Jesus can be your savior, your lamb, your substitution. He is the only sinless, unblemished sacrifice that can assume (absorb) all of your sins. He offers you salvation and eternal life, which is Heaven (see Path Step 8).

We have one choice, and we have free will. Our perfect and holy God gives us the answer.

"This day I call Heaven and earth as witnesses against you that I have set before your life and death, blessings and curses. Now choose life, so that you and your children may live." (Deuteronomy 30:19)

The option is set before you. God provided the answer. Have you made your choice?

THE SALVATION RECIPE

How do we become a follower of Jesus Christ? What must we do to gain salvation? Jesus calls us to make Him Lord and Savior. The Bible teaches the following:

1. Learn from the Bible

"No one can come to me unless the Father who sent me draws him and I will raise him up at the last day. It is written in the prophets: 'they will all be taught by God.' Everyone who listens to the Father and learns from him comes to me." (John 6:44-45)

No one has ever been saved without understanding the truth of the Gospel. You must first learn about Jesus Christ in order to accept Him as Savior. The Bible describes His life, purpose, and teachings. He asks us to follow Him. We must learn the truth about Him to do so.

2. Repent

"Godly sorrow brings repentance that leads to salvation and leaves no regret, but worldly sorrow brings death." (2 Corinthians 7:10)

The Bible teaches that we must turn from our sinning ways and follow the path of Jesus. Repentance is the acknowledgment of and turning from sin; therefore, we must veer from that sinful nature.

3. Confess Jesus as Savior

"That if you confess with your mouth, 'Jesus is Lord,' and believe in your heart that God raised him from the dead, you will be saved. For it is with your heart that you believe and are justified, and it is with your mouth that you confess and are saved." (Romans 10:9-10)

You must realize that you need Jesus Christ as your savior due to your sinning nature. Then, you must confess Him as your Savior. You must believe that Jesus was raised from the dead, and you must accept Him as your Savior, verbally.

4. Obey

"Jesus, once made perfect, became the source of eternal salvation for all who obey him." (Hebrews 5:9)

In the New Testament, Jesus refers to the Lord, or the apostles refer to our Lord Jesus, 384 times. Jesus is to be Lord of our lives. Jesus defines salvation and His plan for humankind. How can Jesus be Lord of your life if you do not obey him? Reading the Bible and submitting to his commands is essential. Jesus wants and knows the best for us. Establishing a close tie with your Lord will add to your fulfillment and joy. Have you made Jesus Lord of your life?

5. Be Baptized

"Whoever believes and is baptized will be saved, but whoever does not believe will be condemned." (Mark 16:16)

In the New Testament Jesus commands baptism. In obedience, we are to be baptized soon after accepting Jesus Christ as our Savior.

6. Become Part of Church Body

Ephesians 5:23 and 25-26 tell us that Jesus is Savior of the body (church), and gave Himself for the church.

Jesus wishes for us to grow as His followers and to spread the good news that He represents. He established His church (His followers) to strengthen our faith, share, and promote His life-saving gift.

REPENT AND BE BAPTIZED

- "Peter replied, 'Repent and be baptized, every one of you, in the name of Jesus Christ for the forgiveness of your sins. And you will receive the gift of the Holy Spirit.'" (Act 2:38)

- "I tell you, no! But unless you repent, you too will all perish." (Luke 13:5)

- "Repent then, and turn to God, so that your sins may be wiped out that times of refreshing may come from the Lord." (Act 3:19)

- "Therefore, go and make disciples of all nations, baptizing them in the name of the Father and of the Son and of the Holy Spirit." (Matthew 28:19)

What does it mean to repent? Definition: to feel such sorrow for sin or fault as to be disposed to CHANGE one's life for the better; be penitent. It is not only being sorry for sins committed. Repentance is turning away from your sinful nature. Jesus was free of sin.

To follow Him we must change our nature. We should be sorry for the sins we have committed, and ask for forgiveness provided to us by Jesus' sacrifice. However, to follow Him, we need to transform. It does not mean that we will never sin again.

Baptism—What Is It?

Baptism represents the transformation of being born again unto Jesus Christ. Baptism is a symbolic gesture declaring that we are following Jesus. When Jesus was baptized, the Holy Spirit anointed Him. When we are baptized, it symbolizes the death of our old self and the renewal of our spirit. See Path Step 8 discussing the loss of the "old man" sin nature in water baptism.

In addition, this is an act of obedience. The New Testament states that Jesus commands His followers to follow Him in baptism. Therefore, after you acknowledge Jesus as your Savior you should submerge in water (see Figure 96). Baptism is embracing Jesus' death and resurrection. The former person dies and then is buried. The water represents the grave. The new (born again) person rises with a renewed spirit as Jesus did when He resurrected (See Figure 97). We will study this in Path Step 8.

FIG 96 - WATER BAPTISM

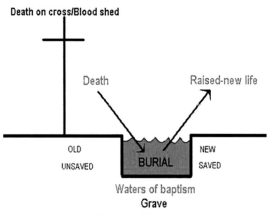

FIG 97 - BAPTISM, "OLD MAN" DIES

Baptism—Jesus' Command

The Great Commission; "Then Jesus came to them and said, 'All authority in Heaven and on earth has been given to me. Therefore, go and make disciples of all nations, baptizing them in the name of the Father and of the Son and of the Holy Spirit, and teaching them to obey everything I have commanded you. And surely I am with you always, to the very end of the age.'" (Matthew 28:18-20)

"Jesus answered, 'I tell you the truth, no one can enter the kingdom of God unless he is born of water and the Spirit.'" (John 3:5)

"Whoever believes and is baptized will be saved, but whoever does not believe will be condemned." (Mark 16:16)

Jesus wants us to obey His teachings and His commands. After confessing Him as Savior, He says there should be a baptism. The New Testament states that if you accept Jesus Christ as your Savior, baptism is necessary. Is there a legitimate reason to disregard baptism?

Baptism—For Obedience

Rom 6:1-4 What shall we say then? Shall we continue in sin that grace may abound? Certainly not! How shall we who died to sin live any longer in it? Alternatively, do you not know that as many of us as were baptized into Christ Jesus were baptized into His death? Therefore, we were buried with Him through baptism into death, that just as Christ was raised from the dead by the glory of the Father, even so we also should walk in newness of life.

Paul states that when we accept Christ as our Savior we receive a renewed spirit, the "newness of life," "just as Christ."

Biblical Baptism

Does baptism involve the sprinkling of water, or is it a full immersion? Some churches sprinkle infants for baptism and then ask the baptized to confirm their decision after the age of consent. Others immerse following a personal decision after the age of consent. The age of consent is when one is capable of understanding Jesus' sacrifice. Are both methods in the Scripture?

Several forms of the word "baptize" exist in the Bible. Let us review the words in the Greek language that are in the original manuscripts:[6]

Βαπτίζω

baptizō, bap-tid'-zo

From a derivative of βάπτω (bapto); to make whelmed (that is, fully wet); ceremonial ablution (cleansing), especially of the ordinance of Christian baptism: baptist, baptize, wash

βάπτω

baptō, bap'-to

A primary verb; to whelm, that is, cover wholly with a fluid; or (by implication) to stain (as with dye): dip

- "One Lord, one faith, one baptism." (Ephesians 4:5) In Paul's letter to the Ephesians, he states there is only one God, one faith (path to Him), and one baptism. The Scriptures state what we are commanded.

- "At that time, Jesus came from Nazareth in Galilee and was baptized by John in the Jordan. As Jesus was coming up out of the water, he saw Heaven being torn open and the Spirit descending on him like a dove." (Mark 1:9-10) Jesus came up out of the water. The implication is that Jesus went into the water; therefore, there was no sprinkling of the water.

- "And he gave orders to stop the chariot. Then both Philip and the eunuch went down into the water, and Philip baptized him." (Act 8:38) The eunuch and Philip "went down into the water" to be baptized.

- "Now John also was baptizing at Aenon near Salim, because there was plenty of water, and people were constantly coming to be baptized." (John 3:23) If sprinkling were the method for baptism, to be in the midst of "plenty of water" would be unnecessary.

The Bible describes an immersive baptism. Immersion is eyes closed, breath suspended, hands folded and to be lowered beneath the water, as in death. Then, as Jesus, one must rise out of the water as He did from the grave. Baptism represents the "old" person dying to Christ and the rebirth of the spirit.

"We were therefore buried with him through baptism into death in order that, just as Christ was raised from the dead through the glory of the Father, we too may live a new life. If we have been united with him like this in his death, we will certainly also be united with him in his resurrection. For we know that our old self was crucified with him so that the body of sin might be done away with, that we should no longer be slaves to sin." (Romans 6:4-6)

Based on verses consistent with that above, some Christian believe that their "old man" actually did die with Jesus on the cross.

Must One Be Baptized?

"One of the criminals who hung there hurled insults at him: "Aren't you the Christ? Save yourself and us!" But the other criminal rebuked him. "Don't you fear God," he said, "since you are under the same sentence? We are punished justly, for we are getting what our deeds deserve. But this man has done nothing wrong." Then he said, "Jesus, remember me when you come into your kingdom." Jesus answered him, "I tell you the truth, today you will be with me in paradise." (Luke 23:39-43)

What is wrong with this picture? "You will be with me in paradise" But how without a baptism? How did this criminal on his cross know the true nature and role of Jesus, and then be in Heaven with Him?

- "Or do you not know that as many of us as were baptized into Christ Jesus were baptized into His death? Therefore, we were buried with Him through baptism into death, that just as Christ was raised from the dead by the glory of the Father, even so we also should walk in newness of life." (Romans 6:3-4)

- "Having been buried with him in baptism and raised with him through your faith in the power of God, who raised him from the dead." (Colossians 2:12)

Jesus had not died yet. He was still on the cross. No one could be baptized into His death. Therefore, the thief on the cross is not a conclusive argument.

"While Apollos was at Corinth, Paul took the road through the interior and arrived at Ephesus. There, he found some disciples and asked them, 'Did you receive the Holy Spirit when you believed?' They answered, 'No, we have not even heard that there is a Holy Spirit.' So Paul asked, 'Then what baptism did you receive? 'John's baptism,' they replied. Paul said, 'John's baptism was a baptism of repentance. He told the people to believe in the one coming after him, that is, in Jesus.' On hearing this, they were baptized into the name of the Lord Jesus." (Acts 19:1-5)

John's baptism, before Jesus' sacrifice, was not recognized.

Jesus was baptized. Jesus and God command baptism. Do we have to be baptized? YES, we should do so in obedience when following Jesus. Can someone be saved by Christ and not be baptized? Debate focuses on this question. The Bible states "faith without works is dead." It is not possible to be saved by good works. We are saved by our faith in Christ. However, good works should result from our faith in Christ. Can someone be saved by Christ and not be baptized? Yes, and faith without works is dead.

A person is saved when he or she accepts Jesus as their personal sacrifice for their sin. The moment they believe in their heart and confess with their mouth, they are saved. If a Christian is not baptized, he or she has not started a walk with God. Jesus may be the Savior, but he has not been made Lord. If you accept Jesus as Lord and Savior, why would you not obey His first instruction?

"His master replied, 'Well done, good and faithful servant! You have been faithful with a few things; I will put you in charge of many things. Come and share your master's happiness!'" (Matthew 25:21)

There is much debate of the many factions of Christianity that surround baptism. One cannot make a case of baptism being necessary or "a good idea." However, faith without works is dead. Christ commands it of His followers. If you accepted Christ as your personal Savior and are not baptized, you should obey His command. It is a public and outward expression of your inner change. Just as Jesus asks us to confess Him with our lips, we are to make a public statement that we follow Jesus by following Him into death and rebirth.

Personal Savior

Jesus believes in the gathering of His followers so we may encourage and support one another (the Church). His focus is to reconcile humanity with God. Jesus' death and resurrection provides a means for each individual (not humanity, as a whole) to obtain forgiveness and fellowship with God from His sacrifice. Those that follow Him represent the Church, or the Body of Christ.

"With the heart, man believes to righteousness, and with the mouth, confession is made to salvation." (Romans 10:9-10)

Since the lamb of the Old Covenant was for a sin offering, is Jesus your "personal" lamb? (See Path Step 9).

You MUST accept Jesus, have a personal relationship with Him, and take Him as your Savior. Association with a church or any denomination cannot save you. The acknowledgment of Jesus Christ as Lord and Savior of your life, and the belief that He died with your sins and rose again (you are renewed), will save you.

PRAYER—TALKING WITH GOD

The promise of the New Covenant is a relationship from the heart and with the Holy Spirit. After accepting Christ, a born-again spirit in Christ lives within us, Jesus lives in us. The New Covenant is a closer connection with God.

"Now this is eternal life: that they may know you, the only true God, and Jesus Christ, whom you have sent. (John 17:3)

How can we obtain this?

The Bible defines eternal life as a relationship with God. For eternity, we have an intimate one-on-one relationship with the creator of the Universe. God seeks communication with us constantly. Prayer is one method of our communication with God and can take on many forms. Prayer can be formal, with praise and request. Prayer does not need to be elaborate and specific. Prayer is a conversation with God. You can tell God what you are doing, where you are going, why you are going there, etc. Ask for His guidance. Ask God to make you aware of His presence in your spirit.

Prayer is communication. Over time and with much prayer, you will recognize God's interaction response with you. God wants to be a primary part of our lives. He took on a human form and gave His life so that we would choose Him, and have an eternal relationship with Him from our new spirit. The purpose of the Bible is for humankind to regain fellowship with the fullness of God. The moment we believe in Jesus Christ with our hearts, we regained that fellowship (see next Path Step). Do not ignore God, fellowship with Him. Talk with Him. Pray!

Prayer is a forum for requests.

- "Do not be anxious about anything, but in everything, by prayer and petition, with thanksgiving, present your requests to God. And the peace of God, which transcends all understanding, will guard your hearts and your minds in Christ Jesus." (Philippians 4:6-7)

- "Therefore, I tell you, whatever you ask for in prayer, believe that you have received it, and it will be yours." (Mark 11:24)

- "If you believe, you will receive whatever you ask for in prayer." (Matthew 21:22)

Prayer is supporting God's will

- "This is the confidence we have in approaching God: that if we ask anything according to his will, he hears us. And if we know that he hears us—whatever we ask—we know that we have what we asked of him." (1 John 5:14-15)

- "It is God's will that you should be sanctified: that you should avoid sexual immorality; that each of you should learn to control his own body in a way that is holy and honorable, not in passionate lust like the heathen, who do not know God; and that in this matter, no one should wrong his brother or take advantage of him. The Lord will punish men for all such sins as we have already told you and warned you. For God did not call us to be impure, but to live a holy life. Therefore, he who rejects this instruction does not reject man but God, who gives you his Holy Spirit." (1 Thessalonians 4:3-8)

- "The LORD is far from the wicked, but he hears the prayer of the righteous." (Proverbs 15:29)

- "Do not be like them, for your Father knows what you need before you ask him." (Matthew 6:8)

Prayer is a vehicle for action (see Path Step 8 for Prayer in the Spirit)

- "And pray in the Spirit on all occasions with all kinds of prayers and requests. With this in mind, be alert and always keep on praying for all the saints." (Ephesians 6:18)

- "But you, dear friends, build yourselves up in your most holy faith and pray in the Holy Spirit. Keep yourselves in God's love as you wait for the mercy of our Lord Jesus Christ to bring you to eternal life." (Jude 1:20-21)

- "Be joyful in hope, patient in affliction, and faithful in prayer." (Romans 12:12)

A means to deepen faith and understanding

- "Do not be anxious about anything, but in everything, by prayer and petition, with thanksgiving, present your requests to God. And the peace of God, which transcends all understanding, will guard your hearts and your minds in Christ Jesus." (Philippians 4:6-7)

- "Therefore, confess your sins to each other and pray for each other so that you may be healed. The prayer of a righteous man is powerful and effective." (James 5:16)

- "Devote yourselves to prayer, being watchful and thankful." (Colossians 4:2)

Jesus tells us how to pray effectively and for what we should pray.

"This, then, is how you should pray: 'Our Father in Heaven, hallowed be your name, your kingdom come, your will be done on earth as it is in Heaven. Give us today our daily bread. Forgive us our debts, as we also have forgiven our debtors. And lead us not into temptation, but deliver us from the evil one.'" (Matthew 6:9-13)

This prayer is not to recite without thought and intention. In fact, Jesus recited the prayer for the Hebrews of the pre-resurrection. Much of what He prayed came to fruition as He resurrected. Jesus gave us the prayer as a guide. What does He teach us about prayer? For what should we pray?

- We should recognize and acknowledge God as all-powerful in Heaven

- We should seek that God's will is done

- Ask for the provision of our sustenance

- Ask forgiveness for our sinful nature

- Ask assistance to forgive others as Jesus did for us

- Keep us strong, righteous, and devoted

- Protect us from the devastating deception of the evil one

PRAYER, FAITH AND BELIEF

"Jesus replied, 'I tell you the truth if you have faith and do not doubt, not only can you do what was done to the fig tree, but also you can say to this mountain, 'Go, throw yourself into the sea,' and it will be done. If you believe, you will receive whatever you ask for in prayer.'" (Matthew 21:21-22)

Faith and belief are required. Belief is confidence in the truth or existence of something with little vulnerability to be disproven. Faith is conviction, but not based on proof. For example, a person can have faith that God, Jesus, and the Holy Spirit are truth, even though they have not seen them. You can employ faith and believe in God, Jesus, and the Holy Spirit. Based on your faith, you can have belief that the Word of God (Bible) is truth, and trust the Bible as fact. If you do not believe that you can move mountains, literal or figurative, as in Matthew 21:21-22 above, moving mountains will not work for you.

"If any of you lacks wisdom, he should ask God, who gives generously to all without finding fault, and it will be given to him. But when he asks, he must believe and not doubt because he who doubts is like a wave of the sea, blown and tossed by the wind." (James 1:5-6)

Do not doubt and pray for what is scripturally sound; your prayers will be answered.

"Jesus replied, 'I tell you the truth if you have faith and do not doubt, not only can you do what was done to the fig tree, but also you can say to this mountain, 'Go, throw yourself into the sea,' and it will be done. If you believe, you will receive whatever you ask for in prayer.'" (Matthew 21:21-22)

Doubt is humanity's downfall. The earth is being deceived and is under the power of the fallen one. Satan is humankind's enemy. Humanity falls prey to his deceit. From our earthly eyes, truth hides. The spirit world was in existence before the earthly realm. The spirit world is the first reality. In this world, what we believe is not entirely real. If God, His Son, and the Holy Spirit are truth, and what we understand on earth is not perfect and not what God intends, then we live a deceived life with only our physical senses. It may seem that God and truth, and the lack of doubt, are simple. However, we are deceived to perceive this world only with our physical senses. Believing the spiritual side, what is "real," requires effort and spiritual provision.

"When they came to the crowd, a man approached Jesus and knelt before him. 'Lord, have mercy on my son,' he said. 'He has seizures and is suffering greatly. He often falls into the fire or into the water. I brought him to your disciples, but they could not heal him.' 'O unbelieving and perverse generation,' Jesus replied, 'how long shall I stay with you? How long shall I put up with you? Bring the boy here to me.' Jesus rebuked the demon, and it came out of the boy, and he was healed from that moment." (Matthew 17:14-18)

Although they may have had faith in Jesus, the disciples were not able to heal the boy due to their unbelief.

"Then the disciples came to Jesus in private and asked, 'Why couldn't we drive it out?' He replied, 'Because you have so little faith. I tell you the truth, if you have faith as small as a mustard seed, you can say to this mountain, 'Move from here to there' and it will move. Nothing will be impossible for you.'" (Matthew 17:19-20)

It is not our faith that limits us. We only need the faith of a mustard seed. We hold back because of what we see, hear, touch, smell, and feel. What is real is the born again Spirit inside us, not this fallen world.

Prayer opens a channel to God for discussion and requests. It opens our sensibilities to the presence of God's Spirit in and around us (see next Path Step). Prayer keeps us focused on our relationship with God and Jesus. Pray for the truth in the Bible, have faith, believe the truth, and prayer will open potential far greater than this world.

PRAYER OF SALVATION

A prayer of salvation must come from your heart, and you must believe it in your mind. Your communication with God to accept Him and Jesus, His Son, can take many forms. Below is an example of a prayer that admits your broken nature and asks God for forgiveness and a relationship with Him.

> **"Father, I know that I have broken your laws and my sins have separated me from you. I am truly sorry, and want to turn away from my sinful life and head towards you. Please forgive me, and help me avoid sinning again. I believe that your son, Jesus Christ died for my sins; He rose from the dead, He is alive, and He hears my prayers. I invite Jesus to become the Lord and Savior of my life, to rule and reign in my heart from this day forward. Please send your Holy Spirit, renew my spirit, and help me obey. I want to do your will for the rest of my life. In Jesus' name I pray, Amen."**

It is important that you do not base your salvation on a narrated prayer. Reciting a prayer cannot save you! If you want salvation, it is through Jesus. Place your faith in Him. Fully trust His death as a sufficient sacrifice for your sins. Completely rely on Him as your Lord and Savior. Trust in His resurrection and ask to be reborn, you will know Him through your renewed spirit. Faith and belief in Jesus Christ and in His atoning blood is the basis of SALVATION.

SUMMARY

We are destined for either Heaven or Hell. To receive salvation:

- Accept Jesus Christ as your personal Savior

- Speak a prayer of Salvation

- Repent of your sinful nature

- Be baptized

This Path Step concludes the SALVATION Phase of A Rational Path to Christ. The third and final Phase centers on applying the principles of the FOUNDATION and SALVATION Phases of the Path. The next Phase examines REALIZATION.

As with each Step on A Rational Path to Christ, this Path Step ends with the same question from when it began. Would your life change IF…salvation reunites you and God? Yes or no? If yes:

- Do you REJECT salvation reunites you and God?

- Do you THINK salvation reunites you and God?

- Do you BELIEVE salvation reunites you and God?

- Do you KNOW salvation reunites you and God?

NOTES

1 James Strong, Strong's Expanded Exhaustive Concordance of the Bible (Nashville: Thomas Nelson, 2009), s.v. "salvation."

2 James Strong, Strong's Expanded Exhaustive Concordance of the Bible (Nashville: Thomas Nelson, 2009), s.v. "Sheol."

3 "The Broken Earthen Bottle – The Book of Jeremiah." James J. Barker. Biblebaptistelmont.org. Web. www.biblebaptistelmont.org/BBC/books/Jeremiah-21.html

4 https://en.wikipedia.org/wiki/Gehenna 4 Gehenna, https://en.wikipedia.org, September 4, 2016, https://en.wikipedia.org/wiki/Gehenna.

5 "The Prophetic Symbolism of Jewish Marriage Customs." AngelFire.com. Web. January 23, 1999, www.angelfire.com/realm2/prophetshare/jewish.html.

6 James Strong, Strong's Expanded Exhaustive Concordance of the Bible (Nashville: Thomas Nelson, 2009), s.v. "baptize."

A RATIONAL PATH TO CHRIST

PHASE 3

8	9
Spirit Will Guide Your Path	**You Can Live "Truth"**

Realization

Path Step 8

Would Your Life Change IF…?

CONTENTS

SPIRITUAL

I am a spirit being!

I believe many Christians fail to realize, at any significant level, their born again divine nature and the power of the Holy Spirit. Our true God is defined as the Father, the Son, and the Holy Spirit. In the beginning, God said, "Let us make man in our image." Based on selections from the Bible, I do not believe that we are fully made in God's image until those inheriting salvation receive a glorified body, a body identical to Jesus following His resurrection. At that point, we have the image of the Father in our soul, the image of the Son, Jesus, in our flesh, and the image of the Holy Spirit in our born again spirit. We are made in God's image. At that point, God (the Father, the Son, and the Holy Spirit) will have "made man in Our image."

If you are born again into Jesus today, you are a spirit being. You, personally, have a spirit born inside you created in the image of Jesus. You are an eternal being and are one with God, as Jesus is one with God. Other Scriptures define that the power that raised Jesus from the dead is present and alive in born again believers. Yet, why is it that we do not see that same power that raised Jesus from the dead, and the power of Jesus born again in us, at work en masse in the world around us? Why are healings, prophecies, and other miracles not commonplace among the believers?

The answer to this question is simple. To varying degrees, we, the born again believers, are deceived. Jesus died to return to us authority over this world. He died and rose again to give us life and make us whole. He rose to make us victorious and to live life more abundant. How many Christians embrace these?

The power of God may seem distant and strange to many of you. I know a man to whom this does not apply. He is a dear friend and brother of mine in Jesus Christ. His name is Don Eagon. Although they may exist on the planet, I have not met anyone who walks more "pressed in" to the Holy Spirit and to His power than Don. He is a humble man who lays hands on people and heals them, who submits himself as a conduit through which God can speak to people, and who loves God so deeply that it is obvious he loves God more than this world.

Don has made evident to me many truths in the Scriptures, which I believe the Church at large has missed or excused away. I would hope that God has used me on occasion to speak into his life as well. With Don's inspiration and the truth in the Bible, I learned that our born again spirit is not a holding place for something greater to arrive later. Although my body has yet to be made like Jesus', my born again spirit will never change. The spirit being that I will be, I already am.

Don and I took a 3 hour road trip to pray over a woman in her thirties who was diagnosed with a brain tumor and told she had only months to live. We arrived to a house full of believers, all with the hope of seeing their miracle. We engaged in conversation to become acquainted. After a bit, Don and I laid hands on her. Don began to pray healing with authority. I did as well, but largely prayed in the spirit. Both Don and I felt an electric-like tingle through our body, and up and down our spine. After 10 to 15 minutes, we stopped praying and watched the young woman. She walked about the room for a minute or so. Then, she asked if someone could provide to her a Bible. She opened the Bible and began to read the text. Although, I am not even certain which Scripture she was reading, or if even she can recall which it was. The woman who hosted the event began to cry and rejoice, as well as others.

Don and I looked at each other puzzled. We said to our host, "What's going on?" Our reply came swiftly, "She is reading from the Bible. The tumor took her sight; she was blind!" Then, Don and I began to rejoice as well. Weeks later, we learned that the doctors were baffled that her tumor had completely disappeared, and this young woman went to Disneyland to enjoy time with her family, including her small children. Wow, my God is an awesome God!

I praise God for Don's obedience to the voice of our God, his hunger for the truth, and his embracing the Holy Spirit so fervently in his walk.

So, what did I learn? Certainly, God does work through the power He placed within us, as defined in Scriptures. In addition, I registered that I had lots more to learn about the born again nature of Jesus Christ within me, and the power of the Holy Spirit enveloping me. Truly, if I am a new creation, I need to understand better who and what I have become through my spiritual rebirth.

I believe you should as well.

Would your life change IF…the Spirit will guide your path?

"There is no such thing as a Holy Spirit."

"If Jesus died for my sins, is that all there is to it?"

"A second coming? Jesus never came to earth the first time."

"I'm going to look into Christianity soon, very soon."

Christianity is true if Jesus lived, died, and resurrected. Why did Jesus have to resurrect from the dead? He paid the penalty for sin with His death. In the establishment of Christianity, why was it necessary for Christ to resurrect?

Realization

In the FOUNDATION Phase, we characterized truth and life's purpose based on truth. The examination showed evidence supporting biblical accuracy and credibility. Founded on overwhelming evidence of Mount Sinai and the Israelite encampment, the FOUNDATION Phase, concluded with a review of God's purpose for humankind, and the Ten Commandments as delivered to Moses and modified later by Jesus Christ in the New Testament. We learned that because of sin, a gap exists between humankind and God the Creator.

In Path Step 4, the SALVATION Phase, we learned the process God requires for the forgiveness of sin. In Path Steps 5 and 6, we examined evidence that verifies the life, death, and resurrection of Jesus Christ, and how He fulfills the New Covenant between God and humankind.

In the final Path Step of the SALVATION Phase, we learned what it means to be saved, what happens to those who are not saved, and the requirements to obtain salvation through Jesus Christ. We will now study the REALIZATION Phase and learn how one can embrace the promises of Christianity, with the renewal and leadership of the Holy Spirit confirmed by Jesus Christ.

PATH STEP 8: THE SPIRIT WILL GUIDE YOUR PATH

The REALIZATION Phase begins with Path Step 8: Spirit Will Guide Your Path.

How is a Christian different from a non-Christian? Most people have heard of the Holy Spirit. If you have accepted Christ as Lord and Savior of your life, does the Holy Spirit communicate with you? Do you have Jesus dwelling within you? When a Christian is "reborn," does he or she receive a new spirit? What does it mean to let the Holy Spirit guide your path? What is baptism in the Holy Spirit?

SPIRIT, SOUL AND BODY

"May God himself, the God of peace, sanctify you through and through. May your whole spirit, soul, and body be kept blameless at the coming of our Lord Jesus Christ." (1 Thessalonians 5:23)

This Scripture says that believers in Jesus Christ, the saved, have a spirit, soul, and body. When the saved receive a new spirit, their born again spirit is free of sin. Sanctification is the progression to conform our soul to our new spirit.

"At the end of your life, you will groan, when your flesh and body are spent." (Proverbs 5:11)

The flesh, our body, is not eternal, but the new spirit of the believer in Jesus Christ is.

"Do not be afraid of those who kill the body but cannot kill the soul. Rather, be afraid of the One who can destroy both soul and body in Hell." (Matthew 10:28)

Two outcomes exist. Our soul will live on with our eternal spirit, or it will be killed by the One who can destroy the soul.

"Jesus answered them, 'Is it not written in your Law, 'I have said you are gods?'" (John 10:34)

When we obtain a born again spirit, we become one with Jesus and God. We resemble Jesus, who resembles God. We are gods because we operate with the authority of man and Jesus, through our new spirit, in Him.

"Then God said, 'Let us make man in our image, in our likeness, and let them rule over the fish of the sea and the birds of the air.'" (Genesis 1:26)

What does God mean by "us" and "our?"

Each of us has a soul and a body. The body perishes and remains in the grave when our time on earth is complete. Our soul remains after we die. Will the soul live for eternity with an everlasting spirit, or it is destroyed in Hell. A true believer in Christianity receives an eternal spirit.

So, what is Christianity?

CHRISTIANITY

Christianity is true if Jesus lived, died, and resurrected. Jesus lived a flawless and sinless life; He was the perfect, unblemished lamb. He died with the sins of many, thus forgiving them of their sins.

Then, why does Christianity need Jesus to resurrect? The answer lies within what happened to Jesus when He resurrected and what happens to His followers the moment they believe.

A definition of Christianity is the belief in Jesus Christ as described in the Bible. To believe in the promise of Jesus as Savior, we have to start at the beginning and then envision the promise of the future.

Christianity is the world's leading religion. Christians believe in Jesus Christ and strive to follow His teachings. Christians believe Jesus is God's son, sent to become human and offer a new covenant for all people. He is human, and God. Jesus is divine. He lived on earth from 2 BC until 33 AD.

Jesus walked the earth, was born a Jew who lived and died in Israel under the Roman rule, in a province the Romans called Palestine. At age 30, He began His ministry, traveling the Palestine region, teaching about God, and spreading a message of God's love, peace, hope, and forgiveness. Jesus performed miracles by healing the sick and feeding the hungry. Jesus gathered a host of followers who were zealous for His teachings.

As His following grew, many of the Jewish religious leaders (Pharisees and Sadducees) became enraged with Him because He threatened their ways and power. Eventually, these Jewish leaders turned Jesus over to the Roman government for they wanted Him killed. The Roman governor of Judea, Pontius Pilate sentenced Jesus to an execution. At Golgotha, the Place of the Skull, just outside the city of Jerusalem, is where they crucified Him. Jesus' burial was in a tomb of a wealthy Jew.

In accordance with Old Testament prophecies, Jesus overcame death. On the third day, the second day after his crucifixion, the day Christians today celebrate Easter, Jesus appeared among His followers as the risen, living Christ, or Messiah. He continued to teach, spreading God's news of redemption for all, sharing the story of His life and resurrection forty days before returning to God in Heaven. The Bible describes His story and teachings in the New Testament. Born again Christians believe that Christ lives inside and amongst them by the power of God's spirit.

Through Jesus, God fulfilled a new foundation for His relationship with humankind. Jesus is a Savior and He is the key to a new relationship and is a means to:

1.   Forgive sin

2.   Be worthy of fellowship with God

We considered that Christianity is true if Jesus lived, died, and resurrected. Jesus lived a sinless life and died as a perfect sin offering for anyone who calls on His name. Jesus' sacrifice removes sin. In addition, He was a Day of Atonement sacrifice to forgive unknown sins, or sins of omission. Then, why did He need to resurrect?

With Jesus as our atoning sacrifice, He forgives our sins. His sacrificial death pays the penalty required by God for our sin. If He forgives our sins, are we worthy of God?

WORTHY OF GOD

God offers a New Covenant for humankind with His divine assistance. The New Covenant and God's laws are in our hearts and minds.

"I will put my law in their minds and write it on their hearts." (Jeremiah 31:33)

We are imperfect beings. Paul tells us that we become perfect with the New Covenant. Consider Christians and non-Christians alike, not one of them is perfect. Then, how is it possible for a man or woman to become perfect?

"His SPIRIT will be UPON them and His words will remain in them." (Isaiah 59:21)

For God, anything is possible. The New Covenant provides us with His divine assistance. Isaiah declares that God's Spirit will be upon us. Is this the divine assistance promised? Yes! God is perfect. If His spirit is in us, are we then perfect?

We established that through Jesus Christ, our sins are forgiven, and we are made worthy to fellowship with God. When Jesus is our Savior, we are changed. Either we receive something or He improves what we already have. Jesus makes us worthy of God!

THE NEW PERFECT COVENANT

The divine assistance of the New Covenant is the Spirit of God.

"And by that will, we have been made holy through the sacrifice of the body of Jesus Christ once for all. Day after day, every priest stands and performs his religious duties; again and again, he offers the same sacrifices, which can never take away sins. But when this priest had offered for all time one sacrifice for sins, he sat down at the right hand of God. Since that time, he waits for his enemies to be made his footstool because by one sacrifice he has made perfect forever those who are being made holy." (Hebrews 10:10-14)

He makes His followers perfect. A perfect covenant, how can this be? How could God make a perfect covenant with imperfect beings? We are sinners and fall short of God's glory. "Perfect" seems garish, but with divine assistance it is not.

When we accept Christ, our "old self "perishes and we are born again. This renewing is a spiritual rebirth. When we accept Christ, the Holy Spirit gives us our new spirit. The Holy Spirit places the spirit of Christ in us; we are made one with Christ. We are born again in the spiritual realm. Now we, individually, are remade in the image of Christ. We become eternal beings. Our spirit is perfect.

If our spirit is born anew and we are with Christ, then we are one with God, because Jesus is one with God. Although our flesh (body) may sin, our born again spirit is perfect like God and cannot sin. He forever linked our new spirit to Himself.

How can God make a perfect covenant with an imperfect being? With Jesus as our Savior, our sin washes away forever. The Holy Spirit gave us our spirit. We are now acceptable to God and perfect, as is He. Our new spirit is perfect because it connects to God and is conformed to the image of Jesus. With a born again perfect spirit, the New Covenant cannot fail.

With our resurrection in Christ, God made the New Covenant with Himself. PERFECT!

BECOME ETERNAL

"And the LORD God said, 'The man has now become like one of us, knowing good and evil. He must not be allowed to reach out his hand and take also from the Tree of Life and eat, and live forever.'" (Genesis 3:22)

Because humankind sinned, God banished humanity from the garden to prevent humankind from eating from the Tree of Life and living forever in a corrupted state. The result, humankind is in a fallen state and would NOT live forever. However, when we accept Jesus Christ, we are reborn with a new spirit. Our new spirit is sinless and righteous in God's eyes. Our new spirit has the mind of God. As we walk this earth, our flesh will continue to sin, but our new spirit in Christ cannot sin. Christ provides a new spirit in us, which is Jesus Christ. When we accept Christ, we have God in us.

While in the flesh (body), we have a choice to accept Jesus Christ as our Savior. The moment we accept Him, we join Him. Our flesh will perish when we die. However, our new spirit lives on with God and Christ for eternity. You become an eternal being when you truly accept Jesus Christ into your heart.

"Therefore, let that abide in you, which you heard from the beginning. If what you heard from the beginning abides in you, you also will abide in the Son and in the Father. And this is the promise that He has promised us—eternal life." (1 John 2:24-27 NKJV)

In the Garden, humankind lost eternity. However, God had a plan for humankind that they may receive "forever." Eternity begins at rebirth by the power of the Holy Spirit!

COMING OF THE HOLY SPIRIT

"Then Jesus came from Galilee to the Jordan to be baptized by John. But John tried to deter him, saying, 'I need to be baptized by you, and do you come to me?' Jesus replied, 'Let it be so now; it is proper for us to do this to fulfill all righteousness.' Then John consented. As soon as Jesus was baptized, he went up out of the water. At that moment, Heaven was opened, and he saw the spirit of God descending like a dove and lighting on him. And a voice from Heaven said, 'This is my Son, whom I love; with him I am well pleased.'" (Matthew 3:13-17)

When Jesus was baptized by John, he was anointed with His mission and purpose by the Holy Spirit.

"But I tell you the truth: It is for your good that I am going away. Unless I go away, the Counselor will not come to you; but if I go, I will send him to you. When he comes, he will convict the world of guilt in regard to sin and righteousness and judgment." (John 16:7-11)

The Holy Spirit would not come until Jesus ascended to Heaven and sent the Spirit.

"He told them, 'This is what is written: The Christ will suffer and rise from the dead on the third day, and repentance and forgiveness of sins will be preached in his name to all nations, beginning at Jerusalem. You are witnesses of these things. I am going to send you what my Father has promised, but stay in the city until you have been clothed with power from on high." (Luke 24:46-49)

The Holy Spirit bestows power from God. Jesus said, He would send the Holy Spirit when He returned to the Father.

"Now the earth was formless and empty, darkness was over the surface of the deep, and the spirit of God was hovering over the waters." (Genesis 1:2)

Two words refer to the spirit, the Hebrew "ruach," and the Greek "pneuma." Ruach occurs approximately 380 times in the Bible and translates to wind or breath. It means to breathe out through the nose with violence. In other words, air or breath that moves.

In the Septuagint (the Greek Old Testament), the Hebrew ruach translated with the Greek word, pneuma approximately 260 times and 50 times as wind. Ruach has many meanings: natural wind, breath of life, temper, disposition, courage, strength, life-giving energy, creating power, overpowering tempests, strength that is beyond the human, and special power of inspiration or enablement. It portrays an idea of violence and power, anything from an impersonal force to a particular person.[1]

Ruach combined with Yahweh, Elohim, or the word with God's spirit specifies a powerful or forceful action of God upon the Universe, an individual, or a group of people (such as the nation of Israel, or the Church-the Body of Christ).

In the New Testament, pneuma occurs approximately 380 times with the idea of wind, breath, human emotions and thought, and the life force of the person, or great power. It comes from the Greek word pneu, meaning a dynamic movement of air: to breathe out, to breathe in, to breathe on, to blow air, blow out, to blow a musical instrument, to inspire, steam, evaporate, radiate, anger, have courage, benevolence, emit fragrance, etc.[2]

Pneuma implies that the air is set in motion—action. Therefore, an inherent power, one that is in the spiritual realm. When referring to God's spirit (approximately 250 times), it indicates activity or action of God or the manifestations that result from the movement of God's spirit.

After the resurrection of Christ, the Holy Spirit is our connection to God and Christ. Upon our belief, the Holy Spirit gives birth to our spirit through Christ.

PURPOSE OF THE SPIRIT

The Holy Spirit has the power of God, and we can receive the power from on high. What is the purpose of the Holy Spirit and what does the Spirit do?

1. Convict the world of sin, righteousness, and judgment

"And when He has come, He will convict the world of sin, and of righteousness, and of judgment: of sin because they do not believe in Me; of righteousness because I go to My Father and you see Me no more; of judgment, because the ruler of this world is judged." (John 16:8-11)

The Holy Spirit convicts us of right and wrong. The closer we are to the Spirit, the closer we are to God's will.

2. Helps us to remember the word of God

"But the Helper, the Holy Spirit, whom the Father will send in My name, He will teach you all things, and bring to your remembrance all things that I said to you." (John 14:26)

God promises in the New Covenant that He would keep His law and words in our hearts and minds. The Holy Spirit, through our new spirit, is the mechanism by which God accomplishes this.

3. Helps us to lead a godly life

"But the fruit (evidence) of the Spirit is love, joy, peace, long-suffering, kindness, goodness, faithfulness, gentleness, self-control. Against such, there is no law." (Galatians 5:22-23)

The fruit of the Spirit allows us to live a transformed life, and to worship and glorify God.

4. Gives us spiritual gifts for the edification of believers

"There are diversities of gifts, but the same spirit. There are differences of ministries, but the same Lord. And there are diversities of activities, but it is the same God who works all in all. But the manifestation of the Spirit is given to each one for the profit of all." (1 Corinthians 12:4-7)

With our new spirits in Christ, we have a purpose in God's Kingdom. He gives us abilities through the spirit. To achieve His calling depends on our decisions and our desire to seek Him.

"Even so, you, since you are zealous for spiritual gifts, let it be for the edification of the church that you seek to excel." (1 Corinthians 14:12)

We should seek to manifest these gifts for strength as a Christian so that when others see the gifts within us, it reveals the nature of God.

"Each one should use whatever gift he has received to serve others, faithfully administering God's grace in its various forms." (1 Peter 4:10)

Just as Jesus served others, we are to use the fruit of the Spirit and spiritual gifts to serve God's kingdom.

5. Empower us to be witnesses for our Lord Jesus Christ

"But when the Helper comes, whom I shall send to you from the Father, the spirit of truth who proceeds from the Father, He will testify of Me." (John 15:26)

The spirit within us will testify to others about Jesus.

"But you shall receive power when the Holy Spirit has come upon you, and you shall be My witnesses in Jerusalem, and in all Judea and Samaria, and to the end of the earth." (Acts 1:8)

Use the Spirit to witness. The Spirit will motivate you in this direction.

"And with great power the apostles gave witness to the resurrection of the Lord Jesus. And great grace was upon them all." (Acts 4:33)

To be born again, the Holy Spirit renewed the apostles so they may perform great works for God's kingdom.

"And my speech and my preaching were not with persuasive words of human wisdom, but in demonstration of the Spirit and of power, that your faith should not be in the wisdom of men but in the power of God." (1 Corinthians 2:4-5)

Paul declares that he did not speak with human wisdom. Rather, he spoke in concert with the spirit of God.

6.   Transform us in the sight of God

"And such were some of you. But you were washed, but you were sanctified, but you were justified in the name of the Lord Jesus and by the spirit of our God." (1 Corinthians 6:11)

The Spirit connects us to Jesus when we are reborn, and it makes us one with Him. We are cleansed from sin. God does not see us in our flesh any longer. After rebirth, He sees our new spirit in Jesus Christ.

7.   Given us our spirit—Our guarantee of eternal life with God

"Now He who establishes us with you in Christ and has anointed us is God, who also has sealed us and given us the spirit in our hearts as a guarantee." (2 Corinthians 1:21-22)

"In Him you also trusted after you heard the word of truth, the gospel of your salvation; in whom also, having believed, you were sealed with the Holy Spirit of promise, who is the guarantee of our inheritance until the redemption of the purchased possession, to the praise of His glory." (Ephesians 1:13-14)

GUARANTEE OF THE HOLY SPIRIT

When one believes in Jesus Christ as Lord and Savior, the Holy Spirit creates in them a new spirit. The new spirit is justified and righteous in God's eyes. God made a covenant with the reborn spirit and promises eternal life. The "new" you, will live forever with God. The reborn spirit is an eternal being.

Is your inheritance of God's kingdom a guarantee? Is it a promise from God for believing in Jesus? When you receive a new spirit, and feel and experience interaction with the new spirit, it is your guarantee of God's promise for salvation and eternity. Since the reborn spirit is eternal, when you receive it you have your guarantee. Your reborn spirit is tangible evidence of God.

Do you have evidence of God? Though our flesh may perish, our spirit will live in fellowship with God after the final judgment. Do you have the Spirit? Do you have your guarantee?

"Those who obey his commands live in him, and he in them. And this is how we know that he lives in us: We know it by the spirit he gave us." (1 John 3:24)

And, what is the evidence you are saved? You need to experience the Holy Spirit, tangibly, given to us by Jesus.

UNIT III: IMPLICATION—PERSONAL MEANING
(CONTINUED FROM PATH STEP 6)

In Path Step 6, we learned the relevance and meaning of the 4th Cup of Passover. The journey splits into four units:

Unit I.   Explanation—Jewish Tradition

Unit II.   Application—Relevance with Jesus

Unit III.   Implication—Personal meaning

Unit IV.   Revelation—Jesus Revealed

We will now conclude the Implication unit and soon examine IV - Revelation in Path Step 9.

SHARED BAPTISM

How do we share baptism with Jesus? Jesus was baptized by John the Baptist in the Jordan River.

"Then Jesus came from Galilee to the Jordan to be baptized by John. But John tried to deter him, saying, 'I need to be baptized by you, and do you come to me?' Jesus replied, 'Let it be so now; it is proper for us to do this to fulfill all righteousness.' Then John consented." (Matthew 3:13-15)

Following His baptism in water, Jesus is baptized in the Holy Spirit from Heaven on High.

"As soon as Jesus was baptized, he went up out of the water. At that moment, Heaven was opened, and he saw the Spirit of God descending like a dove and lighting on him. And a voice from Heaven said, 'This is my Son, whom I love; with him I am well pleased.'" (Matthew 3:16-17)

Can we share either of these baptisms with Jesus Christ? These three verses will enlighten you on this question.

- "I have been crucified with Christ and I no longer live, but Christ lives in me." (Galatians 2:20)

- "We were therefore buried with him through baptism into death in order that, just as Christ was raised from the dead through the glory of the Father, we too may live a new life." (Romans 6:4)

- "Therefore, if anyone is in Christ, he is a new creation; old things have passed away; behold, all things have become new." (2 Corinthians 5:17 NKJV)

Baptism is symbolic of Jesus' death and resurrection—to His glorified state. It also symbolizes receiving a new spirit and the Holy Spirit as Jesus did following His baptism by John. Baptism is death of the "old" person and rebirth of the "new" in Christ. The New Testament comments extensively on this transformation. What does Scripture reveal about the spirit in the believer? The following are verses that define creation, the role, and nature of the born again spirit.

"Do not conform any longer to the pattern of this world but be transformed by the renewing of your mind." (Romans 12:2)

Your spirit renews your mind. Your spirit is perfect. It is like Christ. It thinks like Christ. In time, and with seeking, the spirit can dominate your thinking and actions.

"So then, faith comes by hearing and hearing by the word of God." (Romans 10:17)

The word of God and the Bible behave differently after you accept Jesus and receive your spirit. The Holy Spirit works through your spirit and God's word. Pray for a greater understanding, with intense reading, studying and meditating on His word. It will transform your thinking. Unlike before, the Bible will begin to make sense. You will realize the faith given to you in your spirit.

"I and the Father are one." (John 10:30)

Jesus connects through His Spirit to the father. Jesus declares that He is one with God.

"I have given them the glory that you gave me that they may be one as we are one." (John 17:22)

In the Gospel of John, Jesus states that He shares His spirit with us so that we may be one with Him as He is one with God. When connecting to Jesus, we are connecting to God.

"For you have been born again, not of perishable seed, but of imperishable, through the living and enduring word of God." (1 Peter 1:23)

Our spirits are born again. We learn that the spirit is imperishable and is eternal. Our spirit will live with God forever. What we become in Heaven after accepting Jesus, we have already received.

"Flesh gives birth to the flesh, but the Spirit gives birth to spirit." (John 3:6)

The Holy Spirit births our spirit when we are born again in Christ.

- "By this we know that we abide in Him, and He in us, because He has given us His Spirit. Believers in Christ have the spirit of Jesus in them. They are one with Jesus, recreated in His image for an eternal purpose." (John 3:6)

- "Love has been perfected among us in this: that we may have boldness in the Day of Judgment; because as He is, so are we in this world." (1 John 4:17 NKJV)

These verses are powerful. As Jesus is (right now, not when He walked the earth), so are we in this world. We have the mind, the fruit, and the power of Jesus dwelling within us daily after we have been born again into His spirit.

We will conclude this topic and review with the first verse listed.

"I have been crucified with Christ and I no longer live, but Christ lives in me." (Galatians 2:20)

We undergo baptism as a symbol of Christ's death and rebirth (resurrection). Our new spirit is one with Christ. We are one with Christ.

When we accept Christ, our old self, dies. With a new spirit, we are a new creation, just as Christ at the resurrection. Christ died for the forgiveness of sin, He rose from the dead, and then He was renewed and glorified. When we acknowledge our sinful nature and accept Christ, symbolically we die with Him in baptism. We rise out of the water as if it were an earthen grave; we are a new creation in God. He takes our death. We die with Him and resurrect, are renewed, and made righteous as Jesus in God's eyes.

Many Christians overlook foundational principles described in the Bible. Being born again, having a new spirit where Christ lives inside us, having a life changing experience, and empowerment beyond imagination, is almost inconceivable.

The moment we accepted Jesus as Savior:
Our spirit was reborn in Christ
In our spirit, we are like Christ
Connected one with Christ
For eternity!

Becoming Worthy

Paul referred to the New Covenant as the "Perfect Covenant."

"Because by one sacrifice he has made perfect forever those who are being made holy." (Hebrews 10:14)

To be holy, is to be pure and consecrated for God's purpose.

- "God had planned something better for us so that only together with us would they be made perfect." (Hebrews 11:40)

- "To the church of the firstborn, whose names are written in Heaven. You have come to God, the judge of all men, to the spirits of righteous men made perfect, to Jesus the mediator of a new covenant, and to the sprinkled blood, that speaks a better word than the blood of Abel." (Hebrews 12:23-24)

The Bible states that the New Covenant makes us perfect. However, how are we perfect if we are imperfect beings? We accept the New Covenant and acknowledge our sinful and fallen state. We make a covenant with God. God deposits our spirit and creates in us a new being that is the essence of Christ. We become one with Christ as Christ is one with God.

God makes us perfect with a perfect covenant because He made the covenant with Himself. Under the Old Covenant, man did not ask for divine assistance, so he fell short of God's expectation. Due to man's imperfection, the covenant failed. Under the New Covenant, God made the agreement with Himself; thus the covenant is perfect. God is incapable of fault and imperfection. Since we are one with God, the covenant and the agreement is perfect. It cannot fail.

A Perfect Covenant

By the promises of the perfect covenant, we are made worthy of our God.

Unit IV: Revelation - Jesus Revealed

Sharing The 4th Cup

Jesus celebrated the Passover Feast in the upper room with His disciples. He concluded the feast by drinking the 4th Cup just before he gave up His soul on the cross. At the Last Supper, Jesus Christ told us that He would drink the 4th Cup with us. Following the Third Cup of Passover, Jesus made the statement that He would not drink the fruit of the vine, until a certain time.

"I tell you, I will not drink of this fruit of the vine from now on until that day when I drink it anew with you in my Father's kingdom." (Matthew 26:29)

The following are the stages, exchange, and sharing of the 4th Cup and all that it represents. We will go through the crucifixion and resurrection of Jesus, with a focus of Jesus' sacrifice for each of us. To begin, picture yourself, unsaved, realizing you carry the Cup of God's Wrath in your hand. Next, picture Jesus on the cross at 9:00 a.m. (the 3rd hour) on Nissan 14.

1. Understand what salvation means and the covenant God offers to you through Jesus Christ, the penalty for your sin has not been paid. The wages of sin is death, the soul that sinneth, it shall die. You have earned the Cup of God's Wrath, which you will have to drink when you are judged by God. Before knowing Christ, you carry the Cup of His Wrath with you. Without Jesus, you hold the Cup of God's Wrath in your hand and have the promise of death.

2. "God so loved the world that He gave His only Son that we should have eternal life" (John 3:16). Jesus offers Himself to humankind as a sacrificial substitute. He is without sin and is able to take your sin. He will die with your sin and remove it from existence.

3. You acknowledge your sinful nature and realize the penalty for sin is death. You believe in your heart that Jesus is Lord and call on His name as your Savior. As your Savior, Jesus takes the Cup of God's Wrath from your hand the moment you believe.

4. Jesus is all knowing and omnipresent (see Path Step 9). He reaches through time and takes the Cup of God's Wrath from your hand. He takes this Cup to the cross to fulfill His role and promise as Savior.

5. Before Jesus gave up His spirit, a Roman soldier raised a sour wine-soaked sponge to Jesus' lips. Jesus received the drink. This represents the next time He would drink of this fruit of the vine as promised at the Last Supper in Matthew 26:29. It represented the 4th and concluding Cup of the Passover celebration, the Cup of Redemption and the Cup of God's Wrath.

6. Jesus fulfilled His promise with you as your Savior. The wine, or fruit of the vine, was the Cup of God's Wrath. He took your punishment; He paid the price defined by God for your sin, which is death. At the same moment, Jesus received the Cup of Redemption for you. He drank the Cup of Wrath and Passover Cup of Restoration simultaneously.

7. Jesus took every sin you had ever committed up to the moment of your belief in Him, and every sin you will ever commit in life, here on earth. As the sin offering, all of your sins transferred to Him, and then He paid the ultimate price, once for all time.

8. Jesus received the Cup of Restoration and He was born anew, and then God resurrected Him.

9. By His resurrection, Jesus received a glorified body and spirit. "By this he meant the Spirit, whom those who believed in him were later to receive. Up to that time the Spirit had not been given since Jesus had not yet been glorified." (John 7:39) This verse reveals that prior to His resurrection, Jesus had not been glorified. The resurrection made Him anew.

10. "You cannot drink the cup of the Lord and the cup of demons too; you cannot have a part in both the Lord's table and the table of demons. Paul refers to the believer's drinking the Cup of the Lord, or the Cup of Christ. After propitiating your sin, Jesus made you righteous and justified. He shared with you His cup, or the Cup of Christ.

11. Receiving the Cup of Christ when you first believe, your old self perishes and you are born again, anew. You transform as an eternal spirit unified to Jesus Christ, sharing His resurrection. In your spirit, you are perfect and reconcile to your God (Hebrews 10:14).

12. With Jesus Christ as part of your new spirit, you became worthy of God and a fundamental component of God's Kingdom.

13. When you believe in your heart that Jesus is Lord and confess Him as your Savior, it connects you to God and Christ through the counsel and guidance of the Holy Spirit with your new spirit in Christ.

Beyond the parallels of the 4th Cup of the first and second Passovers, does Scripture provide enlightenment of this process? Yes!

It's Personal

Jesus offered himself as a sacrifice for all of humankind's sins, but not everyone will accept Him. We know some will perish (see Path Step 7). He did not die to save the sins of the church. It requires a personal decision to accept Jesus and the Holy Spirit; He died for all that would accept Him. With the 4th Cup, it is a sacrifice that has a personal meaning. If you were the only person to ask Him to be Savior, still Jesus would have sacrificed himself and received the 4th Cup 2,000 years ago. On a personal basis, you can state the following:

- Jesus heard and saw me **independently** accepting Jesus as Savior and asking Him to be my personal lamb sacrifice.

- He took all of my sins, **specifically** those I have already committed and those I have not.

- He drank **personally** the Cup of Restoration, 4th Cup—He restored me when I first believed, made me accepted by my God.

- He accepted from my hand and drank the Cup of God's Wrath for me **singularly**, the 4th Cup—to take my punishment.

- He gave up His spirit and died with my sins **completely**.

He shared the 4th Cup with me individually, independently, specifically, personally, singularly, and completely. With Jesus, it is personal!

Shared Baptism

"You will drink the cup I drink and be baptized with the baptism I am baptized with." (Mark 10:39)

When considering the Cup of Restoration, we share a life with Jesus. By the 4th Cup, we are restored to fellowship with God. Our rebirth connects us to Jesus with a new eternal spirit.

We also share His death. Through baptism, we are crucified with Jesus. We lose our old self and are reborn (resurrected) anew. The following are two verses in the shared baptism Phase.

- "I have been crucified with Christ and I no longer live, but Christ lives in me." (Galatians 2:20)

- "We were therefore buried with him through baptism into death in order that, just as Christ was raised from the dead through the glory of the Father, we too may live a new life." (Romans 6:4)

- Our old self dies, just as Christ died on the cross. He drank the Cup of God's Wrath for us.

- Being submerged symbolizes when Christ was buried, before He rose from the dead.

- We receive a new life when we rise from the water, just as Christ rose from the dead, and exited the tomb with a gloried body.

Anyone who calls on Jesus as Savior was raised with Him on the third day of the crucifixion. He lives in us and He restored us some 2,000 years ago.

"After two days He will revive us; On the third day He will raise us up, That we may live in His sight." (Hosea 6:2)

We share in Jesus' death and His life, in His baptism. We are anew with Jesus in His baptism.

SPIRIT AND YOU

The moment of Jesus' crucifixion, which was at 3:00 p.m. on April 3, 33 AD, the curtain separating the holy place from the Most Holy Place in the temple of Jerusalem, tore from top to bottom. God's residence on earth ceased to be the most holy. God left the most holy, He no longer compartmentalized with the Jews. He no longer connected with man in one location. Under His new and perfect covenant, God lives in the hearts of those who believe in the resurrection of Jesus Christ. The divine assistance promised in the New Covenant is the new spirit in Christ that exists in each of His followers.

By grace, He gives the Cup of Christ; this is eternal life in a new spirit and fellowship with God through Christ. If we seek it, our new spirit gives us the fruit of the Spirit found in Galatians 5:22-23: love, joy, peace, patience, kindness, goodness, faithfulness, gentleness, and self-control. This is evidence of the Holy Spirit in a believer's life.

- "Love has been perfected among us in this: that we may have boldness in the Day of Judgment; because as He is, so are we in this world." (1 John 4:17 NKJV)

- "The thief does not come except to steal, and to kill, and to destroy. I have come that they may have life and that they may have it more abundantly." (John 10:10 NKJV)

- "And this is eternal life that they may know You, the only true God, and Jesus Christ whom You have sent." (John 17:3)

The New Covenant offers a supernatural existence. You become an eternal being, and are in fellowship with God for eternity. With salvation, we have Jesus living inside us, we have the fruit of the Spirit, and the power that Jesus has in His risen state. Also, the same power that raised Jesus from the dead resides in us if we are born again. This is powerful and life changing!

"And if the Spirit of him who raised Jesus from the dead is living in you, he who raised Christ from the dead will also give life to your mortal bodies through his Spirit, who lives in you." (Romans 8:11)

Many people profess to believe in Christ, but are not aware that their spirit has been born in Jesus. They believe that the Holy Spirit comes and goes. Many Christian prayers center on asking God to send His Holy Spirit to us. God is within all who are saved. We do not need to call or summon Him. If we do not sense His presence, it is because we have taken our focus off Him, and choose to walk under our own power and authority. Your new spirit is always with you, it connects you to Christ, and is one with Christ as Christ is one with God. When we talk with God, we may get intuitions, voices, whispers, etc., it derives through our new spirit. **An ambition for every Christian should be to pierce and enlarge the opening between the physical and the spirit realms.**

"Do not conform any longer to the pattern of this world but be transformed by the renewing of your mind." (Romans 12:2)

When we renew our minds, we gain access to our eternal spirit and are transformed.

"So then, faith comes by hearing and hearing by the word of God." (Romans 10:17)

We renew our minds by reading, studying, and meditating on the Word of God. The Bible is a living document, and it takes on new meaning to the believer. As you read, you renew your mind; you will have a greater sense and understanding of the Holy Spirit.

Following Christ necessitates change. The testament of Jesus, biblical records, and testimonies, all call out to you. You must respond. The spirit will live in you only with your invitation.

Have you invited Jesus into your life?

Accept Christ—Accept The Spirit

When we accept Christ, He shares His eternal spirit. He does not want us to live as if nothing has changed. By His grace, we receive eternal fellowship with Him. His intent was for us to live our lives connected to Jesus, live as Jesus did while He walked the earth. We are an example of Christ by connecting with our new spirit. How do we connect with our new spirit in Christ?

- Accept Christ into your heart as your Savior. Be born again in the Spirit. The Holy Spirit will create in you an eternal spirit. It will communicate to you through your new spirit.

- Repent—turn from your sinful ways. Recognize the sin. Change your behavior. Remove the sin.

- Regularly read the Bible. Renew your mind. Let the Holy Spirit teach you. The Bible is the truth about God; He communicates and teaches His children.

- Regularly pray and talk to God. Open a conversation with Him. Pray to Him. It does not have to be formal. Involve God into your day. Tell Him your plans. Ask him to bless your endeavors in the name of Jesus, your Savior. Thank Him for all you have been given.

- In prayer, ask God to baptize you in His Spirit and anoint you with spiritual blessings and gifts.

- Ask God for guidance on everything you do.

- LISTEN for an answer! It may be an intuition, a feeling, a whisper, or a voice. This may take time to understand. When you seek God, He will reveal himself to you and you will become accustomed to His communication—random thoughts and your flesh.

- Evaluate and test the communication. Ask God to reveal Himself to you in new ways, perhaps a voice, a new intuition, in a dream, through another person or group of people. Learn who God is and how He moves. Soon, it will become a commonplace to you.

As a new creation in Christ, you will live in the Spirit that is in you!

Spirit, Soul And Body—Revisited

When we receive salvation from Jesus Christ, we receive a new spirit in Christ. When we are born, we receive only a soul and a body. When we are born again in Jesus, we receive a perfect spirit, as shown in Figure 98. Our body or "flesh" lives by the rules of the world. What we see, hear, feel, smell, and taste dictate what we believe as the truth.

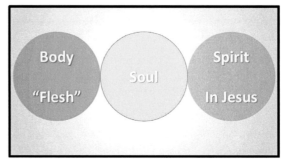

FIG 98

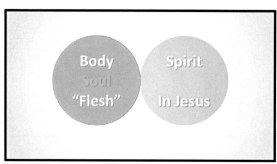

FIG 99

As shown in figure 99, without a spirit our body and soul co-mingle. Our flesh governs our soul with the rules of the world.

We learned in Path Step 3 that the fallen angel, Satan, is in control of this world. The orange circle represents the entanglement, or overlap of our flesh and soul. This is our reliance in the physical realm, where the enemy rules.

"For what the law could not do in that it was weak through the flesh, God did by sending His own Son in the likeness of sinful flesh, on account of sin: He condemned sin in the flesh that the righteous requirement of the law might be fulfilled in us who do not walk according to the flesh but according to the Spirit. For those who live according to the flesh set their minds on the things of the flesh, but those who live according to the Spirit, the things of the Spirit." (Romans 8:3-5 NKJV)

If this world controls you, it also controls your flesh. Living by our senses, we are living in the flesh. When we receive our new spirit, it never overlaps with the flesh; therefore, they are mutually exclusive.

If you live according to the Spirit, your views and mind are set on things of the Spirit. We learned that the Spirit world is the true existence. Our flesh and soul are imperfect, unlike our spirit (See Figure 100). Until death, one who has received salvation and a new spirit will have a battle raging inside them. The flesh and Spirit are competing for the soul as depicted in Figure 100.

When we succumb to our bodily desires, our soul is ensnared by our flesh. When we study the Word of God, strengthen our faith, and seek the Lord Jesus, the soul overlaps to a greater degree with the spirit. Moving our soul closer to our spirit is the life-long process of sanctification. The goal of every Christian should be to overlap their soul and spirit, disregard the urges of their flesh and realize their purpose set by God.

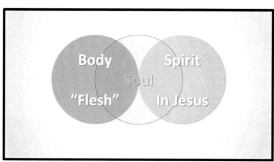

FIG 100

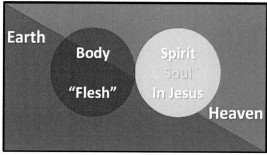

FIG 101

As shown in Figure 101, when a saved Christian dies, their body rests in the grave as defined in Path Step 7. Regardless of the type of death (we may be burned, dismembered, crushed, consumed, etc.), the remains of the flesh reside on earth. However, the soul of the saved and his or her born again spirit goes to Heaven immediately following their death.

Do you ever get your body back? The answer is yes. Just as Christ received a gloried body as He resurrected, so will the saved Christian.

"Listen, I tell you a mystery: We will not all sleep, but we will all be changed - in a flash, in the twinkling of an eye, at the last trumpet. For the trumpet will sound, the dead will be raised imperishable, and we will be changed. For the perishable must clothe itself with the imperishable and the mortal with immortality." (1 Corinthians 15:51-53)

FIG 102

FIG 103

Believers and their resurrected bodies rise into the clouds to meet Jesus and to escort Him back to the earth (See Figure 102). At, the second coming of Christ, our bodies rise from death in a glorified state, and they merge with our soul and our eternal spirit (See Figure 103).

Our perfect body and spirit will guide our soul into eternity. Though Jesus was the first to resurrect and rise to Heaven, we share eternity with Him. Our spirit will connect like His. We will have a glorified body with features as His, and we will become just like Him.

"Then God said, 'Let us make man in our image, in our likeness, and let them rule over the fish of the sea and the birds of the air.'" (Genesis 1:26)

Asked earlier, what does "us" and "our," mean? God is will and decision, not equivalent but similar to our soul. Jesus is the body, the manifestation of God in flesh. The Holy Spirit is the spiritual representation of God. If we have a spirit, soul, and glorified body, we are the image of God who is the Father, the Son, and the Holy Spirit. This is what God intended when He stated, "Let us make man in our image." Remember, before the foundations of the world, God predetermined that those called would be conformed to the image of His son, Jesus Christ. We are not completed in the image of God until we are glorified in Jesus.

The "Last" Adam

"So it is written: 'The first man Adam became a living being'; the last Adam, a life-giving spirit." (1 Corinthians 15:45) Adam sinned and is responsible for the fall of humankind. With His perfect sinless life and sacrifice, Jesus overcame the sin legacy left by Adam.

Why does Paul refer to Jesus as an "Adam" in 1 Corinthians?

Adam of Genesis is a father to all humankind. Each human being is a sinner and has a sinful nature. We received our DNA and sinful nature from the first Adam. The genetics of every human being is rooted in Adam since we descended from him. We share his nature and his body.

Is it appropriate that Paul refers to Jesus as another Adam? All humans follow in Adam's nature and share his body. Do all humans share in Jesus' nature and in His body? No! Then, why is Jesus the "second" Adam? When we accept Jesus Christ as Savior and are born again with His Spirit, we receive His nature and body. With His new Spirit in us, we become one with Christ.

"I have been crucified with Christ and I no longer live, but Christ lives in me. The life I live in the body, I live by faith in the Son of God, who loved me and gave himself for me." (Galatians 2:20)

As the first Adam, followers of Jesus Christ have the DNA of Jesus Christ in them, and His sinless nature. As we are perfect in Him, there is no need for another Adam. Jesus is the "last" Adam.

Faith, Belief, And Knowing

In Path Step 1, we considered Truth. We developed a scale that could help us to learn and evaluate Truth (REJECT, THINK, BELIEVE, and KNOW). Depending on the facts and information supporting a notion, we might find ourselves rejecting, thinking, believing, or knowing the Truth. Scientific concepts such as the Big Bang Theory and the Theory of Evolution are unproven. Neither is based on overwhelming evidence. By our scale, we cannot know they are Truth. However, many think or believe them to be Truth. Evidence goes only so far and leaves a gap between theory and reality.

To support these notions one must make a leap of faith. They must build a bridge of their beliefs, to reach over the gap that exists between evidence and fact. They build a bridge on their faith that their notion is correct. In some cases, the testimony supporting the truth is only their faith. In other cases, faith in a belief or notion is rewarded later with evidence that moves the theory into truth.

To believe, we must have evidence to build a foundation. It may not be indisputable proof, but it is foundational and compelling. To know, tangible evidence must exist to confirm the notion. So, how does faith play a role in this process? Let us consider Christianity.

The following diagrams will help illustrate this point. Before we believe in God and Jesus, we lack information. The gap separates us from knowing the evidence (Diagram 1). To believe, we must take a leap of faith with little to support us. Often, this leap will fall short. However, by seeking, learning, and experiencing, we build our understanding and faith. Faith allows us to develop a relationship with God and Jesus (Diagram 2).

With a relationship based on faith, the Bible will take on new meaning. The chapters and verses will also take on a new meaning with spiritual discernment. We gain a greater understanding as our comprehension grows. We gain insight into God's purpose, salvation, and fellowship with God. However, it is only with a solid grounding or foundation that we have faith in our eternal salvation and fellowship (Diagram 3).

To some, faith is an obstacle that lacks credible verification. By seeking the foundation, connecting the dots of Christianity (your own Rational Path), believing in the promise of the Holy Spirit and renewal from the Bible, God and His Spirit will dwell within you (Diagram 4). Have strong faith, truly seek and ask for guidance.

A new realm opens when you experience the Holy Spirit and believe in God's promises in the Bible. Connecting to God through our new spirit gives us tangible evidence of God, the Bible, and Truth. Faith that God exists is no longer an obstacle because you have a tangible relationship with validation (Diagram 5).

By having a tangible relationship with the Spirit, we know that God and Jesus are Truth (Diagram 6). Because of our tangible relationship with God, we have a foundation from which to have faith in the promise of redemption, salvation, and eternal fellowship (Diagram 7).

In the scientific world, with the burden of theory and proof, there is no knowing without faith and no faith without knowing. You cannot believe something is true unless you take a leap of faith,

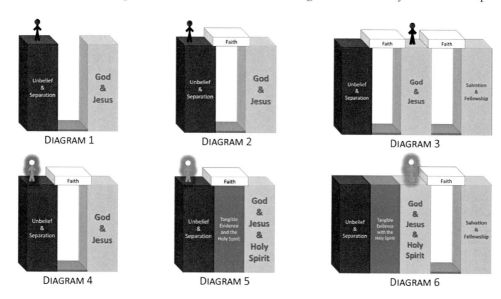

though it is unproven. Further, one cannot have faith in a theory unless there is a solid, tangible foundation of truths. In the days of ancient mariners, those who believed the world was round rather than flat took a leap of faith to circumnavigate the globe. Based on the common notion that the world was flat, they should have fallen over the edge, but they did not because of their theory and faith.

Whether it is faith in God and Jesus, or faith in salvation and eternal fellowship, faith begins after taking the FIRST STEP! One must find a solid and tangible foundation of credible information, such as A Rational Path to Christ (Diagram 8). From there, make the leap of faith (Diagram 9). God took human form, was tortured, died in your place, and He placed in you a tangible spirit that is one with Him so you may fellowship into eternity with Him.

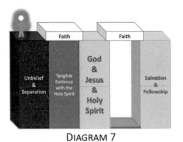
DIAGRAM 7

DIAGRAM 8

DIAGRAM 9

There are nine Path Steps on A Rational Path to Christ. It takes only one step to begin following Him!

Baptism In The Holy Spirit

Three Baptisms

We defined earlier, in Path Step 7, to be baptized means to be immersed within.

The New Testament defines three baptisms.

1. Baptized into Jesus

It is a new day. You have changed. You received Jesus Christ as your Savior and are born again anew in Him. A new spirit is in you, that is you, but born again into the Spirit of Jesus. You are now an important and integral part of a greater existence. You are part of the Body of Christ.

"My prayer is not for them alone. I pray also for those who will believe in me through their message, that all of them may be one, Father, just as you are in me and I am in you. May they also be in us so that the world may believe that you have sent me. I have given them the glory that you gave me, that they may be one as we are one: I in them and you in me. May they be brought to complete unity to let the world know that you sent me and have loved them even as you have loved me." (John 17:20-23)

We are one with Jesus, just as He is one with God. After we believed and asked and welcomed Jesus into our hearts, we were changed. We have been brought into complete unity.

Changed…brought into unity…by who or what? How did this happen? We get a clue from how Jesus was raised from the dead.

"But you are not in the flesh but in the Spirit, if indeed the Spirit of God dwells in you. Now if anyone does not have the Spirit of Christ, he is not His. And if Christ is in you, the body is dead because of sin, but the spirit is life because of righteousness. But if the Spirit of Him who raised Jesus from the dead dwells in you, He who raised Christ from the dead will also give life to your mortal bodies through His Spirit who dwells in you." (Romans 8:9-11)

The "Spirit of Him" is the Holy Spirit. The Holy Spirit raised Jesus from the dead. Jesus did not do it of Himself. We have a triune God in the Trinity: the Father, the Son, and the Holy Spirit. And, each has a role to play in the Kingdom and in eternity, but as one. In Romans 8:11 we learn that the Holy Spirit raised Jesus from the dead in the tomb.

"And God raised us up with Christ and seated us with him in the heavenly realms in Christ Jesus, in order that in the coming ages he might show the incomparable riches of his grace, expressed in his kindness to us in Christ Jesus." (Ephesians 2:6-7)

Despite recognition that we have a triune God, Jesus did not raise himself from the dead. Ephesians describes that we were raised up with Christ. Therefore, we were raised just as Jesus was raised. As born again believers, we were raised by the Holy Spirit in Jesus Christ from our fallen state to eternal life. The verse below validates this reality.

"For we were all baptized by one Spirit into one body—whether Jews or Greeks, slave or free—and we were all given the one spirit to drink." (1 Corinthians 12:13)

1 Corinthians captures the mechanism. One spirit baptized us into one body. In other words, the Holy Spirit baptized us into our new spirits in Jesus, and we became the Body of Christ. The Holy Spirit delivered to us our new spirit in Jesus Christ. Hence, we are born again. We are immersed in Jesus.

Baptism 1 - Summary: The Holy Spirit baptizes us into Jesus Christ.

2. Baptized into Water

The Gospel of Matthew records the final words of Jesus before he arose to Heaven. The religious community in general has termed the following statement by Jesus the "Great Commission".

"Then Jesus came to them and said, 'All authority in Heaven and on earth has been given to me. Therefore go and make disciples of all nations, baptizing them in the name of the Father and of the Son and of the Holy Spirit, and teaching them to obey everything I have commanded you. And surely I am with you always, to the very end of the age.'" (Matthew 28:18-20)

Jesus commands His disciples to go make disciples baptizing them in the name of the Father, and of the Son and of the Holy Spirit. He commanded disciples to baptize disciples, and so on. A priest or official ordained by humankind is not required in order to baptize new believers in water. A disciple of Jesus may baptize one that he or she is training to be a disciple.

- "We were therefore buried with him through baptism into death in order that, just as Christ was raised from the dead through the glory of the Father, we too may live a new life. If we have been united with him like this in his death, we will certainly also be united with him in his resurrection. For we know that our old self was crucified with him so that the body of sin might be done away with, that we should no longer be slaves to sin—because anyone who has died has been freed from sin." (Romans 6:4-7)

- "I baptize you with water for repentance. But after me will come one who is more powerful than I, whose sandals I am not fit to carry. He will baptize you with the Holy Spirit and with fire." (Matthew 3:11)

Water Baptism is immersive (see Path Step 7). It is symbolic of dying and being buried, and then rising again as you surface from under water. Romans 6 refers to the crucifixion and death of our old self. The repentance decreed in Matthew 3 is the turning away from the sin nature, or "old man." Many believe the death of the old man is symbolic, while others believe that their sin nature died along with their sin on the cross with Jesus Christ nearly 2,000 years ago. Bible scholars debate whether the old man died at the moment of water baptism or at the moment of salvation.

In either case, Jesus commands a water baptism. We are immersed in water.

Baptism 2 - Summary: A disciple baptizes us in water.

3. Baptized in the Holy Spirit

"I baptize you with water for repentance. But after me will come one who is more powerful than I, whose sandals I am not fit to carry. He will baptize you with the Holy Spirit and with fire." (Matthew 3:11)

Matthew declares that the one coming after Him, more powerful than him, will baptize you with the Holy Spirit. Who is the He that will do the baptizing? Let us investigate the other Gospels.

"I would not have known him, except that the one who sent me to baptize with water told me, 'The man on whom you see the Spirit come down and remain is he who will baptize with the Holy Spirit.'" (John 1:33)

In each of the Gospels, we learn that John the Baptist baptizes Jesus in water and apart from Jesus receiving water baptism, the Holy Spirit comes down and rests upon Jesus. At this moment, Jesus was baptized in the Holy Spirit, and the Holy Spirit remained upon Him. "The man on whom you see the Spirit come down" was Jesus. Necessarily, Jesus then is "He who will baptize with the Holy Spirit."

This statement is definitive in that Jesus is the one baptizing, not the Holy Spirit. An important statement indeed. Is it possible that the Gospel writers above mixed the subject and object of the statement? Should it be saying that the Holy Spirit will be baptizing us in Jesus?

"I baptize you with water, but He will baptize you with the Holy Spirit." (Mark 1:8)

Here again, He (Jesus) will baptize you with the Holy Spirit.

"John answered them all, 'I baptize you with water. But one more powerful than I will come, the thongs of whose sandals I am not worthy to untie. He will baptize you with the Holy Spirit and with fire.'" (Luke 3:16)

He (Jesus) will baptize you with the Holy Spirit and with fire. Jesus will baptize you in the Holy Spirit, in this verse with the addition of fire (power). Jesus does the baptizing and the Holy Spirit is what is received.

For those trained in grammatical construction, it is obvious that the four Gospels agree Jesus is the object in the declaration; the Holy Spirit is the subject. We are immersed in the Holy Spirit.

Baptism 3 - Summary: Jesus baptizes us in the Holy Spirit.

The Baptisms

Baptism 1	Summary: The Holy Spirit baptizes us into Jesus Christ.
Baptism 2	Summary: A disciple baptizes us in water.
Baptism 3	Summary: Jesus baptizes us in the Holy Spirit.

The Table below lists the three baptisms described by Scriptures. Theologically and grammatically, these three baptisms are separate and distinct. As we will review just ahead, these are three separate events as recounted in the book of Acts. Although, two or more of these baptisms may occur simultaneously depending on the circumstances and context of the believer's journey. The Table below shows that the three baptisms differ in the baptizer and media. The three baptisms are separate and distinct.

Baptism	Baptizer	Medium (In What?)	Baptized
1	Holy Spirit	Spirit of Jesus, Divine Nature	Believer
2	Disciple	Water, Old Man Dies	Believer
3	Jesus	Holy Spirit, Fire & Power	Believer

When we believe, the Holy Spirit raises up our spirit in Jesus Christ.

The Holy Spirit baptizes us into the Body of Christ. Jesus did not raise Himself; nor did or do we.

Then, a disciple of Jesus baptizes us in water, symbolizing the burial and resurrection of Christ. Here it is believed by many based on Scripture that the sin nature of the believer, the old man dies.

After one believes, Jesus intercedes for us and baptizes us into the Holy Spirit. Next, let us review the intercession of Jesus Christ.

Jesus, Our Intercessor

What is an intercessor? One who acts or interposes on behalf of someone in difficulty or trouble, as by pleading or petition, or one who attempts to reconcile differences between two people or groups; mediator.

- "Therefore he is able to save completely those who come to God through him, because he always lives to intercede for them." (Hebrews 7:25)

- "Who is he that condemns? Christ Jesus, who died—more than that, who was raised to life—is at the right hand of God and is also interceding for us." (Romans 8:34)

After Jesus ascended into Heaven, He took His place at the right hand of God to intercede for us. The two verses above make this clear. Further, we learn that Jesus received all authority, both in Heaven and on earth.

- "And Jesus came and spoke to them, saying, 'All authority has been given to Me in Heaven and on earth.'" (Matthew 28:18)

- "However, when He, the Spirit of truth, has come, He will guide you into all truth; for He will not speak on His own authority, but whatever He hears He will speak; and He will tell you things to come. He will glorify Me, for He will take of what is Mine and declare it to you." (John 16:13-14 NKJV)

Of the Trinity, Jesus has all authority in Heaven and on earth, according to Matthew.

The verse from John 16 above records Jesus' words. He shares that the Holy Spirit will take of what is His (Jesus'). Jesus also tells us that the Holy Spirit will not operate in His own authority. Though we have a triune God in the Trinity of God the Father, Jesus Christ the Son, and the Holy Spirit, each of the Trinity has a role to play. Here we can see that Jesus sits at the right hand of God with authority and intercedes for us with God. The Holy Spirit submits to the command of Jesus. This is an important biblical fact.

"Now if we are children, then we are heirs—heirs of God and co-heirs with Christ, if indeed we share in his sufferings in order that we may also share in his glory." (Romans 8:17)

We are co-heirs with Jesus. We cannot do anything through the Trinity unless we and Jesus agree. When we ask to be baptized in the Holy Spirit, Jesus intercedes for us. Jesus then baptizes us in the Holy Spirit, as the Holy Spirit is submitted to the authority of Jesus. Jesus desires that we be baptized in the Holy Spirit. We are co-heirs, and we agree.

The result; when we ask Jesus to baptize us in the Holy Spirit, He baptizes us in the Holy Spirit.

The Baptisms of Jesus and the Book of Acts

Jesus is our example.

"Then Jesus said to his disciples, 'If anyone would come after me, he must deny himself and take up his cross and follow me.'" (Matthew 16:24)

How do we follow Jesus?

"Or don't you know that all of us who were baptized into Christ Jesus were baptized into his death? We were therefore buried with him through baptism into death in order that, just as Christ was raised from the dead through the glory of the Father, we too may live a new life." (Romans 6:3-4)

We need to understand how Jesus was baptized.

- Jesus had His perfect, righteous spirit; at birth, He was holy and blameless

- He was water baptized

- He was baptized in the Holy Spirit

1. Jesus was born divine and human. He was the Son of God and the Son of Man. From birth, He had the divine nature. He had all the fruit of the divine Spirit within Him.

"But the fruit of the Spirit is love, joy, peace, patience, kindness, goodness, faithfulness, gentleness and self-control. Against such things there is no law." (Galatians 5:22-23)

Though in His first thirty years Jesus did not walk in the miraculous, He did embrace and embody the divine nature as defined in Galatians.

Clearly, Jesus was born into the nature of Jesus.

2. Jesus was water baptized by John the Baptist, and God baptized Him in the Holy Spirit.

"Then Jesus came from Galilee to the Jordan to be baptized by John. But John tried to deter him, saying, 'I need to be baptized by you, and do you come to me?' Jesus replied, 'Let it be so now; it is proper for us to do this to fulfill all righteousness.' Then John consented. As soon as Jesus was baptized, he went up out of the water. At that moment Heaven was opened, and he saw the Spirit of God descending like a dove and lighting on him. And a voice from Heaven said, 'This is my Son, whom I love; with him I am well pleased.'" (Matthew 3:13-17)

Clearly, in Matthew, as well as in Mark and Luke, Jesus was water baptized.

3. Immediately following Jesus' water baptism, Jesus was baptized in the Holy Spirit. As noted above in Matthew, after Jesus was water baptized, He came up out of the water. Then, the Spirit of God descended upon Jesus.

At this moment, the ministry commenced of Jesus, the Christ, the Messiah. The New Testament records Jesus speaking and walking in power and authority. He turned water into wine, healed the sick, cleansed the lepers and raised the dead, among a host of other spectacular feats. He preached the coming kingdom of God. The power of the Holy Spirit was evident in the Son of both God and Man.

Baptism in the Holy Spirit – The Early Church

The book of Acts is perhaps the best record of the "acts" of the early Christian body of believers. Before Jesus ascended and departed, He commanded His disciples not to depart and to wait for the promise of the Father.

"On one occasion, while he was eating with them, he gave them this command: 'Do not leave Jerusalem, but wait for the gift my Father promised, which you have heard me speak about. For John baptized with water, but in a few days you will be baptized with the Holy Spirit.'" (Acts 1:4-5)

The gift God the Father promised is the baptism of the Holy Spirit.

"God has raised this Jesus to life, and we are all witnesses of the fact. Exalted to the right hand of God, he has received from the Father the promised Holy Spirit and has poured out what you now see and hear." (Acts 2:32-33)

Jesus told His disciples to await the promise of the Holy Spirit. In Acts 2, we learn that Jesus received the promise of the Holy Spirit, which we learned earlier rested upon Him like a dove. Only after receiving the promise did Jesus walk in power and miracles.

Many Christians believe that the promised Holy Spirit was intended only for those present at Pentecost, as described in Acts 1 and 2. They might claim, "The gifting and power of God was given through the Holy Spirit only to those present to activate the Christian church and call attention to Jesus." They believe the promise was given only to the 120. However, Scripture in Acts appears to disagree.

"Peter replied, 'Repent and be baptized, every one of you, in the name of Jesus Christ for the forgiveness of your sins. And you will receive the gift of the Holy Spirit. The promise is for you and your children and for all who are far off—for all whom the Lord our God will call.'" (Acts 2:38-39)

Verse 39 states explicitly that the promise is for those present, and their children, and for all far off and for whom the Lord will call. This means that all Christians are entitled to the promise of God; the gift of the Holy Spirit.

Acts 2:38-39 offers additional guidance with regard to the Holy Spirit. Peter declares that we should repent, be baptized, and then we will receive the Holy Spirit. Below is the Table summarizing the three baptisms syncing with the three commands of Acts 2:38.

Baptism	Baptizer	Medium	Baptized	Acts 2:38
1	Holy Spirit	Spirit of Jesus, Divine Nature	Believer	Repent
2	Disciple	Water, "Old Man" Dies	Believer	Be Baptized
3	Jesus	Holy Spirit, Fire & Power	Believer	Receive H.S.

"But when they believed Philip as he preached the good news of the kingdom of God and the name of Jesus Christ, they were baptized, both men and women. Simon himself believed and was baptized. And he followed Philip everywhere, astonished by the great signs and miracles he saw. When the apostles in Jerusalem heard that Samaria had accepted the word of God, they sent Peter and John to them. When they arrived, they prayed for them that they might receive the Holy Spirit, because the Holy Spirit had not yet come upon any of them; they had simply been baptized into the name of the Lord Jesus. Then Peter and John placed their hands on them, and they received the Holy Spirit. When Simon saw that the Spirit was given at the laying on of the apostles' hands, he offered them money and said, 'Give me also this ability so that everyone on whom I lay my hands may receive the Holy Spirit.' Peter answered: 'May your money perish with you, because you thought you could buy the gift of God with money!'" (Acts 8:12-20)

In this passage, Phillip was in Samaria. While there, many accepted Jesus as Savior and were baptized, both men and women. Next, Acts 8 states when the apostle heard that Samaria had received Christ, they sent John and Peter, established apostles and disciples. The Samaritans had already been born again in Christ and water baptized. They had already realized the first two baptisms, as defined herein. Yet, in verse 15, it is distinct the Holy Spirit had not come to any them, and Peter and John remedied the shortcoming by the laying on of hands.

As noted above, Samaria had accepted the Word of God. They believed. Only after the apostles arrived did they lay hands on the Samaritans so they might receive the Holy Spirit. Further, the apostles prayed for them because the Holy Spirit had not yet come upon any of them. Not even one of the Samaritans who had received the word of God had received the baptism of the Holy Spirit before the arrival of the apostles. Clearly, as accounted in Acts 8, receiving Christ as Savior is a separate and distinct event from being baptized in the Holy Spirit. These verses in Chapter 8 indicate persuasively for three baptisms, including baptism in the Holy Spirit.

The book of Acts offers additional support for the baptism of the Holy Spirit.

"While Apollos was at Corinth, Paul took the road through the interior and arrived at Ephesus. There he found some disciples and asked them, 'Did you receive the Holy Spirit when you believed?' They answered, 'No, we have not even heard that there is a Holy Spirit.' So Paul asked, 'Then what baptism did you receive?'' 'John's baptism,' they replied. Paul said, 'John's baptism was a baptism of repentance. He told the people to believe in the one coming after him, that is, in Jesus.' On hearing this, they were baptized into the name of the Lord Jesus. When Paul placed his hands on them, the Holy Spirit came on them, and they spoke in tongues and prophesied. There were about twelve men in all." (Acts 19:1-7)

In Acts 19, Paul arrives in Ephesus and finds disciples. A disciple is one who believes in Jesus and has a spiritual understanding of elements of the Word of God and the Gospel sufficient to lead others to a relationship with Jesus Christ, and to further their growth and relationship with Jesus. Why would Paul ask them if they received the Holy Spirit? Did not they receive the Holy Spirit when they accepted Christ as Savior? The disciples answers are enlightening. Even though they had already been born again in Jesus, they replied, "No, we have not even heard that there is a Holy

Spirit." After a discussion of John the Baptist's baptism of repentance, they were water baptized into Jesus. To complete the three baptisms, Paul then laid hands upon them and the Holy Spirit came upon them. The disciples speaking in tongues and prophesying is strong evidence that they received the Holy Spirit.

The baptisms of Jesus, the 120 at Pentecost, the Samaritans and the disciples at Ephesus bear strong testimony that the New Testament proclaims three baptisms, including the baptism in the Holy Spirit, and that the promise from God (the Holy Spirit) is for all, including those far away and for all whom the Lord our God will call.

The New Testament is compelling. But, does the Old Testament establish a foundation for the three baptisms, as well? Yes, it does.

Old Testament Foundations

To understand the foundations of the Old Testament, let us look at several New Testament Scriptures.

"For there are three that testify: the spirit, the water and the blood; and the three are in agreement." (1 John 5:7-8)

1. The blood is the Holy Spirit baptizing us in Jesus, as He shed His blood for the forgiveness of our sins. By the blood, we are reborn and receive the divine nature of Christ.

2. The water is for the water baptism that sheds the sin nature of our old man.

3. The Spirit is the baptism in the Holy Spirit by Jesus as our intercessor. By the Holy Spirit, we receive the power of God.

Only with these three can we receive the fullness of God.

"For I do not want you to be ignorant of the fact, brothers, that our forefathers were all under the cloud and that they all passed through the sea. They were all baptized into Moses in the cloud and in the sea." (1 Corinthians 10:1-2)

The verses above describe the same three that testify to our relationship with God as in 1 Corinthians. Moses was a precursor to Jesus Christ. Jesus is our intercessor and Moses was the intercessor for the Hebrews. The Hebrews were baptized into Moses. Moses was a "type" of the Christ yet to come.

Each of the Hebrews passed through the sea, referring to water baptism. "By day the LORD went ahead of them in a pillar of cloud to guide them on their way and by night in a pillar of fire to give them light, so that they could travel by day or night." (Exodus 13:21)

The cloud is a reference to the Holy Spirit, who guided the Hebrews as they left Egypt and resided at the base of Mount Sinai. In addition, as we noted in Path Step 4, the high priest would enter into the Most Holy Place on the Day of Atonement. However, the chief priest burned incense in order to create a cloud and obscure the sight of God prior to his entering the Most Holy Place. Remember, God existed behind the veil in the Most Holy Place. The Old Testament prepares a foundation for abundant New Testament fulfillment. The chief priest experienced God in full only when he was made righteous by the blood of an unblemished lamb, was washed clean of his filth (his old man), and was fully whelmed in the Holy Spirit. These Old Testament illustrations establish a Trinity and foretell a baptism in the Holy Spirit.

Receive the Baptism in the Holy Spirit

"So I say to you: Ask and it will be given to you; seek and you will find; knock and the door will be opened to you." (Luke 11:9)

God answers all prayers that are consistent with the truth of His Word. As defined above, God wishes to share the promise with all. Receive your born again Spirit in Christ. Now, do you desire the presence and power of the Holy Spirit? If in your heart you fervently desire a tremendous blessing and powerful gift from God, pray this prayer to receive the baptism in God's Holy Spirit:

> **"Heavenly Father, at this moment I come to You. I thank You that Jesus saved me. I pray that the Holy Spirit comes upon me. Lord Jesus, baptize me now in the Holy Spirit. I receive the baptism in the Holy Spirit right now by faith in Your Word. May the anointing, the glory, and the power of God come upon me and into my life right now. May I be empowered for service and gifting from this day forward. Thank You, Lord Jesus, for baptizing me in Your Holy Spirit. Amen."**

Now, having asked and received as defined above in Luke, begin to practice the power of the Spirit. An ideal place to begin is where the first apostles did, praising God in a new language, the gift of tongues. To do this, begin praising God out loud in whatever words come to you. You do not need to think about the words you utter. Let them come from within, not from your conscious intellect. Tell God how much you love Him. Thank Him, worship Him, and yield your voice to Him. Now let Him give you new words of praise and thanksgiving. Praise Him with those words, too. You will learn that this can be a very rewarding experience of communication with God that will strengthen your faith. Continue to pray to God each day in the language that the Holy Spirit has given you.

Chapter 14 of 1 Corinthians describes the gift of tongues offered to all baptized in the Holy Spirit. Study these Scriptures and engage in a new, powerful prayer language. But this prayer language is only one of the gifts that God wants to give you through the baptism in His Spirit.

The Gifts of the Holy Spirit

The Apostle Paul told the Corinthians that the Holy Spirit would manifest Himself among them in special gifts, of which speaking in tongues was only one. "Now about spiritual gifts, brothers, I do not want you to be ignorant." (1 Corinthians 12:1) "To one there is given through the Spirit the message of wisdom, to another the message of knowledge by means of the same Spirit, to another faith by the same Spirit, to another gifts of healing by that one Spirit, to another miraculous powers, to another prophecy, to another distinguishing between spirits, to another speaking in different kinds of tongues, and to still another the interpretation of tongues." (1 Corinthians 12:8-10) "But eagerly desire the greater gifts…" (1 Corinthians 12:31)

In 1 Corinthians, Paul defines the spiritual gifts. They are:

- Words of Wisdom – sharing wise advice with someone God wishes to receive it
- Words of Knowledge – sharing knowledge about the person or their circumstances
- Faith – intense devotion and belief in God and in His full purpose and hope
- Healing – supernatural healing of sickness, disease and infirmities
- Miracles – supernatural generation of extraordinary phenomena
- Prophecy – a reported view into impending events and life choices
- Discerning of Spirits – determining the spiritual or demonic basis for occurrences and beliefs
- Speaking in Tongues – speaking or singing in spiritual languages
- Interpretation of Tongues – conversion of prayer in tongues to prophetic messages

When activated and cultivated in the believer, these are a powerful testimony to the power and reality of our true God. Paul instructs us to desire the greater gifts. Implicit in this statement is that as a born again believer, we can have any or all of the gifts listed above. "All these are the work of one and the same Spirit, and he gives them to each one, just as he determines." (1 Corinthians 12:11) As eluded to above, the Holy Spirit gives gifts to each as He determines. Based on a large contingent of additional Scripture, He determines this based on your desire and motivations. The purpose of the gifts is to serve others, build up the Body of Christ, and glorify and praise God. 1 Peter 4:10-11, Romans 12:4-8, Ephesians 4:11-13 11.

Why Do We Need the Baptism of the Holy Spirit?

If you are born again in Jesus by the Holy Spirit and have the divine nature living inside you, why would you need to be baptized by Jesus in the Holy Spirit? The answer is complex. However, to simplify, being baptized in the Holy Spirit activates the gifting, anointing, and power of God in your life.

We used Figure 104 earlier in this Path Step to describe spirit, soul, and body. The flesh and the born again spirit do not overlap. They are separate and distinct. Further, they battle for control over the soul, or the will, of humankind. We need to overcome the urges and yearnings of the flesh to walk more closely with the born again spirit, fully connected to our God.

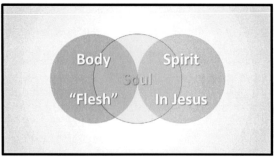

FIG 104

And, in our spirit we have the mind of Christ.

"'For who has known the mind of the LORD that he may instruct Him?' But we have the mind of Christ." (1 Corinthians 2:16)

As depicted in Figure 105, we have the mind of Christ because in our spirit we are one with Him as He is one with God the Father.

"I do not pray for these alone, but also for those who will believe in Me through their word; that they all may be one, as You, Father, are in Me, and I in You; that they also may be one in Us, that the world may believe that You sent Me." (John 17:20-21)

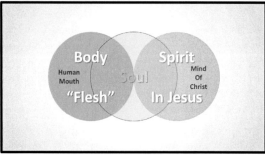

FIG 105

The gifts described above are exercised through the flesh, but they are controlled through the born again spirit in Jesus Christ. Since the spirit and flesh do not overlap, this seems to be an oxymoron.

Enter the Holy Spirit!

As shown in Figure 106, when someone is baptized in the Holy Spirit, it means they are whelmed, submerged, and engulfed by His power and presence. So, let us demonstrate how the Holy Spirit influences spiritual gifting with the example of tongues.

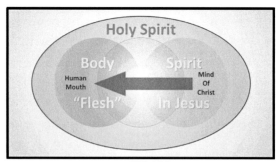

FIG 106

Recall that in our born again spirit we have the mind of Christ. How can the mind of Christ influence that which it does not control (or overlap, as in Figure 105)? The Holy Spirit acts as a conduit by engulfing the flesh and the born again spirit. In essence, the Holy Spirit binds the flesh and spirit as one. In Figure 106, after a believer is baptized in the Holy Spirit, the mind of Christ in the born again spirit of the believer is connected by spiritual means to the mouth of the fleshly body. By yielding one's self to the born again spirit, the Holy Spirit acting as a conduit nurtures the mouth speaking in a spiritual language, called tongues.

With baptism in the Holy Spirit, the same is true for prophecy, words of knowledge and wisdom, miracles, healing, etc. The mind of Christ and power flow freely through the believer and supernatural occurrences result. The flesh alone is not capable of any of the gifting.

Baptism in the Holy Spirit permits the born again to operate in the supernatural power and anointing of God. So, in asking for the baptism in the Holy Spirit you are making available to yourself the gifts for advancing God's kingdom and allowing the Holy Spirit to cultivate further in your life the fruit of righteousness - two critical foundations in living a life God can use mightily for His purpose and glory.

God has given to anyone who would ask eternal life, and every power and tool needed for righteous, victorious, and abundant living. God is offering the baptism in the Holy Spirit to believers who need only to reach out and receive it.

TIMING

Where are you on A Rational Path to Christ? Are you following? Are you on The Path? Have you evaluated EACH Path Step? Has EACH Path Step made sense? Are you beginning to understand God and His plan? If not, have you made a decision about Jesus Christ? Is it TIME to decide?

Revelation And Prophecy

Prophecy reveals that Christ will return (Second Coming) at the end of the age. The age refers to the Church age—the growth in believers and followers of Jesus Christ. His return marks the beginning of judgment as described in Path Step 7. The Second Coming" prophecies and descriptions are in many Old and New Testament books: Revelation, Genesis, Psalms, Isaiah, Ezekiel, Daniel, Zechariah, and most of the New Testament. Revelation has the most descriptive and graphic accounts of Jesus' return. It provides a comprehensive account of what is to occur before, during, and after Jesus' return. Revelation 19:11-16 describes the moment of Jesus' return. "The scepter will not depart from Judah, nor the ruler's staff from between his feet, until he comes to whom it belongs, and the obedience of the nations is his." (Genesis 49:10)

The first book of the Bible predicts that Jesus will come and garner the obedience of nations. Upon crucifixion, Jesus' primary purpose was not obedience. Genesis refers to the Second Coming. "Our God comes and will not be silent, a fire devours before him and around him, a tempest rages. He summons the heavens above, and the earth, that he may judge his people, 'Gather to me my consecrated ones, who made a covenant with me by sacrifice.'" (Psalm 50:3-5)

In the first coming, Jesus was our sacrifice. At the Second Coming, He will gather the saved, His elect, His consecrated. "In the last days, the mountain of the LORD's temple will be established as chief among the mountains; it will be raised above the hills, and all nations will stream to it. Many peoples will come and say, 'Come, let us go up to the mountain of the LORD, to the house of the God of Jacob. He will teach us his ways so that we may walk in his paths.' The law will go out from Zion, the word of the LORD from Jerusalem. He will judge between the nations and will settle disputes for many peoples. They will beat their swords into plowshares and their spears into pruning hooks. Nation will not take up sword against nation, nor will they train for war anymore." (Isaiah 2:2-4) Isaiah refers to the reign of Jesus Christ, which occurs after the Second Coming. "See, the LORD is coming with fire, and his chariots are like a whirlwind; he will bring down his anger with fury, and his rebuke with flames of fire. For with fire and with his sword the LORD will execute judgment upon all men, and many will be those slain by the LORD. ...'And I, because of their actions and their imaginations, am about to come and gather all nations and tongues, and they will come and see my glory.'" (Isaiah 66: 15-16, 18) The Lord will execute judgment upon all men upon the Second Coming. As described in Path Step 7, many will be those slain by the Lord. Other prophecies can be found in Daniel 7:13-14, Zechariah 12:10, and Zechariah 14:4-8.

Jesus comes to the Mount of Olives, accompanied by all the holy ones.

"No one knows about that day or hour, not even the angels in Heaven, nor the Son, but only the Father. Two men will be in the field; one will be taken and the other left. 'Therefore keep watch, because you do not know on what day your Lord will come.'" (Matthew 24:36, 40, 42)

This description indicates "The Second Coming" will be swift and unannounced.

"Now learn this lesson from the fig tree: As soon as its twigs get tender and its leaves come out, you know that summer is near. Even so, when you see all these things, you know that it is near, right at the door." (Matthew 24:32-33)

When the signs and prophecies leading up to Christ's Second Coming are evident, we will know the time is near, but not exactly.

"He said to them, 'It is not for you to know the times or seasons the Father has set by his own authority.'" (Act 1:6)

We will not know the actual time, but we need to be watchful! The Bible provides prophecies as evidence, to know that the predictions are true, and to make us aware as the time draws nearer.

Revelation is filled with prophecy leading up to the Second Coming of Christ and beyond. Many biblical scholars agree that the "end of age" prophecy has nearly reached fulfillment. It is not the intent of A Rational Path to Christ to explore and analyze end-time prophecy. Although we will not know the exact time, many agree that most of the fulfillment of prophecy has transpired. The missing data in predicting the Second Coming is the length of time God plans between those events that already occurred. As of now, very few prophecies remain. When it happens, no one is sure. Nevertheless, we ARE in the season!

Israel (Nation) Prophesied

In Path Step 5, we reviewed the Seventy Sevens, which Daniel prophesied with accuracy, the death of Jesus Christ, and the end of the age in the final seven. Ezekiel recorded a pre-end time prophecy in his fourth chapter, which is the judgment of the Israel nation and its return. This prophecy will occur before the return of Jesus Christ, and as predicted, the formation of the nation of Israel on May 14, 1948.

"Now, son of man, take a clay tablet, put it in front of you and draw the city of Jerusalem on it. Then lay siege to it: Erect siege works against it, build a ramp up to it, set up camps against it and put battering rams around it. Then take an iron pan, place it as an iron wall between you and the city and turn your face toward it. It will be under siege, and you shall besiege it. This will be a sign to the house of Israel. Then lie on your left side and put the sin of the house of Israel upon yourself. You are to bear their sin for the number of days you lie on your side. I have assigned you the same number of days as the years of their sin. So for 390 days you will bear the sin of the house of Israel. After you have finished this, lie down again, this time on your right side, and bear the sin of the house of Judah. I have assigned you 40 days, a day for each year." (Ezekiel 4:1-6)

Ezekiel's prophecy of the rebirth of Israel in 1948 and then the fulfillment on May 14, 1948 is a paramount fulfillment of biblical prophecy. The prophet Ezekiel was a slave during the Babylonian captivity 25 centuries ago (606-536 BC). The Lord revealed to him in the Old Testament, that in the year 1948 Israel would regain the Promised Land.

Israel and the Holy Land are a significant prophecy. In the Old Testament, God specifies the timing and schedule for the banishment of the Israelites from the Promised Land (Jerusalem). This was their punishment until God permitted their return.

In other Old Testament prophecies, God planned a prophetic day to be equivalent to one biblical year. Therefore, Israel was to receive punishment for 390 years, plus an additional 40 because of their disobedience to God's commands. God punishes Israel for 430 years (390 + 40 years = 430 years).

However, as prophesied by Jeremiah, the 70-year captivity in Babylonian that began with Nebuchadnezzar's capture of Jerusalem in 606 BC ended in the spring of 536 BC. This was in the month of Nisan, where only a small remnant of the Jews returned to Jerusalem under the decree of Cyrus the Great.

"In the first year of Cyrus king of Persia, in order to fulfill the word of the LORD spoken by Jeremiah, the LORD moved the heart of Cyrus king of Persia to make a proclamation throughout his realm and to put it in writing: This is what Cyrus king of Persia says: 'The LORD, the God of Heaven, has given me all the kingdoms of the earth and he has appointed me to build a temple for him at Jerusalem in Judah. Anyone of his people among you-may his God be with him, and let him go up to Jerusalem in Judah and build the temple of the LORD, the God of Israel, the God who is in Jerusalem.'" (Ezra 1:1-3)

This is the first 70 years of the exile. Therefore, we must deduct that 70 years, which ended in 536 BC.

> 430 years minus 70 years in Babylon = 360 years.

This assumes that another 360 years of exile remained for the Israelites at the end of captivity in Babylonian.

However, 360 years are not enough. God revealed a principle to Moses who recorded it in Leviticus. In this chapter, the Lord established promises and punishments for Israel based on their obedience and disobedience with His commands. In Leviticus 26, God warned Israel that if after being punished for her sins, and if she still failed to repent, the punishment would be multiplied seven more times (the number of divine completion).

- "And after all this, if you do not obey Me, then I (God) will punish you seven times more for your sins." (Leviticus 26:18)

- "Then, if you walk contrary to Me, and are not willing to obey Me, I (God) will bring on you seven times more plagues, according to your sins." (Leviticus 26:21)

- "I myself will be hostile toward you and will afflict you for your sins seven times over." (Leviticus 26:24)

- "And after all this, if you do not obey Me, but walk contrary to Me, then I (God) also will walk contrary to you in fury and I, even I will chastise you seven times for your sins." (Leviticus 26:27-28)

According to Leviticus, Israel receives seven times the punishment.

> 360 years of Exile x 7 = 2,520 biblical years of additional exile for the Israelites

The length of a biblical year is 360 days. The modern Julian calendar is 365.25 days and represents the solar year. In ancient times, the Jewish year was a lunar-solar year, with 12 months—30 days each, which was 360 days. Therefore, Ezekiel's prophecy reveals that the Israelite's final restoration to their promised land would occur 2,520 biblical years after the end of captivity in Babylonian (in the spring) of 536 BC.

According to the Bible and historical sources, which include Flavius Josephus (see Path Step 5) the end of captivity in Babylon occurred in the month of Nisan, in the spring of 536 BC. This date is the point of departure for our calculations.

- 2,520 biblical years x 360 = 907,200 days

- 907,200 days divided by 365.25 days = 2,483.7 calendar years

It is critical to understand that there is no year zero BC or AD. We must add a year to our calculation.

> 2,438.7 – 536 BC + 1 year = 1948.3

Ezekiel prophesies that the end of Israel's captivity would occur after 2,483.7 calendar years had elapsed following the beginning of the Jewish exile in the spring of 536 B.C. This, by our calculation, is the year 1948.3 or around May 1948.

"And say to them, 'This is what the Sovereign LORD says: I will take the Israelites out of the nations where they have gone. I will gather them from all around and bring them back into their own land.'" (Ezekiel 37:21)

Israel Back in Her Land as a Sovereign Nation on May 14, 1948

Because of the truth and accuracy of the Bible, it predicted and fulfilled a calendar marker, but it does not predict the Second Coming of Christ. At least 64 years have passed since this event. Experts in eschatology agree that a vast amount of end of the age prophecy has already met fulfillment.

The fulfilled prophecy of Israel regaining the Promised Land is both precise and astounding.

Revelation

Israel becoming a nation is a precursor to the Second Coming of Jesus Christ. In Step 7, the Bible predicts the return of Jesus Christ. Old Testament prophets predict His Second Coming, as do the apostles in the New Testament, and in the book of Revelation. The return of Christ marks the end of an era. It is the end of the Church Age, where the Gospel of Jesus Christ spreads throughout the world—expanding the population of believers (the Church). It marks the beginning of the 1,000 year prophecy during which Jesus Christ will rule over the planet. This is the beginning of a new era.

Followers of Christ should not fear the Second Coming. It marks the beginning of the new age, to what God had originally intended for humankind—fellowship between Him and man as one in the Garden of Eden.

No one knows the hour of His coming. The Bible makes it clear that no one will know for sure. However, the Bible cautions us to study the prophecies. God tells us to be watchful for signs of the season. Those who study biblical prophecy and eschatology know that many of the antecedents to His coming have transpired. Still, this does not say that His coming will happen today or in several hundred years.

Understanding the nature of these prophecies and the significance that many have occurred suggests that evaluating the Bible, Jesus Christ, Christianity and salvation is timely to say the least!

Available Sphere Of Influence

We began each Path Step with a list of statements and questions. Who are those from which they originate? Maybe you have family who relate to some or all of these questions. Maybe your friends have made these statements to you. Perhaps a co-worker shared with you a question about God or a discussion of Jesus Christ arose at work. Maybe you learned of a statement made by someone that you did not know. Have you read books and articles that have made similar statements? Have you seen a television program, website, email, social media post, or advertisement containing these statements or questions?

Have YOU made any of these statements? Are YOU asking any of these questions?

Who are these people?

All these people are groups within your Available Sphere of Influence (ASI). These are people you have the ability to influence in your lifetime. Your influence can range from a notion shared in an electronic resource to mutual exploration over time. The people making these statements and asking these questions are in your ASI. They are people whose lives you have the ability to shape. The influence can take on many forms. It can be encouragement, inspiration, or persuasion. It may be friendly, stimulating, or provocative. Whatever method, you CAN influence these people in your life.

Imagine those in your Available Sphere of Influence who are not Christians, who do not know Jesus Christ personally, carrying their Cup of God's Wrath. With that image, understand that a time will come when they are required to drink of it.

Will you choose to influence?

Salvation And The Second Coming

We briefly investigated the arrival of the Second Coming of Christ. As declared in the Bible, we do not know when it will occur. We know many of the signs, know that fulfillment has already occurred and that there is more to come. More so than in ancient times, investigating God, Jesus Christ, and salvation is timely! What would happen to your ASI if the Second Coming does not occur for many years? What would happen to your ASI if Christ returns a few moments from now?

- Estimated Time to Return: 10 Decades—Your ASI remains intact. In 100 years, longer than the average lifespan, your ASI does not diminish. Depending on your age, and those in your ASI, you have time to influence everyone in your ASI.

- Estimated Time to Return: 10 Years—Your ASI remains intact. You can accomplish a great deal in 10 years with planning and technology, ensuring that access to your ASI does not diminish.

- Estimated Time to Return: 10 Months—Your ASI diminishes. In 10 months, your access will begin to shrink. The time-frame for discussion or debate is limited. Your ability to influence reduces—you would have less effect on the others in your ASI.

- Estimated Time to Return: 10 Weeks—Your ASI diminishes. In 10, weeks, your influence will shrink. The time to engage in discussion or debate is drastically limited. You will have moderate effects to your "Contacts" in your ASI, but you may still have influence on your "Co-workers."

- Estimated Time to Return: 10 Days—Your ASI diminishes. Due to your limited time to build a foundation and generate agreement, 10 days will severely limit your time to influence your co-workers. Your friends like and trust you. It is still likely you will influence this group. However, time is short.

- Estimated Time to Return: 10 Hours—Your ASI diminishes. In 10 hours, your many friendships and responsibilities on earth will dramatically limit your ability to influence your friends. Your family may be the only group that will devote the time you demand to hear and consider your declarations. Again, time is disappointingly limited.

- Estimated Time to Return: 10 Minutes—Your ASI diminishes to just YOU. With 10 minutes, do you have enough time to make a decision for God and Jesus Christ; to believe genuinely in your heart? Will you know enough to have faith that the Bible represents truth? Will there be sufficient time to change your heart? Will Jesus Christ hear you admit your sinning nature, and hear you ask Him to be your Savior and sin offering?

Your relationships and surroundings may not agree with the given timescale. You may want to change the nature and order of them. Still, the general principles are pertinent. Do you care for these people? Do they love you? Do you love them?

One fact should be obvious in your ASI. The influence begins with YOU! This is a critical life topic. If the probability is greater than zero that Jesus Christ is truth, this topic should become a priority— THE priority! Due to freedom and free will, the nature of our day is flexible. We do not know what is going to happen next. Events can dramatically change our ability to evaluate and decide. If your ability diminishes, where does that leave you? Where does that leave you and those in your ASI for eternity?

Eternity with God begins the moment your spirit is born in Christ!

A CALL TO ACTION

When you began A Rational Path to Christ, were you unsure about Christianity. Was it difficult to understand why many claim it as their faith? Did you think you were a Christian because you attended a church? Did you not know who Jesus Christ is, or understand salvation. Many believe that Christianity is about attending church weekly. "God sees me in church every Saturday or Sunday, I'm in!" Were you baptized in a church, but in your heart, you were never reborn in Jesus Christ?

Have you accepted Jesus Christ as your Lord and personal Savior, and hold the promise of eternal fellowship with God? Have you read the Bible, studied it to learn more about God, His promises, and the life of your Savior, Jesus Christ? Are you in search of a greater confidence so you are able to witness your faith to others in your family, friends, and workplace? Did you read this book in searching for forgiveness and for an answer? Perhaps you do not know why you are reading this, but you felt compelled to continue reading.

God is offering you a new and perfect covenant to save you from sin and give you eternal life with Him. This New Covenant is perfected with divine assistance for humankind's failings. God offers a better way to live your life that is fuller, complete with His Spirit in you.

Is it time to evaluate all of this for yourself and for those in your Available Sphere of Influence?

Have you learned enough to have faith in Christ?

SUMMARY

Accept Christ earnestly into your heart; connect with your reborn, new spirit. Enjoy the fruits of a tangible relationship with God. Be baptized in the Holy Spirit and begin to walk in the victory and power God intends for us all. Regularly read the Bible, pray and talk to God, and ask God for guidance.

LISTEN for a voice! It may be an intuition or a whisper. Then, evaluate and test the voice. Be prepared for a new, awesome reality surrounding you.

Christianity is Truth if Jesus lived, died, and resurrected. By living, Jesus provided an example of a fulfilled, righteous life. By dying, Jesus, our Savior, removed every sin we ever committed or ever will commit. With His death and bloodshed, He forgives us; He paid the penalty for our misdeeds. He removes our sin and destroys it. His blood is our entry fee to a larger reality. Jesus resurrected to share His glorified spirit with us, to make us holy, righteous, and sanctified. The resurrected and glorified Jesus remade us spiritually into a perfect, eternal creation to coexist with Him and God forever. He remade in us a spirit that can guide our path, and with seeking, can help us to worship and glorify God forever. His resurrection remade us worthy of God. The resurrection of Jesus and the remaking of His followers reconciles us with God. Only with our rebirth can we begin to experience the fullness of God.

The Realization Phase concentrates on applying all eight Path Steps, which explains the nature of Jesus' sacrifice and His relationship with you. Path Step 8 is the first of two Steps in this Phase.

As with each Path Step on A Rational Path to Christ, this Path Step ends with the same question from when it began. Would your life change IF… the Holy Spirit can guide your path? Yes or no? If yes:

- Do you REJECT the Holy Spirit can guide your path?
- Do you THINK the Holy Spirit can guide your path?
- Do you BELIEVE the Holy Spirit can guide your path?
- Do you KNOW the Holy Spirit can guide your path?

NOTES

1 James Strong, Strong's Expanded Exhaustive Concordance of the Bible (Nashville: Thomas Nelson, 2009), s.v. "ruach."

2 James Strong, Strong's Expanded Exhaustive Concordance of the Bible (Nashville: Thomas Nelson, 2009), s.v. "pneuma."

Path Step 9

Would Your Life Change IF…?

CONTENTS

"BECOMING REAL

Every one of us either has read a story or seen a movie where the hero sacrifices his or her life for the greater good. She may have dived in front of the bullet, or he may have thrown himself on a grenade. Maybe the hero was locked away in prison and paid the ultimate penalty on death row, while completely innocent, taking the fall for another. These dramatizations, while entertaining and compelling, do not connect us with the cold reality of these deaths or suffering. We admire these heroes, as they give us a standard for which to strive. "Wow, what an admirable, courageous and just person that was!"

But, how many of us appreciate the cost to the heroes of these noble and captivating stories? For me, these are fantastic, but not personal, nor real. For many years, the crucifixion and sacrifice of Jesus was much the same as these fictional accounts. "Yes, Jesus died for me and my sin. Praise God for that!" I recollect the movies I've seen with blood on Jesus' forehead, hands, feet, and His side. I grew up confronted by crucifixes adorning my home and the homes of my family and friends. They were all decorated the same. "Yup, Jesus died alright!" It wasn't real to me.

For many, watching the movie, "The Passion of the Christ", changed that image. It was so graphic that many closed their eyes in disgust, as it was hard, or for some impossible, to watch. I cried the first time I saw it, and my eyes glass up every time since. It is difficult to watch for certain. However, according to Scripture, it is not graphic enough. As I read the Bible I learned Jesus on the cross was a mass of unrecognizable flesh. Regardless, it still was not real for me.

I realized the gap, or disconnect, arises from my seeing a person die, but not fully appreciating what was happening. When you investigate the sin offering of the Old Testament and overlay it with New Testament Scripture, the death of Jesus becomes far more dramatic and personal. When you understand what Jesus was doing, what was happening to Him and what He was feeling, His death becomes real, or at minimum, more intimate for us. The sacrifice of the Son of God and Man needs to be real to you.

As the transfer of sin occurs and the emotions of the Christ are imagined even remotely, the resurrection of Jesus compels you to walk more powerfully and personally deliberate.

Would Your Life Change IF…You Can Live Truth?

"Is there a Rational Path to Christ or is it all faith?"

Realization

In Path Step 8, the REALIZATION Phase, we explored the reason for Jesus Christ's resurrection, the coming and purpose of the Holy Spirit, and spiritual rebirth through Christianity. In Path Step 9, we will study the nature of Jesus Christ's sacrifice and crucifixion. We will conclude the Path Step by walking A Rational Path to Christ, and with a discussion on Jesus, truth, and life's purpose.

PATH STEP 9: YOU CAN LIVE TRUTH

"I urge, then, first of all that petitions, prayers, intercession and thanksgiving be made for everyone - for kings and all those in authority that we may live peaceful and quiet lives in all godliness and holiness. This is good, and pleases God our Savior, who wants all people to be saved and to come to a knowledge of the truth" (1 Timothy 2:1-4)

Studying Path Step 9 on A Rational Path to Christ, we will identify, understand, and apply Truth to our existence and purpose. We will begin with the personal nature and intent of Jesus Christ's sacrifice for each of us.

DOES JESUS KNOW THE PAST AND FUTURE?

When Jesus came to earth, do you think He knew He would be crucified? Did He know that Adam and Eve would sin? The Bible says that Jesus understood and prophesied of His Second Coming and His fellowship with God and His elect (the saved). Is Jesus omnipresent? Does He know what has occurred and what will in the future? Did Jesus know His future on earth prior to His death and resurrection? "See, the former things have taken place, and new things I declare; before they spring into being I announce them to you." (Isaiah 42:9) God declares His omniscience. "I make known the end from the beginning, from ancient times, what is still to come. I say, my purpose will stand, and I will do all that I please." (Isaiah 46:10) Again, God defines His omniscience. "In the beginning was the Word, and the Word was with God, and the Word was God. He was with God in the beginning. Through him, all things were made; without him nothing was made that has been made." (John 1:1-3) The Gospel of John begins with the pronouncement that Jesus, the Word, was with God in the beginning of all things, was God, and made all things.

Jesus was with God at the beginning of creation. Jesus will be with God at Judgment Day and will fellowship with humankind in the New Jerusalem. Jesus prophesied this in the New Testament Gospels and in Revelation. Jesus is one with God. The Bible is full of explanations of Jesus' omniscience. Throughout Jesus' existence, He was and is all knowing. (Colossians 2:9-10)

Jesus has the Deity living in Him, and He reveals that He and God are one. Jesus Is God. If God is omnipresent, then so is Jesus. The Bible states that God and Jesus are all-knowing. "Jesus Christ is the same yesterday, today, and forever." (Hebrews 13:8) We note also that Jesus had been the same in the beginning at creation, when He walked the Earth, and into eternity. "For by him, all things were created: things in Heaven and on earth, all things were created by him and for him. He is before all things, and in him, all things hold together." (Colossians 1:16-17) Jesus created all things. He governs all for God's will. If He is managing all things, He must know God's will in order to hold it all together. Jesus commanded the beginning, the end, and everything that happens in between. "'I am the Alpha and the Omega,' says the Lord God, 'who is, and who was, and who is to come, the Almighty.'" (Revelation 1:8)

Jesus knows the past, present, and future. He is the beginning and the end. He knows the heart and mind of all creatures, including humankind. Despite our free will, He has foreseen all choices humankind has made and will make. "For those God foreknew he also predestined to be conformed to the likeness of his son that he might be the firstborn among many brothers. And those he predestined, he also called; those he called, he also justified; those he justified, he also glorified." (Romans 8:29-30)

This Scripture is highly debated. Some believe it infers that God chooses who will be saved by Jesus Christ in advance while others believe that God looks forward and sees the decision of all humankind.

The word "foreknew" is derived from the Greek, proginōskō, which means to know beforehand or foresee. With this definition, God had foreknowledge of who would accept His Son for their redemption.[1] The first faction described above believes that He also predestined, meaning that God defined who would be like His Son, Jesus. Rather, this Scripture states that those people whom God saw in advance who would receive His Son as Savior, would be like His Son. Predestined from the Greek word proorizo means "to determine beforehand."

God predetermined that all who accept His Son would be renewed in Jesus Christ's image (see Path Step 8). God offered salvation by grace through His Son to everyone. He was able to see ahead and who would accept Jesus as their sin offering and receive redemption through His grace. God foresaw those who would accept Christ. He predestined that those who accepted Christ would be conformed to the likeness of His Son. He predetermined (predestined) those who follow Him to share a renewed spirit with Jesus.

God called (ordained), justified, and glorified those who accepted His Son whom His Spirit now resides. God intended that those who accept Jesus as a propitiation for their sin be conformed to Jesus. Romans 8 states that God knew and knows everyone who will accept the grace He offers through the sacrifice of His Son, Jesus Christ. Their names are written in the Book of Life referred to in the Gospels and the book of Revelation. God and Jesus are omnipresent and omniscient.

From these verses, we learn the following:

- Jesus is God and is one with God
- Jesus existed before all things
- Jesus has never changed
- Jesus holds all things together
- God (and Jesus) foresaw who would accept Him by their free will
- God predetermined (predestined) those who would follow Him and have a renewed spirit in Jesus ("likeness of His Son)

Prior to Christ walking the earth, and before His crucifixion, God foresaw all who would exercise their free will to choose Jesus as their Savior. When God allowed Jesus to propitiate for the sins of humankind, He foresaw (had foreknowledge of) who would follow Jesus, who would be made anew and connect to Him, and share a renewed spirit in Him. Anyone who chooses Jesus, God called (ordained to be holy) justified and glorified.

Jesus is one with God. He is all knowing. He is omniscient. Jesus knows everyone that ever has or ever will call on Him as Savior. Jesus knew these things at the time of His crucifixion. You will need to recall this point as we continue.

THE "NEW" PERSONAL COVENANT

God intended that those who accept Jesus be conformed to Jesus.

- "I am the gate; whoever enters through me will be saved. He will come in and go out, and find pasture." (John 10:9)

Those who enter through Christ will be saved. Those who do not acknowledge Christ will perish.

- "Jesus answered, 'I am the way and the truth and the life. No one comes to the Father except through me.'" (John 14:6)

You cannot gain fellowship with God unless you are justified by Jesus Christ.

- "If anyone does not remain in me, he is like a branch that is thrown away and withers; such branches are picked up, thrown into the fire and burned. If you remain in me and my words remain in you, ask whatever you wish, and it will be given you." (John 15:6-7)

You must acknowledge Jesus, but also live your life renewed with Him. Jesus defines the need for a personal relationship with Him. Let us examine the sin offering and atonement and understand the personal nature of Jesus' sacrifice.

Was Jesus A Sin Offering?

In Path Step 4, we studied the personal nature of the sin offering. The head of the household, with the blessing of the family, would present the sacrificial lamb from their flock and take it to the tabernacle. After receiving the priest's approval, he would lay his hands on the lambs head and transfer the family's sin to the unblemished life.

Next, he would cut the lamb's throat. The sin offering was not for spectators. Under the New Covenant, God provided a new and perfect lamb in Jesus Christ. However, God did not change the sin offering process. The Old Covenant sin offering is the type to which the New Covenant sin offering is the anti-type. Therefore, the crucifixion needed to fit the description of a sin offering.

"For what the law was powerless to do because it was weakened by the sinful nature, God did by sending his own Son in the likeness of sinful humanity to be a sin offering. And so he condemned sin in human flesh." (Romans 8:3)

The Bible states that Jesus was the sin offering.

"And live a life of love, just as Christ loved us and gave himself up for us as a fragrant offering and sacrifice to God." (Ephesians 5:2)

Isaiah 53:10-12 provides another reference to Jesus as an offering to God.

"Yet it was the LORD's will to crush him and cause him to suffer, and though the LORD makes his life a guilt offering, he will see his offspring and prolong his days, and the will of the LORD will prosper in his hand." (Isaiah 53:10-12)

The prophet Isaiah speaking for God declares that Jesus is an offering.

"But with the precious blood of Christ, a lamb without blemish or defect." (1 Peter 1:19)

In 1 John 4:10 Jesus is described as the perfect sin offering.

"This is love: not that we loved God, but that he loved us and sent his Son as an atoning sacrifice for our sins." (1 John 4:10)

Scripture states that Jesus is an atoning offering for sin, and that He is a sin offering.

Sin Offering/Atonement

The Old Testament describes a sin offering and a Day of Atonement sacrifice for the forgiveness of sins. The God-given details of the instruments used and of the process involved are unique and comprehensive. The removal of specific sins of an individual and sins of omission for the Israelite nation were once a year. The Israelites, God's chosen people, turned the process into a ritual and diminished its significance. Later, the New Covenant promised the forgiveness of sins but with God's law in our minds and in our hearts. How does Jesus' sacrifice accomplish this?

Next, we will superimpose over the sin offering the steps leading to the crucifixion of Jesus Christ. We will list the process and steps of the Old Covenant. We will then examine the stages of the New Covenant and its comparable obligations.

The Old Covenant was made between God and the Israelite nation. Since we defined that Jesus' sacrifice is personal, for purposes herein, the New Covenant is defined as the Personal Covenant. The process begins realizing that we are sinners and that sin blemishes our flesh and souls, and renders us unholy; therefore, we are unacceptable to God and His purpose.

SIN OFFERING PROCESS—OLD AND NEW

The tabernacle was the centerpiece for sacrifices to the Old Covenant. This also included the Tent of Meeting, Brazen Altar, Most Holy Place, and the Ark of the Covenant. The Place of the Skull, or Golgotha, succeeded the tabernacle under the New Covenant. We will begin the sin offering process from Path Step 4. The New Covenant defines a personal relationship. For this assessment, we will identify the New Covenant as the "Personal Covenant."

1. **Old Covenant: Select a young, unblemished lamb**

A young, unblemished lamb symbolizes that it was without sin (defect). Because it was innocent, it was able to assume the sin of an offender. If blemished, its death would pay for its imperfections, and would be incapable of substituting for a person's sin. Only a sinless sacrifice can be a substitute for the sinner.

1. **Personal Covenant: Recognize you need Jesus as Savior**

Under the New Covenant (personal), you must recognize you are a sinner and incapable of living without sin. Sin blemishes you and your sin will result in your death. Jesus Christ is the only sinless human to walk the earth, the only unblemished lamb. He is an available offering to you as your Savior, your unblemished lamb for sacrifice.

2. **Old Covenant: "Is this your personal lamb?"**

Under the Old Covenant, families could not borrow a lamb for a sacrifice. The lamb was required to be the property of the family. A priest greeting those with a sacrifice at the Tent of Meeting asks an Israelite, "Is this your personal lamb?" The sacrifice had to be personal. The sacrifice had to represent a cost and a loss. The price for sin had to be paid.

2. **Personal Covenant: Have you confessed Jesus as your (personal) Savior?**

Do you believe in your heart that Jesus is your Savior? Confess with your lips that Jesus is your Savior.

"That if you confess with your mouth, 'Jesus is Lord,' and believe in your heart that God raised him from the dead, you will be saved." (Romans 10:9) Is Jesus your personal Savior?

"When they came to the place called the Skull, there they crucified him, along with the criminals— one on his right, the other on his left. Jesus said, 'Father, forgive them, for they do not know what they are doing.'" (Luke 23:33-34)

Forgive whom? Was Jesus talking about those who were persecuting Him at the crucifixion? Because Jesus is omnipresent (see Omnipresent Jesus), at that hour, He heard the voices and saw ALL who would ever plead for His sacrifice and confess Him as Savior. He was not speaking to God, the Roman persecutors, or the legalistic Sadducees and Pharisees. He asked for forgiveness of ALL who would call on His name as a Savior.

Jesus was aware beforehand of ALL who would call on Him by choice. He saw everyone who would ever call on Him as Savior. Jesus asked His Father to forgive each of them, for they did not understand the eternal penalty for their actions.

3. **Old Covenant: High priest approves lamb as unblemished**

Under the Old Covenant, the high priest was to inspect the lamb (or other sacrifice) for imperfection (sin). It had to be acceptable to transfer sin as God instructs in Deuteronomy and Leviticus. The high priest under God's authority was to ensure purity so the transfer of sin and would be understood and accepted. The high priest inspected the sacrifice at the entrance to the Tent of Meeting, in the sight of God.

3. **Personal Covenant: God approves Jesus as a worthy high priest**

"As soon as Jesus was baptized, he went up out of the water. At that moment, Heaven was opened, and he saw the Spirit of God descending like a dove and lighting on him. And a voice from Heaven said, 'This is my Son, whom I love; with him I am well pleased.'" (Matthew 3:16-17)

Under the New Covenant (personal), we need the same unblemished sacrifice in the sight of God, a sacrifice that is incapable of sinning to receive our sin. Scripture states that the voice of God approved Jesus Christ as our unblemished, acceptable offering. Many New Testament verses characterize Jesus as the unblemished, pure sacrifice. Jesus is God; He is both man and God. He never sinned, and His sinless blood atoned for our sin.

"Therefore since we have a great high priest who has gone through the heavens, Jesus the Son of God, let us hold firmly to the faith we profess." (Hebrews 4:14)

In his letter to the Hebrews, the author reveals that Jesus was a great high priest who had authorization to designate himself as a perfect offering for humankind.

4. **Old Covenant: Confess sins and transfer to the lamb**

"He is to lay both hands on the head of the live goat and confess over it all the wickedness and rebellion of the Israelites—all their sins—and put them on the goat's head." (Leviticus 16:21)

The laying of hands on the sacrifice with a confession of sin was symbolic and represented the transfer of sin into that sacrifice.

"He is to lay his hand on the head of the burnt offering, and it will be accepted on his behalf to make atonement for him." (Leviticus 1:4)

By the laying on of hands and transferring sin to the animal, a man (family) was able to atone for sin through the sacrifice. When confessing specific sins over the lamb, the sacrifice paid the penalty for them. The life of the sacrifice takes the place of the sinner. The blood transfers sin to the horns on the brazen altar, and then that accumulated sin is removed by the Day of Atonement ritual. Sin died with the sacrifice. Though a transgressor may repeat the sin, the transfer of sin still perished with the sacrifice.

4. **Personal Covenant: Confess sins to Jesus and transfer to Him**

As with the lamb in the Old Covenant as a sin offering, under the New Covenant, a sinner must transfer sin to Jesus. Under the Old Covenant, a sinner would lay his hands on the sacrifice and then confess his sin. The sin, and guilt, was transferred to the sacrifice.

"From the sixth hour until the ninth hour darkness came over all the land. About the ninth hour, Jesus cried out in a loud voice, 'My God, my God, why have you forsaken me?'" (Matthew 27:45-46)

Jesus said this while on the cross. At that moment, God forsakes Jesus. Why would God forsake His son? God did not change. He is consistent throughout the Bible. Because God is holy, He will not tolerate sin. Adam and Eve sinned and "surely died." When Jesus assumed all the sins of those who repented, Jesus was unholy and unacceptable to God.

"My God, my God, why have you forsaken me?"

Prior to His crucifixion, as the sin offering, Jesus witnessed all who would call on him as Savior (see Does Jesus Know the Past and Future?). Jesus heard them plead for His sacrifice and blood. From the sixth hour to the ninth hour, Jesus received all their sins. All sin was on Him that they ever committed and ever will.

Consider what happened to Jesus during this period of the crucifixion (sin offering). Imagine hearing countless pleas, and witnessing every sin committed from the beginning of time to the Day of Judgment. Imagine hearing all those people asking you to die for their sins.

Jesus took on all the sins you committed throughout your lifetime. He embraced the sin you have not yet contemplated. Consider the magnitude that Jesus embraced for those who called on Him as their Savior. During His anguish and torment, imagine being one with God and then abandoned because you are unworthy, you become filthy to Him. After assuming responsibility of all sin, Jesus was unacceptable to God. God forsook Jesus. God abandoned Jesus. The Father abandoned His Son.

For three hours, Jesus heard all pleas for the forgiveness of sin, from then and the future. Any sin is not acceptable to God. If God abandoned Jesus, the truest, purest, unblemished sacrifice, why would He accept you carrying your sin? God abandoned Jesus because, as the sacrificial substitute, He incorporated the sin of His followers. God will abandon you due to sin if you lack the justification by Jesus, the lamb. You need Jesus Christ's sacrifice and blood to make you righteous and holy.

Darkness fell for three hours while the Lamb of God took on the sins of those who would ever call Him Savior.

Darkness came over all the land…

5.   Old Covenant: Sacrifice the lamb and spill its blood

"If the offering is a burnt offering from the herd, he is to offer a male without defect. He must present it at the entrance to the Tent of Meeting so that it will be acceptable to the LORD. He is to lay his hand on the head of the burnt offering, and it will be accepted on his behalf to make atonement for him. HE is to slaughter the young bull before the LORD, and then Aaron's sons the priests shall bring the blood and sprinkle it against the altar on all sides at the entrance to the Tent of Meeting." (Leviticus 1:3-5)

The transgressor was responsible for killing the sacrifice for sin or guilt. The party responsible transferred their sin onto a blameless, guiltless, and sinless animal before slaughtering it. Sin required death and bloodshed. The result of sin is death. God required a transgressor to bring an unblemished lamb to the Tent of Meeting, expecting sacrifice for sin or guilt. The lamb would die for the burden of the sinner.

The high priest brought in the blood of the sacrifice for the nation of Israel into the Most Holy Place, on the Day of Atonement. While sprinkling the blood on the east side of the Ark of the Covenant, it removed all sins of the previous year. This took place at the brazen altar in the sin offering process, for those sins of omission for the entire nation.

5.   Personal Covenant: Sacrifice the Lamb and spill its blood

As the sin offering, we are responsible for our own sacrifice for the remission of our sins. When we ask Jesus to be our Savior, we ask Him to die for us. This is an important detail of the sin offering. Jesus came to earth as part of God's plan to restore His people. He came to die, as the Lamb of God. Jesus knew that many would believe in Him and call on Him as Savior.

"The wages of sin is death!" As our Savior, we ask Him to take our punishment, which is death. Even though the Jewish leaders and Romans sentenced Jesus, He chose to be around them to establish His kingdom and stir their actions. Giving His life on Golgotha was Jesus Christ's plan and choice.

Our behavior and pleadings sent Jesus to the cross. God could have taken back our power of attorney over the earth, rescinded our free will, and removed the effects of sin, but He gave the world to humankind. By free will, we have the choice to choose Jesus, and to worship and glorify God. If only one person asked Jesus to be their Savior, the crucifixion would have still taken place. Jesus died because we selected Him. Each of His followers put Him on the cross.

As the lamb on the brazen altar in the sin offering, a centurion thrust his spear into Jesus' side, and blood and water flowed from His body. His blood flowed as a sin offering and Day of Atonement sacrifice. The blood flowed, and diminished the sins of many.

"Instead, one of the soldiers pierced Jesus' side with a spear, bringing a sudden flow of blood and water." (John 19:34-35)

Symbolically, we are the Roman centurion thrusting his spear. We pierced Jesus' side to let His blood flow for us, like the lamb at the brazen altar.

"And when the centurion, who stood there in front of Jesus, saw how he died, he said, 'Surely this man was the Son of God!'" (Mark 15:39) All saved asked Jesus to die for their sins and to shed blood. When the centurion completed this task, he acknowledged the Son of God.

We turn away when we see Jesus tortured as portrayed in the movie, "The Passion of the Christ." We cannot bear to watch His flesh ripped from His body, exposing blood and bone. We turn away and condemn the Jewish leaders for inhumanity, and the grotesque treatment Jesus received.

"Just as there were many who were appalled at him — his appearance was so disfigured beyond that of any man and his form marred beyond human likeness." (Isaiah 52:14)

Based on the prophet Isaiah's prediction, "The Passion of the Christ" is a cartoon compared to what actually occurred and to what Jesus endured. Yet, we find it difficult to watch because we do not want to believe that WE are responsible for His unimaginable death.

The punishment Jesus received was the sentence of each of His followers. Anyone who calls on Him as Savior deserves and receives what Jesus bore for us. We asked Him to suffer for us. He took our penalty, a savage, painful, and excruciating scourging because we asked Him. He did it because He loves us. Jesus chose to receive our punishment and forgive our sins.

"Father, forgive them, for they do not know what they are doing."

As described in Path Step 5, a total eclipse of the moon occurred on April 3, 33 AD and created a Blood Moon.

- "The sun will be turned to darkness and the moon to blood before the coming of the great and glorious day of the Lord." (Acts 2:20)

- "I watched as he opened the sixth seal. There was a great earthquake. The sun turned black like sackcloth made of goat hair, the whole moon turned blood red." (Revelation 6:12)

- "The sun will be turned to darkness and the moon to blood before the coming of the great and dreadful day of the LORD. And everyone who calls on the name of the LORD will be saved." (Joel 2:31-32)

The prophet Joel states that a Blood Moon would preside the moment of crucifixion. In Acts 2:20, Revelation 6:12, and astronomy in Path Step 5, a Blood Moon did preside over Jesus Christ's death, and everyone who called on the name of the LORD was saved.

- God has shown He will not accept sin.

- Where is the blood to forgive your sin?

- Is Jesus your sin offering?

- Did Jesus die with your sin? Even those you have not yet committed?

- Is Jesus your personal Savior?

- **Even if today, your answer is "No," Jesus may have already received you!**

Everyone Or Anyone?

Jesus died for the forgiveness of sin. There is debate as to whether Jesus died for only those sins of the saved or for all sins of humankind. Both offer an argument and make their claim with the same verses. The Calvinist view is that Jesus died only for the elect and that God pre-selected the elect. The Arminian view is that Jesus took on all of humankind's sin but that each individual through free will must select Jesus as their Savior to gain forgiveness. This text will not support or prove either case. We will consider the crucifixion from a different perspective, the sin offering.

Jesus was a sin offering. "For what the law was powerless to do because it was weakened by the sinful nature, God did by sending his own Son in the likeness of sinful humanity to be a sin offering. And so he condemned sin in human flesh." (Romans 8:3) The Bible tells us so.

If we follow the Hebrew sin offering Scripture and tradition, what does it tell us about Jesus' sacrifice?

Sin was transferred to the lamb so that specific sins die with the lamb. Jesus had foreknowledge of everyone who would accept Him as Savior. For three hours, Jesus took on the sins of those who called Him Savior; all their sin to the end of time.

- Jesus' sacrifice is offered to EVERYONE, but we know in the end some will perish

- Some will perish by free will because of their sin

- Salvation is offered to EVERYONE

"Yet it was the LORD's will to crush him and cause him to suffer, and though the LORD makes his life a guilt offering, he will see his offspring and prolong his days, and the will of the LORD will prosper in his hand. After the suffering of his soul, he will see the light of life and be satisfied; by his knowledge my righteous servant will justify many, and he will bear their iniquities. Therefore, I will give him a portion among the great, and he will divide the spoils with the strong because he poured out his life unto death, and was numbered with the transgressors. For he bore the sin of many and made intercession for the transgressors." (Isaiah 53:10-12)

Isaiah prophesies that Jesus will justify many, and bear their iniquities. Jesus will not justify everyone. As a sin offering, He bears the sins of those He justifies.

- Jesus died for sins that transfer to Him as a sin offering at the crucifixion.

- Jesus died for the sins of ANYONE who received the salvation of His blood.

- Jesus is the personal sin offering for ANYONE who selects Him as his or her lamb.

- He is offered to EVERYONE. He died for ANYONE who confesses Jesus as his or her personal Savior.

WOULD YOUR LIFE CHANGE IF...?

He was before all things. He spoke the world into existence. Jesus was born from a virgin. Jesus took human form. He lived a perfect, sinless life. As a threat to established Jewish religion and tradition, He was flogged by the Romans 39 times (one flogging short of causing death), and flesh was ripped from his body. He was beaten and brutalized so terribly that He was no longer recognizable as a human being.

Jesus carried a 200 lb crucifix into Jerusalem to the top of Golgotha, where they nailed His feet and hands. They spit on Him, laughed at Him, and mocked Him. Connected with God the Father as one, He saw and heard each person who would ever call on His name as their Savior, pleading with Him to die for their sins. He heard all of them declare they were sinners. He saw them humble themselves and request His sacrifice.

He asked His Father to forgive each one of them, as they did not know what they were doing. Then, for the next three hours, while skies grew dark, He witnessed every sin that every person who called on Him as Savior committed throughout each of their individual lives. He bore each of their sins and curse in His own body. With this unholy filth and torment encased inside of Him, Jesus was forsaken by God, His Father. With the sin of many, He was no longer holy, and He was unworthy of God, as are we before Jesus our Savior assumes our sin.

When He was ready, when it was time, He gave up His Spirit, paid the ultimate penalty for sin, which removed the sins from His followers. From His death, their sins are gone forever.

Are Jesus Christ and His sacrifice real to you? Do you know who Jesus is, Yeshua, the Christ, the Messiah? Do you see what Jesus offers you, personally? Have you seen Jesus on the cross dying with your sin?

Would your life change IF…You realized Jesus is your only salvation?

Imagine:

- Being beaten beyond recognition

- Being nailed to a tree through your wrists and ankles, with a crown of thorns pressed onto your head

- Hearing the plea of all the lost sheep calling on you to die for their transgressions

- Feeling the obscenity, guilt, and indignity of heinous acts, omissions, and abominations

- Imagine loving your children so intently that you drink the Cup of God's Wrath on their behalf. You receive God's ultimate penalty. You drink the Cup of Restoration for all your children to restore them to God.

Did Jesus welcome you into His faithful family? Did Jesus hear you call on Him and repent when He embraced the sins of humankind? Did your sins die with Him on the cross? While on the cross, did Jesus see and hear you claim Him as Savior?

4TH CUP: REVELATION—JESUS REVEALED

In Path Step 6, we studied the meaning of the 4th Cup of Passover. We divided it into four units:

Unit I.	Explanation—Jewish Tradition
Unit II.	Application—Relevance with Jesus
Unit III.	Implication—Personal meaning
Unit IV.	Revelation—Jesus Revealed

In Path Step 6, we began study of Implication, and in Path Step 8, we concluded it. Now we will study Jesus Christ and the revelation of the 4th Cup of Passover.

OMNIPRESENT JESUS

"When they came to the place called the Skull, there they crucified him, along with the criminals-one on his right, the other on his left. Jesus said, 'Father, forgive them, for they do not know what they are doing.'" (Luke 23:33-34)

Though many believe that Jesus was making a plea to the Father for the forgiveness of the Roman soldiers and the Jewish leaders, the "them" to which Jesus refers are those who will accept Him as Lord. Previously, we examined Scripture that verifies Jesus was and is omniscient. About this hour, as a sin offering, Jesus saw and heard ALL who would ever plead for His sacrifice and confess Him as their personal Savior (lamb). Connected with God as one, the Lamb of God heard all pleas for salvation with the omniscience shared with God.

A CELEBRATION

Jesus drank the 4th Cup for all who would choose Him. It was a personal moment for Jesus and those who were saved. He took the Cup of God's Wrath and placed into them His spirit of renewal. Let us look at the effect of the 4th Cup.

"I will be their God, and they will be my people." (Jeremiah 31:33)

This is the prophecy of the 4th Cup through Jesus Christ and the fulfillment of the New Covenant. In Path Step 6, we accepted Jesus as our Savior and took Him as our God. He celebrated by drinking the 4th Cup, the Cup of Restoration. To be our Savior, Jesus took from our hands and drank the Cup of God's Wrath. While on the cross, He drank the 4th Cup for us, and we became His people.

Let us review the exact moment of the 4th Cup when Jesus Christ was on the cross about to give up His spirit. What was Jesus experiencing on the cross? Based on Scripture we cannot be certain. However, the Gospels do describe occurrences and issues at the crucifixion. By no means is this a complete list of what Jesus experienced. There are at least four issues and influences Jesus endured:

Omnipresence:

When Jesus stated, "Father, forgive them they know not what they are doing," He was referring to everyone who would call on Him as Savior. He saw each person and heard his or her plea for forgiveness, sacrifice, and salvation. What would your response be to the voices asking you to be a savior and shed your blood? What would be your response? Try to imagine how it made Jesus, the Son of Man, feel. What was His response?

Propitiation:

Jesus was a sin offering. Sins transferred onto Him by transgressors just as at the Tent of Meeting in the Old Testament. Jesus took into his flesh the sins from all who asked Him to be their substitute for the penalty of sin. Consider sins accumulated in an average lifespan. Then, multiply that by the millions or more representing the total of humanity inevitably that accept Christ as Savior. How would you feel witnessing all these sins by humanity, every despicable deed, thought, or emotion? What would be your response? Try to imagine how it made Jesus, the human being, feel. What was His response?

Tortured:

"Just as there were many who were appalled at him—his appearance was so disfigured beyond that of any human being and his form marred beyond human likeness." (Isaiah 52:14)

Jesus was scourged by Pontius Pilate and crucified on the cross. The prophet Isaiah describes Jesus as beaten so severely that he was beyond human recognition. Try to imagine unimaginable cruelty, brutality, and punishment to the point where it causes disfigurement, and you no longer resemble a human being. This level of pain is what Jesus suffered for His followers. What would be your response? Try to imagine how it made Jesus, the Son of Man, feel. What was His response?

Forsaken by God:

"My God, My God, why have you forsaken me?"

Jesus, the unblemished lamb, after taking on the sins of His followers, was no longer pure and holy in God's view. He was rejected because of sin. Jesus was forsaken by God. Though we cannot expect that the Bible is a complete history of Jesus, we can expect that Jesus has never known a time, or the desperation and aloneness, associated with not being bonded to God. What would be your response? Try to imagine how it made Jesus, the human being, feel. What was His response?

Jesus heard countless pleas for forgiveness and for Him to be their sacrifice, an offering. He took into his flesh the sins from all who pleaded for forgiveness. There has been no other human being tortured more severely, and to the point that He was no longer recognizable as human. He then lost the security, glory, and presence of God.

If you were Jesus, how would you feel? What would you do next? Give up in desperation, plead for death, or to be mercy killed? Cry? What did Jesus, the human being and Son of God, do next?

He CELEBRATED our salvation, with each of us, individually!

He said, "I thirst." The Roman soldier raised a sour wine-soaked sponge on a stalk of the hyssop plant to His lips, and Jesus received the drink. He received the 4th Cup with each of us, His followers.

Drinking the 4th Cup is the final act of the Passover festival; it is a **celebration**. The 4th Cup is the Cup of Restoration and is received in celebration of being restored to God. Though Jesus drank the 4th Cup once on the cross, He drank it with each of us individually on that day, at that specific moment we prayed for forgiveness of our sins and called on Him as Savior. At what is perhaps the most desperate moment in the history of humankind, a man sacrificed Himself to restore us to the perfection of our God. When He did this, He crowned the achievement with a cup of wine in celebration of the return and restoration of His children to the kingdom of God. To state this personally, the Lord of Glory celebrated me individually on that day when I accepted Him and His sacrifice for my sins, and He celebrated my reconciliation with God.

If so, what is Jesus' response to our plea for salvation? Does the 4th Cup reveal anything to us?

Jesus celebrated our decision and our reuniting with Him to our God. He was a human being nailed to a cross. He was God. Instead of despair and tears, He responded to our pleas with an act of CELEBRATION. He celebrated our decision, salvation, and the achievement of His purpose on earth, "It is finished."

Jesus completed everything He was required to do to save all of those who would follow Him and call on Him as Savior. Jesus was not waiting to transfer to you His Spirit at the moment you truly believed. He bestowed your born again spirit as He was resurrected. Nowhere in the Bible does it state that Jesus awaits our decision for Him – that Gabriel would need to interrupt a conversation between Jesus Christ and God to inform Jesus that in fifteen minutes both Ted and Sue would accept Him as their Savior, and that Jesus would need to go and deliver His spirit into them. As He completed His sacrifice on the cross, in perfection and in completeness, the Lord of Glory reached out to each of us as we received Him as Savior and He pronounced, "It is finished."

The "New" Personal Covenant

God redeemed and delivered His people from bondage with the first Passover. He chose the Israelites as His elect. He provided this under the Old Covenant to pave the way for a new and more perfect covenant.

He delivered and redeemed His people again with the second Passover, but this time from bondage to sin. Jesus Christ became a Passover lamb. As in the first Passover, we need to seek the protection of the blood of the lamb with our freedom of choice and free will. In the Old Testament, God defined the process of forgiveness, a sin offering for known sins and a Day of Atonement offering for sins of omission. The procedure for the Old Testament sacrifices could not take away sin. God never intended these sacrifices to remove sin. This was a revelation of what was to come.

"And every priest stands ministering daily and offering repeatedly the same sacrifices, which can never take away sins. But this Man, after He had offered one sacrifice for sins forever, sat down at the right hand of God, from that time waiting till His enemies are made His footstool. For by one offering He has perfected forever those who are being sanctified." (Hebrews 10:11-14 NKJV)

The Hebrew's author states that the Old Covenant sacrifices will not take away sin.

So, what was the point of the Old Covenant? How were Old Covenant believers restored to God? Is it personal? The Old Covenant sacrifices were the type to the New Testament anti-type.

"Jesus answered, 'I am the way and the truth and the life. No one comes to the Father except through me." (John 14:6)

Old Covenant sacrifices are a foreshadowing of Jesus' sacrifice. Jesus fulfilled the type perfectly. If no one comes to the Father except through Jesus, and the Old Testament sacrifices did not remove sin, then the believers before Jesus needed access to Jesus' death and resurrection.

"For Christ died for sins once for all, the righteous for the unrighteous, to bring you to God. He was put to death in the body but made alive by the Spirit, through whom also he went and preached to the spirits in prison who disobeyed long ago when God waited patiently in the days of Noah while the ark was being built." (1 Peter 3:18-20) (Path Step 7)

Recall from Path Step 7, Peter says that Jesus was dead in His body, but alive in His spirit before the resurrection. Jesus went to Sheol, or Hades, preaching to the Old Testament souls. He offered salvation that He was the only true unblemished lamb.

"This is why it says: 'When he ascended on high, he led captives in his train and gave gifts to men.'" What does "He ascended" mean except that He also descended to the lower, earthly regions? He who descended is the very one who ascended higher than all the heavens, in order to fill the whole Universe. (Ephesians 4:8-10)

After Jesus' preaching, He ascended on high; he led captives in his train and gave gifts to men. He preached salvation acceptable to God through His sacrifice as the anti-type of the Old Testament type. Jesus preached His message so they could make a personal decision about His sacrifice. Would they accept Him as the true Lamb of God? Moses, Abraham, Joseph, and Joshua, among others, must come to the Father only through Jesus Christ, just as you and I.

God offered everyone His son, Jesus Christ as our sin and atonement offering. Jesus became our personal lamb. He was a sacrifice, a sin offering for our sins. By our free will, He became our Day of Atonement sacrifice for sins of omission. We need Jesus to die for us, shed His blood, and carry our sins. For Jesus to be your sacrifice, your sins need to transfer to Him for redemption, by His unblemished blood.

Is Jesus' sacrifice personal? Did Jesus hear you confess Him as your Savior? Are your sins transferred onto your unblemished lamb?

If the biblical account of Jesus is true and He is the only Savior of the world, should we seek to know Him better? Our time on earth is insignificant compared to eternity with Jesus Christ. We are saved by grace through faith. We need to exercise faith in order to receive the salvation of God's grace.

Who is this Jesus, the Christ who died for me?

Should we learn who Jesus is and what He teaches? If we are uncertain of biblical truth, it is essential to examine the account of Jesus Christ further. It is CRITICAL to know Jesus personally and gain a renewed spirit shared with Him.

A RATIONAL PATH TO CHRIST

We are in the 9th Path Step in A Rational Path to Christ. We began and concluded each Path Step with the question, would your life change IF…if the topic in each Path Step were true, would you change your views on life? Would it motivate you to live differently? If you consider deeply the questions and answers in earnest, you will have an accurate representation of where you are on The Path. You will also better understand why you are positioned at that point on The Path.

Throughout A Rational Path to Christ, you will identify Path Steps that will change your life if you consider them as truth. Are they true? That depends on the evidence. Use the Truth Scale in Path Step 1 to evaluate the truth.

Would your life change IF…? Is the answer "Yes?"

- Do you REJECT it? No evidence or basis exists for the statement.
- Do you THINK it? Evidence and foundation exist, but many questions remain.
- Do you BELIEVE it? Evidence exists to change your system of beliefs. However, you do not find the evidence as Truth.
- Do you KNOW it? Overwhelming evidence exists, and you know it is Truth.

These answers determine where you are on The Path. If on any Path Step you answered, "Yes," you need to evaluate the data available to evaluate the truth of the Path Step. Do you REJECT, THINK, BELIEVE or KNOW it to be Truth. Be honest with yourself.

If you REJECT the Path Step, it is necessary to further your investigation. Study the data from all sources and perspectives. You will remain with your understanding or you may have absorbed enough compelling information to move on to THINK, BELIEVE, or KNOW.

If you THINK the Path Step is Truth, identify the strongest points and principles for that Path Step. Investigate it further. When you discover new points add them to your principles and list of foundations. You might go back to REJECT based on your own knowledge or you may move to BELIEVE.

If you BELIEVE the Path Step is Truth, continue researching the quality and quantity of your data. You may find evidence that strengthens your understanding to Truth (KNOW).

If the evidence you find is unquestionable, you have defined a Truth. You can say you KNOW it is Truth.

With each Path Step, consider the question "Would your life change IF" and assess where you are on the Truth Scale: REJECT, THINK, BELIEVE, or KNOW. If you find yourself on REJECT, continue investigating that Path Step. Either you will consider it not a truth, or the evidence is adequate to raise your truth rating. After you rate, THINK, BELIEVE, or KNOW on the Truth Scale, move on to the next Path Step. However, later, return to those principles that could be strengthened by further exploration.

At the end of this study, you may receive Jesus Christ as your Lord and Savior and a holy, righteous, renewed spirit. Your knowledge attained from walking The Path may have played a big part. This may have progressed from studying new and different information. Perhaps a Path Step generated a new way of thinking, and you defined a new path, rational or not. When was the last time something dramatically changed your life? Whatever it may be, would any of the nine concepts presented on this Path, if they were true, change your life forever; for eternity

Assessing the information and determining what you believe, and why, provides a candid picture of your belief system and the level of your faith in God and Jesus Christ. Walking The Path is a valuable exercise.

As we conclude Path Step 9, let us walk The Path. A Rational Path to Christ has nine Path Steps and three Phases. As you investigate each Path Step following, you may record your answers on the the Path Step Questionnaire.

If you do not "Know," record the primary issues or questions that remain.

A RATIONAL PATH TO CHRIST QUESTIONNAIRE

Phase	Path Step	Step Background	Would It?	Truth Status	Clarity Needed?
Foundation	**1** Truth Exists	• What is your life purpose? • Truth exists! • Is your life purpose based on truth?	YES ☐ NO ☐	☐ Reject ☐ Think ☐ Believe ☐ Know	
Foundation	**2** Bible Is Compelling & Credible	Bible supported by more, factual, historical, prophesy & archeological evidence than any document in antiquity	YES ☐ NO ☐	☐ Reject ☐ Think ☐ Believe ☐ Know	
Foundation	**3** You Lost God Due to Your Sins	Mankind created for worship & fellowship. Mankind sinned & fell short of God. God defined 10 Commandments	YES ☐ NO ☐	☐ Reject ☐ Think ☐ Believe ☐ Know	
Salvation	**4** God Has a Plan to Forgive Sin	God defines Passover, Sin Offering & Atonement for sin redemption. No forgiveness without bloodshed & sacrifice	YES ☐ NO ☐	☐ Reject ☐ Think ☐ Believe ☐ Know	
Salvation	**5** Jesus Lived, Died & Resurrected	Archeology, biblical account, non-biblical writing, Pontius Pilate, prophesy & astronomy evidence is compelling	YES ☐ NO ☐	☐ Reject ☐ Think ☐ Believe ☐ Know	
Salvation	**6** Jesus Is the Key to Salvation	Jesus is Passover Lamb & Sin Offering. He redeems us by receiving the 4th Cup of Passover & with His blood	YES ☐ NO ☐	☐ Reject ☐ Think ☐ Believe ☐ Know	
Salvation	**7** Salvation Reunites You & God	• Heaven & Hell are real places • For salvation, confess Jesus as Savior & pray for salvation • Repent & be baptized	YES ☐ NO ☐	☐ Reject ☐ Think ☐ Believe ☐ Know	
Realization	**8** Spirit Will Guide Your Path	Evaluating Bible, Jesus & salvation is timely. Renew your mind to spirit inside connected to Christ, as evidence of God.	YES ☐ NO ☐	☐ Reject ☐ Think ☐ Believe ☐ Know	
Realization	**9** You Can Live "Truth"	Path to Jesus is personal. Apply Jesus' Truth to Your Purpose, live fulfilled. Is your life purpose based in truth?	YES ☐ NO ☐	☐ Reject ☐ Think ☐ Believe ☐ Know	

FOUNDATION

This Phase represents the foundation of information that leads to an understanding of God, you and your sin nature, and the gap between the two.

PATH STEP 1 - Would your life change IF…Truth Exists? Yes or no?

Does Truth exist? We used a paradoxical exercise to prove the existence of Truth. It did not reveal the meaning of life, nor humankind's origin or destiny. Nevertheless, it is the first Step on a Path to discovering many Truths that reform our thinking, viewpoints, and priorities. Seek Truth and apply it to your life. Truth is the basis of purpose. With Truth, you will discover your purpose!

Do you REJECT, THINK, BELIEVE, or KNOW Truth exists?

PATH STEP 2 - Would your life change IF…the Bible is compelling and credible? Yes or no?

Ancient practices used by the Hebrews to copy and translate biblical texts ensure the accuracy of the Old Testament, as confirmed by the Dead Sea Scrolls. Prophecies cited in the Old Testament that have already been fully realized in history validate the Bible's credibility and indicate the text is of a divine nature. For the last 100 years, proof of biblical accounts through archeology has been plentiful. Facts, history, archeology, and prophecy support the Bible's authenticity more than any other religious or spiritual document in antiquity.

A large quantity of information exists in periodicals, nonfiction books, and on the Internet. One only needs to investigate to learn how the evidence is remarkable and significant. There is overwhelming evidence of the Israelite encampment at Mount Sinai (Jebel Maqla and Jebel al Lawz) that fully complies with the activities and geography recorded in Exodus. Identification of the Mount Sinai site confirms God's delivery of the Ten Commandments to Moses, and the construction of the tabernacle for the sin offering and other forms of worship.

Do you REJECT, THINK, BELIEVE, or KNOW the Bible is compelling and credible?

PATH STEP 3 - Would your life change IF…you lost God due to your sins? Yes or no?

God created humankind for worship and fellowship. The Ten Commandments were stored in the Ark of the Covenant. In turn, the Ark was stored in the tabernacle, in the Most Holy Place. Based on the evidence discovered on Mount Sinai, highlighted by the stone foundation that outlined the tabernacle, we have compelling evidence of the delivery of the Ten Commandments to Moses and humankind. The Ten Commandments state God's instruction for human conduct.

God offered a covenant and in this agreement were His Ten Commandments. Sin is a violation of the character of God and His laws. Humankind sinned and violated God's law. In our fallen state, humankind was no longer worthy of God's fullness and fellowship for eternity. Violating these commandments may be acceptable to the world, but it is destructive to the sinner. Are you guilty of any of these commandments? All of humankind has sinned and falls short of God's glory. We are sinners and need forgiveness.

Do you REJECT, THINK, BELIEVE, or KNOW you lost God due to your sins?

SALVATION

This Phase fills the gap between the Foundation Series (understanding the nature of your sin and separation from God) and understanding how Jesus Christ is the only way to regaining your fellowship with God for eternity.

PATH STEP 4 - Would your life change IF…God has a plan to forgive sins? Yes or no?

God established Passover to deliver His people from bondage. Based on the Ten Commandments, God provided a design for a tabernacle as a means to make atonement for sin. He established the sin offering and Day of Atonement sacrifices for the forgiveness of sin and humankind's redemption. The sacrifice must be unblemished, without sin. If anyone dies with sin, their death pays for his or her own sin. A substitute (lamb) may accept the transfer of sin, only if it is sinless (unblemished). Its death will pay the price for the transferred sin, because it is unblemished. Therefore, there is no forgiveness of sin without sacrifice and the shedding of blood.

Blood is God's key to forgiveness, the key to the Old Covenant, and the key to the New Covenant, for it perfects God's plan for the forgiveness of sin.

- "It is the blood that makes atonement for one's life." (Leviticus 17:11)
- "Without the shedding of blood there is no forgiveness (of sin)." (Hebrews 9:22)

"For the wages of sin is death." (Romans 6:23) Sin results in sacrificial death. With death, blood is shed. Through an acceptable sacrifice and shedding of blood, sin dies forever. Sin perishes with the bearer. Ultimately, all sin will perish. A death will occur for every sinner who has sinned; the only variables are the timing of death and who will realize the death penalty.

Where is the blood that will forgive your sin? Is it flowing through your veins? Alternatively, is there another way?

The Bible states that there is only one man who walked the earth without sin. He is Jesus Christ, the Son of God. He became a vessel for sin, yet He never committed a sin.

Do you REJECT, THINK, BELIEVE, or KNOW God has a plan to forgive sins?

PATH STEP 5 - Would your life change IF…Jesus lived, died and resurrected? Yes or no?

Did Jesus live? The Gospels themselves are compelling evidence of Jesus' life and death. However, there is much more.

The Bible describes redemption and the fulfillment of the covenant at Mount Sinai. Prophecy in the Old Testament describes Jesus as Messiah/Savior over 360 times. All prophecies of Jesus' life and death in the Old Testament fulfilled the New Testament and have been realized in history. Including prophecy, the following is a partial list of evidence for the New Testament and Jesus Christ:

- Eyewitness accounts (Gospels) recorded in the New Testament.
- Disciples wrote the Gospels and Epistles, and died while spreading the good news of Jesus Christ.
- Archaeological evidence validates locations in the New Testament visited by Jesus and His apostles. This includes the remains of two apostles, the Golgotha site and garden tomb, the remains of Caiaphas, the high priest who persecuted Jesus, and Pontius Pilate, the Roman authority responsible for Jesus' death sentence.

- 19 non-biblical writers record Jesus as a real person and comment on His death, and the turmoil it created.

- Proven prophecy—the fulfillment of over 360 prophecies of Jesus' life, death, and resurrection.

- A math analysis evaluating the probability of any man fulfilling by chance even just a few of the Old Testament prophecies of the Messiah is exceedingly small. For any man to fulfill by accident all the Old Testament prophecies of the Messiah is highly improbable; a virtual uncertainty. It is certain that Jesus Christ lived, died, and resurrected as the promised Messiah.

- If Jesus Christ had not resurrected, His body would have been exhumed and displayed.

- Cosmological signs in the heavens cited in the Bible prove the conception, birth, and death of Jesus Christ.

By the standard of a court of law, compelling evidence confirms that Jesus Christ existed. By the same standard, evidence also validates His death and resurrection. Do you know who Jesus Christ is?

Do you REJECT, THINK, BELIEVE, or KNOW Jesus lived, died, and resurrected?

PATH STEP 6 - Would your life change IF...Jesus is the key to salvation? Yes or no?

Jesus celebrated Passover at His death, in a significant manner. Jesus drinking the 4th Cup of the Passover Feast connects Him to the Old Testament as the key to salvation. As He gave up His spirit on the cross, Jesus drank the 4th Cup of the Passover Feast, which was a wine-soaked sponge on a stalk of hyssop. Together, the 4th Cup was the Cup of God's Wrath for anyone who would call Him Savior, and the Cup of Restoration to celebrate a renewal to God. He did this for all His followers who accepted Him as Lord and Savior. By sharing the Cup of Christ with us, He also gave His followers a new eternal spirit connected to Him.

Jesus is our unblemished lamb. He is the sin offering we bring to the Tent of Meeting. When we accept Jesus as Savior, He sheds His blood for the forgiveness of our sins. We can gain salvation and fellowship with God only through Jesus Christ's sacrifice, for He was the only sinless man capable of assuming and shedding blood for our sins.

Do you REJECT, THINK, BELIEVE, or KNOW Jesus is the key to salvation?

PATH STEP 7 - Would your life change IF...salvation reunited you and God? Yes or no?

Heaven and Hell are real places. We are not destined for either. Our free will and choice will dictate our destiny. If you die today, which is your destination? The Bible defines eternal life as "Knowing God." Do you desire eternal life? Do you know God?

Are you saved? Take the steps necessary to receive Jesus Christ as your Lord and Savior. Do you believe in your heart that Jesus lived, died, and resurrected and that His blood is your atoning sacrifice that redeems you from the penalty of your sin? Confess verbally that Jesus is your Lord and Savior, and believe it in your heart and pray a sinner's prayer of salvation. Then, in obedience, be baptized publicly as an outward display of your change and proclamation.

Throughout your life, continue to grow in your relationship with Jesus Christ and seek God's love for you. Renew your mind and learn from the Bible. Repent of your sinning ways. Become part of a church (a Bible-teaching body), become a disciple of Jesus. Be united with God with a reborn, eternal spirit.

Do you REJECT, THINK, BELIEVE, or KNOW salvation reunited you and God?

REALIZATION

The final Phase of A Rational Path to Christ is the realization of a relationship with God through Jesus Christ. The focus is to be connected with Jesus through His spirit and to live a life according to His purpose.

PATH STEP 8 - Would your life change IF...the Spirit will guide your path? Yes or no?

Christianity is Truth if Jesus lived, died, and resurrected. By living, Jesus was an example of how to live a God-motivated life. He removed every sin we ever committed or ever will. With His death, we have forgiveness; He paid the penalty for our transgressions. He eradicated our sin. By grace, this is our entry fee to a grander reality. Jesus needed to resurrect so that He could share His spirit with us, to make us holy, righteous, sanctified, and worthy of God. The resurrected and glorified Jesus re-created us as a perfect, eternal creation to coexist with Him and God forever. He remade in us a spirit that guides our path to worship and glorify God forever.

Accept Christ in earnest into your heart; connect with your new, reborn spirit. Enjoy the fruit of a tangible relationship with God. Ask to be baptized in the Holy Spirit, regularly read the Bible and pray, talk to God and ask God for guidance. Live your life in the power and gifting of the Holy Spirit. LISTEN for a voice! It may be an intuition or a whisper. Then, evaluate and test the voice. Be prepared for an awesome reality.

Given the signs of the season (of the Second Coming of Christ), it is timely to evaluate God, the Bible, and Jesus Christ. God offers a new and improved covenant to save you from your sins. He provides eternal life for you and those in your Available Sphere of Influence!

There is no faith without knowing, and there is no knowing without faith. Have you learned enough to have faith in Christ and welcome your new spirit?

Do you REJECT, THINK, BELIEVE, or KNOW the Spirit will guide your path?

PATH STEP 9 - Would your life change IF...you can live Truth? Yes or no?

We began A Rational Path to Christ discussing influences, stimuli, and information that could change your life.

Have you learned new information? Did you receive something you did not have before? Are you wiser? Did you find a new understanding that influences your plan or your response to what life has dealt you? Did you find Truth? Did you learn a Truth that was unfamiliar? Will the Truth change your life, goals, or priorities?

What are those "ifs" that you now recognize as Truth?

THREE QUESTIONS

We concluded Path Step 1 with three questions:

1. What is the purpose of life?

2. Is there a God?

3. If so, what is His purpose for us?

What Is The Purpose Of Life?

By examining some of the most wise men, we learned the following:

- "Happiness is the meaning and purpose of life, the whole aim and end of human existence." - Aristotle

- "Life finds its purpose and fulfillment in the expansion, happiness." - Maharishi Mahesh Yogi

- "I believe that the very purpose of life is to seek happiness." - Dalai Lama

- "How to gain, how to keep, and how to recover happy is he that will most better at all times secret motive all they do." - William James,

- "Pleasure is the object, duty and the goal all rational creatures." - Voltaire

- "To have a grievance is to have a purpose in life." - Allen Coren

- "Let us rise up and be thankful, for if we didn't learn a lot today, at least we learned a little, and if we didn't learn a little, at least he didn't get sick, and if we got sick, at least we didn't die; so, let us all be thankful." - Buddha

- "The purpose of life is not to be happy is to be useful, to be honorable, to be compassionate, to have it make a difference that you have lived and lived well." - Ralph Waldo Emerson

In Path Step 1, according to these great minds, the purpose of life is either to be happy and useful, honorable and compassionate, or to be thankful. While each of these is admirable, we are not given advice of "how to" or why. We are to seek happiness and pursue earthly fulfillment and then hope for something better in the afterlife.

In Path Step 1, we considered our life purpose.

What Is Your Life Purpose?

Among other choices, we considered the following list of purposes:

- Happiness
- Money
- Spirituality
- Career
- Relationship
- Family
- Health
- Power
- Fame
- Belonging

Were you able to define your purpose? Is it only one from the list or several? What did you describe as your purpose? If you identified it, did it surprise you? On the other hand, are you uncertain still of what it is?

How can we know our life's purpose? This is an important question. But question #2 is more so, "Is there a god?" If there is a god, the creator of all, and he created us, can we presume that he has a purpose for our life? In Path Step 3, we learned that the God of Abraham and Jesus Christ created humankind with the purpose; to share a loving relationship and for us to worship and glorify Him.

If there is a God and the Bible is compelling and credible, what does the Bible teach us about life's purpose? What does the Bible tell you about your purpose in life? We will return to question #1 after examining question #2.

Is There A God?

Path Steps 2 through 6 deal with the issue of God's existence. In Path Step 2, we explored the evidence that supports occurrences in the Old and New Testament. There is evidence supporting the Exodus from Egypt, and the dealings between God and Israel in Mount Sinai. This is where God described the Old Covenant ratified by the Israelites. Fulfilled prophecy in the Bible of individuals, nations, dates and omens, reveals a divine, higher being. Unlike other religious text, the Bible discloses a comprehensive, significant, and perfect plan. The Bible IS compelling and credible and has evidence of the God of Abraham, Moses and Jesus Christ.

You or someone you know embraces these questions and statements:

- "If there is a God, why does He let us suffer?"
- "I can't believe in an unforgiving God who would let people die in Hell!"
- "I refuse to accept a God that destroyed people and cities in the Old Testament!"
- "Christianity is great, but it's just one way to God!"

As you consider these beliefs, on what is their foundation based? None is based on evidence or truth. Each belief results from flawed thinking and a limited perspective. Without evidence, some still hold it to be true. The manufacturing of these Truths is in the believer's mind. The believer creates his or her own personal Truth. They represent an opinion. If a god exists and this god is the creator, would not truth be comprised of this god's design? If compelling evidence defines a god, as the creation of that god, how can we question, or even pretend to understand the potential complexity of the god's design?

Does God let us suffer? People will die in Hell. What happened to the dead of the Old Testament? Why would God create only one method or pathway to Him?

By creating their own Truth with these statements and no evidence to substantiate, they become their own god. If you define the characteristics of your own god, are you not "god" of your god? If you stated that "god lives on Jupiter, is 500 feet tall, and visits earth on leap years," with no substantial evidence to prove your god, that god would be of your own making. You would become the creator of gods and definer of truth. In fact, you would be god!

Of all deities worshiped on this planet, which of them is supported by overwhelming evidence or have a solid foundation? Humankind has limited perspective and judgment. If god exists, it is likely that this god has perspective not shared or understood by humankind. If a deity exists, how can we contend that we can understand the full purpose and inner workings of a Universe? We cannot. Therefore, we cannot understand the complex structure of existence created by such a deity. Our god likely would want us to believe that as our god, he makes sense. A benevolent and merciful god would understand that. We are able to examine the evidence, find a god based on truth, and explore a relationship with that god and the reality that the god created. Though we may not fully understand the commands or doctrines of that god, it is a god of basis and not a god of our own creation.

In Path Step 2, we considered the evidence supporting the God of the Old Testament and of the Israelites. Among many convincing characteristics of this God, prophecies are fulfilled in the Old Testament and strikingly by Jesus Christ in the New Testament.

In Path Step 5, we examined that Jesus Christ lived, died, and resurrected, which is further evidence of God. However, the nature of God's plan, the Word of God (Bible), despite the difference in geography, time, writer, and language, is a consistent, tight story.

Perhaps the most convincing evidence is experiencing the Holy Spirit and the renewing of the spirit as described in Path Step 8. This spiritual renewing and divine experience is tangible evidence of God. Achieving this relationship with God is undeniable and reinforcing.

With this evidence, we KNOW God exists! Man lives in a fallen state encumbered with sin. Therefore, we fall short of God's approval and will perish. However, this merciful God describes a plan for forgiveness, reconciliation, and redemption. This merciful God came in human form and suffered pain, anguish, and death so that humankind could be worthy of Him. He offers a plan to make us holy like Him forever!

"'We are not stoning you for any of these,' replied the Jews, 'but for blasphemy, because you, a mere man, claim to be God.' Jesus answered them, 'Is it not written in your Law, 'I have said you are gods?'" (John 10:33-34)

God exists! Now, on to Question #3

What Is His Purpose For Us?

In Path Step 1, we investigated God's purpose for humankind. We assessed that God created man for a loving, worship relationship. God wanted to create a race of beings that He could love beyond measure. In return, it is God's will that humankind would choose to love God for His great love, His favor, and the blessings He would share. The account of man begins in Genesis.

"Then God said, 'Let us make man in our image, in our likeness, and let them rule over the fish of the sea and the birds of the air, over the livestock, over all the earth, and over all the creatures that move along the ground.' So God created man in his own image, in the image of God he created him; male and female he created them." (Genesis 1:26-27)

Here, in Genesis, the triune God declares, "Let us make man in 'our' image." God did not state that He would make man in "His" or "My" image; He stated, "Our" image. It is God's intent that mankind be made in the image of one being with multiple facets. Earlier in Genesis, we learned that at the dawn of creation, the Holy Spirit was hovering over the waters, much like an expectant mother. In the Gospel of John, Chapter 1, a key truth of creation is revealed.

"In the beginning was the Word, and the Word was with God, and the Word was God. He was with God in the beginning. Through him all things were made; without him nothing was made that has been made. In him was life, and that life was the light of men." (John 1:1-4)

Adding to the first four verses of Chapter 1:

"The Word became flesh and made his dwelling among us. We have seen his glory, the glory of the One and Only, who came from the Father, full of grace and truth." (John 1:14)

The result is a definitive picture. Jesus, the Word, was there in the beginning with God. The Holy Spirit was there in the beginning with God. They were there, because they are God. God defined His will to create humankind in the image of God. Jesus, the Word, spoke creation into existence with authority. The Holy Spirit responded to the authority and created all things. The Holy Spirit and Jesus responded to God the Father, the will.

God the Father provides the will, or soul of the triune God. The Holy Spirit defines the spirit person in the same entity. And, Jesus represents the body or physical nature of God. God said, "Let us make man in OUR image." That includes the Father, the Son, and the Holy Spirit. For God, "Our" image would include a soul, a spirit and a body. The soul defines your will, but is influenced by spirit and body

In Path Step 8, we studied Scripture that defines man is comprised of spirit, soul, and body. So, with this similarity, is man made in God's image?

"For he chose us in him before the creation of the world to be holy and blameless in his sight. In love he predestined us to be adopted as his sons through Jesus Christ, in accordance with his pleasure and will." (Ephesians 1:4-5)

Before anything was created, God defined that His chosen followers be conformed to the image of Jesus Christ, God. God desired to make man in God's image and to be conformed to the image of Jesus Christ. Man is not fully made in God's image until we are conformed to the image of Jesus; Jesus' spirit, soul, and a glorified body.

"Through these he has given us his very great and precious promises, so that through them you may participate in the divine nature and escape the corruption in the world caused by evil desires." (2 Peter 1:4)

The saved have a born again spirit with the divine nature of God that influences our soul, or will. When remade with the divine nature influencing our soul, we are created in the image of God, the Father. When born again with spirit and baptized in the Holy Spirit, we are conformed to the image of God, the Spirit. When Jesus returns and our bodies are glorified and perfected, we are conformed to the image of God, Jesus, the flesh. The spirit is incorruptible and the flesh can and will no longer corrupt the soul. With these, we are made in God's image…fully!

God did not make us in His image in the garden; if we were made in His image fully, could we have eaten the fruit of disobedience? God knew before the foundation of the world, with free will, we would need to understand our need for Jesus to make us righteous; and, that righteousness is the only way with God. The path to Jesus Christ is one that God intended for all humankind to walk. The culmination of the walk is life eternal in His image.

We achieve His purpose for humankind when we are adopted as children in Jesus Christ, and are remade incorruptible.

Conformed To His Image

"Then Jesus said to his disciples, 'If anyone would come after me, he must deny himself and take up his cross and follow me. For whoever wants to save his life will lose it, but whoever loses his life for me will find it. What good will it be for a man if he gains the whole world, yet forfeits his soul? Or what can a man give in exchange for his soul?" (Matthew 16:24-26)

In the Gospel of Matthew, Jesus specifies He wants us to follow Him. We learn that His desire for us is that we make the right choice from free will that will lead to saving, rather than losing our souls. Lastly, Jesus tells us that in order to find our life (or our purpose), we must lose our life and follow Him.

God gives us eternal inheritance when we accept His son, Jesus Christ. We become an eternal being forever. We gain fellowship with God. We are free from sin's bondage and curse. We are capable of achieving our purpose. When renewed, we receive our calling, our purpose to worship and glorify God for eternity (see Path Steps 3, 7-9).

God desires that we coexist for eternity. When we accept Jesus Christ, we receive a spirit that will guide us on a path that God chose for us. If God is Truth, and we worship and glorify Him, and walk His path, by definition we are living the Truth.

If you desire further guidance in a job, to marry, have a family, or where to live, the answer is simple. Whatever job you take, your marital status, your number of children, or your location to live, your purpose should be to follow Jesus and His teachings, and worship and glorify God for eternity.

We need to be conformed to His image!

The Truths Of Jesus

God created the human race for intimate fellowship. He has immense love for us and desires that we have a one-on-one, intimate, personal relationship with Him. God states that this one-on-one path to Him is through Jesus Christ.

"Then Jesus came to them and said, 'All authority in Heaven and on earth has been given to me.'" (Matthew 28:18)

God gave Jesus authority over Heaven and earth. All who follow Him He will justify before His father in judgment. He will determine our destiny, Hell or Heaven, perishing or everlasting life. Jesus has ultimate authority.

We worship and reflect God by living and supporting His truths. He gave us His life as a sacrifice and as an example. What does Jesus Christ's life tell us about living and purpose? This leads to the fourth question.

What Does Jesus Expect From Us?

Before we answer this question, reflect on the life application questions from Path Step 1.

- What is the purpose of your life?

- Is it based on Truth?

- If Jesus is Truth, is your purpose in accordance with His expectations?

If Jesus, the Son of God, Lamb of God, Messiah, and Redeemer is the Truth, His expectations reign. If Jesus has authority over the earth, what does He expect from us? We will concentrate on the following seven categories. The Bible instructs us that Jesus expects us to:

- Worship and glorify God

- Confess and repent of our sins

- Love others and be generous

- Tell others about Jesus' love–make disciples of all the nations

- Be wholeheartedly obedient

- Grow in and act upon our knowledge

- Develop our gifts

NOW LET US REVIEW EACH WITH CONFIRMATION:

1. Worship and glorify God

In Path Step 3, we learned that God created humankind for relationship. Humankind would worship and glorify God in all things. In return, God would provide blessings to humankind. Since the Bible primarily focuses on the redemption and restoration of humankind to God, the purpose for humankind is still intact. It is God's desire that all of us have an intimate relationship with Him in ALL we do.

2. Confess and repent of our sins

"If we confess our sins, he is faithful and just and will forgive us our sins and purify us from all unrighteousness." (1 John 1:9)

"After John was put in prison, Jesus went into Galilee, proclaiming the good news of God. 'The time has come,' he said. 'The kingdom of God is near. Repent and believe the good news!'" (Mark 1:14-15)

By confessing our sins, we acknowledge it. After acknowledging sin, we can repent. Repentance is evidence of your renewed, reborn spirit.

3. Love others and be generous

"But I tell you who hear me: Love your enemies, do good to those who hate you, bless those who curse you, pray for those who mistreat you. If someone strikes you on one cheek, turn to him the other also. If someone takes your cloak, do not stop him from taking your tunic. Give to everyone who asks you, and if anyone takes what belongs to you, do not demand it back. Do to others as you would have them do to you. If you love those who love you, what credit is that to you? Even sinners love those who love them. And if you do good to those who are good to you, what credit is that to you? Even sinners do that. And if you lend to those from whom you expect repayment, what credit is that to you? Even sinners lend to sinners, expecting to be repaid in full. But love your enemies, do good to them, and lend to them without expecting to get anything back. Then your reward will be great, and you will be sons of the Most High because he is kind to the ungrateful and wicked. Be merciful, just as your Father is merciful." (Luke 6:27-36)

4. Tell others about God's love and desire for them to be saved and make disciples of all the nations

"Go therefore and make disciples of all the nations, baptizing them in the name of the Father and of the Son and of the Holy Spirit, teaching them to observe all things that I have commanded you; and lo, I am with you always, even to the end of the age." (Matthew 28:19-20 NKJV) Amen.

Throughout time, humankind designated Jesus' last words before He ascended to Heaven The Great Commission. Jesus commissioned His followers to spread the love of His sacrifice to all the nations and to observe all He shared on earth. His deeds and His message were for the benefit of all humankind, specifically those who would embrace His teachings and love.

5. Grow in and act upon our knowledge

"But grow in the grace and knowledge of our Lord and Savior Jesus Christ. To Him be the glory both now and forever. Amen." (2 Peter 3:18 NKJV)

"For though I am absent in the flesh, yet I am with you in Spirit, rejoicing to see your good order and the steadfastness of your faith in Christ. As you have therefore received Christ Jesus the Lord, so walk in Him." (Colossians 2:5-6 NKJV)

By reading God's word and communing in the Spirit, we get a better sense of our purpose. Jesus expects us to share the Truth and enlighten others of the kingdom of God.

6. Wholehearted obedience

"Remember, therefore, what you have received and heard; obey it, and repent. But if you do not wake up, I will come like a thief, and you will not know at what time I will come to you." (Revelation 3:3)

"Therefore go and make disciples of all nations, baptizing them in the name of the Father and of the Son and of the Holy Spirit, and teaching them to obey everything I have commanded you. And surely I am with you always, to the very end of the age." (Matthew 28:19-20)

If Jesus is Lord and Savior of your life, you will obey His commands, teachings, and expectations.

7. Develop your gifts

"As each one has received a gift, minister it to one another, as good stewards of the manifold grace of God. If anyone speaks, let him speak as the oracles of God. If anyone ministers, let him do it as with the ability which God supplies, that in all things God may be glorified through Jesus Christ, to whom belong the glory and the dominion forever and ever. Amen." (1 Peter 4:10-11 NKJV)

> "There are diversities of gifts, but the same Spirit. There are differences of ministries, but the same Lord. And there are diversities of activities, but it is the same God who works all in all. But the manifestation of the Spirit is given to each one for the profit of all." (1 Corinthians 12:4-7) "Each one should use whatever gift he has received to serve others, faithfully administering God's grace in its various forms." (1 Peter 4:10)

When you accept Christ and then are baptized in the Holy Spirit, you receive a spiritual gift or gifts. The kingdom of God is established and growing, and so that in all things God may be glorified. We have gifts so that we may serve, and for the benefit of all.

Considering the seven expectations of Jesus, what is your life's purpose? What are your gifts? Should you have a ministry? Should you have a job? Should you get married? What purpose will you choose to uphold Jesus' expectations? How can you follow Christ and be significant while not being consumed by this fallen world? What will you do to build God's kingdom?

The Apostle Paul was a tent maker and was able to be significant to others. Paul's ministry did more to spread the truth of Christianity than did any other. How was Paul successful?

"After this, Paul left Athens and went to Corinth. There, he met a Jew named Aquila, a native of Pontius, who had recently come from Italy with his wife Priscilla because Claudius had ordered all the Jews to leave Rome. Paul went to see them, and because he was a tent maker as they were, he stayed and worked with them." (Act 18:1-3)

Paul was a tent maker. He used his skill to provide sustenance until his ministry had enough funds for evangelizing. He leveraged his profession to advance the gospel. Perhaps, what is significant was his approach to ministry.

"Though I am free and belong to no man, I make myself a slave to everyone, to win as many as possible. To the Jews I became like a Jew, to win the Jews. To those under the law I became like one under the law (though I myself am not under the law), so as to win those under the law. To those not having the law I became like one not having the law (though I am not free from God's law but am under Christ's law), so as to win those not having the law. To the weak I became weak, to win the weak. I have become all things to all men so that by all possible means I might save some. I do all this for the sake of the gospels that I may share in its blessings." (1 Corinthians 9:19-23)

Paul became relevant in all situations without fully embracing the culture and society. He gained access to those who needed to be saved. Being relevant (not an oddity), he was able to witness his faith and provide his testimony of God's kingdom.

Paul was able to be all things to all people in his walk. How? Should you be a parent above anything else? Should you make lots of money? Should giving be your purpose? Many other questions are relevant to your purpose. The answer to each of these questions is yes and no and it may change during your life. Follow God's will for your life. What is His will for you? The spirit renewed within you knows His will for you; this is after you receive Jesus as your Savior. You can reach into your spiritual side by renewing your mind. You renew your mind by reading the Word of God, the Bible.

Reading the Bible will not define your life's purpose. However, it teaches you God's will for your life. When you understand His will, you find a purpose that is in accord with His will. What is your life's purpose? What is your life's purpose right now? What will it be in a few years or in ten? Does your purpose now matter to God and to His kingdom? Will it matter 1,000 years from now or until eternity?

Your true purpose, when defined, will make a difference in God's kingdom now, soon, and forever. If you influence God's kingdom through your spouse, a child, sibling, friend, contact, coworker or other acquaintance today, imagine the effect on God's kingdom that they can have with their influence over their lifetime, and the people they touch and so on, and so on, into eternity.

YOUR ACTIONS TODAY MAGNIFY INTO ETERNITY!

When you started this day, maybe, considering your purpose did not matter. Maybe it did, but not so much. Just like every day you have enjoyed, you awoke with a choice to make a difference. You can make a profound difference today that will carry you into God's eternity. When you accept Christ, you change eternity. Moreover, then you are able to influence the lives of others in your Available Sphere of Influence that will dramatically change their lives, their eternities, and the eternities of all others they will influence in their lives, and lives subsequent. Your purpose today, transformed by truth, can have an extraordinary effect on the abundance of eternity.

God already knows your choices employing your personal free will. He has seen your future, the result of your choices. However, He will not interfere with your free will. It is your choice today, and every day, for the rest of your life that will either expand or contract the fullness of eternity.

Truth In Our Lives

What fundamental truths guide your life? A Rational Path to Christ outlined a journey through God's defined truth. Jesus is the way, and the truth, and the life. Accept Jesus Christ, be renewed. Apply the truths and expectations of Jesus. Define your true purpose. Fulfill God's plan for humankind and you. Be conformed to the image of Christ. You can live a life based on truth! Don't forget, who is in your Available Sphere of Influence?

Your path to Jesus is personal. Apply Jesus' truth to your purpose and live fulfilled. Based on truth, what is your life's purpose? What effect will you have on eternity? Will the effect be emptiness or be magnifying?

PATH STEP 9 CONCLUSION

Do you REJECT, THINK, BELIEVE, or KNOW you can live Truth?

The nine Path Steps provide evidence, scriptural arguments, and a certainty of Jesus Christ as Truth and the only path to restoration with God. The information herein is not complete in its extent or depth. You may achieve the same end with a different course. Perhaps, portions of the Path Steps made sense, but others did not; however, you now have a saving relationship with Jesus Christ. If you place Jesus, His life, and His ideals at the center of your life in everything you do, YOU WILL LIVE TRUTH.

As with each Step on A Rational Path to Christ, the Path Step ends with the same question from when it began. Would your life change IF…you can live Truth? Yes or no? If yes:

- Do you REJECT you can live Truth?

- Do you THINK you can live Truth?

- Do you BELIEVE you can live Truth?

- Do you KNOW you can live Truth?

Return to and complete the Assessment Questionnaire, beginning at Question No. 11. Have you gained any Truths? Did you realize a difference? Is there a gain or loss? Are you living Truth?

NOTES

1 James Strong, Strong's Expanded Exhaustive Concordance of the Bible (Nashville: Thomas Nelson, 2009), s.v. "foreknew."

AFTERWORD

As many life paths exist as there are people. The path for many comes from choice and natural forces. However, the paths for others are the result of their choices, and natural and spiritual forces. The word of God is a historical, defensible, and practical guide to your path if you choose to renew your mind and make it so.

"Your word is a lamp to my feet and a light for my path." (Psalm 119:105)

"In the way of righteousness, there is life; along that path is immortality." (Proverbs 12:28)

Jesus is the way of righteousness. Belief and rebirth in Him yields righteousness. By His justification and with spiritual renewal we connect to Jesus. We become righteous and forever immortal! Then, we experience the fullness of God.

If you have found Christ, seek to define your purpose in life. Finding Christ is the beginning of eternity and reconciliation with God. When you have found your purpose on earth in Christ, you will have made your first step on your "Rational Walk with Christ".

"He has shown you, O man, what is good; And what does the LORD require of you But to do justly, to love mercy, And to walk humbly with your God?" (Micah 6:8)

Each Path Step helps with understanding and building credibility for the nine Path Steps. Use your heart and mind. Consider the testimony, meditate on the evidence, and experience the nature and character of God.

Be honest with yourself. Do you hear the calling from within?

Where is your mind? Where is your heart?

Where are YOU on A Rational Path to Christ?

For His glory!

A Rational Path To Christ
Notes

Images used with permission from the following.
Notes include additional Resoures for futher exploration.

John Stott, Basic Christianity, Downers Grove, IL: IVP Books, 1971.

Josh McDowell, More than a Carpenter, Carol Stream, IL: Tyndale House Publishers, Inc., 2009.

Lee Strobel, The Case of Christ, Grand Rapids, MI: Zondervan, 1998.

Frank Morrison, Who Moved the Stone?, Grand Rapids, MI: Zondervan, 1958.

Peter Kreeft & Ronald K. Tacelli, Handbook of Christian Apologetics, Downers Grove, IL: IVP Books, 1994.

Robert Cornuke & David Halbrook, Mountain of God, Nashville, TN: Broadman & Holman, 2000.

Josh McDowell, The New Evidence That Demands A Verdict, Carol Stream, IL: Tyndale House Publishers, Inc., 1999.

Josh McDowell & Don Stewart, Answers to Tough Questions, Carol Stream, IL: Tyndale House Publishers, Inc., 1980.

Penny Cox Caldwell, The God of the Mountain, Alachua, FL: Bridge – Logos, 2008.

Dr. Lennart Moller, The Exodus Case, Strangnas, Sweden: Scandinavia, 2010.

Simon Greenleaf, The Testimony of the Evangelists, Clark, New Jersey: The Lawbook Exvchange, Ltd., 2009.

N. T. Wright, Simply Christian, New York, NY: Harper Collins Publishers, 2006.

Mysteries of the Bible: PC version, 2003. "Disc 1: The Exodus Revealed," "Disc 3 – The Secret of the Dead Sea Scrolls," Questar Entertainment.

Gutenburg.org, May 30, 2012, http://www.gutenberg.org/files/17324/17324-h/v4c.htm.

www.bible.ca/archeology/bible-archeology-maps.htm.

www.arkdiscovery.com

wyattmuseum.com/mount-sinai

www.ancientexodus.com/topics/index/mount-sinai-and-the-apostle-paul/

www.arkdiscovery.com

wyattmuseum.com/mount-sinai

www.ubthenews.com/summaries/garden_of_eden.htm accessed, June 4, 2012

eBibleteacher.com, accessed June 4, 2012

Hebrew4christians.com, June 5, 2012

www.theshofarman.com "The Brazen Altar" DVD, Dr. Terry Harman, 2006.

Associates for Biblical Research, www.biblearcheology.org, June 12, 2012

NOTES

NOTES

NOTES

NOTES

Made in the USA
San Bernardino, CA
31 May 2019